THE
CHAIRMAN

THE
CHAIRMAN

The Rise and Betrayal of Jim Greer

PETER GOLENBOCK

NEWSOUTH BOOKS

Montgomery

NewSouth Books
105 S. Court Street
Montgomery, AL 36104

Copyright © 2014 by Peter Golenbock
All rights reserved under International and Pan-American Copyright Conventions.
Published in the United States by NewSouth Books, a division of NewSouth, Inc.,
Montgomery, Alabama.

ISBN 978-1-58838-308-2 (hardcover)
ISBN 978-1-60306-352-4 (ebook)

Library of Congress Control Number: 2014932728

Printed in the United States of America
by Edwards Brothers Malloy

All photographs courtesy of Jim and Lisa Greer;
additional photographs can be found at
www.newsouthbooks.com/chairman/supplement

To Wendy Sears Grassi, who saved me.
And to Jim Greer, who trusted me.

— P. G.

~

To my loving wife Lisa, who has been with me through the good times and bad, and to my wonderful children Hunter, Amber, Austin, Aidan, and little Hope, I love you all so much.

To my in-laws, Beth and Coy, for all your support during these difficult, trying times.

To my mom Virginia, who was so proud of me.
I miss you so much.

To my true friends who have stood by me, thank you for your support and loyalty; and to all you reasonable-thinking Republicans who really are the majority of the GOP, don't let your voices be silenced.

— J. G.

Storm Warnings

"Get out. Don't run for reelection. Things are going to get bad." — HARRY SARGEANT, *finance chairman of the Republican Party of Florida in late 2008*

"You need to stop defending Crist so much. Separate yourself before you become a target. Charlie has pissed off a lot of people." — TOM FEENEY, *former United States congressman in 2008*

"If you resign, our enemies will take over the party and look for anything to embarrass the Boss. You need to stay as chairman to keep that from happening." — GEORGE LEMIEUX, *Governor Crist's chief of staff and former U.S. Senator*

"Don't resign. If the crazies get control of the party, they will accuse you and Crist of improper things, maybe even illegal things." — CHRIS DORWORTH, *state representative and speaker-designate in December 2009*

"You are all that stands between Charlie and the extremists. You are the last marine at the gate. If they take over, all hell will break loose. You can't resign. You need to go out in a body bag." — JAY BURMER, *media consultant and former advisor to Charlie Crist in December 2009*

"The party has lost confidence in Charlie, and you're his guy. It's not about you. It's about him." — DEAN CANNON, *speaker of the Florida House of Representatives in December 2009*

"The group that wants you out as chairman will say or do anything." — JASON GONZALEZ, *general counsel to the Republican Party of Florida*

"Chairman, when good men do nothing, evil men will prevail. You can't resign or evil men will take over the party and turn back all the good things you and I have done." — GOVERNOR CHARLIE CRIST, *in December 2009*

"You always put Charlie and Carol first. Your loyalty to them is what got you here. You were warned they would come after you, but you wouldn't listen. These people are evil and will to do anything to hurt Charlie and you." — LISA GREER, *every day*

CONTENTS

II—THE BETRAYAL

PREFACE

THIS IS A STORY OF FRIENDSHIP AND BETRAYAL. IT'S A SHAKESPEAREAN DRAMA played out in the political arena about a successful businessman who is plucked from obscurity by a crafty politician to lead his party and to do his bidding, and a loyal follower who in the end finds that the politician who calls himself his "brother" cares more about his political career than he does about his best friend.

With his protégé facing a jail sentence, all the politician has to do is tell the truth about a pact the two of them had made, and the other man will go free.

He doesn't do it. His political future is more important.

His protégé goes to jail.

The politician, Charlie Crist, once considered by John McCain as his vice presidential running mate, currently is running for office in Florida. The former Republican governor Crist—defeated by Marco Rubio for a U.S. Senate seat in 2010—is running as a Democrat in 2014 in an attempt to return to the Florida governor's office.

His protégé, Jim Greer, the former chairman of the Florida Republican Party, accused by his arch-conservative enemies of misusing party funds, at this writing was serving an 18-month sentence. While Crist was free and planning his run for governor, Greer was in prison and then in a halfway house in Orlando, Florida.

The story of how and why party chairman Jim Greer ended up in jail is a page-turner. Before serving his sentence, Greer spent weeks with me detailing his chilling story of how he was railroaded into accepting a guilty plea and a jail sentence.

The corrupt nature of Florida politics is well-known. The book I eventually wrote based on Greer's saga takes the reader into the governor's mansion, into the chairman's office, and offers a rare opportunity to see and hear how politics really works.

The Chairman—named in ironic homage for Greer's former job—tells the insider truth about some of Florida's most powerful people. It details the side deals and the payoffs that greased the once smooth-running machine that was the Florida Republican Party.

The book chronicles Crist's rise and then his fall at the hand of the burgeoning Tea Party and a then little-known South Florida lawyer and state representative by the name of Marco Rubio—now a potential presidential candidate in 2016. Readers will see the inner workings of the party through the eyes of Crist's then-consigliore Florida Republican Party Chairman Jim Greer. He will take them to the back rooms for a behind-the-scenes look at the wheeling and dealing, the backbiting, and the double-crossing that took him to the top for a brief moment—only to come crashing down on him when the wheels fell off and a scapegoat was needed.

SOME OF THE MOST compelling reading concerns personal relationships. No one will want to miss the true story of the relationship between Charlie Crist and his hand-picked chairman, and how Crist stabbed Greer in the back in order to save his political career. People will see that "Sunshine" Charlie Crist was an empty suit who cared more about winning the job than doing the job, just another politician out for his own personal gain and benefit.

On August 26, 2014, Floridians will flock to the polls to select which Democratic candidate will face Republican incumbent Rick Scott in the general election in November. Polls indicate the Democratic front-runner will be Charlie Crist.

It will be interesting to see how voters react after they learn what *The Chairman* has to tell them. As a liberal Democrat, I fear the fallout, but as a journalist I feel honor-bound to report what I have learned. I don't want Rick Scott to win as governor. Jim Greer certainly doesn't either. Perhaps Crist can succeed anyway.

Crist's deceit and betrayal was only the last step in a long and tortuous process that resulted in Greer's incarceration. The reader, rooting for Greer, will understand why in the end he would become the sacrificial lamb. It would not be wrong to call him a political prisoner.

The hatred of the moderate Crist by the hard-right wing of the Republican Party and by the far-right Tea Party was the first step. Crist had run for governor as a "Jeb Bush Republican," but the hard-liners knew that wasn't so. The hard-liners were convinced Crist was gay, and worse, a moderate Republican. When he supported a bill to give felons back their rights, they cringed. When he accepted federal stimulus money from President Obama and then hugged the first black president at a rally, their contempt and rage turned to hatred. The Tea Party tried hard to find a way to indict Crist, but Crist proved too elusive. To gain a measure of revenge against the governor, they went after the next-best target, Jim Greer.

The book shows how the rising star Tea Party favorite, Marco Rubio—a vicious adversary who defeated Crist for U.S. Senator—pushed for Greer's indictment. Florida Attorney General Bill McCollum was a right-winger who while in Congress led the movement to impeach Bill Clinton. Hating Crist and his sidekick Greer, he brought the action, and after the 2010 elections the new attorney general, Pam Bondi, another Tea Party favorite, did all she could to make sure Greer not only was indicted but got hard jail time.

Even with the big guns aligned against him, Greer still could have gotten off. All Charlie Crist had to do was admit that he had authorized Greer to take over the fundraising for the Republican Party. If he did that, the charges that Greer stole money from the party would not have been able to stand.

In backing his friend, though, Crist knew he would have a problem. Running against the Machiavellian Rubio, Crist knew that if he admitted the truth, Rubio would crucify him. Polls already showed that Rubio was beating him in the race to become U.S. Senator. In an attempt to save his campaign, Crist lied, dooming his best friend to jail.

Other political associates, knowing Crist had lied, were willing to testify on Greer's behalf. To make certain Greer wouldn't get off, the prosecutor, at Attorney General Pam Bondi's behest, took depositions of each of them, forcing them under oath to reveal information that potentially could have ruined their lives. In an attempt to insure that Greer wouldn't call them to the stand, the prosecutor promised Greer that he would "destroy them" if they came into court and testified.

His enemies were betting on Greer not being ruthless like them. And they turned out to be right. Unwilling to harm his friends in an effort to save himself, Greer fell on his sword rather than implicate others.

Readers will come to see him as a hero, not a felon.

Before he accepted a plea bargain, rumors swirled that Greer at trial would embarrass his enemies, revealing the behind-the-scenes goings-on of the sharply divided Republican Party during the three years he was state party chairman. There was talk he would spill secrets about lavish spending by top members of the Florida Republican Party, including Rubio, House Speaker Dean Cannon, and Senate President Mike Haridopolos. There was also concern in the Crist camp that Greer—Crist's closest confident during the three years he was chairman—would reveal what he knew about the governor. When that didn't happen and Greer agreed to go to jail, all feared that Greer would write a book about his days in Tallahassee among the rich, famous, and powerful.

This is the book they were fearing. What they weren't counting on was what a great read this story has turned out to be.

THE CHAIRMAN

Prologue

The Pleading

On February 11, 2013, Jim Greer, the former chairman of the Republican Party of Florida, stood before the Honorable Marc L. Lubet in the Orange County Courthouse. Greer had been indicted on six counts of stealing money from the Republican Party and money laundering.

Prosecutors charged that Greer had created a company called Victory Strategies in order to fraudulently obtain money from the Republican Party of Florida, then re-directed the money into his own bank account. They said he twice was paid $10,000 on top of his fundraising commission and put the money in his personal bank account. They said he received $30,000 for a poll he never conducted. They said he requested $21,250 for fundraising commissions, and the next day received $12,250 from the party. Finally, the prosecutors said that Victory Strategies was designed solely to conceal or disguise the personal payments of more than $100,000 over a year's period. They could make this charge because Charlie Crist, Greer's best friend, lied under oath that he had no knowledge of Victory Strategies or of Greer's role as the party's fundraiser. Crist's denial brought headlines in the papers.

The allegations had been brought initially by John Thrasher, a Jeb Bush protégé who had replaced Greer as the Florida Republican chairman. Florida Attorney General Bill McCollum then pursued the charges. Both Thrasher and McCollum were members of the Tea Party faction of the Republican Party. Greer had been the right-hand man of Charlie Crist, whom both Thrasher and McCollum despised.

There was no truth whatsoever to any of these charges.

Greer had two sworn affidavits and a sworn deposition from three wealthy Republican fundraisers who knew better: Harry Sargeant, Jay Burmer, and Brian Ballard. He had proof that Victory Strategies was no secret to anyone. He also had a severance agreement outlining his fundraising role signed by

Thrasher, Florida House Speaker Dean Cannon, Florida Senate President Mike Haridopolos, and GOP party attorney Jason Gonzalez, to prove it.

As a result Greer was certain the charges would be dropped.

"I kept saying, why doesn't John Thrasher go over to the prosecutor's office and say, 'We made a mistake. The contract was approved. We knew about it,'" said Greer. "Jay Burmer knew why. He one time said to me, 'McCollum is using the Florida Department of Law Enforcement (FDLE) as his Revolutionary Guard, like they do in Iran.'"

For the first year after the indictment, Greer waited everyday for someone to come to his home in Oviedo and say to him, "Jim, we're sorry. It got out of hand. The charges are being dropped. We shouldn't have done it."

As it turned out, there were other hidden charges. Delmar Johnson, Greer's right-hand man, had spent about $60,000 of party money after writing out phony invoices that Greer had known nothing about. The prosecutors told Johnson he would get immunity if he gave up Greer.

When Greer's lawyers asked for a bill of particulars behind the charges, prosecutors refused. For a whole year Greer had no idea the prosecution was going after him for Johnson's misdeeds.

"I didn't know that was even an issue," said Greer. "I never knew what he had done. And when we found out, we had to switch gears. My lawyers said, 'We've been fighting the wrong case.' We had to switch gears and say, 'Holy shit.' The whole case would be based on Johnson's telling prosecutors, 'The chairman told me to do it.' I was lucky Delmar wasn't selling heroin out of our office and saying I was telling him to do it."

Naturally, Greer said that Delmar Johnson had been lying, but because earlier Charlie Crist had failed to acknowledge that he had approved Greer's taking over fundraising, few believed Greer. There were more headlines about Greer's so-called misdeeds.

GREER, WHO WAS 100 percent sure he could prove his innocence in court, was in a bind. He realized that McCollum had the force of the FDLE behind him and would do anything—literally anything—to see that Greer lost at trial. If he were found guilty, Greer was looking at more than ten years in jail. The new attorney general, Pam Bondi, who had an allegiance to the Tea Party, as much as told him that through her minions: "Just one count, and you're going to do 10 years." Greer was certain she meant it. He was also sure John Thrasher and others within the party were pushing her.

If he pled guilty, under an agreement with the prosecution, he would spend 15 months in jail and get to see his young children grow up. Against his attorney's advice, Greer decided that the forces unleashed against him were too powerful to fight. Even his mentor, Governor Charlie Crist, had turned his back on him for political reasons. He stood alone, trying in vain to go against a very powerful tide. With his financial resources depleted, his wife in tears every day, and his reputation being smeared by the Republican Party he had loyally served, Greer decided that accepting a plea was best for him and his family.

When the indictment was announced on June 2, 2010, Greer said he was innocent of all charges and would defend himself vigorously. Reporters and interested parties salivated at the prospect of seeing Greer's attorney cross-examine the 117 witnesses on his list, including such figures as Rubio, Cannon, McCollum, Thrasher, State Representative Will Weatherford, Haridopolos, and Crist, plus numerous wealthy lobbyists, Tea Partiers, and law enforcement officers. But when Greer's day in court finally came, he disappointed everyone.

"Have a seat, folks," said Judge Lubet. "Good morning, Mr. Greer."

"Good morning, your Honor," Greer replied.

Up to the podium strode Damon Chase, Greer's attorney. The courtroom was packed. This case would reveal the inner workings of the Republican Party of Florida. The reporters in the gallery couldn't wait.

When Chase spoke, it was though he had let the air out of a giant balloon.

"After consulting with his attorney," said Chase, "my client has decided to plead guilty in the best interests of his family. And at this time, he would enter a plea of guilty, sir."

As part of the plea deal the sixth count, charging Greer with money launder-ing, was reduced to grand theft, a third-degree felony.

Judge Lubet then addressed Greer.

"Pleading guilty to counts two, three, four, five, and six as amended, is that correct?"

After a moment's hesitation, Greer looked down at the photograph of his wife and children that he had brought with him, and said, "Yes, sir."

"Are you under the influence of any drugs, medication, or alcohol at this time?"

"No, your Honor."

"Have you ever been treated for a mental illness, emotional disturbance, or are you suffering from any of those things?"

"No, your Honor."

Greer was asked if he had read the charges.

"I did, your Honor."

"And did you understand everything on this plea form?"

"I did, your Honor."

The judge asked if it was his signature on the second page of the form.

"It is, your Honor."

"Did you sign this freely and voluntarily, understanding everything contained within it?"

"I did, your Honor."

"Are you satisfied with your attorney's presentation?"

"Very much so, your Honor."

"I also have a DNA form. Did you read that over?"

"Yes, your Honor."

"Did you understand it?"

"Yes, your Honor."

"And that's your signature on there?"

"It is, your Honor."

"Okay. All right. Mr. Greer, as to the charge in Count 2 of grand theft third degree, how do you plead?"

"Guilty, your Honor."

And so on with the other counts, until Lubet said, "All right. Are you entering the pleas freely and voluntarily?"

"I am, your Honor."

"Are you entering the pleas because you believe it's in your best interest?"

"Yes, your Honor."

"Has anyone forced, threatened, or coerced you to enter this plea?"

"No, your Honor."

"Do you understand that by entering this plea, we're not going to have a trial. I'll just sentence you based on the plea?"

"Yes, your Honor."

Judge Lubet then accepted Greer's plea and set sentencing for six weeks later.

ON MARCH 27, 2013, Jim Greer, former chairman of the Republican Party of Florida, was sentenced to 42 months in jail. But Judge Lubet noted that Greer had never been in trouble before and suspended 28 months, leaving an effective sentence of 18 months, of which he had to serve 85 percent, or 15 months. Greer would be free on July 5, 2014. Six months of probation would follow. The speculation was great that powerful people had paid Greer to keep quiet and that he had pled guilty to protect the powers of the party.

The truth was that Greer had pled guilty to end the nightmare and to ensure that he would not miss years of his young children's lives.

After sentencing Greer had a little over six weeks to settle his affairs before surrendering to the Gulf Correctional Institution in Wewahitchka, Florida. In those three months, he vowed, he would do what he could to make the world understand that not only was he not guilty of the charges but that there had been an organized scheme by the ultra-right wing of the Republican Party to send him to jail in a vindictive attempt to smear the administration of Governor Charlie Crist. In the greatest of ironies, it was Crist, the man who had chosen Greer as his chairman, whose treachery ultimately sent Greer to jail.

What follows is Jim Greer's story.

I

THE RISE

"If you want a friend [in politics], get a dog."

— Harry Truman

THE GOVERNOR-ELECT CALLS

"CHAIRMAAAAAANNNNNN," CAME THE VOICE BOOMING THROUGH THE phone. The voice belonged to Charlie Crist, the governor-elect of the state of Florida, and he was calling Jim Greer, who was the chairman of the Charlie Crist campaign in Seminole County. "Chairmaaaannnnnn," Crist repeated, adding, "but I don't mean of the county any more. I mean of the state. I'd like you to serve as chairman of the Republican Party of Florida."

Greer was overwhelmed. He didn't know it, but that one call would make him rich and powerful. In three short tumultuous years, it would also ruin his reputation and his life.

After high school, Greer attended Brevard Community College in southeast Florida, with the goal of becoming an attorney. To pay tuition, he worked in Cocoa Beach as a doorman and bouncer for ABC Liquors, a combination liquor store, lounge, and dance club, one of a Florida chain of such popular establishments.

One evening a large group of bikers drove up, and several bikers got into a brawl with the local gentry—"rednecks" as they were called. One biker held one of the locals down, and another picked up a bar stool and slammed it into the victim's face, costing him the sight in one eye.

The man sued for millions, and when the investigators for ABC Liquors arrived to interview witnesses, the customers who had seen the fight clammed up. No one wanted to get involved. One of the store managers referred the investigator to the cherubic Greer, who was friends with many of the customers. Greer accompanied the investigator on interviews, and because the customers trusted Greer, they began to talk about what happened that night in the lounge. The investigator, grateful for Greer's help, told his supervisor from the ABC Liquors Loss Prevention Program about the gregarious kid at the Cocoa Beach store.

Not long afterwards Greer left ABC Liquors and was hired as a store detective with Montgomery Ward. He had been on the job about three months when his mother told him, "The director of loss prevention at ABC Liquors called today," said Mrs. Virginia Greer, "and he wants to talk to you about a job."

"It was a big deal," Greer said later, "because this was the corporate environment versus working at the low level I had been. I went over, interviewed with Dave Castro, the director of loss prevention and legal affairs for ABC Liquors, and he hired me as an investigator for the East Coast."

Greer was 21 years old.

His job was to investigate accidents and to spy on stores where thefts were common occurrences. Another part of the job was to train bartenders, servers, and managers on the laws relating to alcoholic beverages, to make sure they checked IDs, didn't serve minors, and didn't get in any trouble with the law.

Greer was efficient, and because he was the sort of guy who made friends wherever he went, soon managers began requesting that he be the one sent to train their employees.

Greer, a man with an entrepreneurial streak, had an idea. He was working for ABC Liquors, a chain that could afford to pay him for his services. He wondered whether smaller, independently owned establishments which couldn't afford a loss prevention program might pay him to train their employees. His timing was perfect, because around this time the Florida Division of Alcoholic Beverages was getting a lot of press for arresting bartenders, managers, and other employees for not obeying the liquor laws.

Greer quit his job at ABC Liquors on June 18, 1984. He rented a tiny office for $100 a month, bought a desk and a plastic book shelf from Eckerd Drugs, and, to make his operation look official to customers, he brought his mother in to be his secretary. Mrs. Greer started cold-calling bars and restaurants to set up appointments for Jim to pitch his training services. He called his company Florida Beverage Law Consultants, and ten years later renamed it Regulatory Compliance Services, Inc.

Three days after he opened shop, Greer gained his first client when he was hired by the owners of the Thirsty Turtle in Cocoa Beach. He met with them, described his services, and they agreed to pay him $75 a month. His price was reasonable, and local bars began lining up to buy what Jim Greer was selling.

Before long Greer had clients all across Florida, and then in states all across the country. As the money came pouring in, he opened offices in California and Texas. He sold the company in 2007, pocketing several million dollars. He owned a twin-engine Piper Navajo airplane and an expensive power boat.

BY THAT TIME HE had a decade of activity in local and state Republican politics, including work on Jeb Bush's gubernatorial campaigns in 1994 and 1998. A resident of Oviedo, a mostly white community of about 30,000 population 20 minutes from downtown Orlando, in 2004 Greer ran for and was elected to the Oviedo City Council. He became the city's deputy mayor, serving on the metropolitan planning organization and the tourism development council. And he was a former president of the Rotary Club and a director of the chamber of commerce.

Besides his civic duties, he raised money for local candidates and wrote five-figure checks to Republican legislative candidates. Twice he was selected Businessman of the Year. Whenever the business community or a civic organization needed something done right, the man they inevitably called was Jim Greer.

Greer had met Charlie Crist even before Crist decided to run for governor. Crist had been appointed assistant secretary to the Florida Department of Business and Professional Regulation in Tallahassee, the state agency that regulates alcohol and food safety, and periodically Greer, in his travels for Regulatory Compliance Services, would lunch with him.

In January 2005 Greer and his wife Lisa were invited to the Florida GOP's inaugural ball in Washington to celebrate the reelection of President George W. Bush. That night they ran into Crist, by now the Florida attorney general. Crist was developing a reputation for being a hardcore law-and-order Republican. He had brought back the practice of putting orange-suited prisoners along the state's roadways picking up litter.

"Chain Gang Charlie," they called him.

Crist told Jim and Lisa Greer that he was close to deciding whether he was going to run for the governorship: "Would you be willing to help?"

Greer said he would.

After Crist announced his candidacy in May 2005, Greer didn't hesitate. He called Crist and told him he was interested in working with him.

"I don't have any county chairs at this point," Crist told him. "I don't have any staff. I don't have anybody, except a woman by the name of Arlene DiBenigno who's working as my grass-roots director in Tallahassee, but otherwise I don't have any structures in place.

"Would you like to be the first county chairman of the Charlie Crist for Governor campaign?" Crist asked.

"Yes, I'd love to," said Greer.

And thus Greer first earned the right to be called *chairman* when he became head of the Charlie Crist campaign in Seminole County.

THEY AGREED TO MEET for dinner. Jim, Lisa, Crist, and Scott Peelen, a friend and adviser of Crist's from Orlando, gathered at a very fancy, elegant restaurant, Manuel's, in downtown Orlando atop the Bank of America building. Greer brought with him two of his best clients, Tony Davenport and Julian Lago.

Florida candidates for state office can receive a maximum of $500 from individuals, but checks to the Republican Party of Florida can be written for an unlimited amount. That night Greer and his guests, including wives, gave Crist checks for his campaign totaling around $3,000. They also wrote checks for the Republican Party of Florida to the tune of $20,000.

Crist was duly impressed. Greer, he saw, not only was going to help organize his campaign in Seminole County, but he was also capable of raising big money.

Greer was excited because he was impatient to put together a grass-roots volunteer organization in Seminole County. Quickly, Greer saw that Crist had a more important objective.

"The first thing he wanted me to do," said Greer, "was organize a Seminole County fundraiser for him. Charlie was all about the contributions. He knew that money determines the campaign's success rate."

"How much do you think you can raise?" asked Crist.

"A hundred thousand dollars," Greer said.

Crist was skeptical.

"No, no, no, no," said Crist. "Jim, I appreciate it, but I just don't see you raising that kind of money at the first fundraiser for Central Florida."

Crist was incredulous when Jim joined with County Commissioner Brenda Carey and another businessman, Rob Thiessen, and together they raised $118,000.

CHARLIE CRIST WAS BORN in Altoona, Pennsylvania, on July 24, 1956. His family name comes from the Greek Christodoulou. As a child he and his family moved to St. Petersburg, Florida, where he graduated from St. Petersburg High School. He attended Wake Forest University for two years, boasting he had played back-up quarterback on the varsity football team. He graduated from Florida State University, where he was elected student body vice president. He was a member of Pi Kappa Alpha and then received his law degree from Cumberland School of Law at Samford University in Birmingham.

After passing the bar on his third try—a fact critics harped on—he was hired as general counsel to Minor League Baseball, which was based in St. Petersburg. In 1986 he ran for a state senate seat as a Republican and lost. He was then an aide to Connie Mack III in Mack's successful run for a U.S. Senate seat. In 1992, again running as a Republican, Crist was elected to the Florida Senate, defeating longtime incumbent Helen Gordon Davis of Tampa. His was one of the GOP victories that year that ended Democratic Party control of the Florida Senate.

In 1998 Crist began to make headlines when he ran against the popular Bob Graham for the U.S. Senate. He lost that race, then was named Florida education commissioner in 2000. In 2002 he was elected Florida attorney general. Against the wishes of Governor Jeb Bush, Crist ended the nationally controversial attempt by pro-life advocates to keep alive Terry Schiavo, who was in an irreversible coma. He also went after civil rights violators and perpetrators of fraud, a number of them wealthy businessmen, angering the conservative wing of the Republican Party.

Crist wasn't an ideologue, Greer saw. He was a moderate, like himself.

When Greer began to organize Seminole County for Crist, he ran into resistance from old-line Republicans who were backing Crist's gubernatorial primary opponent, Tom Gallagher, the insurance commissioner of Florida. Greer was learning that there was a significant, vocal segment of the Republican Party that didn't much like Charlie Crist.

Greer met with a group of political friends to talk up Crist. Greer's friend, Tom Feeney, an important Republican legislator, hosted a barbeque at his home. Jim Stelling, the party chairman of Seminole County who later was appointed by Greer as the state party's rules committee chairman, was there, as was Chris Dorworth and Jason Brodeur, good friends who became legislators. All were old-line Republicans holding the same conservative social views as Gallagher: there should be a ban on abortions, a ban on gay marriage, and no stem cell research.

When they heard that Greer had joined Charlie Crist's campaign team, they began teasing him about Crist. The gibes came fast and furious.

"Everyone in the party knows he's gay." "He sucks dick. Why are you helping him?" "Why are you working for someone who takes it up the ass?" "Why are you working for a queer? Gallagher is going to kick Crist's ass. And anyhow, Crist is not a Republican. Everyone knows he's not a Republican."

"They called him a RINO—Republican in name only," explained Greer. "It almost came down to a fistfight between me and many of my good friends."

"You're being ridiculous," Greer told them. "We're going to kick your ass in the upcoming primary."

Later Greer said to his wife Lisa, "Did you hear that shit?"

"Yeah," she said. "I did."

Greer began to see the uphill battle he was facing in Seminole County. All the old-school Republicans were for Gallagher. Greer decided to try to attract younger voters. He built a corps of grass-roots volunteers and held events for Crist. On the lawns in his neighborhood there would be ten Gallagher yard signs. His was the only *Crist for Governor* sign.

At the same time, Greer, who saw himself as a moderate Republican, thought it was important to build rapport with the Gallagher people.

"I tried to have good relationships with them," said Greer. "I felt there was no reason to tear the county Republican Party apart."

One morning Greer called Arlene DiBenigno, Crist's lone campaign employee. She was the director of his grass-roots effort, as well as his political director.

"Hey, Arlene," said Greer, "my name is Jim Greer, and I'm the county chairman for the campaign in Seminole County."

"You are?" she said. "I didn't know we had county chairs yet."

"Yes, Charlie asked me to be the first county chair."

"Are you going to be the finance chair or the organizational chair?"

"I'm going to be everything," said Greer.

And he was.

GREER WAS A BUSINESSMAN who knew how to organize. He had run local campaigns, and he didn't need much guidance. Crist recognized that Seminole County was well-organized. He set up a campaign that did phone banking like a campaign was supposed to, and his volunteers walked door to door in support of Crist's candidacy. Greer also was raising money, a lot of money.

Greer was a bundler. Greer liked to say fundraising was more like Amway than a Ponzi scheme. If he enlisted ten people to go out and raise money for Crist, and each of them solicited ten people to raise money for them, then Greer would get credit for *all* of the money brought in from *all* of them. From the beginning to the end, Greer was credited with raising over $200,000 for the Crist for governor campaign.

Often when Crist wanted a big turnout and a great show of support, or if he wanted a rally at which an important person was making an endorsement, he'd call Greer. Even if the rally was held in a more populous city like Miami or Tampa, inevitably Arlene DiBenigno would call Jim and say, "Can you put together a huge rally?"

"Yup," Greer would say. "I sure can."

For one rally featuring John McCain's endorsement of Crist, Greer held it inside an airplane hangar at Sanford International Airport. He called the sheriff, who knew the airport officials, and it was arranged for Greer to use a hangar. He rented a big stage and brought in dozens of flags to fly behind it. He bought hats, T-shirts, and hired a Dixieland band. At the same time, other county chairs were holding rallies for Crist in Pizza Huts and Wendy's.

Hundreds were there to cheer when Crist's private jet rolled up to the red carpet. As he deplaned, the Dixieland band struck up a tune. Crist was overwhelmed by the reception.

When he took the podium and proclaimed, "Everything good starts in Seminole County," the adoring throng went wild.

Crist told Greer, "This looks more like a presidential campaign stop than a governor's stop."

The flamboyant Greer didn't disagree.

Crist gave Greer a promotion and the title of Central Florida Coordinator. Greer was now in charge of not only Seminole County, but also Brevard, Volusia, and Orange (includes the Orlando metropolitan area) counties.

Once a week the county chairs for the campaign from around the state would get on the phone with DiBenigno for a conference call. Arlene would often ask, "Jim, would you tell the county chairs what you did this past Saturday?"

In front of other county chairs, Crist would proclaim, "Jim Greer is the best county chair in the state of Florida."

"I was very proud," said Greer. "We were humming like a well-oiled machine."

Crist began to rely more and more on Jim Greer. If Crist held rallies in any of the other counties, the call would come in:

"Jim, Charlie has asked if you can drive for him."

"Driving for the candidate is a big deal," said Greer, "because you get close interaction with the candidate. I was starting to get called often. If a candidate likes you, he talks to you a lot. Many who drive hope that the relationship will turn into a job in the new administration."

GREER, WHO HIMSELF HAD political ambitions, was being seduced by the headiness of it all.

"There I was the deputy mayor of Oviedo. I was president of a multi-million dollar company, and I would get excited that Charlie wanted me to drive for him. I was ecstatic. I was seeing my political career starting to take off."

Greer was starting to hear rumors from his political friends.

"You're going to Tallahassee with him if he wins," Greer was told. "He loves you."

The Crist campaign began hiring staff. George LeMieux, who had worked with Crist in the attorney general's office, left his post there and began as Crist's campaign manager. He and Arlene DiBenigno hired field directors from around the state. Field directors were getting paid about $30,000 a year, and their job was to work with the volunteer county chairs. Once they became field directors, they worked like dogs, toiling 15, 16, 17 hours a day. At times they had to spend their own money, but they were dedicated, glad to do it.

"They are the political animals who love campaigning," said Greer, "and ultimately if the campaign is successful, they get jobs in the administration."

One day Arlene told Jim, "We're looking to hire a field director by the name of Delmar Johnson." Greer was told that Johnson had a lot of experience and was asking for a $50,000 salary.

"We're negotiating with him, Jim, and once we get him hired, I'll have him contact you and the Orlando chairman," she said.

Delmar Johnson, a large man with a hearty laugh, had worked in the Jeb Bush administration in a low-level position and as a field director for a statewide organization opposing the government's taking of private property by eminent domain.

Arlene was extremely high on him.

"He's outgoing," she said. "He's vivacious. Here's a great field director. Everybody loves him. He's a big guy, weighs about 350 pounds, and he has a great personality."

"I couldn't hear enough good things about Delmar," said Greer.

About a week later Arlene called Greer to tell him the Crist campaign had hired Johnson.

"Delmar came over to my house. I liked him immediately," said Greer. "He was always big on kissing your ass. He'd be like, 'Chairman Greer. You're just the greatest chairman in the world. Everybody says what a great chairman you are.' It was the way he talked. He was lovable, a teddy bear of a guy. And he knew how to suck up. He knew how to make you feel very good."

Greer and Johnson hit it off from the start. Their personalities meshed, and they worked very well together.

The field director would always tell Greer, "I don't have to worry about Seminole County. You're in charge. You're in control. And you're doing it exactly right. Now Brevard and Orange counties, they are all screwed up."

Delmar would then fill Jim in on the inner workings of the Crist campaign, information Greer would not have been privy to as a volunteer chairman.

Quickly they became close friends, in fact, more like family. Delmar frequently ate dinner at the Greer home—especially after a day of problems in another county.

By late July 2005, with the primary coming up in September, Charlie Crist had raised more than $50 million, far ahead of Tom Gallagher. More than anything, Crist was a formidable fundraiser, someone who could sit on the telephone for hours and days calling people for contributions. In that respect he was a rarity. Whereas most candidates hated having to ask for money, Crist loved dialing for dollars. He would go from house to house to house asking for donations without a twinge of embarrassment. To Crist, raising money was a game, and he was very good at it.

After a fundraising event, the question foremost on Crist's mind would be: "How much have we done?" By the time he was in the car getting ready to leave the event, he wanted the numbers: "How much is in hand?"

"A lot of people who do fundraising events will say, 'I've got $22,000 in hand and another $50,000 coming in over the next week," said Greer. "Charlie always said, 'Show me the money now.'"

AT THE SAME TIME Crist was raising a ton of money, his opponent, Tom Gallagher, running as a family values Christian conservative despite a messy divorce, began having problems.

The Crist-driven rumor mill was accusing him of buying and selling stocks using his state-owned computer while he was the state's chief financial officer. Rumors were also being spread of his womanizing and cocaine use.

Crist began to pull away in the polls.

One night in late July Greer got a call from Arlene DiBenigno in Tallahassee. The two had become good friends. If she was having a bad day or wanted to bitch and moan or vent about something, she called Greer.

This night she asked him, "Are you a member of the REC?"

"What's that?"

"The county Republican Executive Committee."

"No," he said. "I didn't even know there was one."

Greer had been deputy mayor of his town, but he had no connection whatsoever to the structure of the state Republican Party.

"What is it?" he asked.

"Every county has a Republican Executive Committee," she said. "Three people from each county—the county chairman, the state committeeman, and the state committeewoman—make up the state Republican Executive Committee. It meets once a month, and you need to become a member of it."

"Why?" asked Greer.

"Because there's talk up here in Tallahassee about making you the chairman of the Republican Party," DiBenigno said. "But you can't be chairman unless you're a member of the Republican Executive Committee. The first thing we've got to do is get the names of the three members of the Republican Executive Committee, and then we've got to find one of the three who will resign so you can be elected to one of those offices."

This came during the primary between Crist and Gallagher as Crist looked to be the sure winner in the election.

"The talk has stepped up," she said, "because there are rumors that Gallagher is going to drop out before the primary."

Greer was so green he didn't realize the prestige of the position he was being considered for.

"That sounds exciting," said Greer. "I don't know what the Republican chairman does, but if that's what you all think would be good . . ."

"It's everything you do so well," she said. "You raise money. You run a good organization."

And then she warned, "But there are a lot of crazies in it. I'll get into all of that later on.

"For now," said Arlene DiBenigno, "get ready."

2

Money, Money, Money

For a week—an eternity—Jim Greer waited for the phone to ring. One thing he had learned about Arlene DiBenigno: when she said "get ready to storm the hill," the matter still might be dropped in favor of something more crucial. Greer knew this was just the nature of politics.

While he waited, rumors that Tom Gallagher was getting out of the race proved false. Though facing crushing rejection, Gallagher stayed in because he wanted to force the hated Crist to spend a few more million dollars.

On September 5, 2006, Charlie Crist won the Republican primary over Tom Gallagher by 300,000 votes. Aware of the bad blood between the candidates, Greer wanted to do something to ease tensions in Seminole County.

The next day Greer called Gallagher's Seminole County campaign chairman and Jim Stelling, the Seminole County Republican chairman, and suggested they have a unity dinner. Greer was the only Republican in the Crist camp to hold such a dinner. He booked the restaurant and on the wall behind them hung a long banner that read "Crist and Gallagher People Together, United on a Path to Victory."

The county chair of the Gallagher campaign got up and made a speech, Jim Stelling spoke, and an after-the-election calm spread over Seminole County, thanks to Greer's conciliatory instinct.

Throughout the rest of the state, the bitterness between the Gallagher and Crist camps festered. The Gallagher people were part of the Jeb Bush group, and most hard-core Republicans had a laundry list of complaints about Crist, as did Greer's Seminole County friends. At the top of the list was that Crist had refused to meet with Jeb's brother, George W. Bush, at a presidential campaign rally in Pensacola in 2004. They were murderously furious about that. Karl Rove vocalized his disdain for Crist.

Crist tried to explain his reasoning for the slight of W, saying that he had a scheduling conflict and that he was appealing to moderate Republicans, Hispanics, African Americans, and Democrats. To the hard-core rightwingers, no explanation sufficed. What he had done was inexcusable. To them Crist was an insult to the party, an interloper, a RINO, and even worse, a RINO fag, who didn't deserve to be governor.

The conservatives' disdain for Crist would grow into a deep hatred.

THE RACE FOR GOVERNOR of Florida was now between Charlie Crist and the Democrats' Jim Davis, a former congressman from Tampa who was a lackluster campaigner. The only chance Davis had to win was that a hefty percentage of Florida voters were sick and tired of George W. Bush's administration—the Iraq and Afghanistan wars and the tax breaks for the rich were putting the country into deeper and deeper debt—and voters were kicking the tires to see if the Democrats could do better. Countering that negative vibe was that W.'s brother, Jeb, the departing governor, was a favorite of 66 percent of Florida voters.

What Crist had going for him was his advantage over Davis in fundraising. Crist would raise and spend many millions of dollars on a wave of radio and TV ads that promoted his populism and his deep love for the state of Florida.

In the contest between Crist and Davis, Jim Greer again was at the top of his game in Seminole County, getting out a mass of volunteers for Crist and turning out big dollars. Among those who started showing up at Greer's events for Crist was George LeMieux, Crist's right-hand man, a veteran politico known as "The Maestro." Much as Karl Rove was "The Architect" behind George W. Bush, so the Maestro was the brains behind the Crist campaign operation.

"During the primary race and all during the general election against Jim Davis, I started running into George a lot," said Greer. "George was always quiet, analytical. You could tell he was the one running the show. George began to see firsthand what I was doing in Seminole County."

The Crist-Davis gubernatorial race was the most expensive in Florida history. According to campaign finance reports, Crist raised $19.6 million, compared to Davis's $6.8 million. That did not count the money raised by the parties: $40 million by Republicans for Crist, and $14.7 by the Florida Democratic Party for Davis, who, unlike Crist, had drained most of his funds battling through a primary.

During the campaign, Crist tried to distance himself from George W. Bush but stay close to Jeb Bush. Crist took a populist stance and wanted Republican voters to think he would continue most of Jeb's policies, including education reforms that favored vouchers for private schools, offshore drilling, and tax cuts. To appeal to moderates, Crist promised that ideology would be less important than it had been under Bush.

"When Charlie would go around during the campaign and say he was a Jeb Bush Republican," said Greer, "he was just saying that. And everybody knew it. But he said it enough that he won the election."

On November 7, 2006, Crist defeated Davis by 52 to 45 percent (2,487,140 to 2,151,597 votes). In his acceptance speech, Crist told his cheering supporters, "Tonight, we all come together as one. Not as Republicans, Democrats or Independents but as one, as Floridians. Each Floridian will have a voice in all we do, and I will serve every Floridian with all my heart."

THE TWO PEOPLE WHO orchestrated Crist's 2006 gubernatorial victory were George LeMieux, the campaign manager, and his relentless, hand-picked fundraiser, Meredith O'Rourke.

LeMieux, the Maestro, was a magician who had a way of making problems go away. In early November, close to Election Day, a video surfaced that suggested that Crist had had sexual relations with two men. One of the men identified on the video was Bruce Carlton Jordan, a travel aide to U.S. Representative Katherine Harris. Jordan had been on probation after convictions of grand theft and forgery.

The other was Jason Wetherington, a young political gadfly out of South Florida who showed up at a lot of fundraisers. The former GOP staffer and Broward School Board student liaison boasted of having an affair with Crist. After the story was made public by Broward County blogger Bob Norman, Wetherington disappeared until the election was over. But the enterprising Norman tracked him down in Georgia and talked to him briefly. Norman reported that Wetherington said that he was being "taken care of very well."

Crist vehemently denied he was gay, even denied he had ever met Jordan, though many of Crist's friends had seen them together often. The matter seemed to go away after Jordan and Wetherington suddenly were nowhere to be found. Greer said DiBenigno had told him that LeMieux had gotten the two to leave Florida in the last few weeks of the campaign, and that each had been paid $100,000 by a wealthy donor.

With the absence of the two alleged lovers, the issue of Crist's gayness died as quickly as it had sprung up.

As good as LeMieux was at making Crist's problems disappear—literally—O'Rourke was equally good at making money appear. A former fundraiser for the Republican National Committee, she was paid $30,000 a month by the Crist campaign to be its chief money raiser. Greer thought she was worth every penny.

"In politics today," said Greer, "it's all about who gave the most, and who is going to give more." As he explains it, today's high-stakes campaign fundraising works a lot like the multi-level marketing of companies like Amway and Mary Kay.

"It's interesting that the most wealthy of the wealthy are always interested in the little trinkets, the lapel pins, the cuff links, the Republican ties. Me, too. I liked to be able to go to a Charlie Crist event and wear my Founder lapel pin so people knew I was a money person. Other people who gave $100,000 had a different-looking pin, and finally I got one after I moved up to the next level."

For the Crist campaign, O'Rourke gave the big money raisers personal tracking numbers and continually prodded them to reach the next level. Legally, individuals could only give the candidate $500, but "bundlers" could get friends and business associates to give, and all that money was credited to the fundraiser's tracking number. "Another tactic is to form a corporation, something that's very easy to do in Florida. Then you can write a check to the Crist campaign from your company," Greer said.

"Some people find all kinds of ways to get that $500 check to the campaign. They will ask everybody in their family to write a $500 check. If they have a company, they write a company check. Through the year and a half of the campaign, they turn in all the checks, and then everyone gets to see who are the top contributors and fundraisers. They get special rewards like tickets to the inauguration and VIP seating to the inaugural ball."

Lobbyists and persons who have business with state government are different. They aren't raising money for a lapel pin but to get a contract approved, a law passed or killed, or an issue handled by a state agency.

"It's all about personal relationships, so a lot of lobbyists will support candidates and do things so they are seen at the events. If the candidate wins, and the lobbyist happens to need help for a client, there will be a mental note in the successful candidate's head: 'Hey, I saw you during the campaign. You raised a lot of money for me. What can I do for you today?'"

In other words the more money a person raises, the more influence that person will have if his candidate gets elected. Meredith O'Rourke managed those expectations for the Crist campaign and used them to push fundraisers to higher levels.

"Let's say you have a tracking number and you've raised $15,000," said Greer, "and you're trying to get to the next level at $25,000. Meredith is calling you all the time, because one thing she does, she is constantly running the numbers. She is constantly exhorting you to raise more. You could have raised money for an event on Saturday night, and three weeks later Meredith is on the phone telling you about a Disney World fundraiser, and she needs to raise $100,000. It's always more, more, more, more."

Greer said fundraisers could get angry if they weren't getting the credit they felt they deserved.

"Here's why. Say I call you up and say, 'Hey, John, we're friends. Listen, I'm working on Charlie Crist's campaign. I'm doing some fundraising. He's coming to Tampa. I can't be there Saturday night. So if you can raise me $5,000, you'll get to go to the VIP party. I'll make sure your name is on the list. I need ten $500 checks. Can you do it, John?' He says he can.

"Sometimes you tell John about your tracking number, and other times you don't, because you don't want John to know he can get a tracking number of his own. So sometimes you say, 'Make sure you put this number on your checks.' And sometimes you just tell Meredith, 'John is my guy, and all the checks he turns in I want credited to my tracking number.'

"What happens sometimes is John shows up to an event, and he starts mingling, and he's feeling good over the fact people are treating him well because he's one of the people who brought in $5,000 that night. Someone might say to him, 'Hey, John, why don't you become a bundler? We'll give you your own tracking number.' All the checks then get credited to John's tracking number and not to the person who brought John into the game. That person gets all pissed off and calls Meredith, saying 'He was my guy. His checks need to be credited to me.'"

"Usually," said Greer, "they just go in and fix it. Unless the complainer is a pain in the ass or a bull shitter and he isn't going to raise a lot of money—and there are a lot of people out there like that. But the ones who have the potential to raise even more, you try and make them happy. Because if a guy raises you $5,000, you're going to try to get him to raise another $25,000 over the course of the campaign."

Jim Greer held very successful events for Crist in Seminole County, but no matter how successful he was, O'Rourke was always pushing him to raise more.

"Can you do another event for us in Seminole County?" she asked.

"You were here just three weeks ago, and we sucked the county dry."

"Charlie is really asking," she would say.

And sometimes Crist would get on the phone and make the request himself.

"Charlie was on the phone all the time with potential donors and with donors," said Greer. "If you had the capability of hosting a big event and you were on the fence as to whether you wanted to host it, the next thing you knew, Charlie would be calling you. One of the big marketing tools Meredith and Charlie used was the call for *just one more* event before they closed out the quarter."

At the end of every quarter every campaign and every political party had to file with the Florida Division of Elections a financial report, and every candidate running for governor wanted to be able to show he had bigger fundraising numbers than the other candidates.

"Charlie would call and say, 'Listen, John, we need a million this quarter. We have $900,000. We need one more big fundraiser. And I won't forget it, John, if you can pull it off. Can you do it?' Of course he'll say he'll do it.

"And so," said Greer, "during the campaign I got to know Meredith, and we got along well. I worked on the campaign along with her. There was a lot of pressure. She called you all the time. If you agreed to do an event in your home, Meredith would be there with her crew of young girls who would run around, pick up checks, make deposits and help her out.

"Meredith had a welcome table out front. She got everyone to sign up for emails, and she was the one who took the checks at the door. Two weeks before the event she'd give you a call to make sure everything was going well in preparation for it, to make sure the invitations went out, that you had enough RSVPs.

"She'd ask, 'Is there anyone Charlie Crist needs to call?'

"If you knew John Smith could bring in a lot of checks, you'd say to Meredith, 'I got a fish on the line who can raise a lot. I need Charlie to call him himself.' And Charlie would do that.

"She managed all this with the Crist campaign, and there's no doubt she had a lot to do with Charlie Crist winning in November of 2006."

3

CAROLE JEAN JORDAN

TOLD BY ARLENE DIBENIGNO TO "GET READY," JIM GREER HAD HIGH HOPES that Charlie Crist was taking him to Tallahassee. Looking to the future, Jim Greer turned his attention away from Oviedo politics and began to focus on the bigger picture. Rather than attend the celebration for his reelection as Oviedo's deputy mayor, Greer and Lisa drove west to St. Petersburg where they attended governor-elect Charlie Crist's victory celebration at the stately Vinoy Hotel.

"I was riding high in Seminole County," said Greer. "Everyone knew I was county chairman of the Crist campaign. George LeMieux made nice comments about me. Everyone was kissing my ass and saying 'Jim is going to be the guy.' My head got a little big, and I was thrilled with the direction I saw my life taking."

On election night everyone started asking Greer, "Where're you going? What will you be doing? Are you getting a cabinet position? Are you going to be chief of staff?"

Greer knew for certain he wasn't going to be chief of staff because that job was going to LeMieux. But he thought he might be named the secretary of business and professional regulation because that was his training. And yet he knew if he was offered that job, his competitors would blow a gasket.

That night at the Vinoy, Greer and LeMieux stood together at the top of the stairs of the fancy restaurant on the second level. LeMieux said, "Charlie wants you to come to Tallahassee with us. What do you want to do?"

"I don't know," said Greer, "but I'd like very much to come to Tallahas-see with you."

"I will call you in a week," LeMieux said.

Greer had heard that before.

During the longest week of his life, Greer was kept apprised by friends inside the Crist camp. "They told me they were seeing my name penciled in for different positions, but nothing had been finalized," said Greer. "I just sat at home excited, but at the same time wondering. In politics a lot of things are promised but never done."

In the meantime, Greer was appointed by Jeb Bush to the Central Florida Planning and Development Commission. Greer had helped Jeb raise money in 1994 and 1998, and this appointment by the lame duck governor was a reward for past service.

Greer was attending his first meeting of the commission when he got a phone call from Lisa: "George LeMieux is trying to get hold of you. He says he has something for you."

LeMieux had said he'd call in a week, and it was exactly seven days since their talk at the Vinoy.

Greer called him back.

"Jim," said LeMieux, "the governor-elect is going to be calling you in a few minutes. He would like you to serve as chairman of the Republican Party of Florida."

Flabbergasted, all Greer could say was, "Okay."

Lemieux told him, "I think you have an entrepreneurial spirit, your business experience . . . all those things can be brought to the Republican Party to make it a better organization."

Then he added, "It has problems. The Republican Party has problems."

As to what those problems were Jim Greer had no idea. He learned some of them in his subsequent phone call to his friend, Congressman Tom Feeney, asking whether he should take the job of chairman.

"Don't do it, and I'll tell you why," said Feeney. "There are two main reasons. Number one, Charlie is going to have trouble with the base of the party. The base is not happy, and that's going to put whoever is chairman in a bad position, and number two, when the governor is of the same party, the chairman doesn't run the party, the governor and his chief of staff do. I wouldn't do it."

Greer dismissed the advice.

"I felt it was a position in which I could use all of my skills," said Greer.

"I thought it was a reflection of what I had already done on a local level: rallies, raising money, organizing, leading."

ANOTHER OF THE PROBLEMS LeMieux had alluded to, one which would plague Greer during his entire time as chairman, was that too many of the grass-roots, old-time Republicans who worked for the state Executive Committee (REC) were right-wing, hard-core conservatives who didn't want Charlie Crist as their governor. Another problem was that the state REC was the body that actually voted for the chairman of the Florida Republican Party, and many REC members resented being told by Crist whom to vote for. They felt that Crist, the RINO (Republican in name only), the imposter, was dictating to them by plucking Greer from obscurity and naming him to the position. They had come up through the ranks of the Republican Party. Jim Greer, the deputy mayor of Oviedo, was unknown to them.

Getting elected chairman would be an ugly fight, and Greer would have to mount his own campaign to win it.

Arlene DiBenigno had been named as Crist's incoming deputy chief of staff. "Congratulations," she said somewhat sarcastically, "but we're going to have our work cut out for us."

DiBenigno was all too familiar with the state REC membership because she had been the REC's grass-roots contact during the Jeb Bush administration. Jeb had been well liked by the state REC, so she and the members had gotten along well. With Crist's election, all had dramatically changed.

"The first thing you need to do," she told Greer, "you have to become a member of the Republican Executive Committee. You need to get elected to the precinct."

Greer looked up whether his precinct was vacant, and it was. First hurdle cleared.

"Next," she said, "you have to ask the Seminole county chairman or the state committeeman to resign, so they can hold a special county election to elect you and make you eligible to run for state party chairman."

"Oh my God," said the new kid on the block. "Becoming chairman isn't as simple as it appears."

"Oh, no," said DiBenigno. "There's going to be trouble because they're not happy with Charlie Crist as governor."

If that wasn't bad enough, there was one other impediment. The current party chairman, Carole Jean Jordan, a stern, serious woman, was one of those Jeb Bush grass-roots, conservative, hard-liners who had visible contempt for Crist. And she had announced that she intended to run for reelection even if Crist didn't want her. It was unheard of, a slap in the face to Crist that she was even thinking of running for another term, a direct challenge to Crist's ability to govern, and his position as the titular head of the party.

Jordan, like most chairs, had worked her way up over the last 20 years, starting as a precinct person, then was elected to state committeewoman, and then chairman of the party. She had been working for Tom Gallagher behind the scenes. Crist and LeMieux, knowing this, wanted her out but she wasn't ready to go.

Greer, a neophyte, had no knowledge of any of this. He was flying blind. As far as Greer was concerned, when the governor-elect called him and said, "I want you to be chairman of the party," it was end of story.

When Greer contacted Jordan and asked for a meeting, she flatly refused to meet with him.

Greer was surprised at the vehement negative feedback coming from Jordan. "We have all kinds of problems," he was told. "Carole Jean doesn't like you."

"She doesn't even know who I am," said Greer.

"That may be true," he was told, "but she doesn't like Charlie Crist, and she hears you ran a company that puts beer in bars."

FIRST THINGS FIRST.

Greer called Ray Valdez, the state committeeman of Seminole County, one of a handful of elected officials who had supported Crist over Gallagher and had helped Greer in the campaign.

Greer was aware that Valdez loved being state committeeman. Even so Greer said to him, "Ray, I need you to do something, and I'm asking you on behalf of governor-elect Charlie Crist. Will you resign as the state committeeman so I can run in a special election, so I can run for state party chairman?"

"Absolutely," said Valdez. "Anything for Governor Crist."

Greer was surprised and gratified.

Two weeks later Greer was elected the new state committeeman of Seminole County. It was the first time any of the grass-roots Republicans in the room had ever met him.

Now eligible to run for state party chairman, Greer would face the incumbent Jordan in an election on January 22, 2007.

"We want to assign you a staff person. Who do you want?" Arlene DiBenigno asked.

Greer didn't hesitate. "I want Delmar Johnson. Everybody loves him. We work well together. I'll make him the campaign manager for the Jim Greer for Chairman campaign."

Greer and Johnson hit the road to meet as many members of the Florida REC as possible. There are 67 counties in Florida, and Greer was determined to meet as many of the REC's Big Three—county chairman, committeeman, and committeewoman—as they could from each county. Greer campaigned hard. He and Johnson raised over $200,000 to pay campaign expenses—hotel rooms, political consultants, bonuses, and the big election party Delmar intended to hold if Greer won.

One thing Greer noticed about Johnson: the big man liked to do things big. He didn't scrimp when it came to spending money. For long road trips, Delmar would rent an SUV, not a compact car. If they were having dinner with someone deemed important, Delmar would make the reservations at the Capital Grill in Tallahassee or at an expensive steakhouse—not at Carrabba's or the Olive Garden. Their guests, who had to decide between voting for Greer or Jordan, would appreciate the extra elegance.

Greer's nomination and Crist's support were by now public knowledge. Everyone in the Republican Party of Florida knew that Crist had handpicked Greer, even if they had never heard of him.

Greer quickly was learning what it was like to be a public candidate on a big stage. Carole Jean and her supporters were spreading malicious untruths about him. She was making his business, advising bars how to stay out of trouble, into an election issue by twisting the facts about what he had been doing.

Two weeks after Crist announced Greer's appointment as chairman, the Republican Party of Florida held its quarterly meeting in November of 2006 at the Rosen Hotel in Orlando. Greer and his wife Lisa were asked to attend.

JIM AND LISA GREER had met eight years earlier at a McDonald's, of all places. Jim, then 36, had picked up his then two-year-old daughter Amber from daycare and taken her for a hamburger. Lisa, then 26, had picked up her son Hunter, the same age as Amber, from daycare, and met her mother at that same McDonald's.

Lisa first noticed Amber, who was waddling around the main part of the Mickey D's carrying her soda and drinking it from a straw while her father was talking on a cell phone. He continued his conversation when he sat at a table adjacent to Lisa, her mother, and Hunter.

Hunter and Amber went into the ball pit to play, and when the irresistibly sociable Hunter left the pit, he took a surprised Jim by the hand and brought him and Amber over to meet his mom.

While Lisa was talking to Hunter and Amber, Lisa's mother began talking to Jim, who told her all about his business and his divorce. Lisa's mother let Jim know that Lisa wasn't married or involved with Hunter's father.

Lisa returned to the table, and when Jim first began talking to her, she was rather quiet. She thought him to be too old for her and not her type. She was also a little put off because she could see that her mother was trying to get them together.

When Jim began to play with Hunter, she softened. But she had to go back to work and when she told Jim she and Hunter had to leave, he walked her to her car.

"It was very nice to have met you," Jim said. "Maybe I can see you and Hunter again soon."

Lisa was at her desk when the receptionist informed her that she had a delivery. Lisa's mother had told Jim where she worked—at Pro Staff, a company that helped find temporary and long-term employees for accounting firms—and he had sent her a dozen red roses and a note that included his phone number and, "It was nice meeting you and Hunter." She was touched that he had remembered Hunter's name.

She called him that day.

The date was July 1, 1998, and on the phone Jim told her he had to go out of town on the third, so they better go out for dinner the next day, "because I can't wait that long to see you again."

By their fourth date Jim told Lisa he intended to marry her. He saw they were a good team. Not only was Lisa a beauty pageant winner, she was also a lifelong Republican.

Two years later he proposed, and six months after that they were married. Lisa had no idea what she was getting herself into. In a way, neither did Jim.

"YOU'RE GOING TO MEET with the governor-elect," said DiBenigno. "Then we're going to introduce you to the state committee."

"I was excited," said Greer. "I put on my suit, my red tie, and my cuff links. My wife had her high heels on and her Republican pin. We brought our baby boy, Austin, who was as cute as can be. I had never been to a RPOF meeting, so I didn't know what to expect. Delmar was briefing me."

As the Greers pulled into the hotel, Arlene called Jim on his cell phone.

"There are a lot of people really upset over the way Charlie has done this," she said. "There are 500 or 600 people coming, and a lot of them are trouble-makers. They're all griping about how Charlie hadn't consulted them about you."

"Okay, what should I do?" Greer asked."

"Come into the lobby," said Arlene. "Don't talk to anybody. Just sit there until I call you."

Greer and his wife sat in the hotel lobby until Arlene arrived and began introducing them to some friendly delegates, who treated the Greers well.

"Hey, Jim, we don't know you. But we're told you're a great guy."

The reception was called for 7 p.m., and at 6 Arlene ushered the Greers upstairs. As Greer walked down the corridor leading to Crist's suite, he noticed FDLE officers standing in front of the door.

When Greer entered the suite, Crist boomed, "Hey, Chairmaaaannn," putting his arm around Greer. "You're going to be a fantastic chairman. You're going to be the best chairman the party ever had."

Greer, Crist, and LeMieux sat at the dining room table in the suite, and they talked about how they would like Greer to reform the party.

"The party has a lot of problems that you're going to find out about," said Crist. "We wouldn't want to be you!" Crist joked with LeMieux.

"Is there anything you'd like to ask us?" said LeMieux.

"I would like to have assurance that I will have direct access to the governor," Greer said. "If I'm going to run the party, I'd like to know that I can talk to the governor when I need to talk to him."

"Yes, that's fine," said Crist, "but George speaks for me. George and you will be working together very closely."

Greer's impression that night was that Charlie Crist didn't think very much of the grass-roots members of the Florida Republican Party, and neither did George LeMieux, himself a former county chairman, who told Lisa Greer, "We'll win in spite of them, not because of them."

There was a knock on the door. It was Carole Jean Jordan, who had been invited to the meeting. When she walked in, Greer, amazed he was standing in the same space with the governor-elect and his incoming chief of staff, was grinning from ear to ear, not believing his good fortune. Jordan quickly threw a damper on his exuberance.

"Governor," she said sharply, "I normally don't say this to governors, but you've really messed this one up. The way you've announced Jim as chairman has really upset a lot of members. I can't tell you how many angry people there are downstairs."

Greer didn't yet know it, but Jordan had asked Crist's people to get her a job—with benefits, because she had a sick husband—in return for not running against him. In an effort to nail down this job, she had been arm-twisting Crist.

Crist's people had gotten a tentative commitment from U.S. Senator Mel Martinez's office to hire her, but it wasn't yet a sure thing, so while she stood there Charlie Crist did what he did best: he deflected the situation.

"You're going to love living in Washington D.C., Carole Jean," he said, without even acknowledging the problem she was addressing.

Jordan turned to Greer and said, "This is not about you, Jim. Nobody knows you. You've never been involved in our state party before."

"Yes," said LeMieux, "but he's going to make a great chairman."

Greer was briefed on the agenda for the night. Jordan was to introduce Crist, who would make a speech and then introduce Jim Greer, his new Republican Party of Florida chairman. Part of Crist's task was to talk about Greer in a way that would make him more acceptable to the opposition.

Shortly, the group walked down to the meeting of the party. Greer saw that he wasn't getting the warm, fuzzy reception he had expected as the new chairman. He was shaken.

As Jordan rose to speak, Greer could feel the hostility in the room. Jordan was brief, and when Crist took the stage, he said simply, "You know, it's great to be your governor. Thank you for your help. Get to know Jim—he'll be a great chairman. Good night, everybody."

DiBenigno was panicking because Crist hadn't done what he said he would, tell the crowd all about this newcomer Jim Greer and explain why he was going to be a terrific chairman.

"Don't go anywhere," Arlene said to Jim. "Stand right here. I'm going to talk to him."

A few minutes later she returned.

"Nope," she said. "He's not saying any more. He's leaving."

And then Charlie Crist left to catch a plane.

THAT NIGHT THE AFFABLE Jim Greer walked from table to table introducing himself to as many Republican Party members as he could. He received many favorable comments, while also experiencing standoffish slights. He was not only meeting supporters of Carole Jean Jordan—and she had a lot of them—he was also encountering followers of Tom Gallagher, the right-wing Republican who had lost to Crist in the gubernatorial primary.

"It was a very interesting night," Greer recalled.

Later that night, Greer held a reception in his suite for state committee members—those who would be voting for the next chair. Jeff Kottkamp, the lieutenant governor-elect, spoke and said very complimentary things about Greer, but few state committee people heard his comments because few actually came to the reception.

The next morning, Sharon Day, one of Jordan's biggest supporters, asked to have coffee with Greer. "I don't know who you are," Day said. "I've been the national committeewoman for four years. Carole Jean Jordan is one of my best friends. And I think the way Charlie has done this is just terrible. He's caused so many problems with the state committee. He should have put out feelers to see how people felt about you. Instead he suddenly announced you were going to be the next party chairman, and that's upset me and many people on the state committee."

"Sharon, I'm sorry," Greer said. "Nobody asked me. I'm just following along."

"I just don't know what's going to happen," Day said. "I have to tell you. I don't know if you're going to be elected."

"I have to tell you," Greer replied, "I've always taken the position that the governor runs the party."

Greer explained later that he wouldn't allow Sharon Day or anyone else to put him or Charlie down.

Said Greer, "Whenever someone played that card with me, my answer was always the same: if he's the governor, I believe the governor gets to decide who's going to run the party."

Greer's next meeting was with Paul Senft, the Republican national committeeman. Senft would turn out to be one of Greer's staunchest allies.

"I'm a Charlie Crist guy," said Senft. "Charlie says you're the guy to be chairman, and I'm with you a hundred and ten percent."

"That's great," Greer replied, "because I just left having coffee with Sharon . . ."

"Sharon's a bitch," said Senft. "The reason Sharon is upset is because she's been up Carole Jean Jordan's ass for the last four years. They go shopping together. I'm the national committeeman, and yet I've been cut out of the loop for the last four years, and Sharon Day has been in the loop. What you're seeing, Jim, is Sharon losing her power and influence because Carole Jean isn't going to be the chair anymore."

Greer was pretty sure he would get ten votes from the members of the Florida senate and ten votes from the Florida house, because they were going to vote for whomever the governor wanted. Still, to win he figured he would need many of the votes of the grass-roots party members throughout the state as he could get.

"I knew I had problems," said Greer. "I knew I was absolutely going to have to run a campaign for chairman versus just being anointed."

FOR THE NEXT 45 days Greer and Johnson continued their tour of Florida, going to every county and meeting with every county chair, state committeemen, and state committeewomen who would see them. The more Greer traveled, the more he found out just how dysfunctional the Florida Republican Party was. For example, Delmar would schedule Jim to go into a county in the Panhandle and tell him: "We're going to meet the county chairman at 8 at the Waffle House. We're going to meet the state committeeman at 9 at Denny's, and we're going to meet the state committeewoman at the Cracker Barrel at 11."

"Why can't we meet all three at the same time?"

"Because they hate each other," said Johnson.

"They're supposed to be the Big Three of the REC from the same county, and we can't all have coffee together?"

That's how dysfunctional it was.

"In most cases the county chairs didn't like the state committeemen and women," said Greer, "because the state committeemen and women don't have a specific area of responsibility, the way the county chair does. A county chair runs his county. He does all the work. So normally, if there was a troublemaker in a county party, it was the state committeeman or woman. The way the county chair sees it, after he's done all the work, the state committeeman and woman show up to steal the credit."

While Greer was touring the state seeking votes, incumbent chair Jordan sat on her throne in Tallahassee not letting anyone know her intentions. When asked if she was running for reelection, she'd say she hadn't made up her mind. But Jim learned that Carole Jean was in fact getting some of her longtime cronies to call REC members, soliciting votes on her behalf. She also sent out a questionnaire asking, "If Carole Jean does announce she's going to run against Jim Greer, who will you vote for?"

Meanwhile, Crist had assigned Jim Rimes, a member of his transition team, to deal with Jordan. Rimes would call and ask what her intentions were, but she was as vague with him as she was with everyone else.

One day Rimes called Greer. "I spoke to Carole Jean today," he said. "She talks very negatively about you. She says you shouldn't be chairman. You run a company that teaches bars about alcohol laws. You had a DUI 20 years ago."

"What does this all mean?" asked Greer.

"It means nothing," Rimes said. "We're just keeping you apprised that she's being a real bitch."

"Okay," said Greer. "I'm out here campaigning. Today I'm going to Gainesville."

On the plus side, Greer received the endorsement of the Federation of Young Republicans, who complained that Carole Jean had treated them poorly. Other organizations and segments of the party that had not been treated well by Carole Jean also started coming out and endorsing Greer.

Jordan remained mum.

Ten days before the Greer-Jordan election, anonymous emails attacked Greer and his family, saying his son Austin was illegitimate, which was a blatant lie. Another email told of Greer's police record from his DUI 20 years earlier.

Crist and Greer knew it was coming from Jordan or her supporters, but they weren't able to prove it. Jim Rimes said to Carole Jean, "If you know where this is coming from, you need to tell them to stop. It's terrible what you're doing. This isn't Jim's fault. Jim was picked by Crist."

"It's not me," Carole Jean said. "I have nothing to do with it. I don't know who's doing it."

The Crist camp didn't believe a word of it. The anonymous emails continued.

Jordan knew enough about Charlie Crist to know he wasn't a loyal guy. She figured that if she could create enough negativity, Crist might drop Greer as a candidate.

"It wasn't out of the question that she was right about that," said Greer.

For two weeks the governor had gone silent with Greer, who wondered whether Crist would stick with him. During this time a story was making the rounds that Crist and LeMieux had interviewed former House Speaker Alan Bense, a well-liked conservative, about *his* becoming the chairman.

Unfortunately for Bense, Greer was to find out later, the outspoken House speaker was too much his own man.

LeMieux later told Greer, "Bense was never seriously considered. You were always the only one he wanted as chairman of the party."

"Whether that was true," said Greer, "I'll never know."

Ten days before the vote, the Crist administration gave Jordan an ultimatum: "We're tired of playing this game. We're the new administration. We want you out as chair, and we want Greer in. And we want you to endorse him as chairman."

Jordan refused.

In retaliation, LeMieux, with Crist's knowledge, ordered Jordan ejected from her office on the second floor of Republican Party headquarters. Quietly, confidentially, Crist's staff was ordered to intercept all her mail to stop her letter-writing. The staff was ordered to stop communications with her.

Jordan packed her stuff into her car and drove off, never to return. She called all her cronies on the state committee and told them of her shabby treatment by the Crist administration.

"I can't even send letters out any more because they are all scrutinized, just like they do in prison," she said.

Carole Jean Jordan went back to her home in Vero Beach. She took Republican Party of Florida letterhead with her, and she sent out letters intimating she intended to run against Greer.

"Charlie Crist has a right to recommend who he'd like as chair," she wrote, "but you as the voting members have the ultimate choice."

It seemed clear that Jordan would run for reelection. How bad would it be for the incoming governor if his nominee lost? It would be the first ding in his armor. The message would be, *His own party won't listen to him.*

The guessing game continued. Would she or wouldn't she?

4

'The Greatest Day of My Life'

The annual meeting of the Republican Party of Florida convened at Disney World's Dolphin Hotel on January 22, 2007. As Jim and Lisa Greer entered the building, Greer was taken aback when he noticed people wearing "Draft Carole Jean for a Third Term" buttons. But he also could see that Delmar Johnson, his campaign manager, had worked his magic. Big banners proclaimed, "Elect Jim Greer Chairman of the Republican Party of Florida." Volunteers wearing "Elect Jim Greer" T-shirts were shaking hands and handing out flyers in every corner.

The whole Republican Party is divided, Greer thought to himself, *and my family and I are in the middle of this thing.*

The election was imminent, but despite the "Elect Carole Jean" hoopla, she still hadn't announced whether she intended to run. No insider was openly campaigning for her because she hadn't even told her state committee buddies what she was going to do.

Johnson's poll numbers showed that Greer would win overwhelmingly against Jordan. As it turned out, a lot of those polled weren't telling the truth.

The night before the Saturday election, Johnson booked the huge Dolphin Hotel ballroom. He spent $30,000 to promote Jim Greer for chairman. A live band was on stage. Balloons dotted the entranceway. It looked like a presidential campaign stop.

Long tables held vast quantities of shrimp and prime rib. Drinks and fine wine flowed. Gift baskets were sent to the room of every voting member.

Just about everyone came to the party: Governor-elect Crist, every cabinet member, many of the state legislators, and, of course, most of the 400 members of the state committee. Whether they intended to vote for Greer or not, all came to eat the jumbo shrimp and prime rib and to drink the expensive wine.

The next morning, two hours before the scheduled election, Jim Rimes, who worked for Crist and answered to George LeMieux, told Greer, "You're probably going to be elected chairman, and I just want to take a few minutes to tell you that the chairman's role is ceremonial."

Greer bristled. "That's not what the constitution says. That's not what the bylaws say." He understood instantly what this meant: George LeMieux intended to call the shots for the party.

"Jim," said Greer, "in that case I may not be the guy for the job. For good or for bad, I'm a take-charge kind of guy. I've come from being a CEO of my own business. When George and the governor asked me to take this position, they told me they wanted me to reform the party, to do good things."

"This doesn't mean you can't do it," said Rimes, "but you're going to have to coordinate a lot of things with the governor's office."

"Fine," said Greer, and they left it at that.

Years later, Greer reflects that if he had accepted being just a ceremonial chairman he "never would have had the problems I had."

Charlie Crist took the podium on the main stage of the huge ballroom. Carole Jean Jordan sat at the head of the dais and presided over the meeting. The 250 voting members sat at tables. Many more who came for the spectacle stood behind ropes that kept them apart. An air of suspicion permeated the room.

Crist began, "Madame Chairman, it's great to be your governor. Ladies and gentlemen, I now nominate Jim Greer to be the chairman of the Florida Republican Party."

Greer, sitting with the contingent from Seminole County 15 rows back, was heartened when the crowd began to roar their approval.

Tom Feeney, a congressman and a friend of Greer's, seconded the nomination, as did Mario Diaz-Balart, a congressman from Miami. Delmar Johnson arranged for one of the state committee members to also second Greer's nomination so it wouldn't appear that just high-ranking politicians favored Greer.

The crowd was going crazy. The Jim Greer bandwagon was on a roll.

Carole Carter, a longtime friend of Carole Jean Jordan, stood at a microphone amid the delegates on the floor and said, "I nominate Carole Jean Jordan for another term."

Greer had heard she would be nominated, but the scuttlebutt held that she intended to turn down the nomination. An elderly gentleman from the Panhandle walked up to the microphone and seconded the nomination. The photographers were clicking away. The room was hushed.

Carole Jean Jordan walked to the podium.

"I want to thank those who nominated me for a third term," she said. "We cannot afford on-the-job training."

Greer turned to Jim Stelling sitting next to him.

"That bitch is going to do it," he said.

Whereupon Carole Jean Jordan said, "I hereby accept the nomination to run for chairman again."

She's throwing down the gauntlet. I wonder what she's going to do if she gets elected because the governor's office won't take her phone calls. And the governor won't raise her any money.

After the ballots were distributed around the room and everyone had voted, the ballots were taken to a side room and counted. For 33 long minutes Greer held his breath as suspense filled the room.

Clay Ingram, one of the vote counters, winked and smiled at Greer when he walked by him.

Finally it was announced—out of 266 votes cast, Greer had defeated Jordan by eight votes. Applause filled the room. "Get up so you can wave at everyone," Greer was commanded. As he did, Carole Jean Jordan made a quick exit out the side door and left the building.

Before entering the following luncheon in his honor, Jim, Lisa, Amber, Austin, and Hunter held hands in a circle and prayed that Greer serve the party well.

I've just been elected chairman. This is the greatest day of my life.

As Charles Dickens once wrote and as Jim Greer would come to find out: It was the best of times; it was the worst of times.

5

'I'm Not Going to Be a Jeb Bush Republican'

Two weeks before Jim Greer's election, Charlie Crist was sworn in as Florida's 44th governor. Jeb Bush, his predecessor, was up on the main stage with him, as was Tom Gallagher, the loser to Crist in the primary. Greer, accorded VIP seating, sat in the sixth row in the front of the stage. After the ceremony he stopped by the governor's office and met Crist's parents and sisters. He extended his congratulations and left.

The inaugural ball which traditionally followed the governor's victory always was a *big* deal. Women went out and bought long gowns, and men rented or put on their own shiny tuxedos. Everyone involved in the winning campaign was to be a guest that night.

In preparation for the great event, Meredith O'Rourke, Crist's lead money-raiser, and Brian Ballard, a wealthy lobbyist, raised millions of dollars from their major donors, including $50,000 from Florida Light and Power; $100,000 from Disney; and $100,000 from Universal Studios. The Governor's Ball was to be a gathering of the money people and the hundreds of Crist's grass-roots supporters. Major donors would receive neckties emblazoned with the emblem of Florida and special cuff links, too. Newspapers began to write about the extravagance of the party.

And then Charlie Crist, the consummate politician, aware that the country's and the state's economy were going into the tank, abruptly canceled the inaugural ball.

"He decided against it," said Greer, "because his whole mantra was, 'Charlie Crist is a man of the people and for the people.'"

The bellows of Republican fury were heard all over the state of Florida. The lobbyists who had raised the money for the ball were outraged. Even more furious were the grass-roots Republicans who already had spent their hard-earned money on non-refundable airline tickets, room reservations, and fancy clothes.

Crist's cancellation of the inaugural ball put Jim Greer in a bind. It was still two weeks before the election between him and Carole Jean Jordan, and the night of the Inaugural Ball he had arranged a party at the Silver Slipper Restaurant in Tallahassee to woo Republicans to side with him as party chairman.

When asked about his plans, Greer told reporters, "We're going to continue to celebrate the Republican Party, and I'm going to continue to have this celebration."

Charlie Crist didn't show up for Greer's party, but Crist campaign manager George LeMieux and lieutenant-governor-elect Jeff Kottkamp did. When LeMieux arrived, everyone in the room understood that the governor still supported Greer as chairman. But Crist not making an appearance showed Greer something else.

"It told me at the very beginning that when things get tough," said Greer, "Charlie Crist is not the one to take the hill with you."

When Crist became governor, there were still hundreds of pending appointments made by his predecessor, Jeb Bush. Ordinarily these appointments would go to the Senate for confirmation during the coming legislative session. But Crist did something very unusual. He pulled all of Bush's pending appointments, something that's usually only done when the opposing party takes over.

In rescinding them, Crist said he wished to look at each appointment individually and decide whether he'd continue with the appointee or name someone else.

"And that alienated a lot of people," said Greer. "That was an insult to Jeb Bush."

ON THE BRIGHT, BLUE sunny day of his inauguration Crist called an afternoon staff meeting to talk about a pet project, a Clean Energy Climate Control Summit. He invited California Governor Arnold Schwartzenegger to be the keynote speaker. Schwartzenegger had convened a similar summit in California. The Governator was demanding $300,000 be given to a political organization that he supported. The money was raised privately.

Why is the issue of clean energy so important? The Republican Party has no interest in those things. The Republican Party doesn't believe in global warning or in providing resources to those types of liberal issues. We're the party that takes big campaign contributions from Big Oil, electric companies, and coal-burning companies. We're not geared to have a Clean Energy Summit with a governor of California who isn't liked by his own party, thought Greer.

From day one Charlie Crist started down a path to show he was a "Man of the People," that he wasn't a hard-core, right-wing Republican, like most of the Republican leaders in Florida. During the campaign he had often said, "I am a Jeb Bush Republican." But now he was making an about face, telling the public in effect, "I'm *not* going to be a Jeb Bush Republican like I said I would be on the campaign trail."

To further emphasize that point, Crist made it very clear to Greer just how he felt about Jeb Bush. Shortly after Greer became chairman, Crist sat with Greer in the chairman's office on the first floor of the Republican Party Headquarters in Tallahassee. On the walls were dozens of photographs of Jeb Bush.

"There are a lot of Jeb Bush pictures around here, chairman," said Crist.

Greet understood the message: *Get rid of them.*

Even though the political staffs of the Republican House and Senate supposedly worked for Greer as chairman, whenever he went to visit them on the second floor of the same building, he always felt like an outsider. The house and senate staff weren't Crist people. They were Jeb Bush people.

Not only did they not take down the Jeb Bush photographs, they put up bigger ones. The schism within the party was growing.

Greer, who had supported Jeb Bush during both of his campaigns for governor, followed Crist's lead, buying into what Crist was advocating.

"I began to distance myself from Jeb because I had become a Charlie Crist guy," said Greer. "I wasn't anti-Jeb. In fact, shortly after becoming chairman, I had this idea of going down to Miami to brief Governor Bush about our party's plans. But I was rebuffed by Jeb every time I made the effort. One night I sent a text to Jeb: 'I'd like to come down and talk to you about the minority outreach program we're doing and how I'm restructuring the Republican Executive Committee.' He wrote back, 'I appreciate your thoughts, Jim, but it's best I stay out of what's going on.' What that meant was, 'You're Charlie Crist's person, and I hear Charlie and others are saying unkind things about me, so . . . good luck.' We'd hear from Jeb Bush's people later."

The next important policy decision Charlie Crist made as governor was to restore the rights of convicted felons. When Greer was still with the Seminole County Crist for Governor campaign, Crist and he were riding together when Crist said, "Jim, let me ask you a question. What do you think of felons getting their rights back after they serve their time and after they've made restitution and done everything they should?"

"I think that's absolutely right," said Greer. "I don't think people should have a ball and chain around their leg the rest of their life. I don't see why Florida isn't like most states where after you serve your time, your rights are automatically restored."

"I agree with you," said Crist, who recounted a story of a man he met on the campaign trail, a convicted felon. He told Crist he never thought about the loss of his rights as a citizen on any day of the year except Election Day.

Crist said the man told him, "'I feel like half a human being on Election Day.' This man touched my heart, and I'm going to propose it." This was a liberal stance for a Republican governor, but shortly after his election, he proposed it, and the cabinet reluctantly agreed and the policy was adopted.

Here we go again. We're a law and order, throw the key away party. We're not a rehabilitation, compassionate, circumstances occur, people should get a second chance party.

Crist, having set himself up as a Populist progressive governor, a moderate who reached out to everyone, had a 70 percent approval rating with the public, and when he proposed the law to give felons back their rights, everyone in the state cabinet voted for the measure—except Attorney General Bill McCollum, the golden boy of the conservative movement of the Florida Republican Party. McCollum, a former Florida congressman, had been a floor manager of the Bill Clinton impeachment. Perhaps because of that he had lost his reelection bid to Congress.

But thanks to Crist, the rights of nonviolent felons automatically would be restored. The citizens of the state of Florida loved their new governor. The Old White Men—the hard-core Republican base—hated him with a rage and a passion.

WHEN CRIST CAME INTO office, he and his sidekick George LeMieux generally left the day-to-day running of the Republican Party to Greer. Everyone knew Greer was the governor's guy, so whatever Greer wanted, Greer got.

One early decision Greer had to make was whether to give money to ultra-conservative organizations that backed causes like the Defense of Marriage Act, which defined marriage as between a man and a woman. Under Greer's predecessor, Carole Jean Jordan, and at the direction of Jeb Bush, the Republican Party of Florida donated $300,000 a year to such groups.

"Are we going to continue to spend money to promote the Defense of Marriage Act in Florida?" Greer's staff, including Delmar Johnson, Jim Rimes, and Andy Palmer, wanted to know.

Greer said no.

"I don't think the party should be involved in those types of issues," he said. "I'm not saying I don't believe a marriage is between a man and a woman"—he didn't want to alienate them all—"but I don't think the party should be spending money on it. And I'm sure neither does Governor Crist."

Later over dinner Greer told the governor of his decision.

"Great decision, Chairman," said Crist.

Later a number of the Christian fundamentalist groups would work openly against Crist and snub the governor and Greer by not inviting them to their big statewide dinners.

JIM GREER, LIKE CHARLIE Crist, had big ideas on how to improve the Republican Party of Florida. But first he had to make some important appointments. One of the most important positions was finance chair, a person who is typically a multi-millionaire who can raise a ton of money from his colleagues. Usually it's a close friend of the governor. It was no different this time around.

Crist strongly suggested that Greer hire a Pi Kappa Alpha fraternity brother of his at Florida State University, an ex-Marine, a top gun pilot, a guy who flew for Delta Airlines before he joined his father's shipping company and turned it into a billion-dollar oil business called Sargeant Oil. His company won the contracts for providing oil transfers to Iraq.

Harry Sargeant III was a man's man.

Crist told Greer, "I want you and Meredith to meet with Harry Sargeant at lunch, and I want you to ask Harry to be the finance chairman of the party."

They went to the Governor's Club in Tallahassee. Sargeant, a tall, distinguished, handsome man, and Greer hit it off. They were both entrepreneurs and leaders—though Sargeant had made far more money.

Crist had said to Greer, "Ask Harry to make a commitment of writing a $250,000 check for the Republican Party to show he's really going to buy into being the finance director."

"This was the first time in my life I had ever asked anyone for $250,000," said Greer. He was sure Crist had laid the groundwork, but the formal request was to come from the chairman.

Toward the end of the lunch Greer said to Sargeant, "You know, there are a lot of major donors around Florida who will want to see that the finance chairman has stepped up to the plate, so I'd like to ask if you'd write a $250,000 check to the party."

Greer held his breath. He needn't have.

Sargeant pulled out his checkbook and wrote him a check for $250,000.

"I was flabbergasted," said Greer, "but he did ask me one thing I will never forget. He said, 'Before I do that, how much have you given to the party?'

"I said, 'I don't have the resources you do, but over the years, I've given between $25,000 and $50,000 to the party.' I didn't find his question offensive. It showed him I walked the walk."

Greer said he recalls thinking that they were off to a great start. *Charlie Crist is governor, I'm chairman, and Harry Sargeant is the finance chairman of Florida.*

Greer also had the responsibility of appointing the general counsel to the Republican Party. He had someone in mind from the law firm of Gray, Robinson, but Crist made it clear that he was going to make the appointment.

Crist said, "I think you should really consider Jason Gonzalez," who had been a Crist campaign chairman from Leon County, where Tallahassee is located. Beholden to Crist, Greer had no problem taking his suggestion. "I went back and met with Jason. I liked him a lot and appointed him general counsel."

WHEN GREER WAS ELECTED party chairman, few statewide knew who he was. He was described as being "plucked from Seminole County," and some grass-roots veterans, who had spent 20 years with the party, derided him as being unqualified to be chairman.

"What they failed to realize," said Greer, "was I had been running a multi-million dollar organization, a company I had grown from one client to thousands across the country. I had VPs and field managers and a large staff and my own corporate headquarters building. I was on the city commission. I had raised money for Republicans. I just hadn't been part of their day-to-day world."

Greer felt he was one of the most qualified people to take over an organization like the party. The problem was that he wasn't prepared to deal with the viciousness of some of the people in the party organization. He also didn't understand just how dysfunctional the Republican Party had become. Trying to fix it would cause him serious problems.

"When I came to the job as chairman," said Greer, "I found the party structure and the performance of the staff—and how they interacted with the counties—to be very strange and *not* very productive. To always be fighting with each other, complaining about each other. There was a real disconnect between the paid staff in the headquarters in Tallahassee and the Republican Executive Committee and all their volunteers."

Greer learned that Carole Jean Jordan—and the chairs before her—had essentially avoided these issues. Greer would learn too late that Jordan and her predecessors knew that by interfering with the status quo it would stir up a hornet's nest. Greer didn't know that because he hadn't come through the ranks. Nor did he care. *If it was broke, let's fix it,* was his attitude.

As a result Greer didn't realize that in the normal course of events, everyone hated everyone, everyone complained about everything, and everyone fought—all the time.

"That's just how we are," is how Greer put it looking back.

Greer decided that when he became chairman he would work to develop a closer relationship with the state committee members of the party. The perception at Republican Party headquarters was that the paid staff did its thing, the donors did their thing, and the volunteers from the counties did their thing, and it was best if the three groups stayed away from each other—except during the quarterly meetings.

Greer saw that the paid staffers in Tallahassee were condescending to the county volunteers, while the county Republicans were suspicious of the Tallahassee staff.

He instituted a conference call the first Tuesday of every month in an attempt to bring the paid staff and the volunteers closer together. He, Executive Director Andy Palmer, and Political Director Pablo Diaz would sit by the phone in a conference room and any state committee member could join the conversation. Greer would give an update on party activities and plans and at the end of the call would field questions.

He wanted to make sure that the state committee members had access to information on budget and finances. In the past the chair had provided only sketchy details.

"Chairman," his staff would tell him, "you're giving them too much information. It's going to come back and haunt you."

To the newcomer Greer, that was inconceivable. Why shouldn't he keep the grass-roots volunteers up to speed with what he was doing? Later he'd come to deeply regret his naivete, but back in 2007 the grass-roots Republicans were praising Jim Greer to the heavens.

One of Greer's most innovative business-inspired ideas was to create training and attendance requirements for the state committee members. He created a task force made up of some 42 county chairs and state committeemen and women for the purpose of creating performance requirements such as recording attendance and codifying duties.

Even though many participated, putting down recommendations on paper, and everyone said what a great idea it was, in the end it may have been one of Greer's worst mistakes. The animosity between the county chairmen, the state committeemen, and the state committeewomen only worsened.

"They didn't want any training," he would reflect later. "They didn't want any attendance requirements. They wanted the organization to operate the way it always had."

In March 2007, two months after his election as chairman, Greer held a Club Summit. In counties throughout the state, there are Republican Clubs, Women's Republican Clubs, Young Republican Clubs, and clubs like the Ronald Reagan Club of Hillsborough County. They operate under the oversight of the individual county's Republican Executive Committee. They are supposed to operate in a very cooperative manner because they're the backbone of winning elections. These clubs all have volunteers.

What Greer had discovered was that half of the clubs didn't get along with their county chairs. The club presidents, rather than kissing the rings of the county chairs, held them in contempt. The Club Summit was supposed to lessen the animosity.

The Republican Party chairman was supposed to sign a certificate chartering all the clubs every two years. Jordan had just stamped their names, sent them out to the clubs, and didn't get involved. She was smarter than Greer, who decided it would be a good idea to train the club presidents by making them attend an all-day seminar. Rather than arbitrarily charter the clubs again, he wanted to know if they had done anything in the past five years. If they were serious about getting along with their REC's.

Once again, at the time everyone thought it was a brilliant idea.

Three hundred club presidents met on a Saturday in Orlando. Greer got up and talked about his goals for the summit. He held sessions to air the gripes of the county chairs and the gripes of the grass-roots volunteers.

Towards the end of the session Greer personally signed each of the club charters, and he had a photo of himself taken with each club president. They stood in a long line as each was introduced. At the end of the event Greer received a standing ovation.

The *Orlando Sentinel* gave Greer glowing press for his efforts. The newspaper headlines were right on: "Greer Shaking Up How GOP Does Business"; "Greer Makes Republican Party in Florida More Relevant."

Among those in attendance at the Club Summit was Carole Jean Jordan. Though defeated by Greer, she was still the state committeewoman from Indian River County. She never again came into the Republican headquarters, but for a month after her defeat she refused to vacate the condo in Tallahassee given to her by the party because she was the chairman.

After the Club Summit, she said to Greer, "This was a very good idea."

"What she meant," said Greer, "was 'this was a very good idea, and I wish I could put a knife in your back right now.'"

GREER INSTITUTED ANOTHER INNOVATIVE program called Headquarters for a Day. His goal was to bring the chairman and the Republican headquarters closer to the county grass-roots organizations. He, his assistant Delmar Johnson, his political director Pablo Diaz, and executive director Jim Rimes traveled the state, briefing the Big Three of each county and other party people on what the Republican Party intended to do for the coming 2008 presidential election.

Many of the Big Three—the county chairs, state committee men, and state committee women—embraced the program, and Greer began receiving loud ovations whenever he presented his ideas. The locals asked to have their photos taken with him. Things were beginning to change for the better.

Yet some county chairs still refused to meet with him. "Some egomaniacs resented my coming into their fiefdoms," Greer explained. "They were like dictators of Third World countries. They didn't like being told what to do. They would tell my staff, 'We don't have the time.'"

Greer would respond, "I don't give a shit what the county chair in Pasco or Hillsborough wants. I'm the chairman of the party, and we're going down there to meet those local Republicans."

In one battle between two statewide rival women's clubs Greer tried everything he could to lessen the animosity between the leaders who hated each other. He had women from both groups, including Cindy Graves and Linda Iveil, the two warring leaders, come to a meeting. All were hostile.

Greer sought a compromise, where women of both groups could attend the Republican Party of Florida's quarterly meetings. Peace was attained for a *short* period of time. Behind his back the fighting continued. He threatened to revoke the charter of both groups because of all the fighting and backstabbing.

"In fact," said Greer, "they weren't doing anything to help Republicans get elected. They were just causing trouble."

After he made the threat to revoke their charters, all quieted down. By 2008 only a few isolated clubs calling themselves the Republican Women's Club of Orange County or Pinellas County were not members of the state Federation of Republican Women. The dissidents had been fanatical and hostile, but as new leaders came in, the bitterness ebbed and even more clubs joined the majority.

Greer had done a good thing, but he continued to make enemies. When he chose the Federation over the other groups, the rejected outsiders got mad and held grudges. And grudges can last a long, long time.

ANOTHER OF GREER'S PLANKS when he ran for chairman was his insistence that the Republican Party reach out to African Americans.

"I was a very strong believer that the Republican Party had to broaden itself and become more inclusive," he said. "That was not the way the party was operating when I got there. I wanted it to be known for being compassionate, for one that embraces minority voters, and as I looked around the party headquarters, we had seven departments and there wasn't one minority director in any of them."

Moreover, there was no outreach department.

When Greer asked, "Who handles minority outreach?" he was referred to Vivian, the African American receptionist on the first floor of the Republican Headquarters.

Greer hired John Davis, a former Florida State University football star to be the head of minority outreach. Davis had worked in the Crist gubernatorial campaign with Greer.

"He was a tall, strapping handsome bald black man," said Greer. "He was in his 30s, with a nice personality, a very hard worker, and I liked him a lot." In addition, Davis was intelligent and articulate with all the right ties to the black community, someone the party needed.

When he announced that Davis would head up the minority outreach program, some of Greer's staff cringed. Jim Rimes, one of the political consultants told Greer, "Your approach to minority outreach is going to bring the blacks out from under every rock at election time, and they're only going to vote Democrat."

Greer disagreed. "How can anyone vote Republican if they don't know what the Republicans stand for?" he argued.

Greer didn't stop with African Americans. He set up what he called Leadership Councils and chose about 20 volunteers from different voting groups to lead them. Among the groups were Hispanics, African Americans, Jews, and women. He created advisory councils to advise him on issues that were important to these groups.

His Leadership Council idea didn't go over very well with the political consultants, either.

"The people you're trying to reach out to," he was told, "don't vote Republican. They are never going to vote Republican, and all you're going to do is get them interested in the political process."

This push for inclusiveness was only partially successful. After three and a half years of cajoling, only 13 of the 67 counties ever took up the cause of Leadership Councils or appointed outreach coordinators as Greer had asked. Clearly, a large contingent of old-line Republicans didn't care a whit about inclusiveness. To them, the party was for those who all their lives had clung to a belief in the superiority of white men and a few docile but dedicated white women.

Despite the skepticism, in time Greer's work to change the ethos of the Republican Party of Florida became a focus for other states interested in minority outreach. Greer would go to Republican National Committee quarterly meetings and be asked to make presentations about his youth and minority outreach programs.

He was gaining some attention among Republicans nationally.

6

'We Eat What We Kill'

Jim Greer was elected on a Saturday, and on Monday he sat in his high-backed leather chair at his desk in the Republican Party of Florida chairman's stately, elegant office in the Republican Party Headquarters Tallahassee, a room with mahogany paneled walls, parquet floors, and the flags of Florida and the United States on poles behind him. It was not unlike the office of a reigning monarch.

"I was elated," said Greer. "This was the big world. I had been a success in the business community, but now—sitting in that office—it was overwhelming."

Greer's secretary showed him line by line his date book that noted everything he was to do from the moment he woke up in the morning to the time he went to bed at night. The daily log went to Greer and all of his senior staff. It included his travel, who he had meetings with, who would be picking him up, who'd be dropping him off, and so on.

This morning it said on his line by line, "Meeting with Speaker of the House, President of the Senate."

When he entered his conference room that first day, seated there were two of the most powerful people in Florida politics, Ken Pruitt, the president of the Senate, and Marco Rubio, the speaker of the House.

Pruitt, a Republican, was a moderate like Governor Crist. He was the father of Florida Bright Futures, which rewarded high school students who performed well with grant money to go to college. He had also sponsored a bill to reduce the phosphorous which polluted Lake Okeechobee.

Rubio belonged to the ultra-right wing of the party. His parents were Cubans who had left the island in 1956, three years before the Castro revolution. Nevertheless in his speeches he would talk about their escape to freedom. He went to Tarkio College in Tarkio, Missouri, to play football, but after one year transferred to Santa Fe Community College in Gainesville. He then transferred to the University of Florida, got his BA, and went on to the University of Miami Law School where he graduated cum laude.

At age 28 he was elected to the Florida House of Representatives. The issues Rubio focused on were reducing property taxes and decreasing the size of government. For a long time he fought immigration reform. On any choice between supporting big business or the lower and middle classes, Rubio always opted for the companies, at the same time calling for cuts in all government programs to the disadvantaged. He was named Freshman Legislator of the Year by the Florida Petroleum Marketers Association.

The meeting began, and the first thing Rubio said to Greer was, "Chairman, we want to make sure that things that were done in the past will continue to be done under your chairmanship."

"Exactly what are you talking about?" said Greer.

"We want to make sure that how we raise money, how we spend it and funnel it through the Republican Party will continue as it's been under other chairmen."

"We eat what we kill," said Pruitt.

Today Greer translates this as "if we raise a million dollars and we park it here at the party, and then if we decide we want to take it into the parking lot and burn it or, more to the point, use it to take a trip to Paris or to buy a new roof for a legislator's house, I as chairman won't interfere. Here's what you have to understand: the Republican Party has three checking accounts. It's really one account, but internally it's maintained in three separate categories. One is for the general party, the part of the party that the governor and chairman raises money for. The second part is money for the House of Representatives, and the third part is kept for the Senate. The House and Senate go out and raise their own money, and then they park it with the party. It's all done under the auspices of the Republican Party of Florida."

He says it's not supposed to be done that way. The law says that if money is put into the general account, it can be spent any way the chairman of the party wishes to spend it. But if Greer did that, he understood, the political fallout would be swift and deadly. As a result, money put into the party's general fund by Republican members of the House or Senate always is earmarked for a particular use, even though the word "earmark" never is spoken.

Said Greer, "One of the things I was briefed on when I became chairman: "Don't ever use the term 'earmarked accounts.' Say a major corporation like Florida Power and Light or Progress Energy wants to influence legislators in the House of Representatives. They give $100,000 to the Republican Party of Florida with a wink and a nod that the money will be earmarked for House of Representative campaigns. If they want to influence the Senate, they still make the check to the Republican Party of Florida, but the money ends up going to Senate fundraising events.

"That's how it's done, but it's quite illegal."

It's illegal because federal law and Florida law say a political party may not earmark funds. If the money goes to the Republican Party of Florida, under the law the chairman has total discretion as to where the money goes and how it's to be spent.

"But in reality," said Greer, "when I'd be briefed by the party's chief financial officer Richard Swartz, he'd say to me, 'We have $3 million in the account. A million belongs to the House, a million belongs to the Senate, and a million belongs to the general party."

That is why one of the first things Greer was told was, "Don't ever mention to anyone that any contributions are specifically earmarked because that would be in violation of the law."

It was why Rubio and Pruitt wanted to see the new chairman at their first opportunity.

"All the expenditure checks have to be signed and approved by the chairman," said Greer, "so Rubio and Pruitt wanted to make sure if they raised a million dollars and put it in the account of the Republican Party of Florida and they wanted to go to New York and sit in George Steinbrenner's private box and they wanted to hire a limousine and stay in a five-star hotel—something legislators had been doing for years—they wanted to make sure the new chairman would play ball."

And Greer did play ball. He told Rubio and Pruitt, "I see no reason to make any changes in how the party spends its money. The term 'we eat what we kill' won't end."

"If we raise a million dollars and park it here at the party," said Rubio, "you will *not* tell us what we can and cannot do with it." It was a statement, not a question.

"I won't," said Greer.

This agreement would come back to haunt him, but in reality he had no choice in the matter. Had he not gone along, he would have started World War III within the party.

Greer was learning all of this in his first month as chairman.

"They were telling me how it all works," said Greer. "I was slowly learning this was just a money-laundering operation, because in Florida a candidate can only get a contribution up to $500. I can give a candidate $500 for the primary election and another $500 for the general election. But I can write a check for an unlimited amount of money to the Republican Party of Florida.

"A candidate will say to a donor, 'Why don't you write a check for $10,000 to the Republican Party of Florida, and I'll make sure it goes into the House campaign account, and then I'll get it back?'

"The candidate will say, 'The money will be used to elect Republican candidates.' And then there's a wink and a nod that says, 'We're going to make sure it goes to your district's election,' and with that money the Republican Party will hire poll workers, floor walkers, phone callers, canvassers, and be able to do all the things it takes to benefit the particular candidates.

"For example, a campaign manager of a particular candidate will be hired. He'll actually be an employee of the Republican Party, not the campaign. His paycheck will come from the party. They can do that. They can do things through the party that a candidate can't because he doesn't have the money—because of that limitation of a $500 individual contribution."

According to Greer, the Republican Party became expert at changing the reporting laws over the years by passing laws that deliberately make their expenditure reports vague, protecting party leaders like Rubio, Pruitt, and Greer.

"What you would see on the report, for example, might be $5,000 for the Don Cesar Hotel," said Greer. "You wouldn't know who in the Republican Party actually went to the Don Cesar. You wouldn't know what the $5,000 was for. If someone rented a limo, you'd see $1,200 to Fugazy Limousine. You didn't know who did the renting or why."

The only way Greer, Rubio, or Pruitt could get in trouble would be if one of them chose to leak what might be called "inappropriate expenditures" to the media and reveal who did the spending.

As Greer would learn over time, Marco Rubio, soon to be anointed the Crown Prince of the Tea Party, was himself an expert in leaking such damaging information to the media and charging the party for personal expenses.

7

Crist Endorses Giuliani

In March 2007 the Florida legislative package crafted by the Republican majority in the House and Senate included a bill that said a candidate who ran for federal office did not have to resign from the statewide office he held.

"There was some talk that Marco Rubio wanted to run for a higher office," said Greer. "There were rumors, and then all of a sudden the House proposed a bill in committee. Crist liked that law too, because one thing was true with Charlie Crist, he was always looking for the next office to hold."

The package also included a bill that would increase the power of state political party chairmen, allowing them to remove party officeholders who were perceived to be disloyal or disruptive within their county executive committees.

"This was a bill brought to me by Tony DiMatteo, the chairman of Pinellas County, Bill Bunting of Pasco County, and Lou Oliver of Orange County," said Greer, "because they had troublemakers within their Republican Executive Committee, and they needed to get them out."

The state executive committee consisted of the county chairman, county committeeman and committeewoman from each of the 67 counties in Florida. A number of these volunteers were ultra-conservatives who were upset by the spending of the elected officials of the party, including Rubio, Pruitt, Ray Sansom, Dean Cannon, and soon Greer. They were calling for audits and greater oversight of spending by the House and Senate side of the party. They were demanding less spending by the government and the party, and they wanted to see exactly how their officials were spending the Republican Party funds. The elected officials categorized these disparate characters as "troublemakers" who to them were royal pains in the ass.

These far right-wingers were also disrupting meetings of the local county officials. The standard process for removal was too long and vague, and the county chairmen who were having to put up with them wanted to be able to have the party chairman remove these people so they no longer were able to come to meetings. Pinellas County Chairman Tony DiMatteo, for one, had had enough of these rabble-rousers.

"Later," said Greer, "when I actually threatened to use the power given me by the bill, the county chairs no longer remembered they had crafted the rule. It had become 'Greer's idea.'"

The top elected officials, Sansom, Rubio and Pruitt, along with Crist, had national politics on their agenda. They wanted the Florida primary to have more of an impact on the presidential election than in the past. The thinking was that since Florida was an important, populous state, its primary should have more clout.

The Florida lawmakers seeking to move back the date of the Florida primary were being arrogant, but they didn't care. In 2007 Florida's legislative package included a bill that moved the presidential primary in Florida from March back to January, two weeks before Super Tuesday when a group of more than 20 states hold presidential primaries.

Crist and Rubio, two leaders who wanted Florida to have a stronger influence on the outcome of the primary election, were strong supporters of the bill. Greer, doing as Crist asked, signed off on it, too. In some states the party chairman decides when the presidential primary will be, but in Florida it was the legislature.

The Republican National Committee had decreed draconian penalties for states that moved their primaries before the Super Tuesday. The Florida legislators knew this, but they did it anyway. The man who was unfairly blamed was Jim Greer.

"I was facing hostility from many of the National Committee members from other states," said Greer. "They felt Florida always did what it wanted and had no respect for the rules. Florida for eight years had a governor who was President George W. Bush's brother, and there was animosity that Florida got preferential treatment because of Jeb. They were out to get us. They were going to cut our delegation in half, give us a shitty hotel for the convention, and reduce the number of VIP passes for our major donors to attend the convention."

Greer would spend a great deal of the time leading up to the convention fighting with the Republican National Committee's rules committee to lessen those penalties.

Not since Calvin Coolidge in 1924 has a Republican won the presidency without winning Florida. "It's stupid for the national Republican Party to penalize the one state that's probably going to decide who the next president will be," he'd argue.

"I was very defensive about Florida's rightful place and how much influence we had in the process compared to New Mexico or another state. I told them again and again that as party chairman I don't get to decide when the primary is. It was done by the Florida legislature. They never wanted to swallow that pill. They wanted to penalize Florida because they thought I was the one who moved the primary up. They'd say to me, 'You need to go back and tell them to move the primary . . .' 'This is the law now,' I said. 'This is a law passed by the Senate and House and signed by the governor.'"

For a solid year Greer and Florida received national media attention. Everyone wanted to know: *What is the RNC going to do to Florida?*

When the 2007 Florida legislative session ended in early May, the presidential campaign was the major focus of the news and the daily focus of Greer's life. All the Republican presidential candidates—the three most prominent being Mitt Romney, John McCain, and Rudy Giuliani—were visiting Florida frequently.

Members of the Crist administration were split in their loyalties. The old Jeb Bush crew, including George LeMieux, was supporting Romney. LeMieux was hoping to play a major role in a Romney administration, so his goal was to bring Crist to the table, because he knew Crist's endorsement could decide which candidate would win in Florida and probably in the nation.

Lobbyist Brian Ballard, one of Crist's most influential backers, supported McCain. Ballard, who aspired to be an ambassador if McCain won, was the senator's finance chairman in Florida. McCain also had the ear of Crist, who was being coy as to whom he intended to endorse.

Greer and Harry Sargeant, the state party's finance chairman, supported

Giuliani. Greer felt that Giuliani was more moderate than Romney or Mc-Cain on the social issues, not so far to the right that he'd alienate voters. Greer didn't want to support Romney who catered to what Greer saw as the right-wing nuts who drive the primary votes. In addition Greer felt that Crist was leaning towards and directing him towards Giuliani.

Greer had hopes that if Giuliani were elected, he would support Greer for chairman of the National Republican Party.

All the candidates were after one prize: Crist's endorsement. With Florida's primary now coming before Super Tuesday, they realized that if they could get Crist's endorsement, important to winning Florida, they would have the momentum to win on Super Tuesday and take the nomination.

Grateful for having been supported for chairman by Crist, Greer always kept his eye on working to benefit Crist politically.

"I was focused on getting Charlie Crist what he wanted more than anything, and that was a vice presidential nod," said Greer. "Crist wanted to be vice president, and he intended to use his endorsement as a tool to get it."

Every week, it seemed, a presidential candidate visited Florida. They all stopped at Crist's office in Tallahassee to kiss his ring and tell him how great he was and how much he would be valued in their new administration.

None committed to making Crist vice president, but each said he was on their "short list." In turn Crist was vague about who he was going to endorse.

In late summer of 2007 Greer and Harry Sargeant were meeting more and more with Giuliani's right-hand men, Tony Carbonetti and Mike Du-Haime. Carbonetti, a New Yorker, had been the city's deputy mayor, and DuHaime was a respected national political adviser. The bait they were using to get Crist's endorsement was the constant talk of what a great pairing a Giuliani-Crist presidential ticket would make.

Crist asked Greer to go down to Palm Beach during a Giuliani campaign swing and gauge how serious Giuliani was about asking Crist to be his running mate.

On a sunny Thursday afternoon Greer went to the Marriott Hotel in West Palm. After he was ushered into Giuliani's suite, he was asked to come into the bedroom where Giuliani was sitting in a big reclining chair over in the corner.

"Giuliani proceeded to tell me what a great governor Crist was and how crucial it was that he get his endorsement," said Greer. "He said his campaign would use Charlie around the country to get national media."

"He'll be a major part of the campaign," Giuliani promised Greer.

"Crist loved the idea of traveling around the country to be on the national talk shows," said Greer. "In fact, all three of the candidates promised him that. Whether he was going to be VP or not, they all knew how to push his hot buttons. Everybody knew that Charlie Crist was after one thing: Charlie Crist," said Greer. "They knew how to bait him for his endorsement."

"The governor loves you," Greer said to Giuliani. "The governor wants to help. We need a couple of commitments though. I'd like to be the RNC chairman, and the governor needs the commitment that he'll be your VP pick."

Again Giuliani told Greer, "Charlie's a great guy; he'll play a major role in the campaign. You'll be the RNC chairman. I've heard wonderful things about you."

But Giuliani again stopped short of committing to name Crist his vice-presidential candidate.

"He'll be on my short list," said Giuliani. "I just cannot lock myself into that choice right now."

"Sorry to hear that," Greer told him, "but I certainly appreciate everything you've done."

Said Greer, "I was terribly disappointed, because one thing people have always said about me from a business standpoint: Greer can close the deal."

Greer came back home and told Crist, "You're going to be on the short, short list, but Rudy wouldn't commit to making you the VP."

Crist too was disappointed. "Let's think about this," he said. "We have lots of options."

After thinking it over, Crist decided to back Giuliani, the most moderate of the candidates.

In August 2007 Giuliani, Crist, and one of Crist's chief fundraisers and supporters, Harry Sargeant, played a round of golf at a tony course in the Hamptons. During the game Crist committed to endorsing Giuliani for president without receiving in return a promise of the vice presidential slot. He and Giuliani shook hands on it.

"You can count on me and my commitment," Crist told him.

Only five people knew: Giuliani, his two politicos Mike DuHaime and Tony Carbonetti, Sargeant, and Greer.

From then on, Giuliani based his entire campaign strategy on the little secret that Charlie Crist was going to endorse him.

It was, as he would learn too late, a serious, even fatal, mistake.

8

The Mirror Cracked

What Greer was starting to see was that Crist was remarkably good at raising money. He was a natural. Crist actually enjoyed calling people on the phone to ask for money. His fundraising sidekick Meredith O'Rourke and his top fundraiser Harry Sargeant also were whizzes— a formidable two-some who knew how to part wealthy donors from their money.

In August 2007 Crist, Greer, LeMieux, O'Rourke, Sargeant, and lobbyist Brian Ballard flew to New York to attend two fundraisers on Long Island, one at the Hampton mansion of Mori Hosseini, an Iranian-American who was the chairman and CEO of ICI Homes, one of the largest residential home builders in Volusia County in Florida. In 2004 Hosseini gave President George W. Bush $200,000. Crist knew Hosseini would be generous to him as well. The second stop was at the home of Ronald Perelman, the former husband of actress Ellen Barkin, and once the head of the fabled Revlon cosmetic company.

The night before the fundraisers the group stayed in Manhattan at the W Hotel. Greer was becoming intoxicated by the class of his company and the level of luxury they all enjoyed.

"We were all at the bar drinking, Charlie, Brian, Meredith, and me," said Greer, "and there were two women at the bar, both attorneys, and we invited them to join us in the Hamptons the next day. Meredith, whose job it was to make all the arrangements, told me the next day that a car was going to pick me up at eight in the morning and take me to the heliport pad along the FDR drive for our trip to the Hamptons."

They were taking a helicopter because a Saturday car ride across the Long Island Expressway would be bumper to bumper and could take six hours. Crist had raised the money, and if travel was expensive, it was part of the job.

Crist, Ballard, O'Rourke, Sargeant, and Greer were scheduled to fly out together, and everyone showed up on time. Greer knew everyone well except Ballard, who at 30 had been the youngest Florida gubernatorial chief of staff under Governor Robert Martinez. Greer knew only that Ballard was a powerful lobbyist and a major fundraiser. They sat across from each other on the helicopter.

"He seemed to be a nice guy," said Greer. "We got along."

The helicopter was getting ready to take off when Meredith said, "Chairman, I have to rent another helicopter because the baggage won't fit on this one." Greer, green in his new job, didn't think anything of it. If Meredith said she needed another helicopter, she needed another helicopter. He didn't ask the cost, which came to another $12,000. "Go ahead," he said.

Their helicopter flew off. When they arrived at the Hamptons, the Florida Department of Law Enforcement had a motorcade of SUVs ready for the governor and his entourage, as it always did. Meredith stayed at a small hotel nearby. Crist, Greer, and Ballard stayed at a mansion they had leased for the week. LeMieux came later and stayed with them.

Greer was ecstatic, if still a little reserved, to be hanging out with the governor and his millionaire friends.

In the late afternoon the two women lawyers from the bar at the W Hotel from the night before showed up at the mansion where the group was staying. Greer was sitting by the pool thinking *it was obvious to me why: They want to party with some very wealthy guys.*

At some point, one of the girls grabbed one of the Crist partygoers by the hand and said, "Take me on a private tour." They then went downstairs. When they came back still holding hands, he joked that "my wife never does that for me."

That evening, "We were sitting around," said Greer. "The other girl, short but cute, was sitting out by the pool drinking when Governor Crist announced he was going to bed. Moments later, she told us, 'I'm going to go in the house and use the restroom.' She left and never came back."

"The next morning while the governor went for a swim, I walked out into the hall, and I noticed that her suitcases had been moved into his room. She had obviously spent the night with him.

"After that first day the girls went back to New York City. It was my first picture of what life was going to be like from a social standpoint—expensive cigars, mansions, and eager women."

It was Sunday, and Greer's infant son Austin was being christened. Greer was anxious because there are no commercial flights from the Hamptons to Florida. You have to go back to New York City and fly from there, and Greer didn't know how he would get back home in time for the christening.

Sargeant, a Marine pilot and a wealthy and powerful man, solved Greer's problem. His private jet was at the ready, and he instructed his crew to meet Greer at the Hamptons' airport and fly him home in time for the 11 a.m. ceremony in Oviedo.

"I was the only person on the jet," said Greer. I couldn't thank Harry enough."

Later that month Crist, Sargeant, and Ballard returned to New York City for a dinner at an expensive Italian restaurant. Invited to that dinner was a New York socialite, recently separated from her wealthy husband and with a taste for money and power. As Ballard explained it later to Greer, "It was supposed to be a one-night stand with Charlie."

Greer said Ballard told him "that if Crist hadn't been there that night, she was so attractive that he would have taken her out himself." The woman was Carole Rome, and her ex-husband, Todd Rome, was the president of Blue Star Jets, a manufacturer of private jets. They had two daughters, Jessica and Skylar.

"I was told it was never intended to be anything long-term," said Greer. "Well, they hit it off immediately."

About a month later the governor was scheduled to go on a trade mission to Brazil. Arlene DiBenigno, his deputy chief of staff, was assigned to go with him in part because she spoke Spanish—yes, they speak Portuguese in Brazil. Arlene had worked with Jeb Bush, and she was familiar with overseas travel and the procedures of embassies.

Late every night during the five days of that trip, Arlene would phone Greer on the brink of tears. The first night she called with a question. "Jim, do you know who this woman Carole is who showed up down here?"

"I heard he met this woman," Greer said. "Is she down there?"

"Yes," Arlene said, "and she brought a girlfriend, Mary Ann, and they're acting like they're on a college outing. He's showing up drunk and late, and she's staying in the room with him. They have their own rooms, but Carole is showing up in his room every night.

"It's embarrassing," she moaned. "It's terrible."

It was embarrassing and terrible only because Arlene thought Carole was still married to Todd Rome, and she was afraid the press would find out her boss was traveling with another man's wife, and worse, because of their carousing, Crist was showing up late for his appointments with the Brazilian officials and business leaders, whom he was there to convince to do business with the state of Florida.

"We were an hour and a half late for dinner with the ambassador!" Arlene told Greer one night.

Another time she called Greer and pleaded, "I need your American Express card number, and don't ask me why."

"I need to know why," said Greer. She wanted his personal Amex card.

"You have to swear never to tell anybody this," she said.

"Okay."

"They have destroyed their hotel room," she said. "They've broken a huge mirror; it's cracked in two. The hotel says the governor can't leave until he pays for the damage. The bill is $12,000."

"I don't know if I can pay that," said Greer.

"It gets worse," she said, clearly distraught. "There was drug use. There was cocaine on the mirror."

"Who's cleaning it up?" asked Greer.

"The FDLE has taken care of the problem," she said.

"I'll call you back," said Arlene. "I've never seen anything like this. I went on five trade missions with Jeb Bush, and nothing like this ever happened. This is just terrible."

She never called back.

After Arlene returned to Tallahassee Greer asked what happened and was told it had all been "taken care" of. "That meant 'Don't talk about it anymore,'" said Greer.

Carole Rome wasn't the first good-looking woman Crist had dated.

"Charlie had a reputation for being a womanizer," said Greer. "He had been dating a lot of good-looking women." This despite the whispers that Crist was gay. Years earlier in St. Petersburg it was rumored he had fathered a child with a woman he had met in a bar. It hadn't stopped the whispers. Before he became governor he had dated Katie Pemble, an executive vice president and chief operating office of the Bank of St. Petersburg. Dating Katie allowed him to go in front of the Tiger Bay club of St. Petersburg and when asked if he was gay, to better be able to declare, 'I'm not.' It made headlines. Charlie and Katie dated for about a year, and she was standing with him when he was elected governor, but as soon as he was elected, he dumped her. She was devastated.

"There was a little bit of talk that he had used her for the campaign," said Greer. "There were the usual whispers he was gay and needed to have a woman on his arm at events. And then for three months he went out with Kelly Heyniger, a 36-year-old knockout from Palm Beach. She had been on a reality show called *The Hottest Mom in America*. I met her a couple of times. They had seemed so lovey dovey. That didn't last either. And then came Carole."

After Crist met Rome, they were inseparable. Where in the past Crist spent most of his time either in the governor's mansion in Tallahassee or at the one-bedroom condo overlooking Tampa Bay in St. Petersburg he was renting, now on Fridays he and Carole Rome flew down to her $2 million condo on Fisher Island, a barrier island off Miami.

Recalled Greer, "Fisher Island has the highest per capita income of any municipality in the United States. No road or causeway connects to the island. You can only get there by ferry or boat. You get around by golf cart. There's a beach, a Tiki bar, the Gar Wood Lounge, which is elegant, and there's an Italian restaurant. You have to use a credit card because no money is exchanged on the island. I loved it when Lisa and I would visit Charlie and Carole there. It's paradise. It has a nine-hole golf course and tennis courts. It has big pelicans walking around spreading their wings over the golf course. There's a huge dock at the marina. When you cross over that little inter-coastal waterway to Fisher Island, you literally have died and gone to heaven. It was Fantasy Island. All that was missing was Tattoo to welcome you."

In some ways it was an interesting pairing. As wealthy as Carole Rome was, that's how tight Crist was.

"Crist didn't want to have to pay out of his own pocket to travel, so he had his staff book an event in south Florida so it would look like he was on government business, and he could get the Florida taxpayers to pay for it," said Greer. "He would stop by a state office in Fort Lauderdale or Miami for a three o'clock meeting with the regional director, who couldn't figure out why in the world the governor was there. The governor showed up, spent 15 minutes shaking hands, and told them, 'Everyone keep doing what you're doing,' then left at five. He then ordered the FDLE to drive him to Fisher Island."

All at taxpayer expense.

At first the governor's staff, including LeMieux and Eric Eikenberg, his assistant, lacked information about the woman Crist was dating. "Everybody was asking me, 'Do you know Carole Rome? Who is this woman?'" said Greer. When the staff discovered that she might be married, all were deeply concerned about what would happen if their relationship became public.

"Oh my God," said DiBenigno, "he's inviting her to events, and she's not divorced."

"George felt that Charlie was going to be president," said Greer. "All of us did, and we were all going to be on his staff. George was very worried about this woman. Naturally conservative by nature, George was concerned she didn't meet the criteria of a future first lady—she was married, or recently divorced, she was sexy, and she liked to wear sexy clothes."

Greer became concerned when he learned that LeMieux had hired a private detective to investigate Carole's past. LeMieux wanted to build a case against her that he could bring to Crist to convince him to drop her.

"Carole was starting to have influence in Charlie's decision-making process, which was alienating George tremendously," said Greer. "George had been the one the governor had always listened to."

Greer called Jay Burmer, the wealthy GOP fundraiser who was friends with Crist, to ask Burmer to let Crist know what LeMieux was up to. Burmer did.

"Jay told me that Charlie, being Charlie, didn't get upset," said Greer.

"He told Jay he was frustrated that George would do something like that. I doubt that Crist even mentioned to George that he knew. But I thought it was outlandish that George was investigating the woman Charlie was seeing."

Of all things, Crist's staff was also concerned about Carole's dildos.

Carole's family owned the Franco American Novelty, a company that made costumes. Her grandfather had started it, then her father ran it, and when he died, he left it to his two daughters. Carole was technically the president, but her sister ran it. Carole had added a line of sexy items. In the Halloween catalog there was a picture of rubber dildos. LeMieux was concerned that it could be disastrous for Crist if this went public.

At a meeting of Crist's political staff (sans Crist), LeMieux brought up the topic of Carole as the Boss's girlfriend. "This is going to be bad," he said. "First of all, she's not a Republican."

They had learned that not only was she a Democrat, she was a screaming liberal. "She has very liberal ideas, and she's beginning to influence the governor," said LeMieux. "And now we've got this problem of her company selling dildos."

"George saw Carole as a major threat to Crist's political future, more than I did," said Greer. "George was a *very* astute individual."

One night in November 2007 LeMieux and Greer left the governor's mansion after a meeting with Crist. They were standing on the cobblestone bricks of the circular driveway, when LeMieux said, "Jim, we've got to do something about this Carole."

"George," said Greer, "he says he loves her."

"I don't care about that," said the straight-laced LeMieux. "We need a first lady who can be on the cover of House and Garden, not House and Whores."

"Well, what do you want me to do?"

"He listens to you," said LeMieux. "You need to put the kibosh on this relationship."

But Greer and the governor were forming a close relationship, and Greer didn't feel it was his place to interfere. He cared about Crist and was beginning to like Carole, too.

Crist and Greer often traveled together on party business—and at the same time would attend fundraisers for the Florida GOP. As usual, Crist was having his staff set up these trips so he wouldn't have to pay his expenses out of his own pocket or have Greer set up some type of party meeting so the Republican Party of Florida would pay his expenses.

"If you're on state business," said Greer, "you should stay at the Ramada Inn, not the Beverly Hills Hotel. But the way you get around that is you find someone to give you a $5,000 donation for the party and then the party can arrange the flights and the hotel rooms, and the party will pay for everything. All it takes is for the chairman of the party to say okay."

It wasn't hard to get Chairman Greer to buy into such an arrangement; all the governor had to do was tell him he needed him to come along.

"Can you come with Carole and me to New York, Jim?"

He'd say yes, even though he really didn't want to leave Lisa and the kids alone for the weekend.

"Do you think you can set up a little fundraiser for the party up there?"

Greer recalls, "Sometimes someone would give us a check for $2,500 on a trip that cost the party $10,000, but at least back at party headquarters, nobody really minded because it looked like some kind of fundraiser for the governor and the party."

Crist almost never, if ever, took out his credit card and paid the bill. It was just the way he was. In the end his parsimony—there would be no paper trail—kept him from the scrutiny that Greer later was to undergo.

Greer was sure that part of Carole Rome's attraction for Crist was her wealth. "That Carole had a lot of money must have greatly added to his attraction to her," said Greer. "Later Carole started to complain to Lisa and me that Charlie never paid for anything, even after they were married, and she would say, 'I can't keep picking up the tab.'"

One night Crist and Greer were flying home on a private jet after a fundraiser in New York. The plane was parked at Teterboro Airport in New Jersey, and it was snowing. While they were waiting for the snow to ease so they could take off, the governor left the plane to buy a bottle of wine. Crist and Greer sat in the airport's conference room, drank and talked.

They were cleared to take off around nine at night. Crist and Greer were sitting in the back drinking Merlot and chatting. For the first time, Greer felt, they were bonding as brothers. Out of the blue Crist said, "They don't like Carole, do they?"

"Well," said Greer. "Some people have concerns about her."

"George doesn't like her, does he?" Crist asked.

Greer had been hesitant to discuss the subject of Carole with Crist. He really didn't want to acknowledge who liked her and who didn't, but he felt he had to be honest with his mentor.

"No, he really doesn't," he admitted.

A Florida Department of Law Enforcement agent was on the plane with them, and Crist didn't want the officer to hear their conversation, so he whispered to Greer, "But I love her."

"If you love her," Greer whispered back, "then fuck them all."

After Greer returned home, he said to Lisa, "They're all upset and looking to me to do something about Carole, but he says he loves her. It's not for any of us to tell him he can't be in love with Carole Rome."

Before long the governor began bringing his flashy new girlfriend to a few of the Republican Party of Florida functions.

"When I met her," said Greer, "she was very pleasant and very nice. She was quiet, not coming into her own yet. She was recently divorced from Todd Rome, and Charlie didn't bring her around a lot because of that. LeMieux and others were hoping Carole'd just be another three- or four-month relationship and it would end, but I knew this one was something special."

9

CRIST KILLS THE STRAW POLL

(AND MITT ROMNEY'S CHANCE TO BE PRESIDENT)

THOUSANDS OF REPUBLICANS ACROSS THE STATE OF FLORIDA WERE LOOKING forward to the huge mini-convention of grass-roots volunteers called Presidency 4 in early October 2007 at the Rosen Hotel in Orlando. Much like a national convention it was a gathering at which all of the GOP presidential candidates would speak, but the audience was Florida Republican voters only.

The highlight of the three-day affair was to be the fervently awaited straw poll, in which the delegates would vote for their favorite candidate.

The straw poll was extremely important for two reasons: The candidate who won would go into the Florida primary as the front-runner. Also it provided for the grass-roots volunteers, county chairs, members of the Republican Executive Committee, and precinct workers to be wined and dined and courted by the presidential contenders.

At the previous Presidency 1, 2, and 3 gatherings, candidates had sent huge gift baskets to delegates' rooms and held lavish reception parties for them in the evenings. When else and where else could a delegate from the Panhandle get up close and personal with a presidential candidate?

Heading into the event, Jim Greer was agitated because he had known for months that he would be stirring up a hornet's nest when he had to announce that there would be *no* straw poll.

Once he canceled the straw poll, Greer knew, there was no reason for the candidates to shower the delegates with presents, food, and drink. He had a public relations disaster on the horizon.

Charlie Crist, a most astute politician, had been the one to call it off. He didn't want the straw poll because the tea leaves told him that Mitt Romney would win it. He wanted Rudy Giuliani or John McCain to be the nominee, because he felt it was much more likely one of them would pick him to be the running mate. Romney was in with the Jeb Bush crowd. There was no way Romney would consider Crist for dog catcher.

Greer was upset because he felt the straw poll was the most important part of the three-day event. But when Crist had asked him, "Why should we have a straw poll?" he really wasn't asking a question. Rather, he was making a statement: *we're not having a straw poll.*

Said Greer, "What I learned is that when Charlie Crist says, 'Why?' he already knows why. He's playing you, trying to make you feel like you're telling him something. When you asked him a question, he'd ask the same question back to you."

"What do you think? Greer would ask.

"Well, what do *you* think?" Crist would reply.

"That way he doesn't have to take a position. He always has plausible denial."

George LeMieux, the strategist, was also pushing Greer to cancel the poll.

"Charlie and George wanted flexibility to negotiate the VP slot down the road," said Greer. "They didn't want constraints, and they certainly didn't want some stupid straw poll from Presidency 4 giving them heartache."

Greer tried to push back, cognizant of the great disappointment the grass-roots volunteers would feel. As chairman Greer could have held a straw poll against the governor's wishes, but that would have been treasonous. He chose instead to be a good soldier. "I was Charlie Crist's chairman," said Greer. "I believed that if the governor asks, you do it."

When Crist informed his senior staff that there would be no straw poll, they panicked. "You're kidding," was the response. "This is terrible—there will be a riot."

"They're going to blame you, chairman," Andy Palmer, the executive director, whispered to Greer.

A FEW DAYS AFTER Greer canceled the straw poll, he got a call from Sally Bradshaw, Mitt Romney's Florida campaign director, asking for a meeting. Bradshaw had been Jeb Bush's chief of staff. She was well connected and her husband, Paul Bradshaw, was a major lobbyist in Tallahassee.

Greer and Bradshaw chitchatted for a few minutes, then she got to the point. "We're very upset that you decided to cancel the straw poll," she said.

"I understand that," said Greer, "but that's what we're doing. It's a waste of a lot of money. "

Greer, unhappy with what Crist wanted him to do, went home that night to his little condo in Tallahassee and opened a bottle of wine and started drinking.

"I sat and I kept thinking about how I had just ruined Presidency 4, how I was never going to be forgiven, and how I was being told by my staff that this was the worst thing I could have ever done."

He thought to himself: *What can I do to fix this?*

"It was one in the morning, and I posited, *I wonder if I could put together a live presidential debate from Florida at Presidency 4? I wonder if I could call up Fox and ask if they would like to co-sponsor a presidential debate with me?*

Greer had no idea whether he could do it or who to talk to. He was sure of one thing: if Fox was the host, the candidates would all come.

The next day he told his staff the idea and got the telephone number of Peter Gold, Fox's senior political producer. Gold not only was willing, he jumped at the idea. Fox would co-host the debate with the Republican Party of Florida.

As a provision of the debate, Greer—always thinking of the best interests of Charlie Crist—arranged for the governor to have airtime before the debate so he could invite people to visit the state of Florida.

Greer faced another problem. Each grass-roots delegate was being asked to pay $200 to go to Presidency 4, but without the straw poll he was sure not enough of them would show up to cover the cost of the gathering.

His ingenious solution was to charge each candidate $100,000 to take part in the debate. Fox told Greer that if a candidate refused to pay, he could not be barred from the debate. But he reasoned that he could "still stop them from coming around to the receptions and the rest of Presidency 4," and he wouldn't let them rent a room or have their own reception.

Greer called the campaigns of each of the nine Republican presidential candidates and set up the ground rules. When he mentioned the hundred grand, Romney and McCain didn't bat an eye. At first Giuliani said no, but he couldn't afford not to take part, and it wasn't long before he anted up as well. Five of the six lesser candidates, knowing they were dead in the water if they didn't participate, also agreed.

"We made a ton of money," said Greer.

When Mitt Romney arrived at the hotel for Presidency 4, Jim Greer met him at the elevator and escorted the Massachusetts governor up to his room.

"Governor," he said. "It's an honor to meet you. I'm Jim Greer."

"I know who you are," said Romney brusquely. "Why didn't you hold that straw poll?"

"He was very cold," said Greer later. "He knew about the straw poll. He knew the value of it. His staff told me they had spent millions of dollars in developing relationships in Florida in anticipation of the straw poll. It was going to be a major feather in their cap for the national media to report, 'Mitt Romney won the Florida straw poll from the state's Republican Party convention.'"

What it did was set the stage for a bad relationship between Greer and the Mitt Romney people, and, worse, with the Jeb Bush people, the conservative wing of the Republican Party, who were working for the Romney campaign in Florida for the last year and a half.

With some 1,000 members of the Republican Party of Florida in attendance at the debate in the ballroom of Orlando's Rosen Hotel, the nine Republican candidates and Governor Crist took to the stage. After Lisa Greer sang the national anthem to kick off Presidency 4, Crist took a few minutes to welcome everyone, and party chairman Greer went to the stage to say, "Isn't it a great day to be a Republican in Florida!"

The debate was a huge success. The grass-roots volunteers, furious at not having a straw poll, were assuaged when Greer made sure each had a ticket to the debate.

The big winner that day was the party chairman. "We can't believe Greer pulled off a live presidential debate from Florida," was the general feeling.

BEHIND THE SCENES, CRIST handed Greer another political football to kick around. Two weeks before the scheduled Fox debate, CNN, which is more moderate than the right-wing, red-meat Fox, home of Glenn Beck, Bill O'Reilly, and Sean Hannity, called the governor's office directly. Crist, who was rarely called upon to be a commentator at Fox, was a favorite of CNN.

CNN had a relationship with Governor Crist's communications director, Erin Isaac.

"Erin," she was told, "we want to do a debate, co-sponsored with the Republican Party of Florida and Google."

A day or two later Crist was riding with Greer to a fundraising event in Fort Lauderdale, and Crist said, "Have you heard that CNN wants to do a debate?"

"Yeah," said Greer, "I talked to Erin about that, but there's a problem. Fox is supposed to host the only debate. If Fox gets wind I'm talking to CNN, I may have a problem with the debate coming up in two weeks."

Crist did what he always did. "Chairman," said Crist, "Don't you think that we should let anyone and everyone who wants to hold a debate, have one?"

Greer knew there was only one answer to that question: to make a second debate happen. That this complicated Greer's life immensely was of little or no concern to Crist, who wanted to placate his friends at CNN.

Greer called Steve Grove, the CNN political producer, who confirmed that CNN wanted to hold a second debate two weeks later at the Mahaffey Theater in St. Petersburg, moderated by Anderson Cooper.

"That's great," said Greer, who afterwards sat and stared at the phone because he knew that within a day or two CNN would start to advertise the debate and Roger Ailes and the boys at Fox would explode in anger over Greer going back on his word that theirs would be the only debate.

Sucking it up, Greer called Fox and told them about the second debate. The Fox people, as expected, weren't happy and said they believed they had an exclusive. Greer responded that he never said they had an exclusive.

That afternoon Ailes, the architect behind the constant drumbeat of anti-Obama and anti-Democrats "news" on Fox, called Greer.

"Ailes used the word *fuck* more than any person I ever heard," said Greer. "He screamed at me, 'Do you know who the fuck I am? Do you understand what the fuck Fox is? This is fucking outrageous. Charlie Crist

*Crist and Greer, flanked by the 2008 GOP presidential candidates
before their debate in Florida.*

and you have fucked us . . . and I'm not sure whether we're going to do the
fucking debate. Matter of fact, I don't think we're going to do it. We'll let
you know tomorrow."

Oh my God, thought Greer, *the world is falling apart.*

Around eight that evening he was at home pacing around his pool as he
tried to figure out what he was going to do. He decided he'd try bluffing Fox.

Greer called Steve Grove, the CNN producer, and told him that Fox was
threatening to pull out of the first debate. He asked Grove if CNN would
go ahead with its planned second debate but also hold the first debate if
Fox bailed.

"I don't know, Jim," said Grove. "These debates cost us millions of dollars."

"Listen," Greer said, "It's eight o'clock at night. Fox is calling me back
tomorrow by noon, and I need to know because I'm going to call them
tonight and call their bluff. I'm going to send you an email tonight listing
the five things you need to do if Fox pulls out, and I need an answer tonight,

or you're not getting the debate, and Fox is going to get a call saying they still have it."

Greer's email was sent on to the CNN's legal counsel in New York. Two hours later Grove told Greer, "If Fox pulls out, we'll take over that debate as well."

Greer now had the leverage he needed. He called Fox the next morning and told a producer, "Here's the deal. If you guys pull out, I've got somebody ready to step in. I'll just change the logo on all the mailings."

"Who is it?"

"It's somebody."

"It's CNN, isn't it?"

Greer wouldn't say. "I'll give you until noon tomorrow to tell me whether you'll accept having the debate," Greer told Fox. "You know my people love Fox more than any other network. So don't think it's going to be anywhere near as prestigious or as large. But I have to do this because the governor wants me to do it. We can't do it as an exclusive debate. There are Republicans, Democrats, and Independents throughout Florida, and they're not all tied to Fox. So I need to hear by noon tomorrow whether you're going to continue with this debate in two weeks at Presidency 4, or whether I'm going to drop you."

Fox called back at 9:30 the next morning to say the debate was on. Greer had turned the tables on the powerful media mogul and political guru Roger Ailes.

"I kissed their asses as much as possible," Greer said later, and the debate went on, though he felt his relationship with Fox went sour from that day forward.

CNN held its debate two weeks after the Fox debate. Once again Charlie Crist was making decisions to run middle of the road, as always angering the hard-right wing of the party, going against what the base of the party and Fox news wanted.

And once again Crist's hand-picked party chairman managed to save the day.

10

THE ENDORSEMENT

CHARLIE CRIST AND RUDY GIULIANI HAD SHAKEN HANDS ON THE GOLF course. Governor Crist would endorse Giuliani, so Rudy knew he had a secret ace in the hole. As a result, Giuliani would pull his TV ads in New Hampshire and Iowa to save his money, he'd stay out of South Carolina, and he'd focus all his efforts on winning Florida. If Giuliani could take Florida, he figured he'd go on to win on Super Tuesday and from there sew up the GOP presidential nomination.

"The problem," said Jim Greer, "was that Rudy didn't know that a promise from Charlie means absolutely nothing if it comes in conflict with Charlie's interests. Charlie will not only violate the promise, he will tell you he never made it and won't recall ever being there on the day he made it."

John McCain also visited Florida often. McCain and Crist had a prior relationship. When Crist was running for governor against Tom Gallagher, McCain had flown into Florida and endorsed Crist. Now he was expecting Crist to return the favor.

Even Mitt Romney, miffed by Crist's canceling the straw poll, stopped by the governor's office with his wife Ann to kiss up to Crist in hopes of getting his endorsement, as far-fetched as that seemed.

Greer and Harry Sargeant continued to advise Crist to stick to his endorsement of Giuliani, while almost all the other Crist advisers including Arlene DiBenigno and Brian Ballard were telling Crist that he needed to endorse McCain, who was further to the right than Giuliani but better financed.

Meanwhile, Giuliani's right-hand men, Tony Carbonetti and Mike Du-Haime, having heard that Crist would throw anyone overboard if it served him, were calling Greer and Sargeant frequently to ask if Crist was still on board. "We're hearing rumors," Carbonetti would say.

"Everything's still a go," Greer reassured them.

At the same time, Ballard, who had a great deal of influence with the governor, was whispering in Crist's ear that endorsing McCain was his best shot at being vice president.

Greer and Sargeant went to New York City in late November for fundraising events, and Carbonetti and DuHaime, asked to meet them for coffee. "Is there anything we need to be worried about?" they wanted to know.

Greer told them no, because he hadn't had any clear confirmation that anything had changed.

When Carbonetti called Greer in early December, Greer said Crist still intended to endorse Giuliani, and he added, "We can lock this down if the mayor would guarantee him the VP slot."

"He's not going to do that," Carbonetti said. "But Rudy has told you Charlie's going to be with us, and he's going to be on the very short, short list of vice-presidential candidates. And you will be the RNC chairman."

BY MID-DECEMBER GREER SENSED that the governor's support for Giuliani was fading. "Charlie started doing what he did best, planting little seeds of misdirection. One time we were at the governor's mansion sitting in the study, and I said, 'You know, Giuliani is asking when we're going to do a fly-around,' the tour in which Crist would endorse him in different cities. Charlie said, 'Let's hold off and see how he does in South Carolina.' So it had started."

Greer knew two things were true. One, Ballard, who was pushing Crist to endorse McCain, was gaining influence with the governor; and two, the governor was not showing his cards.

After Giuliani did poorly in South Carolina, he began talking about putting all his energies into Florida. Crist, noticing Giuliani's drop in popularity, told Greer he had decided he wasn't going to endorse anybody.

"It's best to stay neutral," he said.

Greer then had the task of informing the Giuliani camp that Crist was reneging but there was good news in that he would remain neutral and not endorse anyone.

Greer called Carbonetti to give him the news.

"Carbonetti was very upset," said Greer, "but he wasn't out of his mind because I promised we weren't going to endorse anyone else."

Crist told the press, "It's probably best I just stay out of it. I'll wait around to see what the message is from the people, but it's best that I as governor remain neutral."

Since no one knew that Crist had promised Giuliani his endorsement, the announcement created very few ripples. Giuliani's people couldn't cry foul for fear that might push Crist into endorsing the competition.

"I'm sure they felt totally betrayed," said Greer, "but they couldn't say it. Because Charlie Crist had a 70 percent approval rating, and you don't say anything to piss him off even though at that point you probably despise the man."

11

'A Backstabbing, Lying Son of a Bitch'

Through December and into the first week of January 2008, Crist maintained his neutrality. Crist and Greer went to a fundraiser in Tampa thrown by cardiologist A. K. Desai. The event was at a home on a lake, and Crist and Greer sat on the deck overlooking the water to have a glass of red wine. It was Thursday before the Tuesday Florida presidential primary.

"I still don't think I should endorse anyone," said Crist. "I'm going to stay neutral."

That was on the Thursday before the Florida primary.

Two days later, on the Saturday before the primary, Romney enjoyed a six-point lead in the polls over McCain. Giuliani was trailing badly—mostly because he'd run out of money for the TV and radio spots needed to capture the attention of Florida's voters. Giuliani's people were frustrated and angry that Crist hadn't endorsed their candidate.

LeMieux told Greer: "It would be best if you not talk to the Giuliani people anymore."

Greer didn't feel right doing that. When he called Carbonetti, the Giuliani strategist felt he knew what was coming next: "We're going to get fucked, aren't we?"

Not having heard differently from Crist, Greer continued to say, "We're staying out of it. The governor isn't endorsing anyone. That's the word. He's told that to all his senior staff."

The Orange County Lincoln Day dinner, a gala fundraiser for the local Republican Executive Committee, was held that Saturday night at the Rosen Hotel in Orlando. Crist wasn't on hand, having accepted an invitation to speak at the Pinellas County Lincoln Day dinner. St. Petersburg, Crist's hometown, is in Pinellas County.

Giuliani was the keynote speaker at the $50 a plate Orlando event, drawing a crowd of more than 700. Greer was also to speak at the event. Just before his appearance, the Giuliani people held a photo op with the candidate, where a supporter could pay $250 to get his picture taken with Giuliani. Lisa and Jim Greer stood nearby and watched people line up for their photos. Carbonetti and DuHaime were standing off to the side.

It was six o'clock when Greer's cell phone rang. Dinner was supposed to start at seven. He looked down at his cell phone and saw it was Crist calling. No matter what Greer was doing, if his cell phone read "Charlie Crist," he took the call. He could be playing baseball with his kids or having a romantic dinner with Lisa. It didn't matter. Jim Greer took Charlie Crist's call.

"Chairmmmmaaannn, Where are you?" boomed the familiar voice.

"I'm in Orlando with Giuliani getting ready to go to dinner," Greer said.

"Step away for a few minutes," said Crist. "I need to talk to you."

Greer went out into the hall.

"I'm doing the Pinellas Lincoln Day dinner tonight," said Crist.

"Yeah, I know," said Greer.

"You're going to be seeing this live on television in about an hour," said Crist, "so I'm giving you a heads-up. I'm going to endorse John McCain for the presidency."

Greer did what he always did. He bowed to Charlie Crist's wishes.

"Well, sir," he said, "If that's what you think you need to do, I'm sure it's the right decision."

"But I need you to tell the Giuliani people," said Crist.

"Okay."

"You ought to tell them soon, before it hits the TV channels," said Crist. "Because I'm going to do it in my speech."

"Okay," said Greer. "I'll do it right now."

"Thanks."

After he hung up Greer went looking for Carbonetti and DuHaime.

DuHaime, seeing the concerned look on Greer's face, didn't mince words.

"That piece of shit is going to fuck us, isn't he?" he asked.

"Well," said Greer, "the governor is going to endorse John McCain."

DuHaime could not control himself, calling Charlie Crist every foul name he could think of including "a back-stabbing, lying son of a bitch."

Carbonetti, very upset, said that Crist had betrayed them twice, the first time by rescinding the endorsement, but then a second time by not staying neutral as he had promised.

Crist's endorsement of McCain would prove the death blow to the Giuliani campaign as well as to the Romney campaign. DuHaime, who had little respect for Crist to begin with, let Greer know, "I will never forget this, and no matter what happens, I will make sure that Charlie Crist pays a price for what he's done to us tonight."

"I need to tell the mayor," said Greer.

"Come with us, and we'll tell the mayor," said Carbonetti. They pulled Giuliani out of the receiving line. "Crist is going to endorse McCain," they whispered to him. Greer was impressed that Giuliani showed a great deal of dignity. He didn't use foul language. He took it like a man.

"Well, that's very disappointing," Giuliani said. "Charlie had committed to us, but let's get back to the receiving line and finish the dinner."

Carbonetti and DuHaime were red-faced with anger.

"I could tell they were starting to look at me and blame me," said Greer.

DuHaime said, "You told us he was going to stay out of it."

"That's what I was told, Mike."

DuHaime kept repeating that "Charlie Crist is a backstabbing lying son of a bitch."

Before too long Giuliani would gain his revenge *big time*.

"One thing I remember about that night," said Greer, "was that all these people in the dark ballroom were at tables with spotlights on the big dais. You could only see the candles on the round tables of eight. About halfway through my short presentation, I started seeing people getting up and going to different tables and squatting down and holding their Blackberries. And what they were seeing, they were getting messages that Charlie Crist had just endorsed John McCain. And it was spreading as I stood up talking at the podium. I could hear the sighing and then people leaving the ballroom because they couldn't talk while I was speaking. I always thought it was a very sad night for Giuliani, though he showed a lot of dignity. He gave a great speech without any attacks on Crist knowing that Crist, at that very moment, was publicly endorsing John McCain."

Greer's world was turned upside down that night.

"We lied to Giuliani, stabbed him in the back," said Greer. "Crist endorsed John McCain because Brian Ballard had convinced Charlie that McCain was the right man."

CRIST AND GREER MET the following morning. Crist explained, "John Mc-Cain is an American hero. He'd been in prison camps. He'd supported me in my race for governor. And it was just the right thing to do."

Said Greer, "It was the right thing to do because Charlie saw it was the right thing to do *for him*."

For the next two days Crist traveled with McCain throughout Florida, announcing his endorsement over and over again at a series of rallies.

Supporting McCain badly hurt Crist with the base of the Republican Party in Florida. The base—the George W. Bush and Jeb Bush hard-liners who supported Mitt Romney—didn't want John McCain, the Maverick. In October Greer had gone to a Republican National Committee meeting in Washington, and he had been told by a former Texas national commit-teeman, a member of the hard right, "It will be a cold day in hell before John McCain is the party's nominee."

The RNC people were mostly George W. Bush people, and Bush and McCain didn't get along. The animosity went back a long way. McCain had said some pretty derogatory things about Bush in South Carolina in 2004. McCain was considered a maverick, but worse, like Crist, was thought of as a moderate who went against the party on a regular basis.

"They just didn't like him," said Greer. "A lot of the Florida state com-mittee members who opposed Crist didn't like McCain either—he wasn't their kind of Republican."

Yet again, Crist and Greer were making the conservative base of the Republican Party of Florida very unhappy.

Bolstered by the popular Crist's ringing endorsement, McCain overcame Romney's lead and won the Florida primary.

"The way it works, when you win in an important state primary, the money comes pouring in from donors for the next primary," said Greer. "Those people assume they are backing a winner."

Millions of dollars flooded into the McCain coffers. Two weeks later he won Super Tuesday, 24 additional states, locking up the nomination. One could certainly argue that Crist's endorsement had won him the Republican presidential nomination.

A year later, Gene Collins, one of Greer's closest friends, said, "Jim, have you ever given enough attention to the fact that Charlie Crist may have been—just may have been—the sole reason why Barack Obama is president?"

"Why do you say that, Gene?" asked Greer.

"Because isn't it true on the Saturday before Crist endorsed McCain, Mitt Romney was ahead in Florida by nine points?"

"No doubt," said Greer. "But you'd have to assume two things if you buy into that one: that Romney would have won Florida on that Tuesday, and that whoever won Florida would win Super Tuesday two weeks later, which is what happened. But then you'd have to assume that Romney could have beaten Barack Obama in the general election."

"I'm not sure of that," said Collins, "but you saw what happened when McCain became the nominee.

"Obama steamrolled him."

12

Vamping to Be Veep

When Charlie Crist endorsed John McCain, he was expecting a quid pro quo that would dramatically enhance his political career. At best Crist was hoping he'd be chosen vice president, a stepping stone to the presidency. At the very least he was expecting that McCain would promote him on national TV, fly him to the big northern states for rallies, and make him a key element in the presidential campaign, insuring his bright future as a national candidate.

None of that happened.

McCain was running as a hard-right, kill-the-moderates Republican, and Crist was too moderate to fit into his campaign plans. "As you looked at the campaign," said Greer, "you started to see that the McCain people weren't keeping any of their commitments. John McCain had meant those promises when he made them, but the McCain staff, led by campaign managers Steve Schmidt and Rick Davis, never liked Charlie Crist. They never acknowledged that if it hadn't been for Charlie, McCain wouldn't have won the nomination.

"When Arlene DiBenigno became the McCain person for the Florida campaign, she focused on the candidate and conveniently forgot she had any allegiance to Crist. The commitment that Crist was going to be a major player never materialized."

"How come I'm not being used?" Crist kept asking Greer. "How come I'm not on *Meet the Press*?"

Crist was invited on a campaign trip to Washington, D.C., and one to California, but otherwise he was rarely used outside of Florida. "That always pissed me off," said Greer, "and it later caused me to do battle with them. They weren't giving Charlie the credit he deserved."

Greer often reminded McCain's staff that without Crist, they would not have gotten the nomination. Crist himself couldn't complain because he was boxed into a corner. He had to hold onto the belief that he had a realistic shot at becoming the vice presidential candidate. But when newspaper reporters asked McCain about Crist's chances at the VP spot, he would respond, "Charlie Crist is certainly a person who needs to be considered."

McCain, like Giuliani before him, wasn't making any commitment.

Greer saw that McCain's people were playing Crist. They needed Crist's money machine to raise a lot of money in Florida, so they continued to hold out the VP carrot.

Meredith O'Rourke, Crist's chief fundraiser, Harry Sargeant, Brian Ballard, and Crist himself called all of his major donors and raised millions for McCain. Crist spent his weekends attending fundraisers for McCain in Florida. Sargeant did a fundraiser in his Del Ray Beach mansion that raised a million dollars in just one evening for McCain.

"Despite that," said Greer, "there never seemed to be a loving, appreciative relationship. Later Arlene, who by then had gone to work for the McCain campaign, told me they really had no respect for Charlie Crist. They said they saw Charlie as an opportunist, which politicians are. Whether he was an opportunist or not, Charlie was the one who got McCain the nomination and raised him a ton of money in Florida."

When the McCain staff came to Florida to set up their campaign organization, they set it up apart from Crist, Greer, and the Florida Republican Party. George W. Bush's campaign had worked closely with the Florida Republicans in 2000 and 2004. Crist had excellent advisers who had worked on the Bush presidential campaigns, men like Rich Heffley, Randy Enright, and Jim Rimes, politicos considered to be some of the best in the business. But the McCain campaign wanted to run its own show and pretty much made a hash of things.

"If they had listened more," said Greer, "they might have won the general election in Florida. Not in the nation necessarily, but in Florida."

Along the way, the McCain camp brushed off criticisms made by Heffley, Enright, and Rimes. They saw mistakes being made in Florida, but any time they raised their hands to give suggestions, the McCain people arrogantly shot them down.

"They weren't focusing on voter turnout," said Greer. "And they weren't focusing on coalition building or reaching out to religious groups, to Hispanics, to African Americans, to the military. The Crist campaign knew how to do all of that, but the McCain people, Rick Davis on the national level and Arlene DiBenigno and Buzz Jacobs on the state level, weren't working with the party structure like they should have. And they didn't have the nitty-gritty stuff of Florida politics—brochures, yard signs, bumper stickers—like they should have had and state committee members demanded."

There was a reason for the latter deficiency: as Crist himself liked to do, the McCain people based their whole Florida strategy on raising money for television ads, especially along the I-4 corridor from Tampa to Daytona Beach and then down to Miami. Because Florida is a media-driven state, McCain funneled all his money into TV.

McCain might still have won, but he had a serious problem. The party's grass-roots workers weren't enthused about McCain the way Democratic workers were about Barack Obama. When Republicans would come into a McCain headquarters and ask for a bumper sticker or a yard sign, there weren't any, and they mistakenly blamed Greer and the Florida Republican Party. When Greer asked Arlene DiBenigno, the Florida campaign manager for McCain, for bumper stickers or signs, she would say "I couldn't get approval for those things."

Ironically, the main reason McCain didn't excite the Republican base in Florida was that as hard as he tried to appear to be a hard right-winger, he was still seen by the far right as a moderate.

"You have to remember," said Greer, "the person who shows up on Saturday morning to walk precincts, to make phone calls, is a totally dedicated Republican. And dedicated Republicans are generally *very* conservative. They believe in what the Republican Party stands for with little variance. Passionate Republicans are *not* moderate."

THE BIG QUESTION CONTINUED to be whether McCain would choose Crist as his running mate.

"Charlie Crist was always on the minds of everybody," said Greer, "but there were still a lot of people who didn't think Charlie would get it because he too was a moderate. It wouldn't have made political sense to put two moderates on the same ticket. People who had a brain, who were in the political world, would quietly tell me, 'Jim, I don't think it's going to happen.'

"But there was always hope."

13

FISHING IN THE BAHAMAS

ONE OF CHARLIE CRIST'S TOP PRIORITIES AS A CANDIDATE IN 2006 AND AS governor in 2007 was the push to lower Florida's property taxes. The initiative was on the ballot as the Florida Save Our Homes amendment—the first ballot initiative. Their slogan was "Yes On 1." Arlene DiBenigno, then Crist's deputy chief of staff, was assigned to coordinate the "Yes On 1" campaign. Greer worked closely with her at Crist's request, and Crist raised millions of dollars for the initiative.

If approved, the initiative would have increased Florida's homestead exemption from $25,000 to $50,000 and would have provided incentives for homeowners to reduce their property taxes, including moving the exemption from one property to another.

"The 'Yes On 1' initiative was more smoke and mirrors than anything else," said Greer. "It never did lower property taxes. But Charlie had a campaign slogan. He would say, 'The taxes are going to drop like a rock if you pass "Yes On 1."' And people started believing that."

Opposing Crist was conservative Republican Marco Rubio, speaker of the Florida House of Representatives. Rubio's own plan to lower taxes was to increase the sales tax, which would have put the burden on the middle and lower classes. It was a consumer tax, and Crist opposed it.

Either Rubio's or Crist's plan was going to be voted on by Floridians on the same day as the presidential primary on January 29, 2008.

Greer was out to dinner one night in July in Orlando with Lisa and a few friends, when around eight o'clock George LeMieux rang his cell phone. "Are you aware that the Republican Party is paying for a website that challenges Governor Crist's idea of how to lower property taxes?" said LeMieux.

Greer was not aware and quickly agreed with LeMieux that it was something he should do something about. Greer looked at the website promoting

Rubio's position. Sure enough, under it were the words, "Paid for by the Republican Party of Florida."

The website had been up about two weeks, and Republicans were getting conflicting opinions about what the Republican Party of Florida was supporting. Why was Crist out raising money for "Yes On 1" when here was Rubio with a website attacking Crist's idea of how property taxes should be lowered?

"They had never asked my permission," said Greer. "They had done it just because Rubio—as speaker of the House—wanted them to." Greer called Andy Palmer, executive director of the Florida Republican Party, and told him, "We need to take that website down."

"That's not going to make Speaker Rubio happy," Palmer said. "They've never had a chairman tell them they can't do things on their own."

"This is the governor's party," said Greer. "This is not Speaker Rubio's party. The governor runs the Republican Party, and we're not going to have the speaker and the governor out there with websites that counter each other."

Palmer called back and said the site would be "down within the hour," but three hours went by, and it still wasn't down. When Greer demanded to know why, Palmer said Rubio was upset.

"I'm sorry about that," said Greer, "but we're not going to have Governor Crist out raising money for 'Yes on 1,' and Rubio . . ."

The website was taken down around midnight. It was put back up under a different aegis paid for by backers giving money directly to Rubio's initiative. The website no longer said, "Paid for by the Republican Party of Florida."

A month later Greer and Rubio ran into each other. Rubio told Greer how disappointed he was that the website had been taken down.

"I tried to explain it to him," said Greer, "but he just repeated, 'The chairman lets the house do what the house wants to do, and he lets the senate do what the senate wants to do.'"

Greer would face the full force of Marco Rubio's vindictive wrath at a later date.

Crist and Rubio had a passive-aggressive relationship. Rubio was a follower of Jeb Bush and as a result felt that Crist was too moderate for the party. In fact, in his good-bye session as governor in the chambers of the House of

Representatives, Bush presented Rubio with the "Sword of Conservatism." It was a show of affection that designated Rubio as Jeb's soldier and successor.

Rubio, who came from a conservative delegation of Miami politicians, didn't like Crist and never trusted him. David Rivera, a state legislator who became a one-term U.S. congressman and is currently under investigation, was Rubio's right-hand man. Greer had been warned that Rubio and Rivera could be vicious and nasty when challenged.

Two of Greer's friends, Chris Dorworth and Jason Brodeur, had been elected to the Florida House of Representatives, and not long afterward Greer was advised by Lieutenant Governor Jeff Kottkamp to warn them about Rubio and his Miami-Dade delegation buddies.

"Jeff used terms like sleazebags and slime balls. He said that Rubio, Rivera, and their cohorts would take new house legislators to topless bars in Miami, get them drunk, and then take compromising photographs of them. Rubio would then use those photographs to control the legislators to vote the way he wanted them to," said Greer.

WHEN GREER CHALLENGED RUBIO and ordered the removal of the website championing his tax measure, he seethed. But Crist's high poll ratings made it difficult for Rubio to do anything about it; he and his followers were quiet for a while. They lay in wait, looking for their chance to strike.

"Charlie really got behind 'Yes on 1,'" said Greer, "because it was a feel-good measure. It was something that didn't require a lot of thought—not one of Charlie's strong suits. And Charlie loved to campaign. He traveled the state to promote 'Yes On 1,' shaking hands, promising people at every stop, 'Property taxes are going to drop like a rock.' Behind the scenes people bit their tongues when he said that because nobody really believed that was going to happen, but it sure sounded good."

Crist needed 60 percent of the voters to approve the ballot measure, and that wouldn't be easy. He determined that he needed between $3 million and $5 million to get "Yes On 1" passed. He tapped a lot of his major donors for the funds.

One other important aspect to "Yes on 1": Crist needed it to pass because his reputation was at stake. If it failed, his political influence and his reputation would be diminished, which would leave him devastated.

The Yes On 1 campaign was faltering because Arlene DiBegnino couldn't get answers from Crist or George LeMieux. Greer, forced to step in and make those decisions, got the campaign back on track.

Greer was willing to help raise money for "Yes On 1," though he felt some pangs over the fact he was spending more time on the initiative and less on raising money for the Republican Party of Florida.

"People who had been giving a hundred grand to the Republican Party of Florida now were being asked to give a hundred grand to 'Yes on 1,'" said Greer. "They were giving the money to make one person happy, Charlie Crist."

It would not be for the last time.

In December 2007 Crist held his annual Christmas party at the governor's mansion in Tallahassee. It was a night for wooing major donors, though they weren't allowed to be called donors because the party was held on government property. As a result it was called the "Business Leaders Christmas Party."

After the party the celebration moved on to the Governor's Club, a private club with a cigar bar on Monroe Street. Greer, Harry Sargeant, and Brian Ballard mingled among the guests and whispered to about 30 of them, "We're going to have a little get-together in a private room upstairs. The governor wants us to talk to you."

Crist wasn't actually in the private room, but Greer and Sargeant stood in for him to tell the select major donors about an exclusive fishing tournament. Crist came in afterward to seal the deal.

Earlier that month Greer and Sargeant had dinner in Fort Lauderdale with Randy Perkins, one of Crist's big donors. Perkins owns a disaster recovery company. Greer said, "We need a big push. We need another million dollars by the first of January for the 'Yes on 1' campaign."

Perkins said, "Why don't you guys organize a VIP fishing trip with Charlie Crist for anyone who gives $100,000 or more for 'Yes on 1'? After the thing passes, we'll put together a fishing trip, and they can go deep sea fishing with Crist in the Bahamas."

Greer and Sargeant thought it was a great idea.

Now, in the private gathering, Greer and Sargeant made a pitch for money to support "Yes On 1." Greer told the select group of the urgency of the next three weeks, the goal of raising a million dollars, and the reward of the fishing trip with Crist in the Bahamas after the initiative passed.

"Everybody loved the idea," said Greer, "because you have to remember in this world it's all about access—spending time with the governor so you can whisper in his ear what you want from him. Whether it's a contract you want to acquire with the state, whether it's your company—Florida Power and Light or Walmart—lobbyists will pay the money to get time with the governor."

Everyone ponied up.

On Election Day the "Yes On 1" passed with 64 percent of the vote and the fishing trip in the Bahamas was on!

This trip would become a major source of controversy. For one, it was highly criticized because the invitees were only men. Greer claims that was largely because some of the major donors had beseeched Greer not to bring along Meredith O'Rourke, Crist's chief fundraiser. They said they were tired of the drama that often surrounded her.

"It would be better if it was a guy's trip," Greer was told. Later, Greer would be criticized for this decision.

"It wasn't intended to be some salacious boys-only trip," he said. "It was merely a man's trip—smoking cigars, fishing, drinking beer, that type of event."

The three-day trip was held at an exclusive resort in the Bahamas. Most of the donors, flying in on their private jets, converged on the little airport in Freeport. Fishing boats were waiting for them.

Some of the wealthy donors brought women with them. Some were their wives, and some weren't. Some of these women later would be trumpeted in headlines alleging they were prostitutes, headlines resulting from statements made by a traitor looking to protect his own butt from prosecution. The headlines were provocative but false: these were girlfriends and wives, not hookers.

"When rich men show up, women show up," said Greer. "You don't ask them, 'Is that your sister? Is that your daughter?' You figure that some of these women aren't these men's wives, but as far as I was concerned, it was none of anybody's business. We had a great weekend."

Along on the trip was Greer's right-hand man and travel aide, Delmar Johnson—the Judas who a few years later, after being given immunity from prosecution, testified in court the men had brought prostitutes with them.

"Delmar didn't have a clue who those women were," said Greer. "He had not one iota of evidence that any of the women were prostitutes. But he told people in the prosecutor's office they were to make himself seem like an important witness, and that made every national paper in the country."

A few of the women that weekend had arrived unattached and looking for a good time. They weren't prostitutes, either. As history shows, wealthy men draw beautiful women.

"When women see big yachts," said Greer, "they start hanging around. You will read that I hosted men's-only trips for major donors and provided prostitutes for them. Women did show up—it was a resort and plenty of women were there on their own—but that weekend was just a bunch of guys who went on a deep sea fishing trip.

"If it wasn't such a serious charge, it would be laughable."

14

GEORGE LEMIEUX DEPARTS

IN JANUARY 2008 GEORGE LEMIEUX, CRIST'S CHIEF OF STAFF, LEFT TO RUN the Gunster law firm.

"When LeMieux was Charlie Crist's chief of staff," said Greer, "everyone knew George was the guy. Whenever you asked George something, he would say, 'Let me run it by the boss.' But you pretty much knew if George thought it should be done, it would be done. Charlie would always defer to George. You always had a feeling that Charlie and George had a secret; that they were the only ones who knew what was really going on. They kept their cards so tightly to their chests."

LeMieux's deputy, Eric Eikenberg, took his place.

"Eric was George's guy," said Greer. "George had brought Eric up with him from Broward County. Eric had been involved in George's unsuccessful race for the Florida House. They were close."

However, as soon as LeMieux departed, Greer could see the governor's office fall into disarray. Crist was paying most of his attention to becoming vice president. His gubernatorial duties fell by the wayside.

"When I look back," said Greer, "at all the points on our timeline, this is where things started to go wrong. George was a take-charge guy. George was smart. He had good political instincts. He was a substantive guy on policy. Eric Eikenberg is one of the nicest people in the world, but Eric is very quiet, not a strong take-charge guy. He was young, in his thirties. He wasn't able to advise and influence Crist the way George did."

LeMieux went to work for Gunster, a large, influential Florida law firm. Because of his connections in the governor's office, he was able to get big contracts from state government, which is how the game is played. LeMieux's clients obtained a multi-million dollar contract with the Department of Transportation.

Other clients also benefitted from his relationship with the governor's office. George then became the chief negotiator for the Seminole Indians in a deal between the state of Florida and the Seminole Indians that allowed gambling for the tribe. The federal government approved the deal saying that gambling would be "a means of promoting tribal economic development, self-sufficiency, and strong tribal governments."

"George was making a lot of money," said Greer.

Even though LeMieux had left the governor's office, he was still running things behind the scenes, according to Greer.

"George was talking to Eric a lot," said Greer "and Eric called him often. Because Eric deferred a lot of questions to George, George continued to call the shots in the Governor's office."

ONE DAY GOVERNOR CRIST called Greer in for a meeting.

"I want you to give George a contract for $10,000 a month." Crist said.

"I didn't inquire why," said Greer, "because I always felt, and do to this day, that the governor runs the party. If the governor tells you to do something, you do it. But this was very unusual because guys who get contracts usually do something for their money. George didn't have to do anything for it. He just got a check for ten grand a month."

In July 2008 LeMieux and Greer were in Washington together, and LeMieux said, "You know why I'm getting this $10,000 a month, don't you?"

"No, not really," said Greer.

"I'm getting it because I was supposed to get another $250,000 as a bonus when Crist won the governor's office, and there wasn't enough money to pay me," said LeMieux. "So this is the money owed to me from the governor's race."

Greer thought it unusual that LeMieux had bothered to give him this explanation. "George had been a big deal," said Greer, "but now he had a different role. Technically he was a consultant to the party and to me, so I guess he felt he ought to explain it to me."

In 2009 when the hard-liners took over the Republican Party of Florida, they questioned LeMieux's $10,000 a month contract.

"George called me up," said Greer, "and said, 'Listen, there's a lot of scrutiny going on about this contract I've got with the party. Let's just end it. Don't send me any more checks.' LeMieux had been getting those checks for 14 months, but he never did one thing whatsoever for it. But that's common. People who are close to the governor, people who want a ride on the gravy train, one of the ways it can be done is getting paid through the Republican Party of Florida."

15

The VP Questionnaire

After Crist endorsed McCain, the governor and his staff began in earnest to raise money for the presidential candidate. Crist attended McCain events, and solicited donations from most of his most prominent fundraisers. Meredith O'Rourke and her mentor, Brian Ballard—the man who recommended her to Crist—began raking in the dough for McCain.

At the same time Crist's new focus on helping McCain impacted negatively the coffers of the Republican Party of Florida. Greer saw how badly Crist wanted to be McCain's vice president, and he realized that no amount of cajoling or begging would get Crist to take his eyes off the prize.

"I was caught in a bind," said Greer. "What was I to do? Everyone who was supposed to be raising money for the party was now doing so for Mc-Cain. But I couldn't squawk because I was supposed to be helping McCain, too. If Charlie were to make it to Washington with McCain, I would be going with them.

"If I had started whining, 'Hey, you guys are supposed to be holding events for the Republican Party of Florida,' I'd have been told by Charlie, 'Jim, you don't understand. The big picture is to raise money for McCain.'"

At one point a donor pledged $100,000 to the Republican Party of Florida. A couple weeks went by, and the money never showed up. Greer asked O'Rourke, who was being paid $30,000 a month by the Republican Party of Florida, "What's the deal with the hundred-grand contribution?"

"Brian had that person give the $100,000 to McCain, not to the party," she replied

"Holy shit," was all Greer could utter.

This would occur on a regular basis.

"Ballard, who had been a major fundraiser for the party in 2007, was now all-in for McCain," said Greer. "He wanted a role if McCain won.

Meredith was really working for Ballard, and she did everything he wanted.

"It was as if locusts had descended on a town and eaten up all the money for McCain, and nothing would be left for my little RPOF fundraiser the next Saturday," said Greer. "It was extremely frustrating, but I had to live with it, even though it was hurting the state party and its operations. The big picture was raising money for the presidential candidate."

When Greer was forced to cut back on the expenditures of the RPOF, critics began to harp that the "party is in financial straits" and "Greer isn't managing the money properly." If he took steps to correct the deficit he would be criticized for cutting back on staff. If he kept to the status quo, he'd face a serious financial shortfall. Greer was damned if he did and damned if he didn't.

Greer's problem was that he had little ability to raise money for the party on his own. That was Crist's job, and the governor wasn't doing it. As a result, a strain developed between Greer and chief fundraiser O'Rourke, who was powerful in her fiefdom. Along with O'Rourke's total focus on raising money for McCain, she was stubbornly resistant to any of Greer's innovative suggestions for raising money for the party.

"Meredith took the position, 'I'm the fundraiser. I've been doing this for years. I don't want anybody telling me how to do it," said Greer.

Greer was also frustrated because Meredith dealt primarily with the richest donors while he wanted her to reach out to the thousands of middle- and lower-bracket Republicans. She gave no nod to the grass-roots donors who might write a $100 check for which they'd get a membership card and a small plaque.

"That wasn't Meredith's game," said Greer. "She was a big-money person. She didn't give a shit about the little donor. She wanted to go to some rich guy's nice house and raise $50,000 in one night. Meanwhile Al Austin, who lives in Tampa and had been the finance chairman under Jeb Bush, was calling me saying, 'You really need to bring back these lower-donor programs that I created when I was finance chair.' And I agreed with Al, but Meredith had absolutely no interest in it."

Another problem for Greer was that O'Rourke was making it very clear that she was working for Ballard, even though Greer as the chairman of the party was paying her salary. Greer felt the need to remind her that he was the one writing her checks.

"Another mistake on my part," said Greer. "Fundraisers are autonomous. The chairs don't usually bother them too much. I had a relationship with the governor, and we were close enough that I could stick my nose in that arena. Because I came from a business background, I understood the chain of command. But I should have been smart enough to realize that Meredith was out of that chain."

Whenever Greer and Meredith had a blow-up, he'd get a call from Brian Ballard, the wealthy lobbyist and fundraiser who always seemed to have Meredith's back.

"Hey, Jim, what's going on with you and Meredith? Why don't you guys get along?"

"Brian, I'm trying to get Meredith to do certain things that would benefit fundraising, but she refuses to go along."

"Well, she's got a lot on her plate," Ballard would say. "Her daughter isn't doing well. She does a good job. I like her. You really need to get off her back."

"That pissed me off even more," said Greer. "I started telling the governor about it."

To no avail. In a way, Greer and Ballard were rivals for Crist's attention. Who was the bigger dog? In the end it turned out to be the powerful millionaire lobbyist.

Before it came to that, Greer and Ballard had been arms-length buddies. In July 2008 Greer was invited to go along with Ballard, Ballard's billionaire oil man golf buddy Harry Sargeant, and Governor Crist to a trade mission to London, Paris, and Russia.

Greer could not justify having the Republican Party pay for a trip to Europe, and going on a trade mission is really not the function of the chairman, so he declined. "I really can't afford to go," he told them.

"Charlie would like you to come," said Sargeant. "Carole is coming. Everybody's coming. We're going on a private jet. We'll take care of your hotel. I'll pay for it. Don't worry about it."

"I've done that for people but not on that level," said Greer. "It's all relative. Millionaires can do certain things. Billionaires can do other things."

Lisa Greer wasn't able to go because she had given birth two weeks earlier. Greer knew he should stay home, but the governor wanted him to go, and he relished the idea of seeing Europe with the others.

"It was not the smartest thing for me to do," he says in hindsight.

They flew into Paris. Ballard, Sargeant, and Greer stayed at the elegant Ritz-Carlton Hotel. Sargeant paid all of Greer's expenses. Greer never paid for one thing. Neither did the Republican Party.

ON THAT TRIP, ONE night in St. Petersburg, Russia, Greer and Eric Eikenberg, Crist's new chief of staff, met the governor and Carole for dinner After dinner, Greer was in his room when the phone rang.

"Can you come down to the bar?" Eikenberg said, "because I need to talk to you about the most confidential thing in the world."

Greer went down to the bar. Eikenberg pulled out a fat packet and threw it on the table. Crist had received a questionnaire from the McCain campaign.

"Even Crist's press secretary didn't know about it," said Greer. "Not even the governor's inner circle, except Harry Sargeant, me, and probably George LeMieux, knew that we had received a vice-presidential questionnaire—because that's considered the secret of secrets. The most important thing is if it's leaked that you're filling it out, you're off the list."

It was what Charlie Crist had been eagerly waiting for.

The questionnaire was about 40 pages. It asked the vice presidential candidates the most intimate questions about their lives.

"Jim" Eric said, "the governor wants you to help me fill this out."

The two were sitting at the hotel bar filling out routine questions when they encountered two consecutive questions that they stared at for the longest time. The first question: Have you ever been accused of or had rumors circulated about your being a homosexual? The next question: Have you ever been in any precarious situations that could cause embarrassment?

"You have to remember," said Greer, "that when Charlie Crist ran for governor, there were all kinds of rumors he was gay and that two men he had had sex with had been asked to leave the state of Florida during that campaign."

"What are we going to do?" asked Eric. "We need to talk to him."

"No," said Greer. "I'm not talking to him. Here's what we're going to do. We're going to leave those questions blank. We're going to talk to the McCain campaign verbally about those questions, because let me tell you what those questions are going to do, Eric. He's probably not going to be picked, and for the rest of his political life he's going to risk that the answers to this questionnaire might be leaked if someone wants to hurt him."

Which is exactly what Dick Cheney did years before when he strategized to select the VP.

Greer and Eikenberg skipped those questions. The questionnaire was submitted with the two answers blank when they returned to the states. Later, they laughed about the predicament those questions had put them in.

Charlie Crist, everyone in the trade mission now knew, was definitely in the running to become the nominee for vice president of the United States.

"I didn't think he was going to get picked," said Greer. "He and McCain were both moderates. It didn't make sense. Others didn't think he'd get it, either. But it was in McCain's best interests to keep the mindset running that he might, because Charlie was raising a hell of a lot of money for the McCain campaign in Florida."

WHENEVER GREER INTRODUCED CRIST at fundraisers and political rallies, he would always say, "Charlie Crist has the highest approval rating of any governor in the nation."

As it turned out, that wasn't true; there was one other governor who had a higher one, Sarah Palin of Alaska.

"I had heard of her only because I had to look her up," said Greer. "She had the same high approval rating as Charlie Crist. I didn't know a thing about her." But after that, when he introduced the Governor, Greer, who was uncomfortable stretching the truth, would say "he has *one of the* highest approval ratings in the nation."

On August 29, 2008, early in the morning of a blue, sunny day in Florida, John McCain announced his choice for vice president. Governor Crist had no warning except for a quick phone call from McCain a few minutes before the announcement.

The candidate told Crist, "We're going in a different direction."

"In waiting to the last minute to tell Crist, McCain did to Crist what Crist had done to Giuliani," said Greer, "except that McCain got more milking out of Crist than did Giuliani, who was never able to play the Crist endorsement card. Rudy thought he'd be able to, but he never got to use it."

Greer watched TV that morning in a hotel room. He was attending the quarterly meeting of the Republican Party of Florida. He stared as Sarah Palin come out on the stage with McCain to a tremendous ovation.

"I called Crist," said Greer. "'Governor, I'm very sorry,' I said. 'I know this was something you wanted very badly.' I told him, 'When one door closes, another door opens,' putting on it the most positive spin I could come up with."

"Yes, Jim, you're right," said Crist. "I'm sure this is going to turn out well. I don't know anything about her."

"Charlie didn't say anything else about McCain or Palin," said Greer, "but I didn't expect him to. I was calling because I knew the guy was hurt, and I cared about him. By that time Charlie and I had become very good friends, and I could tell he was depressed that morning.

"Things will get better, and who knows where this is going to take you," Greer told him.

Replied Crist, "Who knows where this is going to take *us*, chairman."

16

Dumb as a Box of Rocks

When John McCain chose Sarah Palin, the curvaceous, fast-talking, governor of Alaska, to be his running mate, the enthusiasm of Republicans all over the country was boundless. McCain had been something of a dud as a candidate. The rabid Tea Party Republicans who were taking over the party nationally thought him lame and without sufficient backbone to stand up to the Democrats.

He refused to question whether Barack Obama was an American citizen, as the far right was questioning (even though Obama was born in Hawaii, had graduated from Columbia University, then Harvard Law School, and was president of the Harvard Law Review). The red-meat Republicans kept questioning why Obama was keeping his birth certificate hidden from the public. They were cocksure he had been born in Kenya. They disdained his middle name, Hussein, saying he was a Muslim and clearly un-America. And never mind the Republican-inspired posters that showed the African American Obama with a bone through his nose or eating a watermelon.

McCain refused to go there. But his VP choice, sassy Sarah Palin, would. Palin had no problem expressing her contempt for Obama and the Democrats.

"This is not a man who sees America like you and I see America," she said. "Our opponent is someone who sees America, it seems, as being so imperfect that he's palling around with terrorists who would target their own country. Americans need to know this."

Her constant attack on the Democrats and the media excited the Republican base, even Republicans who saw McCain as a party maverick and, worse, a moderate. Palin, a good-looking, sexy woman, was also a hard-right Republican, a born-again Christian who didn't believe in birth control, abortion rights, equality for gays, or giving amnesty to Hispanics who had entered the U.S. illegally.

"McCain didn't bring a lot of enthusiasm with his candidacy," said Greer. "He had tangled with George W. in the 2001 primary, and the Bushies never forgave him for it. For Floridians, McCain had a questionable reputation. Understand, most volunteers at the local Republican level, the people who do the legwork on gubernatorial and presidential campaigns, are political purists. They believe in everything their party stands for and does. McCain didn't create much enthusiasm because he had bucked the party system.

"But Palin said everything they wanted to hear," said Greer. "The problem was, she was dumb as a box of rocks. Every time I met with her, I could not believe that this woman was our vice presidential candidate. I always said that Palin reminded me of the girl in high school you wanted to sleep with. When she asked you, 'Do you love me?' You'd say, 'Yes,' even though you didn't. You just wanted to get in bed with her. Maybe Palin had some street sense, though I even question that because she had no idea what went on in the street."

A few days before Palin's first visit to Florida, the *New York Times* called Greer. It was in October right after the famous Katie Couric interview in which Couric asked Palin what newspapers and magazines she read, and Palin answered, "All of them." The *Times* reporter asked Greer's opinion of the Katie Couric interview.

"I thought she could have been better briefed by her staff," Greer replied. He said Palin would make an excellent vice president of the United States.

"Was she prepared to become president?" The reporter wanted to know if Greer thought Palin was prepared to be second in line for the presidency.

"I said she was, but of course I knew she wasn't," said Greer. "I was more ready to become president than she was. At least I understand the branches of government and the process. But I thought what I said to the *Times* was perfectly fine. I didn't think I said anything that would offend anyone."

When Palin arrived in Florida, Greer was supposed to attend each of her rallies with Crist. Greer's role was to warm up the crowd for the governor. His big line was, "Isn't it a great day to be a Republican in Florida!" The thousands of people at each event would cheer, and so he'd repeat the line two or three more times to get them really going.

Greer was supposed to fly from stop to stop with Crist in Palin's jet.

"It's a big deal to fly on the candidate's plane," said Greer. "There are always seats for local congressmen, the state party chairman, the governor, and the lieutenant governor. Florida Senator Mel Martinez sometimes went, and so did Jeb Bush. It was important who was on the plane because you're in what's called the bubble. If you're out of the bubble—say you're not in the lead car of the motorcade—if there's a traffic light, you stay behind while the candidate continues forward. Being in the bubble means you're 'inside,' that you're in the caravan when the candidate gets off the plane, that you'll have access to the back of the stage when the Secret Service is there."

Greer had been told by members of his staff that he was going to be in the bubble with Sarah Palin. Then the article in the *Times* appeared.

Arlene DiBenigno, who was now part of the McCain-Palin campaign, called Greer to tell him, "There's no room for you on the plane tomorrow."

Greer met with Delmar Johnson and Jim Rimes and told them, "I'm supposed to introduce the Governor and warm up the crowd."

After Rimes went upstairs to talk to Arlene, he told Greer, ""Yeah, but there's no room. Something happened. It's overbooked. But they still want you at the rally."

Greer could feel coldness from Arlene and the McCain people. Something was up. He asked Jim Rimes, now the "Florida Victory" director of the McCain-Palin campaign, "What's the real story?" And he was told that Palin was upset about the *New York Times* story. "She didn't like your comments about her not being prepared," said Rimes.

"I didn't say she was unprepared," said Greer. "I said her staff didn't prepare her."

"They interpreted that to be the same thing," said Rimes, "and they thought it was disloyal."

Recalled Greer, "I was sure some of this had to do with Charlie not being picked as vice president. They must have been wondering if he'd stay loyal and help them in Florida. They were probably wondering, *Did Greer do this because Charlie Crist didn't get picked?*

"In my mind," said Greer, "I didn't do anything wrong. I could have said, 'She's an idiot who shouldn't be more than a mayor of a small Alaskan town,' but of course I didn't. The thing was, they still wanted me at the rallies. No one was going to keep me from a rally I was supposed to speak at because *she* was upset at one statement I made in the *New York Times*."

"I said, 'Fuck it, we're going to go,' I'm still going to get the national exposure I want and I'm still going to get up and talk about how great Charlie Crist is."

Greer owned a twin-engine Navajo and told Rimes he would fly himself. But when Greer told Delmar Johnson of his decision, Johnson, who was expert at the logistics of political travel, quickly disabused him of that notion.

"The Navajo won't get there in time because of the bubble closing the airport down," said Delmar, who was always thinking big. He said he'd call Bear Air, the leasing company from which Greer bought his plane, to ask if they had a small twin-engine jet for rent—one that could get him there in time.

The cost was $12,000 for the day. Greer went to Rimes, who apologetically agreed that the McCain campaign would foot the entire bill because Palin had thrown Greer off her plane.

Unbeknownst to Greer, the McCain campaign never did pay for the rented plane. Later they would plant stories that Greer's ego was so big he had to rent a private jet at the cost of $12,000 to fly around after he was kicked off Palin's plane.

Said Greer, "They painted this picture of this egotistical crazy man who said, 'If you're going to throw me off the plane, I'm going to charter a jet.' In hindsight I wish we hadn't spent $12,000 to rent the jet. I should have known they weren't going to reimburse us—that they were lying to us."

Greer flew with Lisa in the rented jet to the McCain-Palin rally in Palm Beach.

At the rally Greer and Palin talked about the campaign.

"She was a little bit cold to me. She knew who I was. She talked about abortion in our conversation, how important it was that we overturn *Roe v. Wade*. I stood there and listened, and I said, 'Oh yes, absolutely, very important that that happens.' And she was saying how important it was that we appoint conservative judges and not activist judges because that was one of the major issues at the time—one of the big issues Republicans were talking about at that time. It was an awkward meeting."

When Greer went to the podium to introduce Crist, he brought Lisa up with him. He told the crowd, "I want to introduce you to the first lady of the Republican Party, Lisa Greer." The crowd went crazy.

"I was so glad Lisa was with me," said Greer. "She was a strong supporter. She was attractive and articulate and projected a great image. She wore a big Republican pin. They loved her everywhere she went."

Greer couldn't help thinking that Lisa would have been a far better choice for vice president than Sarah Palin.

Greer was uncomfortable listening to the Tea Party rhetoric. He recalled, "Palin thought the Queen of England ran England, but she said everything the right-wing crazies wanted her to say."

17

KIDS' PLAY

ONCE MCCAIN CHOSE PALIN, CRIST LOST ALMOST COMPLETE INTEREST. His enthusiasm waned, and he stopped being available for McCain's events. When McCain and Palin were scheduled for stops in the Panhandle, the McCain camp sent a request that Crist join them at two of their stops. They waited for confirmation, but none was forthcoming.

"Is he going to attend?" they wanted to know.

Silence.

On the Friday before the events Crist called Greer. "Why don't we take our families to Disney World?" said Crist. "Carole's coordinating it."

The Crists and the Greers stayed at the Grand Floridian Hotel. As they were sitting on the veranda having a glass of wine one night, Crist finally acknowledged that he had been gulled by the McCain campaign, that despite his endorsement and all the money he had raised for McCain, Crist wasn't going to be going on *Meet the Press* or any of the national talk shows as promised. Sensing he wasn't going to be used for much except raising money for McCain, he expressed a tinge of regret. "Jim," said Crist, "It probably would have been best if I had just stayed out of it."

For the trip to Disney World in Orlando, the Greers brought their two teenage children, Hunter and Amber, and Carole brought her two girls, Jessica, 15, and Skylar, 11. They went on a private tour of Disney World (no standing in the long lines under the hot Florida sun). They were taken to a suite for special guests at the top of Cinderella's castle where there's a bedroom suite and a sitting room with a view overlooking the theme park. Once a year the one millionth guest to come through the gates is selected to stay there for a night in honor of Walt Disney's birthday.

"Can we stay here?" Carole asked the young woman who was serving as their guide.

"No, I'm sorry," she said. "It's really, really selective. Only the Disney family." The guide evidently had no idea she was taking around the First Family of the state of Florida.

Carole said to Crist, "We could stay up here one night, couldn't we Charlie?"

Greer immediately intervened—not only was he chairman, but he was also the unofficial concierge for Charlie and Carole. Greer said to the guide, "I'm sure the Walt Disney Company would accommodate the governor of Florida and his family."

"I guess so," she said, unimpressed. "That would be something you'd have to talk to them about."

After they took the elevator back down to the ground, Crist turned to Greer and, miffed that the guide hadn't recognized him, said, "What the fuck was that?"

"It was Charlie's favorite line," said Greer.

Carole and Todd Rome had separated, and it would not be long before they were divorced. Most weekends, Carole's two girls, Jessica and Skylar, would fly down to the wealthy Miami enclave of Fisher Island and stay with their mother. After Carole was divorced, Crist would fly down there too.

The girls and Charlie didn't get along.

"They did not like Charlie," said Greer. "Charlie does not understand or like kids. What would generally happen when the girls came down to Florida, Carole would call me up and say, 'How about you, Lisa, Hunter, and Amber coming down and joining us for the weekend?' You might have thought it was two couples with kids getting together, but what Carole was really saying was, 'We need your kids to occupy my kids because Charlie doesn't want to spend any time with my girls.'"

The Greers and Crist, Carole and her kids would go on family outings. What would often happen was that two hours in, the governor would announce to the group, "I'm going back to the hotel." And he'd say to Greer, "Chairman, would you like to come? We'll have a glass of wine and watch some football."

"Sure," Greer would say, angering Lisa no end. Carole, Lisa, and the four children would then spend the rest of the day at an amusement park or other activity.

Crist followed suit that day they all spent at Disney World. After leaving Cinderella's castle, he wanted to visit the Hall of Presidents.

"He didn't like waiting in line, and it was very hot, and he asked if there was a way they could do a private showing for us," said Greer. "I went and talked to the Disney people, and they agreed."

After leaving the Hall of Presidents, the kids were jumping up and down that they wanted to ride Thunder Mountain.

"I want to go back," said Crist. "My leg is bothering me."

"He had a bum leg that he used whenever it was convenient," said Greer.

"I want to go back to the hotel," said Crist. "You guys go on."

Carole showed her frustration. "He doesn't want to be with us," she said to Lisa. "He doesn't understand the girls. He doesn't understand what it means to be a father."

"It got even worse in 2009," said Greer. "But during this time it was still all pleasant. Everybody loved him. But he just didn't understand families being together."

Greer could see that there was little to no interaction between Crist and Carole's girls. "I didn't fault Charlie under those circumstances," said Greer. "He just doesn't understand affection, particularly teenage kids. Also they had a dad, and Charlie couldn't relate to that. I don't think the girls ever gave him much of a chance either.

"When he was on those trips, Charlie had his guy friend—meaning me—and all he wanted to do was sit at the hotel bar and drink some wine. He wasn't feeling a lot of love walking around with the whole family. He never bonded with them."

Later Carole would ask Jim if he'd teach Charlie how to be a dad. But Greer never felt comfortable in that role, and their conversations on that topic were very limited.

"If, for example, Jessica and Skylar wanted ice cream and told their mother what they wanted to do, Charlie didn't understand a child making demands. If they wanted to eat at one place, he almost always wanted to eat a different place. When the girls were told they couldn't have their way, they

Jim and Lisa Greer and Charlie and Carole Crist, in happier times.

might pitch a fit, which was normal, but Charlie didn't understand any of that. To him, her kids were misbehaving, and instead of trying to discipline them, which he didn't think he had the right to do, he'd just leave."

Crist also had a thing about food.

"I'm a big guy," said Greer. "I like my food. Charlie likes food, too, but he calls it nosh. He's a grazer. He'll say, 'Let's get some nosh, chairman.' In other words, let's order a little bit of this, a little bit of that. He's big on taking food back to the room. He's always very cheap. He wants to box stuff up and take it home."

Charlie, who rarely ate a meal, felt the need to control Carole's eating habits as well as that of her girls. Jim and Lisa noticed that Carole often was hiding from Charlie the fact she was eating something.

"One time we were at the Old Ebbitt Grill in Washington, D.C., while the governor was on official business. I was there on Republican business, so Lisa and I met up with Carole before Charlie arrived. I had potato skins as an appetizer and some chicken wings, and Carole said, 'Charlie's going to be here in a little while. I'm starving. Can I eat some of your potato skins and chicken wings, but you can't tell him I ate them.' She quickly shoveled the food into her mouth and then ordered the waiter to take the plates away."

If Charlie was trying to keep Carole from eating, she was doing the same thing to her daughters.

Her notion that her girls were fat was an obsession. One time Greer's two children and Carole's two girls met to play tennis on Fisher Island. After about an hour, Jim and Lisa drove their golf cart to find them. When they got to the courts, they found Carole running the four children around and around the court. She was screaming, 'Run, run, run.'

"Dad, thank God you're here," said Greer's daughter Amber.

"What's going on?" Greer asked.

"She's making Skylar and Jessica run so we ran with them because she said they're fat."

On one occasion Jim, Lisa, Charlie, and Carole were having dinner, and the children were back at Carole's condo watching *Roots.*

Greer's phone rang. Hunter, the Greers' oldest boy, was on the phone. He was the sort of kid who asked permission before he did something. "Dad," he said, "Skylar and Jessica want to order food but they want to put it on our room because they can't let their mom know they ordered food. Can they get some food?"

"Yeah, of course," said Greer.

"They don't want you to tell their mom they ordered food."

"Okay fine," Greer said. "I'll keep it secret."

When Greer got back to the room he found they had ordered chicken wings and pizza, and most of it was gone. Greer's kids said Carole's girls were starving. It wasn't the only time Jessica and Skylar asked the Greer kids to order them food.

"Carole would always blame Skylar for being fat," said Greer. "It was just weird. She'd say terrible things about her. Maybe she was saying it because Skylar wasn't healthy. I try not to make judgments. All I know is what happened. Parents can judge the circumstances. My kids felt the food issue was very strange. You could understand why the girls were reluctant to spend those weekends with their mom. Not only did they not get along with Charlie, they always came away feeling fat because their mother was telling them so."

The animosity between Charlie and the girls continued to grow.

"What was interesting about this," said Greer, "was that Carole was always put in a position of trying to please him and at the same time trying please her girls. In most cases Charlie won out. Carole was not about to let her girls cost her Charlie Crist. Later she stopped calling her children, stopped having anything to with them until finally her ex-husband in New York got a court order severing the kids relationship with their mother. Carole had made the choice of Charlie over her own children.

"Looking back, when we were all together at Fisher Island, which was often, we'd show up on Friday night and the four kids would leave at nine in the morning to go ride bikes, or go to the beach, or do whatever. Charlie was never with them. His big question always was, 'What are we doing for dinner?' When the girls were there and he did show up, it was a big deal.

"He and I spent a lot of time together. We'd meet for lunch and go to the Tiki Bar. In hindsight I think I was blinded. Here were two couples who I thought were close, but really what was happening was that Charlie was using our kids. Our kids were the pawns to keep their kids happy—and keep him happy."

18

ON TO THE CONVENTION

WHEN THE FLORIDA LEGISLATURE VOTED TO MOVE ITS DATE FOR THE PRESI-
dential primary from March to January, the Republican National Committee
had a conniption fit. Here was a battleground state that had intentionally
violated its primary schedule. The guidelines were clear, calling for Florida
to be stripped of half of its 100 delegates to the National Convention. They
were also to lose floor passes for their major donors, and they were to be
banished to an inferior hotel far from the convention site.

The person who fought back against the wrath of the Republican
National Committee was Florida's chairman, Jim Greer, who bluntly told
the committee, "We're Florida. Stripping our delegates will do nothing to
motivate Republicans to work hard for the candidate. Are you willing to
let the party lose the White House just to penalize us?"

He had one other cogent argument. "At the end of the day," said Greer,
"the eventual nominee is going to step in and direct the RNC to restore all
the things you have taken away from Florida."

Recalls Greer, "I didn't play that up as much as I wanted because I was
told by the McCain people I shouldn't. They felt it would alienate some
people. They wanted it quiet. But I knew there was a general assumption
that the nominee would do just what I was saying. What I hadn't counted
on was the fact that McCain had his own problems with the RNC and with
the Republican National Convention."

Throughout 2008 Greer made a number of appearances on national
talk shows to discuss the penalties the RNC was going to levy on Florida.
Everyone wanted to know if Florida would be stripped of half its delegates.

Every three months there was an RNC meeting to discuss the issue, and
Greer attended each one. He would stand at the microphone in the middle
of the room and plead with the RNC members to be reasonable.

"Is the RNC more interested in imposing and enforcing rules than in winning the White House?" he would ask.

The answer always came back, "Rules must be obeyed."

Friends at the RNC informed Greer that certain members were hostile towards Florida in part because they felt Florida had received special treatment because former Governor Jeb Bush was President George W. Bush's brother. Some wanted to put Florida in its place.

Greer took a belligerent defensive stance.

"As Florida chairman, I wasn't going to swallow that pill," said Greer. "No way was I going to tell them, 'Yes, we violated the rule so beat us to death.' I aggressively defended the fact that 'We're Florida. You want to penalize Kansas, that's your prerogative. But don't mess with the big boy.'"

This did not sit well with the RNC.

"I met with RNC Chairman Mike Duncan, a very powerful guy," said Greer. "We sat down at the RNC headquarters, and he laid out the penalties. He said, 'You are new to this, Jim, but you have to understand the committee has rules, and though Florida is important, you're going to have to abide by them.'"

Greer fought back. "I understand that, Chairman Duncan. Every organization has to have rules. But penalizing Florida will do nothing to help the nominee."

"Republicans don't care about voters in Florida." Duncan shot back. "We are sticking to the rules versus caring about the Republican voters."

Greer pleaded with Rick Davis of the McCain campaign to intervene and tell the RNC, "Stop this—don't penalize any of the states."

Davis told Greer, "We have our own problems at the RNC. We don't have control over the convention the way George Bush did."

"There was so much in-fighting," said Greer. "Some of the more conservative members didn't even want John McCain on the stage at the convention, so they weren't going to listen to him when he discussed Florida's penalties."

The RNC even released a statement saying, "The nominee will have no influence or authority over the rules and penalties of the convention."

In the end when Greer saw he couldn't win, he proposed a novel idea to Duncan and the RNC. He asked if the RNC would allow the delegation to remain at 100 with 50 voting delegates and 50 on the floor as 'honored guests.' That way when the TV cameras panned the Florida delegation on the convention floor, at least it would look like Florida had all its delegates.

Greer also told them, "We need to continue to get passes for our major donors. Money is going to be all important."

The RNC agreed to Greer's compromise—and his request for free passes for major donors—and Greer wound up receiving kudos in the press for his leadership.

The Republican National Convention took place in September 2008 at the Xcel Energy Center in St. Paul, Minnesota. The night before the convention began, the throng of Florida delegates converged on the Minneapolis Airport Marriott Hotel. Because Florida was being punished for moving its primary, its delegates had to bus about an hour to the convention site.

In addition to fighting the RNC over Florida's penalties, Greer was charged with organizing all the events for the 700-member Florida delegation, a tall order.

"Six months out I appointed staff to the convention committee," said Greer. "I assigned Delmar Johnson, who was a terrific organizer, as my convention director. He and his staff took charge of the entertainment, the press, the credentials, transportation—everything. I can't convey what a huge task all of this is.

"You have to have something for them to do every minute of the day at the convention," said Greer.

To finance the week the Republican Party of Florida sold tickets. Delegates paid $150, while major donors paid $10,000. All the Republican members of the Florida congressional delegation, all Republican members of the Florida House and Senate, and the entire Florida cabinet were there, and each needed a hotel room.

"Every morning we had a Florida orange juice breakfast sponsored by the Publix Corporation and other major Florida companies in the ballroom of the hotel," said Greer. "One morning Michael Steele was our guest speaker. Florida Commissioner of Agriculture Charlie Bronson spoke. After breakfast

Jim and Lisa Greer with President George W. Bush.

everyone headed off to the convention center for the business of the day, and then at night, we put on a concert.

"One night we took over a museum and showed the movie *National Treasure* with Nicolas Cage and Jon Voight. We served hors d'oeuvres and wine and brought in Voight, a big Republican who was a star in the movie. He made a speech and posed for photographs. The reason I chose that movie was I wanted to promote Charlie Crist as a 'national treasure.' Since Charlie had such high approval ratings, as far as I was concerned, he was our national treasure." Unfortunately, Crist wasn't there; he was on hurricane watch back in Florida. There were 300 people at the museum, all partying with champagne. At the end Lieutenant Governor Jeff Kottkamp, his wife, Cyndie, my wife Lisa, and I toasted the Florida delegation from the main stage. We toasted John McCain, and we drank a toast to our national treasure, Charlie Crist."

Greer noticed that a lot of the people in the room either weren't very enthused or weren't joining in when he toasted Crist. "They had an unspoken opinion that Crist was an opportunist, that he wasn't a real Republican, certainly not in the style of Jeb Bush. That sentiment permeated the National Convention. They were all Republicans, but many weren't Charlie Crist fans."

When Greer got up to the podium and announced, "The Republican Party has great leaders like Theodore Roosevelt, Abraham Lincoln, Ronald Reagan, and our very own Charlie Crist," which was what he always said in his speeches, he could see people snicker and roll their eyes.

One of Greer's most difficult assignments was satisfying both the major donors and the grass-roots volunteers. Greer went to extraordinary lengths to entertain the major donors.

"A lot of the big donors didn't stay at the hotel with the Florida delegation," said Greer. "They had suites at the Ritz-Carlton or the Marriott. We had to make sure we took care of our major donors. One of the things I knew they were expecting was cigars. We bought fine cigars and found a company in Ocala that would put the Republican Party of Florida's logo on each cigar. Those cigars cost us $3,000. Later I would be accused of shipping those cigars to my home for my sole benefit—so I could have cigars with my bourbon wherever I went in Florida. The truth was I ended up with two cigars with the RPF logo on them, and I still have them.

"There is always a class difference between the donors and the grass-roots members of the state committee. They don't mix. The grass-roots activists and members of the Republican committee think they're the big shits, the ones who actually win elections because they do the grunt work—putting bumper stickers on cars and campaign signs in our yards. As far as they're concerned, the major donors don't do anything except write a check. To the donors, on the other hand, the grass-roots people are just a bunch of crazy activists.

"The major donors want nothing to do with the worker bees because they don't understand them, don't talk their talk, and they aren't on the same level financially or socially. In return the grass-roots people have a real animosity toward the party's big donors. The grass-roots don't understand why we can't have a $10,000 a plate fundraiser at the Waffle House instead of the Vinoy."

Greer said that one way he tried to bridge that gap was to invite the county chairman, the state committeeman, and the state committeewoman to attend for free if there was a high-dollar Republican Party fundraiser in a county. "They didn't have to write the $5,000 check to get in the door. Before, they had never been invited. They'd hear about an upcoming fundraiser that Governor Jeb Bush was having at a famous cardiologist's home, say, but they were never invited, and they'd complain."

Greer's organizing fingerprints were all over the Republican National Convention for the benefit of his Florida delegation. It was his idea to put the Florida delegation in colorful shirts with a motif of oranges, sunshine, and pelicans, shirts usually worn by Florida toll booth operators. One afternoon Greer had a photo taken of the entire Florida delegation wearing their toll booth shirts.

Another Greer idea was that when Palin came out to make her speech, the entire Florida delegation would consist only of women wearing orange scarves so the delegates would have something to wave in a show of solidarity and so TV viewers would see a sea of orange from the floor.

"It got us a lot of attention," said Greer. "It was in all the Florida papers. I was very surprised when some of the men in the delegation didn't immediately say, 'Great idea.' In fact, one of my staff members came and told me there were some men who refused to give up their seats to the women. Adam Hasner, a state representative from Palm Beach, the majority leader, looked at me with disdain when I told him he needed to give up his seat that night. Bill McCollum, who placated the right-wing crazies of the party, was another, and I was told he and Hasner refused to leave and sat in the front row when Palin came out."

McCollum would get back at Greer later in other ways.

19

Moment of Triumph

Before the Republican National Convention, Greer spent an inordinate amount of time and effort talking with the McCain staff about what role Crist would play at that important gathering. Because Crist's ringing endorsement and his fundraising were major factors in McCain's victory in Florida—which then led to the Maverick's big win on Super Tuesday—Greer felt that Crist should get a speaking role in prime time.

"It was crucial to Charlie's national aspirations," said Greer.

When Greer consulted with Rick Davis, Arlene DiBenigno, or Buzz Jacobs of the McCain campaign as the convention was being organized, he kept hearing, "He's going to get something, but we can't make any commitments. It's a tight schedule. We're not sure how it's going to go."

Greer was becoming more and more concerned as the convention neared.

"What's the convention look like?" Crist would ask him.

"I'm not really sure," Greer would say, "but I'm pushing for you to get a key speaking role."

"Great," Crist would say. "Keep it up."

Crist believed his closest conduit to the McCain campaign was Brian Ballard, the powerful lobbyist, the big money man, and the person who collected hundreds of thousands of dollars from his many contacts around Florida and throughout the country. Ballard was the finance chairman of the McCain campaign in Florida.

"Charlie thought he had all of his bases covered with me talking to the McCain people and Brian talking directly to others in the McCain camp, but I never believed Ballard was going to back Charlie like Charlie believed," said Greer.

"Ballard was always telling me I was pushing Charlie too much, that I needed to back off. One time Ballard said, 'Charlie is starting to make himself look needy. He should look more like he's governing Florida.'

"I thought that Ballard always told Charlie what Charlie wanted to hear. When I hung up the phone after speaking with Ballard, I never felt he represented Charlie's interests. Ballard had his own self-interests. Ballard wanted to be an ambassador. He actually told me that. So if the McCain campaign didn't view Charlie favorably, Ballard was not going to go out on a limb to protect his friend, the person who had given him so much."

WITH A WEEK TO go before the Republican National Convention, McCain and his staff, prodded endlessly by Greer, finally decided that the convention would feature speeches in prime time by several Republican governors, including Charlie Crist, Louisiana Governor Bobby Jindal, and Mississippi Governor Haley Barbour.

"Which was fine," said Greer, "because a lot of presidential candidates become the nominee four years after they give their speech at the convention. Barack Obama was the keynote speaker of the 2004 Democratic Convention in Chicago. Everybody in Charlie's little inner circle, including myself, felt this was his time to get national exposure. Okay, he wasn't going to be vice president, but at least the nation would begin to get to know Charlie Crist."

As the convention approached, so did hurricane Gustav, threatening Florida and some of the other southern states including Louisiana, Mississippi, and Arkansas. Hurricanes allow governors to shine. They give a governor a chance to visibly take charge. The governor is the commander of the National Guard. Charlie Crist, expert at showing compassion, could go to the Emergency Management Center and stay for hours and days at a time. It was a great press and public relations opportunity.

With the warnings of this hurricane, the question arose as to whether Governors Crist, Jindal, and Barbour would remain in their states and keep watch or whether they would go to the convention.

Charlie Crist made the decision to stay home. So did Governor Jindal.

"Most of Gustav didn't hit Florida," said Greer. "We only got a bit of it. But George LeMieux always took the position that Charlie should appear to be focusing on Florida. When stories began appearing about the governor's light schedule, it was George who would warn, 'He's looking really bad. What's he doing all day? He's got to get a fuller schedule.'

"So George thought the governor should stay back in Florida and skip the convention. Charlie would be seen as concerned about Floridians rather than his own political career."

Greer tried to change LeMieux's and chief of staff Eric Eikenberg's minds. He wanted Crist at that convention.

"Florida wasn't devastated at all by this one," argued Greer. "And it's only one day. Fly him up and back."

But LeMieux wouldn't budge, and Crist remained in Florida.

"Charlie was not the type of person to make this decision on his own," said Greer. "He talked to George. He probably talked to his father, and they all agreed from a PR perspective that he should stay back in Florida and appear to be governing."

With Crist and Jindal not in attendance, the McCain camp decided to have Crist and Jindal pre-tape interviews which would then be aired in prime time during the convention. Crist taped a ten-minute speech. According to chief of staff Eric Eikenberg and his press secretary, Erin Isaac, Crist "wasn't very good."

"He was off," said Greer. "His words didn't flow. It just wasn't the usual Charlie Crist."

McCain's people must have been turned off by what they saw because they began telling Greer that "because of the tight schedule, we're not going to be able to show Charlie Crist's taped address."

Greer blew a gasket.

"I called the governor all day long," said Greer. "I called him outside a port-a-potty. I said, 'They're fucking you.' And I told him, 'I can't believe we're standing by and letting this bunch do this. Governor, you need to become more assertive with them."

Crist would reply, "But Brian said . . ."

"I don't care what Brian said," said Greer. "I don't think Brian has your interests at heart, and I don't think he's reminding the McCain people of all the money you've raised for them and the fact he wouldn't be the nominee if it wasn't for you."

Greer called several of McCain's top people including Rick Davis and Charlie Black. Nobody returned his calls. So Greer, Katie Gordon, his press secretary, and Jeremy Collins, his travel aide, headed over to the hotel where the McCain camp was staying.

As he was walking into the hotel, Charlie Black, one of the men Greer had been fruitlessly calling, was walking out. When their eyes met, Greer could see he looked uncomfortable. He knew what Greer wanted. Greer stopped him.

"What's this shit about not letting Governor Crist on tonight?" asked Greer.

"We're thinking about not letting any of the . . ."

"I don't care about Bobby Jindal," said Greer. "I don't care about Haley Barbour. They didn't do anything to get John the nomination the way Charlie Crist did."

"You have to talk to Rick [Davis]," said Black. "You have to talk to Bill Harris upstairs. I'm just an adviser."

Greer says he knew "that was a bunch of bullshit" because a lot of the decisions were made by Black.

In the lobby Greer had the Secret Service call Davis and Bill Harris, one of McCain's top people in charge of the scheduling logistics for the convention.

Davis and Harris agreed to meet with him.

"Jim," said Davis, "It's just not going to happen."

Greer lost his cool. "None of you," said Greer, "would be in this hotel room right now if it weren't for Charlie Crist. And I can't believe you're fucking him the way you are."

Greer returned immediately to his hotel and called Crist. "They're not going to do it," said Greer.

As soon as he hung up, the phone rang. It was Brian Ballard. "Jim, you really need to calm down," said Ballard. "You need to back down. You're pissing people off in the McCain campaign. Charlie's good with the video not being shown."

"No he's not," said Greer. "I just talked to him. He's as upset as I am."

"No," said Ballard, "he just told me he understands."

"That was typical," said Greer later. "You couldn't get a straight answer from anybody."

"He's not," said Greer. "He told me he's not."

"You ought to drop it," said Ballard, "because it's having an adverse effect on you. You're promoting Charlie so much it's causing them to have problems with you."

"I'm just trying to make sure the guy who helped them get there gets his shot at national exposure," said Greer.

"Well, just let it go."

Delmar Johnson reiterated what Ballard said.

"Apparently," said Delmar, "back in Florida they want to let it go."

"And we did," said Greer. "It didn't happen. Charlie is the type of person who wants everyone else to do his dirty work. He doesn't ever want to be perceived as a guy who's trying to storm the hill. He wants other people to do it for him. I was always willing to take that role because number one, it was my job, and number two, I really believed in him and thought he had a great future if not as vice president then one day as president. And these people were trying to screw him."

DESPITE HIS ANGER, THE Republican National Convention was a lifetime highlight for Jim Greer.

As the Republican delegates were nominating John McCain for president, going from state to state, when the call came for Florida to announce its vote, the person who stood at the mike wasn't Governor Charlie Crist or Lieutenant Governor Jeff Kottkamp. It was Republican Party of Florida Chairman Jim Greer.

"The greatest honor I've ever had, something I never thought would ever happen, came out of that convention," said Greer. "With the lieutenant governor and the state cabinet standing behind me, I stood there as the head of the Florida delegation and I began, 'The great state of Florida, where Governor Charlie Crist is putting the people first and partisan politics aside . . .' And I finished by saying, 'Florida casts all its delegate votes for John McCain and Sarah Palin.'"

Standing beside Greer was his wife Lisa and his children, who had been

*Greer at the 2008 Republican National Convention, announcing
Florida's delegates for the John McCain/Sarah Palin ticket.*

invited onto the floor so they could watch their father announce the vote.

"It was the greatest honor," said Greer.

The Republican National Convention would serve as Greer's moment
of triumph as party chairman.

"The events we organized for our delegation were fabulous," said Greer.
"The hotel was perfect—everything was top-notch. I rode on buses with
our people. We sang songs together, we were thrilled to be there, and everything ran on time.

"When that convention ended, our state committee members compli-
mented us on the best organized, most efficient convention they had ever
attended."

20

Perks of Power

By dint of his being the chairman of the Republican Party of
Florida, Jim Greer was able to make a number of his dreams come true. One
was going to the White House as an insider—not once, but several times.

The first visit came in 2007 when he was still deputy mayor of Oviedo.
"That was always a dream," said Greer, "because I always had this great
interest in politics, and here I was walking down the hall to the Oval Office. It was very serene. The lights were dim. They opened the door to the
Oval Office, and it was just amazing to stand there and think, *This is where
the president works every day. This is where the power is and where everything
happens.* I had a photograph of myself taken standing in front of the presidential seal at the White House. Then we were escorted out the side door
to see the Marine guard standing at attention."

His second visit came during Easter week in 2007 after he was named
chairman of the Republican Party of Florida. He and his family were invited
to the annual White House Easter egg hunt. "Austin was less than a year
old," said Greer. "I have a picture of him sitting in front of a bunny on the
White House lawn."

That day the Jonas Brothers, teen heart-throbs, were playing. Greer's
older children, Amber and Hunter, were taken behind a tent to meet them.

"They didn't care about meeting the president," said Greer, "but when
it came to the Jonas Brothers, they were very excited."

Throughout 2007 and 2008 Greer flew to the White House several
times for awards ceremonies honoring Florida sports teams. He was there
to celebrate the University of Florida Gators winning the national cham-
pionship in basketball, and he watched as the Miami Heat professional
basketball team was honored.

On the latter day Lisa and Jim were in the East Room of the White House, where Abraham Lincoln and John Kennedy had laid in state. Lisa was carrying their infant son Austin, who began to cry. So as not to disturb the gathering, she took the baby outside and walked him down a long hall.

While she was walking, President George W. Bush finished his speech praising the players, and he left. A few minutes later Lisa returned.

"You won't believe what just happened," she said. "The president walked down the hall, and he picked Austin up out of my arms and walked him around and patted him on the back and calmed him down, and he called for a photographer to come and take a picture of them."

A few weeks later the Greers received in the mail the photo of President Bush and baby Austin (wearing a Republican bib). The portrait was signed, "To Austin Greer, Best wishes, George W. Bush."

In 2008 Jim returned for a reception for the Republican National Committee members. This time he brought Lisa and his mother along.

"The Marine band played 'Fly Me to the Moon,'" said Greer. "My mother loved that song. I danced with her to that, and then they played another Sinatra song, and Lisa and I danced.

"I said to Lisa, 'Can you believe that we're in the White House?'"

Greer also was able to hang out with President Bush during some of the fundraisers for the Republican National Committee held in Florida. The call would come into his office: "The President is in town. Would you like to come?"

IN 2007 GREER WAS invited to Israel as a guest of the National Republican Jewish Federation, along with California Republican Party chairman Ron Nehring. Greer, his sidekick Delmar Johnson, and other Republicans from around the country visited Israel for eight days. Greer, on a panel to discuss U.S.-Israel relations, talked about how important it was for America to support Israel and that the U.S. and Israel should have a strong mutual defense relationship.

Nehring, whose boss was Governor Arnold Schwarzenegger, couldn't believe how close Greer was to Governor Crist. One afternoon Greer was sitting in the back of a tour bus with Nehring when Greer's cell phone rang. It was Crist, who had just been on a trade mission to Israel a few months earlier. He had traveled to many of the sites Greer was visiting including Bethlehem and the site where Jesus was crucified.

"Have you been to the Wailing Wall?" Crist wanted to know.

When Greer hung up, Nehring said, "I haven't spoken to Arnold Schwarzenegger in nine months. I can't believe you just got a call from the governor."

After Greer returned home to Florida, Nehring, who with Greer's support became the chair of the chairman's caucus of the Republican National Committee, periodically asked Greer to make presentations about minority and youth outreach to the other chairs.

GREER ALSO TRAVELED QUITE a lot with the Florida governor outside of Florida. One time in California, Crist and he attended an exclusive luncheon with George Schultz, the former U.S. secretary of state, and prominent business leaders.

"Schultz was talking to the governor," said Greer, "and he told the governor and the small group of us at the table how 'Charlie Crist reminds me of Ronald Reagan.' He was saying that Crist, like Reagan, had a broad approach to things, that he wasn't much of a detail person."

Hmmmm, Greer thought. *That's interesting.*

One of the more intriguing political personalities Greer had the privilege of meeting was former President Bill Clinton. While Greer was attending a fundraising event for John McCain at the Del Ray Beach, Florida, home of the party's finance chairman, Harry Sargeant, Sargeant said to him, "I've got to run up the street to another home here on the ocean and do something quick. Do you want to come?"

"Sure," said Greer. They got into Sargeant's Bentley with his driver, and they were taken to a gorgeous mansion on the ocean not far from the Kennedy Estate in Palm Beach. When they arrived, a sign out front said, "Hillary Clinton for President."

It was a fundraiser for Democratic presidential candidate Hillary Clinton.

"The first thing I did," said Greer, "was take my RPOF chairman's pin off my lapel. Harry had a little grin on his face because of what he'd gotten me into." Jay Burmer, another of Crist's political consultants, had also gone along, and Greer told Burmer, "Oh my God, if people find out I'm here, it's over."

"It may be over already," said Burmer. In the car Greer and Burmer had been talking about how much heat and opposition Crist was getting from the hard-right-wing members of the Republican Party. His comment was addressing that fact.

As the three men approached the front door, Sargeant said, "Let's go downstairs. The owner of the house says there's a little private room where we can have a drink."

On the way downstairs Greer could see that Terry McAuliffe, then chairman of the Democratic National Committee, was making a speech in the large living room to about a hundred guests.

Greer poured himself a drink from a well-stocked bar. No one was in the room except a tall gentleman with white hair—former President Clinton. They were soon joined by Sargeant, Burmer, and, after he finished his speech, McAuliffe.

"President Clinton was drinking a diet Coke," said Greer. "We were standing in a little circle, and I was just amazed to be meeting Bill Clinton. One thing I always liked about Bill Clinton: he always talked about the positive side of the Republican Party. He didn't believe the Republicans were the enemy. I always felt that way about the Democrats."

Greer and Clinton had a heartfelt conversation about the presidential election.

"I found him to be what people say about him," said Greer. "You feel like you're talking to a friend. He makes you feel very much at ease. He's a great conversationalist. We had a great time."

McAuliffe interrupted their conversation. "Tell the president what you do," he said, smiling broadly.

Clinton was wondering what was coming when McAuliffe finally said, "He's the chairman of the Republican Party of Florida."

"Can I put you on the list of endorsements for my wife since you're here tonight?" asked Clinton.

"Please don't," Greer said.

DURING 2007 AND 2008 Greer realized another of his dreams when he found himself quite often on national television, usually talking about Charlie Crist's future.

"In February 2007 a major story came out that Crist was moving the Republican Party of Florida to the center," said Greer. "When that happened, a lot of people wanted me to talk about it."

When Greer appeared on national TV, he'd say, "Here in Florida, under Charlie Crist's leadership, we concentrate on solving problems. The governor is focused on serving all the people, not just one political party."

Later Greer would be harshly criticized for saying that. But in the summer and fall of 2008 Charlie Crist had high popularity ratings, and Greer was always his most visible cheerleader.

Said Greer, "Those were not the type of things the party chairman should be saying. A political organization's chairman should always be promoting the party line. Under the political party system, especially with the Republicans, it's Republicans good, Democrats bad. Republican Party policy: good. Democratic Party policy: bad. We don't generally meet in the middle."

That's not to say that Greer didn't advocate Republican positions. One of his lines was, "Less taxes. More freedom." But when he talked about Governor Crist, he would talk about how focused Crist was on serving the people. One of Greer's most popular lines was, "He puts the people first and partisan politics aside."

Greer didn't yet know it, but by championing Crist's centrist and sometimes left-leaning positions, he was slowly but surely digging his own grave.

21

THE HATRED FOR OBAMA

ELECTION NIGHT IN THE JOHN McCAIN-BARACK OBAMA PRESIDENTIAL race was Tuesday November 4, 2008. The week before, Greer and his political staff, Victory Director Jim Rimes and consultants Rich Heffley and Andy Enright, the people who had successfully run Governor Crist's political campaign and who knew Florida politics like the back of their hand, knew that McCain had serious problems.

"We were going to lose," said Greer. "We still had faith and hope, but the McCain campaign didn't have a clue as to what they were doing, and they had made it clear they didn't want any help. They didn't want any advice from us in Florida. They were running the show.

"Weeks earlier I had called a meeting to see what we could do to straighten them out. I invited Arlene DiBenigno, the McCain Florida director, and Brian Ballard, the finance chairman for McCain, and Buzz Jacobs, a young guy about 30 years old who was his Florida campaign manager. Buzz didn't have a clue as to what he was doing. They sent him down from another state, and Buzz and Arlene didn't get along.

"They all came into the conference room. All of my staff, Heffley, Enright and Rimes were sitting with their chairs up against the wall, when I said, 'The reason I called this meeting today is I'd like to see if there's anything the Republican Party staff can do to help the McCain campaign, because I'm concerned that we have some issues here.'

"Rather hostilely, angrily, Arlene spoke up and said, 'John McCain is going to win. He's a war hero. Everybody loves him, and I don't know why you've called this meeting.'"

Greer said he responded to Arlene, "Why don't you let Rich, Jim, and Randy tell you what they think?"

Greer recalls that the McCain campaign was offended and that after the meeting "Arlene hardly spoke to me again. She had had a lot to do with my becoming chairman, and she and I had been very close. The McCain campaign caused a lot of bad blood."

Money was another issue that caused a rift between Greer and the Republican Party of Florida and the McCain campaign. McCain was running out of money, so Jacobs asked Greer if he would give the campaign whatever federal money the party had in its bank account.

Greer told Jacobs he would only give him half, because he needed to hold back some of the money for the House and Senate races in Florida. Greer was responsible for those races, not the presidential race.

Half, it seemed, wasn't good enough. "They got mad at that," said Greer.

On election night Greer sat in his conference room surrounded by large television sets. Republican Party workers manned their computers, checking the Florida counties as they came in.

"You get the results rather quickly," said Greer. "As we were looking at what was happening around other states, around 9:30 Rimes, the data guru, told me we were going to lose and by bigger margins than expected. By 11 o'clock Barack Obama was our 44th president-elect. John McCain had lost, which was very bad for me, because I was the chairman of the party. I'm supposed to win Florida, even though McCain's people didn't want my help, and even though I had no control over the McCain campaign. For the record, I did win every one of the Florida House and Senate races."

Losing the election to a young African American brought incredible anger to the Old White Men of the Republican Party around the country and especially in the southern states like Florida.

"The GOP's issues with Obama had to do with his not just being a Democrat," said Greer. "Two, he's a liberal Democrat, and no matter what anyone might say, he's black. The Republicans were not ready for the first liberal black American president. Three, his middle name was Hussein. I used to be told all the time by my political staff, 'Every time you talk about him, you should say Barack Hussein Obama.' And the fact he was going to take our country away from us. He was anti-American, and the question was in the air, 'Is he really an American citizen?'"

Even though Obama was black, had a middle name of Hussein, was accused of not having a birth certificate and not being an American, and even though McCain was a respected U.S. Senator and war hero, Obama won by a wide margin. Republicans across America refused to believe or accept it.

"All the election did was bring hurt feelings," said Greer. "People stopped being friends, which can happen easily during a political campaign. People become angry. If you lose, everybody is looking for someone to blame."

Not long after McCain's defeat, Greer was invited by Katon Dawson, chairman of the Republican Party of South Carolina, for a gathering of some state chairmen to have a discussion about what Republicans had done right and what they had done wrong.

Dawson was running against Michael Steele for the chairmanship of the National Republican Party in an election that would take place two months hence, and mostly what he was doing was drumming up support for his candidacy.

"I went to the meeting," said Greer, "and the most important thing they showed was Americans were scared to death about the economy, that they would have followed anyone who had a plan, and Obama had a plan and McCain, if he had a plan, didn't make his plan clear. One political strategist I met told me that many conservatives voted for Obama because he had a plan to fix the economy, and they couldn't decipher McCain's plan. That told us a lot. If the voters can understand your policy, don't bank on them always voting the political party."

What Greer also saw was that after the election the grass-roots Republicans now had but one goal: to defeat the hated Obama in 2012.

"Clearly the political pundits, strategists, consultants, and the grass-roots Republicans became obsessed with winning the 2012 election and getting Obama out," said Greer. "What they looked to do was blame McCain. They wanted to believe that Obama won because McCain was a bad candidate.

"Now it's true the McCain campaign was not run well. It's also true that if we had had the best candidate, the American public was tired of a Republican in the White House. Under George W. Bush we had a bad economy and a war, but it wasn't a war the people felt we needed to keep the current president in like in FDR's time. It was a war that was winding down, a war the American public had no real enthusiasm for. Even Bush supporters were ready to make a change.

"Social issues like abortion and gays, issues the Republican Party always thought were going to save our ass, weren't talked about. I'd say to the press and in my speeches, 'The American public is not sitting at the dinner table talking about gay marriage or abortion. They are talking about where dad's going to get a job. How are we going to pay for college?' And when I would say that the Republicans within the state committee in Florida would interpret that as, 'He's not a conservative. He's not taking the party line.'

"I talked about winning elections, but clearly I was beginning to see that for these hard-right conservatives winning elections was no longer as important as keeping the party pure. And they could see that I was not working, and Charlie Crist was not working, to keep the party pure. I was expressing opinions about minority inclusion and outreach to blacks, women, and gays the hard-core Republicans didn't get. They wanted to talk against gay marriage. They wanted to talk against *Roe v. Wade*.

"Those are important issues when everything is going good, but not when the country is collapsing economically. Americans prioritize. And the Republican Party didn't get that fact. They are not the priorities when dad is unemployed, when houses are being foreclosed on, when families are losing their homes, and as I was saying all that, I was putting a nail in my coffin.

"They were always obsessed with and furious about Obama winning. They were obsessed with removing him in four years. They were sure he'd be a one-term president. They really did believe it. They thought Obama's winning in 2008 was a fluke.

"But the strategists knew why Obama won. It was because he ran a much better campaign than McCain. Obama moved his campaign out of the Washington, D.C., bubble, relocating to Chicago so he could see things more clearly, while McCain kept his headquarters in Washington.

"Also the Obama team was a whiz using new media. His was the first campaign in history where the new media played a major role in winning an election. The Republicans looked at Twitter and Facebook and email as something they didn't understand, and their attitude was, *If we don't understand it, no one else can be using it either.*

"'That's for the newer generation,' was how we thought. And in our thinking the newer generation doesn't vote. The Democrats, unlike us, saw that young people were crucially important. Get them to register, get them to the polls. Bill Clinton used Rock the Vote, and Obama took it further. He took it up many levels to everything the young people were doing: emails, Facebook, and Twitter. While the Republican Party was still thinking, *That's not important. We're still the party of conservative Old White Men. That's what will carry the vote.*

"And we lost. And we lost again in 2012 when Obama beat Mitt Romney, when we were *absolutely* sure there was no way Obama was going to be reelected. To this day we can't understand what happened on election night, except to say, 'It was the candidate. It was Romney's fault.'"

Greer sees irony in his conviction that the more conservative Romney would have been a better candidate in 2008 than McCain.

"Romney at that time was perceived to be the conservative, the person who would get out the passionate activists in Florida," said Greer. "It would have opened up the Jeb Bush and George W. Bush money vault much more than they opened it for McCain.

"In 2008, Jeb endorsed McCain, but he didn't do much beyond that. It worked both ways, because the McCain campaign was hesitant to be seen at the White House with President Bush because of voter animosity toward the president. That meant McCain wasn't going to get the Bush money for the campaign. But the McCain campaign had one major ace in the hole when it came to raising money: Florida's number one politician when it came to raising money: Charlie Crist.

"Charlie is a fundraiser like no other fundraiser. He doesn't mind dialing for dollars. Charlie was the leading force in raising money in Florida for McCain.

"But we still had a problem in Florida when it came to Barack Obama. We just couldn't get people to come out and volunteer for McCain. The few bumper stickers and signs we did have sat in the offices around Florida not being picked up.

"Obama ran a very sophisticated campaign, much more sophisticated than the Republican Party, and we saw ourselves as the elite party across the country. The Republican Party's belief that we were the top when it came to sophisticated Get Out the Vote programs turned out not to be true. The Democratic National Committee was doing things on the national level that we weren't doing. The Democrats nationally were so much better prepared. Most importantly, the enthusiasm for McCain wasn't nearly as significant as it was for Obama."

THE TEETH GNASHING BY Republicans after Obama's victory over McCain in 2008 was great. In Florida the hard-right critics, people who didn't like Governor Crist and Chairman Greer in the first place, sought to place blame of McCain's defeat on Greer, who hadn't given the McCain campaign all the RPOF funds when asked. The Republicans had won every House and Senate seat in the Florida legislature, Greer's domain, but no matter. Within days of the McCain defeat, the discussion began among the hard-right grass-roots Republicans that Greer should step down as party chairman in January.

Greer was in Los Angeles with Governor Crist, staying at the Beverly Hills Hilton, when his cell phone rang. It was Allison DeFoor, who had been vice-chairman of the Republican Party under Greer's predecessor, Carole Jean Jordan.

"Carole Jean and Allison didn't get along," said Greer. "Allison was Bob Martinez's lieutenant-governor candidate when Bob ran for governor the second time and lost. Because Allison has that history, he thinks he's an expert who knows everything about politics. He's about four foot eight, wears Tommy Bahama shirts and shorts. It's odd, because no matter how formal the event, he shows up in sandals, shorts, and a Tommy Bahama shirt."

DeFoor asked Greer, "What are you planning on doing with respect to your reelection in January?"

"I plan on running," said Greer. "I won all my House and Senate races. I picked up two Republican Congressional seats. The governor wants me to run again."

"I don't think you should do that," said DeFoor. "You lost Florida, and I think you should fall on your sword."

"Well, Allison," said Greer, "I'm not falling on my sword because Mc-Cain lost. If I had had a miserable election night, if we had lost House and

Senate seats, I'd agree with you. But just because the top of the ticket lost, I'm not going anywhere."

"I really think you ought to consider stepping down," DeFoor repeated.

"I'm not going to do it," said Greer. "If it had been an off-year election where the president wasn't on the ballot, they would have said, Chairman Greer had a hell of an election night last night."

DeFoor's call for Greer to resign was followed soon thereafter with an anonymous email sent to Republicans throughout the state. It said: "Don't reelect Jim Greer for chairman. He withheld funds from the McCain campaign. He didn't pay for bumper stickers. He's an asshole."

"We never really knew who sent it," said Greer, "though I had thoughts it was Arlene. I don't know if that's true. The person supposedly worked for the McCain campaign."

The next salvo came from Brian Ballard, who when asked by a reporter, "Should Greer be reelected?" answered: "I'll leave that to the governor."

"That's not a ringing endorsement," said Greer. "I could see that Brian was maneuvering to get me to leave, too."

Greer knew what he had to do to save his job. He needed a letter of endorsement from Governor Crist, and he made certain he got one

"I was with Charlie and Carole at an event in Fort Lauderdale at the Bahia Mar, a boat marina and hotel," said Greer. "We stopped at a round table with some people who wanted to discuss something about energy with him, and before the evening was over I had his letter of endorsement in my briefcase. I had typed it out for his signature. I wanted to make sure I didn't get screwed, because Charlie had the habit of promising you something and then letting you twist in the wind.

"As we were leaving, I said, 'Governor, you mentioned to me that you wanted me to seek reelection as chairman.'"

"Yes, absolutely, chairman."

"Would you sign this endorsement letter?" Greer asked.

Greer felt it important to get his signature on the endorsement because he wanted to keep it under wraps until his enemies felt they were winning and the time was right for him to unveil it, which he did.

Crist's letter went out to all the state committee members saying, "Jim

Greer should be reelected. He has done some excellent work with minority outreach. He won all of our House and Senate elections on election night. He's a good chairman. He works diligently and hard."

"Once it was received," said Greer, "they all quietly crawled back under their rocks where they came from."

22

THE WEDDING PLANNER

SOME AMONG CRIST'S STAFF WERE HOPING THAT HIS INFATUATION WITH New York socialite Carole Rome would peter out. They were wary of her because she was a New Yorker, a Democrat, a ladder climber—some said— and she was a sexy woman who loved to show off her body. Not only that, but at the onset of their relationship, they believed she was still married, a situation that Crist's advisers worried could derail a political campaign.

But Greer quickly saw that not only was Rome no mere infatuation, she wasn't going anywhere; in fact, she would be an important figure in Florida politics if the relationship was what he thought it was.

Greer wasn't wrong. In the fall, Charlie proposed and Carole accepted. Greer saw that each was getting something important from the relationship. "You certainly had a feeling that the wedding was occurring for a lot of different reasons," said Greer. "He was enjoying the good life with her. They were going to New York a lot. She was introducing him to her socialite friends and her TV reality show friends, like Jill Zarin from *Real Housewives of New York*. It was becoming a celebrity governorship because he really became obsessed with her lifestyle."

For Carole, she had status that she had never had before. She would become the First Lady of Florida.

"She was writing checks to various New York charities so she could be seen at charity events," said Greer. "She would take the governor along with her. They invited us to go to some of these, and we enjoyed ourselves. The governor spoke at several; they used his stature to help raise money for the arts in New York City."

Greer felt that Crist's timing was partly political—he announced before the 2008 election he and Carole were going to be married. Many questioned his motives, wondering if he was trying to overcome the single or gay issue to make himself more attractive to McCain as a potential running mate. "When he didn't get chosen, politicos as well as close friends were asking me, 'Is there still going to be a wedding in December, Jim?'"

Greer knew there would be.

The wedding of Charlie Crist and Carole Rome was set for December 12, 2008, at a little church in Crist's hometown of St. Petersburg. The reception was at the Renaissance Vinoy Resort Hotel. Crist asked one of his sisters and Greer to help with the arrangements. Once a week Greer and the sister would discuss questions like the band to be hired, the wine to be served, the china to be used. "Here I am the chairman of the party, and I'm becoming a wedding planner," said Greer.

It was a time consuming job, requiring him to leave Tallahassee and go to St. Petersburg for once-a-week meetings with the Vinoy's wedding planner. Carole and he were on the phone constantly.

The arrangements were made with care and precision. Charlie and Carole had the chef at the Vinoy prepare different dishes to sample and wines to taste. Greer came along as a judge. He booked the band—the Buzzcatz. He handled the tedious, difficult seating arrangements for the 300 guests coming to the reception. "Charlie had his Pike fraternity brothers from FSU coming," said Greer, "and Carole's sisters and family would be there. The lobbyists were all coming. To be on the governor's wedding list was a big thing in Tallahassee. Only the top lobbyists, the top supporters, were invited. The question in Tallahassee became, 'Are you going to be invited?'"

He checked every detail with Carole, who usually would tell him, "Talk to Charlie." During the wedding planning Greer and Crist were becoming best friends. "I'd talk to Charlie, and he'd say, 'Whatever you think, chairman,' said Greer. "I appreciated that he trusted me so much. Charlie and I were together all the time. He had a great sense of humor and could tell good jokes. We would laugh and laugh together. We were drinking buddies, too. He'd open a bottle of red wine, and we'd drink it together. He started inviting me over to the mansion one or two times a week to have a glass of wine or a martini. We were really becoming close. I really felt good about that."

TWO DAYS BEFORE THE wedding Jim and Lisa checked into the Vinoy. Carole had taken over the task of arranging the seating at the reception. This was her time to be in the spotlight for all her New York friends. She wanted to make sure everyone sat next to the right person. Carole would call Greer and ask him about some person Charlie had invited. He would reply, for instance, "That's a lobbyist for Florida Power." Greer kept saying, "Carole, this is a *large* project. You've got to draw a seating chart of the tables with numbers at each table, and then you can start . . ."

The day before the wedding Carole summoned Greer.

"Can you take this over?" she asked.

Greer immediately phoned Lisa.

"I need you to do me the biggest favor in the world," he said. "Will you please do the seating chart because I'm busy with so much other stuff?"

Carole dumped a pile of papers with lists of guests written on them for Lisa and Jim to arrange.

"You couldn't decipher some of the names, couldn't figure out who was who," said Greer. "Up to the day of the wedding Lisa sat in a room for hours upon hours putting together this huge seating chart—to the point where she and I would begin to argue. 'I'm not a paid employee here,' Lisa would say.

"Carole had a tendency to take a favor and turn it into your job. Carole would look at the chart and say, 'Oh no, they can't sit there. You can't put them there. Tiffany from the Hamptons can't sit next to Mary—they don't like each other.' Lisa then would have to figure out what to do."

ON THE DAY OF the wedding, several groups of protestors gathered across the street from the First Presbyterian Church in St. Petersburg, where the wedding was to take place. One group railed against the death penalty, another protested the Defense of Marriage Act, and a feminist group protested the anti-abortion laws coming out of the Republican-dominated Florida legislature.

Inside the church, the power elite of Florida was arriving all decked out in tuxedos and ball gowns. To the guests it felt like a Kennedy/Camelot wedding as limousine after limousine pulled up to the church, the distinguished guests exiting in their finery.

A minister presided at the ceremony with Carole's daughters as her attendants.

"It was a very elegant, sweet time," said Greer. "Charlie and Carole looked like they were in love. After the ceremony they came out on a balcony and waved as photographers were clicking. There was a very elegant, prestigious feel to it."

One thing no one could help but notice—the role Greer had played. "Two things were happening that night," said Greer. "One group of guests was thinking, *'My God, look how close Greer is to the governor—he's handled his whole wedding.'* Another group that had known Charlie Crist for years was saying to themselves, *'Look how Greer has been suckered into running the wedding.'*"

As per Lisa's seating chart, at the head table were Charlie, Carole, and their families. At Table 1 next to them were George and Meike LeMieux, Harry and Deborah Sargeant, Jim and Lisa Greer, Jay Burmer and his wife Linda, and Brian and Kathryn Ballard.

Ballard, one of the most powerful and important lobbyists in Florida, had RSVP'd that he and his wife Kathryn would be in attendance, so when he arrived for the reception, Lisa announced to her staff, "Brian Ballard, two."

"We don't have two," said Ballard. "We have five."

The Ballards had brought their three daughters without letting anyone know they were coming. "Five? Hold on a minute," said Lisa. "Let me figure out what I can do."

Ballard's wife Kathryn became impatient. "My husband is Brian Ballard . . ."

Staffers ran to get Greer. "Lisa needs you to come to the table right now," he was told. "There's a big problem." Greer went to see what the fuss was all about. Lisa explained to Jim, "Mrs. Ballard wants her daughters to sit with them, but there's no room at the head table for all five."

Greer and Brian Ballard walked off to the side. "How about if we do this," Greer said. "You two are at the head table with Harry and me. But there's a teenage table right over there, five tables away. Can we put your daughters there?"

"He didn't say anything at first," said Greer. "He was more scared of his wife than anything else. Then he said, 'I think so.'"

The guests were taking their seats. Ballard's daughters headed to the teenagers' table. A few minutes later Kathryn Ballard got up from her seat at the head table, pointed to her daughters, and said, "Let's go. We're leaving."

Ballard, his wife, and the three daughters stormed out.

A few minutes later Greer, seeing the two empty seats at the head table, asked Lisa, "Has Brian left? Where's his wife?"

"Yeah," said Lisa, "they left a little while ago. I think she's mad. She didn't like the daughters being at the other table."

"It doesn't work that way," said Greer.

Greer said he heard later that Ballard was "really pissed." Still later, he would learn that Brian Ballard was a bad man to have for an enemy. Gary Rutledge, a lobbyist who had worked with Greer for many years, once told him, "Ballard is the most disliked lobbyist in Tallahassee. He would run over his own mother to get what he wants."

"AND SO LISA AND I did the wedding," Greer recalls. "The one thing that always bothered me and hurt Lisa was that night before the wedding, Charlie and Carole held a rehearsal dinner at the nearby St. Pete Yacht Club. And here Lisa and I were doing everything for the wedding, and they didn't invite us to the rehearsal dinner. Some people wondered why we weren't invited. Others said, 'Jim, it was family and close friends.' A lot of people think I was a fool, that I was used. But I was doing it for a friend. And, as I reminded Lisa periodically, he was the governor of the state of Florida. Yes, I went overboard doing everything I could for him, but I thought we had become very good friends."

After the rehearsal dinner was over Crist and Greer met at the Vinoy bar and had a drink.

"The problem was that Charlie and Carole—they never think things out. I met a friend who had known Charlie for years and who had known Carole in New York. 'It's a perfect match,' my friend said to me. 'Two of the most selfish people in the world found each other.'"

23

FLYING HIGH

As 2008 was coming to a close, things were looking up for Charlie Crist, Jim Greer, and the state of Florida. Greer's minority outreach program for the Republican Party was showing results, and he was getting high marks in the press for the improvements he was making for the GOP in Florida.

A number of political consultants including Jim Rimes and Randy Enright as well as some grass-roots members of the Republican Party of Florida, suggested that Greer consider running for the chairmanship of the Republican National Committee.

"I felt we were on top of the world," said Greer. "Even though the Republicans had lost the presidential election in November, we had won all the key legislative races in Florida. We had picked up Congressional seats. Crist's future looked bright, despite not having been chosen as the vice-presidential candidate. Several of the presidential campaigns stated they would endorse me and support me to be the next RNC chairman. I thought I had a real shot at it. Most importantly, though, I felt we were doing what had to be done for the party in Florida. The state party was becoming more progressive, relevant, and inclusive and that's the direction I believed it should head.

"At the same time, I was seeing no growth in the national party. I had witnessed this for the last two years as an RNC member. The Republican Party had become the 'Party of No.' It had become the party of 'What's wrong with the Democrats?' but not what was right about us. And we were a party that still wasn't very inclusive. Were we striving to broaden our tent? No, we were shutting the flaps of the tent. I felt the party needed to be one with an optimistic, not pessimistic, view of things.

"The Republican National Committee had become a bunch of Old

White People with no interest in broadening the party. I wanted to change things on a national scale, just as I was trying to do in Florida."

For about two months Greer debated whether to seek the chairmanship of the national Republican Party.

"I knew it would take a lot of money," said Greer. "When I ran in Florida I had to constantly drive around the state and campaign. When running for RNC chairman, I saw I would have to fly all around the country, holding one reception after another, kissing everyone's ass in all those states, just as I had to do in Florida."

Greer felt there were a number of deciding factors negating a run. First off, he was from Florida, and since the Bush years, quite a few RNC members had had it with the state of Florida; they felt Florida received special treatment.

Secondly, Greer had not been one of *them.* He was a member of the RNC not because he had worked his way up through the ranks, but because he had been plucked out of obscurity by Charlie Crist.

Third, Greer was a Charlie Crist guy, and Crist wasn't one of *them* either.

And fourth, Greer had replaced Carole Jean Jordan, a longtime RNC member. Carole Jean had made it known throughout the RNC that she had been forced out by Greer and Crist.

What Greer did have going for him was that at age 48 he was young, energetic, and had new ideas. He had been innovative in Florida, and other state chairs liked his energy and views enough to want to learn from him. Whenever Greer attended a party chair caucus, he would be asked to make a presentation. He would tell the party leaders how his effort to reach the African American, Jewish, and Hispanic voters was a valid attempt to broaden the party.

"I was putting Florida out there," said Greer. "I was putting myself out there. I thought I had a lot going for me."

As 2008 CAME TO a close, other candidates were making it known they wanted to run for national chairman.

One was Saul Anuzis, the party chair of Michigan. Anuzis stressed the importance of social media like Facebook and Twitter. People liked him because he was an IT guy who knew and appreciated computers and computer systems. He had ideas about how the Republican Party should move forward in those areas. After the Obama victory, Anuzis felt the Republicans needed to move quickly to catch up.

"I liked Saul," said Greer. "He always invited me over for drinks at the different RNC functions. We'd go out to dinner together. He was a guy who liked to talk about new and innovative ideas, a very exciting guy."

Katon Dawson, longtime chairman from South Carolina, was another candidate. Dawson, a man with a distinct Southern drawl, had been entrenched with the RNC for years.

"Katon was from the Good Old Boys side of the party," said Greer. "He never came out and said anything racist, but I could picture him running a plantation. He was also a know-it-all. I could see him wanting the party to remain as it was. He never struck me as anyone with new ideas or a new approach to moving the party forward. But Katon was well-liked with the old guard."

A third candidate was Michael Steele. Steele, the former lieutenant-governor of Maryland, was the first African American ever elected to such a high office in that state. Steele had been instrumental in promoting affirmative action in the business community in Maryland.

"Steele was thought of as a conservative, a good Republican," said Greer. In late 2008 there was a lot of turmoil within the party because George W. Bush was leaving, and Mike Duncan was a Bush person. Mike was a nice man, but he was a weak leader. Some liked him because he didn't rock the boat. The ultra-conservative wing of the party definitely wanted him to stay on. But since we had lost the 2008 election to Obama, there was general acceptance that new blood was needed at the RNC. I had talked to Michael Steele on the phone. He voiced the same concerns about the Republican party that I had—that we weren't being aggressive enough about becoming a more inclusive party. We had let—and were continuing to allow—social issues overtake what should be our primary issue: fixing the economy."

To run or not to run, that was the query. Greer knew he'd have to raise at least $200,000. In his favor was the race for chairman wasn't a political campaign, so donors could contribute unlimited amounts.

What troubled him most was that he was up for reelection as chairman of the Florida Republican Party at roughly the same time. He definitely had to raise funds for that campaign. Raising money for both would be a huge challenge.

One morning early, Greer was at the Orlando airport waiting to catch a flight to Tallahassee when his cell phone rang. It was Michael Steele, who said he was in the midst of packing his suitcase to go out of town. "I'm going to run," Steele said. "Are you going to run?"

"I'm just not sure," Greer said. "I'm considering it."

"I need you on my team," Steele went on. "You're just the kind of person, the way you think, your views of the future direction of the party, what will happen if we don't change it."

Greer had wanted to run for national chairman to change the look and feel of the party and make it more inclusive. Here was a fellow Republican seeking to do the same thing. If Steele were to win, the same goal would be in sight, only Greer wouldn't have to go through the torture of running a long campaign to win the post. Greer, relieved really, told Steele that he would support him and endorse him—a big deal in that Greer's endorsement would be Steele's first and because Florida was a hugely important state.

IN JANUARY 2009 DURING an annual meeting of the Republican National Committee in Washington, D.C., a luncheon was held next door at the Capitol Hill Club, a private restaurant. Greer had rented a private room with a podium, and after lunch, Steele and Greer held a press conference at which Greer announced, "As you all know I have considered running for RNC chairman myself. But I found someone who has the same views on the party's principles as I do, someone who is committed to changing this party, somebody who has a vision for the future of the Republican Party similar to mine, and who recognizes we must be a party that reaches out to everyone if we're going to have future success. I would like to endorse and throw my support to Michael Steele for chairman of the RNC."

Steele took the microphone and thanked Greer for doing a great job for the party in Florida. He said Greer had shown the way for the future that others in the party could now follow.

News of the endorsement spread throughout the building where the other RNC candidates were debating. Saul Anuzis touted technology. Mike Duncan and Katon Dawson stressed the status quo. Dawson was overheard saying about Steele, 'Just because we have a black man in the White House doesn't mean we need to have one as head of the party.'

Michael Steele talked about the future and the need for a more inclusive party.

"You had to be careful not to alienate any segment of the voting group," said Greer. "You couldn't say, 'We have not done well because we haven't expanded and not been inclusive enough.' It was very dicey. You couldn't say anything negative about George W. Bush because there were Bush supporters in the audience. You couldn't say, 'We can't keep pushing moderates out of the party or we won't have a party,' because the conservative bloc would cause trouble."

Duncan, the incumbent RNC national chairman, was part of the debate because, like Carole Jean Jordan in Florida, he wasn't ready to step down.

Recalls Greer, "Nobody in Washington seemed to be telling Duncan that as chairman of the Republican National Party, he had lost the presidency. They wanted to keep him on because the segment of the party that Duncan represented saw that the party was going in a more moderate direction and they just couldn't allow that to happen. If that happened, this group would lose power. They were also convinced there'd be an abortion in the U.S. every ten minutes and gays would take over the country. It would be the end of the world if this new progressive element took control of the party."

Prior to Greer's endorsing Steele, all the candidates and Katon Dawson had wined and dined him to try to get his endorsement. They all stressed how important Greer was to the future of the Republican Party.

When Greer endorsed Michael Steele, the other candidates' reactions ranged from deeply disappointed to royally pissed off. "Saul was nice to me, but I could see he was genuinely disappointed," said Greer. "After my announcement, Katon had nothing to do with me, wouldn't talk to me, and avoided me completely." Katon, in fact, would become an enemy.

Before the election for RNC chair, Michael Steele asked Greer, "What would you like to do?" Two years earlier George LeMieux, representing Governor-elect Charlie Crist, had asked Greer the same question.

Greer not only was gaining power in Florida, but he was becoming a force in national Republican politics as well.

"I want to be the national rules committee chair," said Greer. "I want to serve on that committee that gave me such shit over the last year and a half just because Florida held its primary early, and I want to run the committee. I want to stick it to them."

"Okay, it's yours," said Steele. "If I get elected chair, I'll make you national rules committee chairman."

Greer would soon learn Steele could only endorse him for the post; he couldn't appoint him. Greer would have to get himself elected.

IT WAS TIME TO elect the new RNC chairman, but a couple of days before the January 30, 2009, vote, a new candidate appeared. Ken Blackwell was also African American, but Blackwell represented the hard-right conservative element of the Republican Party. Ohio secretary of state 1999–2007, Blackwell had been a strong supporter of George W. Bush. He not only was sued for attempting to disenfranchise Democrat voters, but he was fiercely against same-sex marriage and civil unions. Because of his strong right-wing positions, he was defeated in his bid for reelection as mayor.

Now Blackwell was challenging the more moderate Steele for national party leadership.

It was anyone's guessing game as to how the balloting would turn out. There were 186 votes to be cast. The first candidate to get more than 93 would win.

Said Greer, "I was downstairs one night having a drink at the bar of the JW Marriott Hotel, and people were saying, 'Here's what's going to happen. Mike Duncan is going to have a good show of support on the first ballot, but it will only be out of appreciation for his service. People know he's not going to get the majority.'"

And that's what happened. Steele led by more than 30 votes after the first ballot, with Duncan trailing. But there weren't enough votes for Steele to win. On the second ballot Steele continued to lead as Duncan lost support. Blackwell had 26 votes. He was way behind but he stubbornly refused to quit the race.

Reince Priebus, Steele's campaign manager, who later himself would put a knife in Steele's back, asked Greer if he'd negotiate with Blackwell's team in an attempt to get Blackwell to throw his votes to Steele. Greer was told that Blackwell was angling to be appointed "general party chairman."

"General party chairman?" said Greer. "I don't think there is such a thing. If Steele gets elected chairman, he's chairman."

"You guys have got to do something to take care of Blackwell," said one of Blackwell's political consultants.

"The consultants are the campaign people," said Greer. "It was now time for them to wet their beaks in all this. He said to me, 'I and the other members of the political staff, we've got to get some money, because Blackwell has promised us that if he wins, we'll get jobs with the RNC. We'll get consulting contracts. If we get Blackwell to drop out, what are you people going to do for us?' They were saying, 'You have to do something for Blackwell' as an afterthought."

"I don't know," said Greer. "Let me go talk to Steele."

Greer told Steele of Blackwell's desire to be "general party chairman."

"Absolutely not," said Steele. "I'm not going to share the chairmanship with anybody. I'm going to win this thing on my own."

"Another problem," said Greer. "For them to get Blackwell out, his consultants were asking for contracts. They said they were going to lose $200,000 if they got out."

The negotiation for the size of the payoff to sacrifice Blackwood was under way.

Blaze Underwood, who was running Steele's campaign, authorized Greer to offer them contracts worth $100,000.

Greer told Blackwell's people that.

"We want $200,000," they said.

"I don't know if that's going to fly," said Greer. "The Steele people say they have limited control over contracts. They aren't sure they can do it all."

There was a 45-minute break between ballots. Greer was going back and forth, trying to strike a deal to get Blackwell to get out of the race and to throw his support to Steele. Paul Senft, Greer's friend and another member of Steele's team, asked Greer what was going on.

"I'm being shaken down over there," said Greer, "because the Blackwell people, the consultants and the campaign people who are getting paid by Blackwell to run his RNC race, they're interested in feathering their own nest."

"We'll help them out," Steele's people told Greer. "We'll give them money, but we're not going to make a big commitment about what they're going to get."

Greer, an excellent negotiator, won the day when the Blackwell people told him, "Here's the deal. You as chairman of the Republican Party of Florida have to guarantee us that if we get fucked by the RNC, you will give us some consulting work in Florida."

"Yeah, absolutely," said Greer.

Greer returned to the Blackwell camp only to learn that Blackwell himself was upset because Steele wasn't giving him the appropriate respect that he deserved.

Greer wondered whether race was playing a role in all of this. "What I was seeing," said Greer, "was a pettiness between Steele and Blackwell that came down to: *I've had a greater career as a black man than you have.* It looked like Blackwell was grasping at straws. He was demanding things he wasn't going to get, and every time I'd go over to talk to Steele, he'd just shake his head no. Steele sensed the momentum was going in his favor."

Blackwell then asked for a paid position at the RNC.

"If Steele puts me in charge of minority outreach at the RNC, I'll support him," Blackwell said.

Greer got about halfway to where Steele's group was congregated when he noticed the Blackwell people waving furiously at him. He returned.

"It's got to be at least $100,000 a year."

"We don't know what revenue we have," Steele told Greer. "We have no idea how much we're going to have even for salaries. Tell him there'll be something for him. But we're not making any firm commitments."

When Greer returned to speak to Blackwell, he didn't say it quite that way.

"Yeah," said Greer, "there will be something for you, but I don't know if it will be $100,000. It could be $75,000. It could be $50,000."

Greer was flying high after sealing the deal for Michael Steele.

"I figured if they weren't interested in who was going to be the best RNC chairman, if they were more interested in lining their pockets, then they weren't playing by the rules. So I didn't always tell them what Michael told me. When Michael would say, 'Absolutely no,' I would say, 'Probably not.' I had to get Blackwell out."

After four rounds of voting, Duncan withdrew from the race. The bulk of his votes went to South Carolina party chairman Katon Dawson, giving Dawson 62 votes, Steele 60 votes, Saul Anuzis 31 votes, and Blackwell 15.

After Greer had one more conversation with Blackwell's people, Blackwell finally withdrew from the race and threw his votes to Michael Steele, who won the election.

Greer had negotiated Steele to victory.

"The consultants were going to get $100,000, and Blackwell was going to get some kind of job at the RNC, a paid job," said Greer. "He was going to be on the inner team, and all the political consultants were going to get paid off somehow, one way or another, through the RNC. And if the RNC failed to do it, somehow they'd get paid through the Florida party."

Michael Steele, an African American progressive, was the new chairman of the National Republican Party. When the celebratory photo was taken, Greer was standing by his side.

Because Greer had enhanced the communications department of the party in Florida, he was also put in charge of the 20-man communications department for the National Republican Party. Greer decided who should stay and who should go in that department.

"They gave me an office to use in Washington," said Greer. "I'd fly up to Washington, spend a week at a time—they put me up at a hotel—and I'd go into the RNC every day. I had a big flip-chart where I wrote down goals and objectives that the department should focus on. I brought my press secretary, Katie Gordon, with me. She was energetic and smart.

"One of the things I thought important was to have better communications with the state parties. I felt there should be an RNC message of the day that the state party could then send out to all of its people. I thought the press secretary of the RNC should bring his counterparts from around the states together to talk about working closer together and weighing the good, the bad, and the ugly. Everybody liked that idea."

Steele also named Greer to serve as the co-chair of his transition team.

Articles began appearing in Florida newspapers with stories, "Greer Is Steele's Right Hand Man." "Greer Picked the Right Person to Get Behind."

Later, Greer would win the election as chair of the rules committee.

"I felt my career had reached a high," said Greer. "I was Florida chair. I was on Michael Steele's transition team. I was making decisions about how the Republican National Committee would get its message out, how it was going to talk to the press and the voters nationally.

"I was flying high."

24

THE RISE OF THE TEA PARTY

ON JANUARY 11, 2009, TWO WEEKS BEFORE STEELE'S ELECTION AS CHAIRMAN of the National Republican Party, Greer had to face his own reelection as Florida chair. With the moderate Steele in charge of the national party, Greer was glad he had not run a second race. One was tough enough.

"I felt good going into reelection," said Greer. "I didn't think I was going to have a problem. People felt I had done well. People were behind me. Overall I was generally received as being a good chairman."

Greer once more raised money for his campaign and traveled the state seeking support. "People were willing to give," said Greer, "but most importantly, people knew Charlie Crist was still supporting me for a second term. Once I made his endorsement public, the deal was done."

Meanwhile, with John McCain having lost, Greer was envisioning an upcoming race in which the Republican candidate for president would be Charlie Crist.

"Everyone was sure Charlie would be president one day," said Greer. "I was telling him, George LeMieux was telling him, and other people were saying, 'McCain losing the election may well set it up for you to be president in 2012.'"

But there was still that ultra-conservative element out there in the rural areas of Florida and throughout the party that didn't support Crist and that wished he and Greer had never shown up two years before. Some of the criticism came from McCain supporters.

The fiercest criticism came from Arlene DiBenigno, who had been McCain's Florida political director. Someone was writing nasty anonymous emails about how Greer had refused to fund the McCain campaign. Members of Greer's senior staff were sure the emails were coming from Arlene.

"Remember, Charlie had stopped working hard for McCain once he wasn't named his running mate, so there was some legitimacy to their claim," said Greer. "But that wasn't what cost McCain the election. They were just looking for someone to blame."

Others were becoming more and more vocal in opposing Crist on some of his policies. There were also those who felt Greer should step aside because the Republicans had lost Florida to Obama. "I disagreed," said Greer. "We had won everything there was to win within the state. Losing Florida to Obama hadn't been within my control."

Yet another group opposing Crist and Greer came from a new type of Republican who was unhappy—no, mortified and furious—because McCain had done the unthinkable—he had somehow lost to the African American without a birth certificate. These people hated Obama so much they were foaming at the mouth. Crist called them "the crazies." They called themselves the Tea Party, and their positions were so off the wall that at first they weren't taken seriously. They made arguments that had been voiced in the slave states before the Civil War began. They argued that the federal government should be stripped of its power and that the states should have complete authority to do as they wished, particularly on issues like birth control, gay rights, and immigration policy.

Through the Tea Party the deep racial hatred in America, hidden since the 1960s, reemerged with vehemence. These people were old-line segregationists who didn't—couldn't—hide their racist nature.

"We had two segments coming together in Florida," said Greer. "You had the Ron Paul people, the so-called Liberty Caucus, who believed in no government regulation at all, and then you had the Tea Party. Those two groups disliked the direction the Republican Party was taking."

They were beginning to cause the moderates in the Florida Republican Party a lot of trouble.

"I was being told by my consultants, staff, and many county REC chairs—Jim Rimes, Rich Heffley, Delmar Johnson, Kirk Pepper—and by legislators—Chris Dorworth, Jason Brodeur, and Peter Nehr—that I needed to start removing these people from around the state because they were causing trouble," said Greer. "I had been given authority by the legislators to remove anyone I thought was wreaking havoc on the party, and they were urging me to oust these troublemakers from their local Republican Party committees.

"There was a Ron Paul guy in Kissimmee causing trouble. Gary Lee, from southwest Florida, a former congressman and a Tea Party guy, was a real pain. Another big Tea Party guy named Eric Miller came from down south in Indian River County. He had just been elected state committeeman, and he was telling people he was going to call for an audit of the party. 'The party needs to be taken back by the conservatives,' he kept saying. He was a big-mouthed person who believed Republicans needed to take action against Charlie Crist. He was *demanding* changes."

Greer, who may have been naïve, didn't listen to his consultants. He felt it was wrong to arbitrarily remove people simply because they had different political views. "If I had removed everyone they wanted me to," said Greer, "there'd have been no one left in the party in Florida."

At the same time, Greer found the criticisms unjust and unsettling. These big-mouths were thorns in his side, but his belief in the fine job Crist was doing overrode any negative feelings brought on by the criticism from the Ron Paul critics and the Tea Party crazies.

"I perceived all these naysayers as leftovers who wanted the party to stay where it was. These people were just anti-change," said Greer.

Meanwhile, Tea Party member Eric Miller announced he would run against Greer. "We're not going to make this the party of Charlie Crist," Miller announced. "And I'm going to demand an audit of spending by Chairman Greer. If you elect me chairman, I'm going to keep our party out of the presidential primaries."

Miller was aggressive in his rhetoric, but Greer had sewn up support from the leaders and the delegates. Among those supporting him were Governor Crist, Lieutenant Governor Kottkamp, President of the Senate Mike Haridopolos, Speaker of the House Dean Cannon, and governor-in-waiting Bill McCollum.

GREER RAN OVER MILLER by a vote of 169–52, or 77 percent of the vote.

On that same day, Jim Rimes, executive director of the Florida Republican Party, stepped down. Rimes had been one of Greer's top political consultants, so one of the first decisions after reelection was to find a replacement.

Greer had two choices. One was Kirk Pepper, the current deputy executive director for political affairs. Pepper was a political wonk. Greer didn't much like having wonks around him. They were too serious, too conventional, too boring. His other choice was Delmar Johnson. Say what you wanted about Delmar, the plus-size man was anything but boring. He knew how to have fun and have people around him have fun.

"As Charlie Crist used to say," said Greer, "'If you don't like Delmar Johnson, you don't like life. Because Delmar would bellow, 'Mr. Chaaiiirrrmannnn. Good to see you.' He was that kind of guy. He could have been a circus ringmaster."

There had been a lot of animosity in Florida during the McCain campaign about the way it was run. The McCain people didn't consult the county leaders, and it had little contact with grass-roots volunteers. Republican Floridians, including a lot of talented consultants and members of the party, were left with nothing to do.

"All I kept hearing was that the McCain campaign was taking the people element out of the campaign; that it was all about technology," said Greer.

Keeping that in mind, Greer stood in front of the microphone and told the crowd of delegates, "Ladies and gentlemen, I'm going to appoint Delmar Johnson the executive director of the party. We're going to put the people back into the political campaign."

It brought the house down, and when Delmar came out to take a bow, he received a standing ovation.

Greer asked Kirk Pepper to stay on as deputy executive director of political affairs. Most of the political consultants on Greer's staff were unhappy with his choice of Johnson over Pepper.

"You have to realize that some of these political professionals are not generally people persons. They are more the data kind of people. If you wanted to know who had voted Republican in the last city council race within a three-mile radius of your house, they could tell you, and with great zeal. That's not to say they didn't have good personalities, but they were not outgoing. Delmar was the kind of guy if you gave him a stage, a band, and campaign hats, he would put on one of the best damn events you'd ever see. He was just an outgoing guy and funny. I loved him. We spent great times together. Delmar was like a son to me."

After Greer was reelected chairman of the Republican Party of Florida and after Michael Steele was elected chairman of the National Republican Party, the two developed a close bond. Clearly Greer was going places in terms of the national stage, and Delmar Johnson was going with him.

During the meeting of the Republican National Committee, Steele and Roger Villere, the chairman of the Republican Party of Louisiana, and Villere's political staff, asked Greer if he would be in charge of the Southern Republican Leadership Conference that would be held in New Orleans April 8–11, 2010.

During the conversation Villere said to Greer, "We wanted to sit down and meet with you because we truly believe Charlie Crist is going to be president someday."

"That could be," said Greer.

"And we think you're going to be the guy sitting outside the Oval Office deciding who's going to get to see him."

Recalls Greer, "That was a kiss-my-butt type thing, but I was really excited I had been asked to chair the Southern Republican Leadership Conference."

A week later Greer went to Charlie and told him about his great opportunity.

Charlie Crist said no.

"You need to focus on Florida," said Crist. "We have a lot going on here. You'll be taken away a lot, out of state too much."

In other words: *If you go, you won't be here to look after my interests.*

"I swallowed it gracefully and never looked back," said Greer. "I might have been mad for an hour or two, but when it was all over, as always, it was whatever Charlie Crist wanted."

II

THE
BETRAYAL

★ STATEWIDE OFFICIALS ★

GOVERNOR
CHARLIE CRIST

LT. GOVERNOR
JEFF KOTTKAMP

ATTORNEY GENERAL
BILL McCOLLUM

COMMISSIONER OF
AGRICULTURE

CHARLES H. BRONSON

Crist, Kottkamp, and McCollum all played key parts in the Greer saga.

25

Mel Martinez Steps Down

Jim Greer was sitting on top of the world as 2009 began. He was the well-respected chairman of the Republican Party of Florida, a trusted ally of Michael Steele, chairman of the Republican National Committee, and he was working alongside Governor Charlie Crist, whom he and others were certain would be president of the United States one day. Were that to happen, Greer believed he too would be going to the White House.

But life can throw you a curve ball, and Greer's undoing had begun innocuously enough when in late November 2008 U.S. Senator Mel Martinez made two phone calls.

Greer was meeting with some local dignitaries in his office when the phone rang. "I have made a decision," Martinez said. "I want to retire and come home to Orlando."

Immediately after Martinez hung up, Greer's cell phone rang. It was Crist, who was out of town. Martinez had called the governor as well.

"What do you think of the news?" said Crist.

"It's interesting," said Greer. "It provides a lot of opportunities."

"Do you think it provides a lot of opportunities for me?" asked Crist.

"Yeah, it sure does," said Greer. "The question is, 'What do you do with it?'"

"I'm flying back into town tonight," said Crist. "Let's get together and talk about it. Come over to the mansion around six o'clock."

That evening, over martinis, wine, and cheese and crackers, Greer and Crist strategized about their futures. Martinez's decision to step down wasn't a done deal yet, but Greer advised Crist that he should run for the seat if Martinez stepped down before his term was up.

In addition to a U.S. Senate seat possibly becoming a steppingstone to the presidency, Greer realized something else. The winds were changing around the country. Problems were looming; the economy was tanking. The crazies were getting crazier.

"I had the gut feeling that governors—especially one heading into his third and fourth year—were going to encounter a lot of problems," said Greer. "And Crist wasn't really interested in policy. That had been the purview of George LeMieux."

In addition, Greer knew that he and Crist weren't making a lot of friends among Republican Party stalwarts in Florida. The Governor and the Chairman had endorsed McCain against the wishes of the Jeb Bush crowd; they had campaigned hard for McCain; McCain had lost. Greer and Crist were getting a lot of blame from the hard-right conservative Republicans, unfair as it might have been.

"I felt we needed to get out of town before things got worse," said Greer. "This was our chance."

ON DECEMBER 1, 2008, a few days after his calls to Crist and Greer, Martinez announced publicly he would not run for reelection. He would step down at the end of his term because he wanted to spend more time with his family. The announcement sparked a series of events that would ultimately tumble both Greer and Crist out of politics and put Greer behind bars for more than a year.

Martinez's decision coincided with the emergence of the Tea Party as a ruthless, brutal wing of the Republican Party. Intrigue, political dirty tricks, deceit, and treachery would all play a role in what happened to Greer. Worst, the revenge and betrayal would come from those closest to Greer. It would be a Shakespearean tragedy with a Florida twist.

In the end, as the judge brought down the gavel sending him to prison, Greer never knew what hit him.

MELQUIADES RAFAEL MARTINEZ RUIZ, better known as Mel Martinez, emigrated in 1962 from Sagua La Grande, Cuba, at the age of 15 as part of a Catholic humanitarian effort called Operation Pan Pedro. Catholic charities provided Martinez, who spoke only Spanish, a temporary home at a youth facility. He then lived with two foster families until he was reunited with his own family four years later in Orlando.

After earning his JD at the University of Florida, he began his political career as the Republican chairman of Orange County. While in office he promoted the "Martinez doctrine," which prohibited development from taking place unless there was adequate school capacity for newcomers. He was chairman of the Orlando Housing Authority before President George W. Bush tapped him to be the Secretary of HUD in an attempt to attract more Hispanics to the Republican Party. He was a key fundraiser for Bush when he ran for president in 2000.

In November 2004 Martinez was the Republican nominee for U.S. Senator to replace the retiring Bob Graham. A favorite of the Bush people, Martinez had wanted to run for governor in 2006, but he was asked to run for the Senate in 2004 instead.

His challenger was Bill McCollum, a hard-liner whom Martinez nonetheless accused of being "the new darling of homosexual extremists." Martinez's ads accused McCollum of sponsoring hate crimes legislation and protecting gays while McCollum was a member of the House of Representatives. When Governor Jeb Bush asked Martinez to retract the ads, he did so.

Martinez beat McCollum badly. He then went on to win the Senate seat against the Democratic nominee Betty Castor.

As a United States senator, Martinez was valued by President Bush because he was Republican and Hispanic. In 2006 Bush had asked Mel to meet with him at the White House.

Greer recalled what Martinez later told him about the meeting. "Mel didn't have any idea why he was going to the Oval Office. Bush asked him to become general chairman of the Republican National Committee. Bush wanted him to be the face of the RNC—to court Hispanics and to be their spokesperson on immigration. He wanted to have confidence in the person running the RNC."

The problem was that the RNC already had a chairman, Mike Duncan, so they created a new title and made Martinez the general chairman of the Republican National Committee. (That precedent was why Ken Blackwell later asked for that title as a concession for yielding to Michael Steele.)

Greer said Martinez told him, "I had no idea what the hell the general chairman of the Republican National Committee did." When Martinez showed up at the RNC for the first time, he was treated terribly.

"He had to fight to get an office," said Greer. "He had nothing on his desk. He had to beg for a telephone. When Duncan held staff meetings, he didn't have the decency to invite Mel's staff. Mel realized quickly that his title meant nothing. The president's appointment hadn't guaranteed acceptance."

Greer could identify with that; he faced the same difficulty after being handpicked by Crist to run for the Florida chairmanship.

"It never worked out for Martinez," said Greer. "The powers that be among the Republican Party didn't like him. They thought he was too moderate, especially on immigration. He had everything—except the support of the right-wing of the party."

In 2009, after Martinez had announced he wouldn't be seeking reelection to the Senate, Greer ran into him at an RNC meeting.

"He told me how happy he was not to be running for reelection," said Greer. "He missed living in Orlando, going to ballgames with his kids, spending time with his family. A lot of people in politics say they want to spend more time with their families, but Martinez really did. He loved his wife, Kitty, and he loved Orlando. I think he just got weary and he had no enthusiasm for the job.

"He also told me, 'I will not miss going to those RNC meetings. I won't miss having to deal with the crazies—the wackadoos, he called them. There are a lot of normal, reasonable people in the Republican Party, but because of the crazies, they generally want to get the hell out of it once they get in. Mel Martinez was one of those people.

"It's a shame."

26

DREAMING OF THE WHITE HOUSE

FOR MUCH OF 2008, FLORIDA GOVERNOR CHARLIE CRIST WAS FOCUSED ON being chosen as John McCain's running mate. Unfortunately for Crist, McCain picked Sarah Palin and the ticket then lost badly. Some of Crist's closest advisers, including Greer, viewed McCain's loss as an opportunity for Crist to run for the presidency in 2012.

"A lot of us thought he would have a good shot at it," said Greer. On the day McCain picked Palin, Greer optimistically reminded a crestfallen Crist, "One door closes and another door opens."

Then began the clamoring of various segments in the Florida Republican party for Crist's attention as to what he should do next. The lobbyist crowd, led by Brian Ballard, who had a personal interest in Crist's staying put, wanted him to run for another term as governor. Recalled Greer, "They had raised a lot of money for him, had invested a lot of money in the man, and had easy access to him. They were cozy with his chief of staff and all the agency heads and knew how to use these people to ramrod through what they wanted."

Ballard's clients were far and wide. One of his biggest was gambling interests, and Governor Crist had put out feelers about expanding gambling. Ballard also represented Florida Power and Light and had been promoting the raising of rates. He was involved with U.S. Sugar in its battle with environmentalists over the Everglades. U.S. Sugar didn't want Crist going anywhere, either.

George LeMieux also wanted Charlie to stay as governor because it was in his best interest. LeMieux had joined the prestigious Gunster Law Firm, and he was getting his clients lucrative contracts with the Florida Department of Transportation.

"These people were making millions for clients, not only through contracts but by influencing legislation that could hurt or help a client, or by preventing an agency from over-regulating you," said Greer. "Major figures like LeMieux and Ballard could pick up the phone, and the next thing you know, the problem would go away. Brian had raised millions for Charlie. George had been the de facto governor—the Maestro—the guy closest to Charlie Crist. So don't screw with any of their clients.

"After LeMieux resigned as chief of staff, he brought in Eric Eikenberg to replace him, so all George had to do was call Eric, who then would call the secretary of that agency and say, 'Hey, I understand your Miami office has an issue with Clean Energy Incorporated.' And the next thing you knew, the secretary would be told subtly to get off the back of Clean Energy Incorporated, because it was a client of George LeMieux."

Greer had no such personal financial interest in Crist's career, except that he knew that if Crist became president, he would be going to Washington, D.C., with him.

By January 2009 Crist and Greer had become like brothers. Unlike others close to the governor, Greer had only Crist's political interests at heart. He knew Crist wanted to be president, and he was determined to do what he could to help his friend get there.

"What is Charlie Crist's best strategy?" was the question the political insiders were asking. If he were to run for the presidency in 2012, should he run as the lame-duck governor of Florida or as a sitting U.S. senator?

Greer led those who argued that Crist's path to the presidency would be best served by becoming a U.S. senator. He was thinking that Crist could be seen as a candidate who had experience being both a governor *and* a senator.

"When Mel resigned and this question became central, I said, 'All of Charlie's experiences are beneficial,'" recalled Greer. "One of the big arguments made against Obama—it didn't carry any weight—was that he didn't have executive experience. The same was true of McCain, which enabled Palin's supporters to argue that as a governor she added value to the ticket."

Greer knew that U.S. senators don't make executive decisions beyond the staffing of their own offices. But governors run the entire state government, and Crist already had that under his belt. So in strategy discussions with LeMieux, Ballard, Jay Burmer, and Harry Sargeant, Greer argued to

Crist, "Okay, if you run for Mel's seat in 2010 and you get elected, you have two years as U.S. senator before the presidential election, plenty of time to get national exposure. You'll have one term as governor, two years as U.S. senator—you'll have perfect qualifications to be president."

THERE WAS ANOTHER PERSON who was intensely focused on Charlie Crist's future: his wife, Carole.

"Carole was excited throughout the whole process," said Greer. "My phone would ring at ten o'clock at night, and Carole would want to know what being a U.S. senator entailed. 'Does a senator get a driver?' she would ask me. 'Does the Senate pay for a security detail?' 'Do senators have to stop at the TSA at the airport?' 'What kind of expense account is there?'"

Crist himself had larger concerns. "He was interested in big picture issues like having a political action committee. He talked about raising money through a PAC, something senators do so they can have political action committees and pay for things they can't afford on a senator's salary."

IN THE PRESS, MEANWHILE, speculation was rampant about Crist's intentions.

"People who knew Charlie over his entire political career recognized that he was always looking for the next political opening," said Greer. "He went from state senator to education commissioner to attorney general to governor. People would say, and it was true, 'Crist loves campaigning more than he likes actually holding office.'

"Charlie was coy about his plans. He talked to everybody; he listened to everybody. He consulted with Brian, with George, with me, and he was having intense discussions with Carole. But even those closest to him never quite knew what he was thinking."

At the same time Crist was deciding what to do, the Democrats, anticipating a run for the suddenly open seat, were beginning to plant stories criticizing Crist as "empty chair Charlie." Crist had made the same charge against Congressman Davis in the 2006 gubernatorial election. Now the tables were being turned.

"They went after him," said Greer, "but he had friends like Brian and George who were protecting him, who had relations with people who could kill some of those stories. But the negativity was starting: 'Did Charlie Crist Work as Hard as He Could Have?' the Palm Beach Post wanted to know, and 'Charlie Crist Goes to Disney World the Last Two Weeks of the Mc-Cain Campaign.' And that one was true.

"The shield around him was being poked at," said Greer, "but he was very popular and had incredibly high approval ratings. They were in the 70s. And he still believed his own press. The media loved him, everybody loved him. People believed he had a great future. And so did he. And so did I. We were spending a ton of time together. I was saying all the things he liked to hear. I was trying to guide him in the right direction, but he had another major influence on him now, and that was Carole."

THOUGH CRIST WASN'T ANNOUNCING his intentions publicly, he was putting out feelers to John Cornyn, then the chairman of the Republican National Senatorial Campaign. It was Cornyn's task to find the best Republican candidates across the country to run for the U.S. Senate.

In early January Senator Cornyn contacted Crist about running for the seat. Cornyn publicly stated that he thought Charlie Crist would make a great senator and could win.

Crist loved that.

Around January 15 Cornyn told the press that he was having conversations with Crist about running for the Senate, but when the press asked Crist about it, he demurred. Asked what he thought of being a U.S. senator, Crist answered, "Not much," but few believed him. Everyone knew he was looking into running. Meanwhile, Crist had Greer call Rob Jesmer, Cornyn's number one guy, to get Cornyn's feelings.

"At this time," said Greer, "everyone thought that if Crist did run for the Senate, then Marco Rubio would run for attorney general or governor."

27

OBAMA'S MAN HUG

As 2009 DRAGGED ON, GREER WORRIED THAT GOVERNOR CRIST WAS IN-creasingly indecisive and that the executive office was being run with little direction. Charlie Crist had lost interest in the job, Greer thought.

"Eric Eikenberg was not a strong chief of staff. He'd call me up all the time to get the governor to do things. LeMieux was no longer there to tell Charlie right from wrong, and Charlie was incapable of making a decision. Eric couldn't wrest any answers from him."

With LeMieux gone and Eric not someone Crist would turn to, Greer became Crist's sounding board.

"The governor and I were spending a lot of time together," said Greer. "He was asking my opinion on all sorts of things, and he would regularly invite me over to the mansion for dinner. I have to say it was always impressive when I'd drive up to the mansion, go over to the left side of the building where the personal quarters were, pull up to the big gate, hit a box, and hear an agent say, 'Good evening, chairman. The gate will be opening momentarily.' I had always wondered how it all worked, and now I was part of it."

As Greer got closer to Crist, he also became much better acquainted with Carole. What he soon discovered was that Carole, a New York City Jew and a liberal, was pushing Crist hard to see things from her left-leaning progressive point of view.

"Carole was dangerous," said Greer. "There were times we'd be together, and she'd say things about abortion—she was pro-choice—and quite often Lisa, knowing how Republicans would react, would say, 'Carole, you can't say those kinds of things in public.'"

Greer observed that one of Carole's tricks to get her point across to Charlie was to get others to agree with her first—to then influence Charlie.

"She would call me and give me her take on certain issues she didn't want to express to Charlie directly," said Greer. "She'd try to convince me first so that I would become her ally. Most of the time, though, I strongly disagreed with her. I would tell her it would cause a lot of trouble with the Republican Party, which she didn't understand because she didn't understand the people on the state committee."

One time Carole called Greer and suggested that Charlie should say something positive about President Obama. He had to explain Crist couldn't do that because he was a Republican governor.

"A lot of people already believed we had elected the anti-Christ," said Greer, "and I didn't want Charlie to destroy his entire career by taking objectionable positions. Carole was *very* liberal in her thinking. She was a Democrat, and she had no understanding of the political ramifications of what she was trying to do. Nor did she understand a thing about the party and the organization I governed."

CAROLE CRIST AND THE Greers spoke almost every day for a year and a half, sometimes three times a day, sometimes well into the night. Often it was social. She would ask if Lisa and his kids could come to New York for the weekend because her two girls were going to be there. Or could they come to Fisher Island? Or could Jim get a reservation at some fancy restaurant for her and Charlie?

Greer said he came to see Carole as "a female Rasputin." Like Rasputin, Carole had a vision. "One time over dinner at Disney World, Carole told Lisa and me there was no way in hell Jeb Bush was not going to endorse Charlie. Of course, it didn't happen."

Greer had no way of knowing just how much influence Carole had on her governor-husband, but Greer wasn't surprised when on January 22, 2009, before a crowd of more than 700 at the nonpartisan Forum Club of the Palm Beaches, Governor Crist praised President Obama's stimulus package, saying that the infusion of federal money would ease the pain of Florida's $2.3 billion budget deficit.

"About this time Crist was talking about Florida getting $13 billion in stimulus money," said Greer. "And he really believed, and I did too, that if they were giving out money in D.C., we ought to get some."

Crist was one of the few Republican governors who supported the stimulus. President Obama announced publicly that he wanted to personally thank Governor Crist for his support. This made the Florida Tea Partiers and ultraconservative Republicans apoplectic.

The governor was telling the public that the stimulus would prevent tax increases, but Republican legislators—outraged that Crist would take federal money—started mumbling that this wasn't really true.

Letters came pouring into Greer's office. His secretary, Lela Whitfield, would deliver them to Greer. Some said, "We're never giving to the party again because of Charlie Crist."

Greer, Delmar Johnson, and Kirk Pepper took phone calls from screaming Tea Party members and state committee members such as Gary Lee and Peter Feaman.

"In the first week of February 2009 a poll gave Charlie a 73 percent approval rating," said Greer. "Charlie felt this high rating allowed him to do anything—that it freed him to be the Charlie Crist that both he and Carole wanted him to be. He even said to me at one point, 'With my approval ratings in the seventies, I don't have the hindrance of having to deal with the Republican crazies who are so anti-Obama.' He felt he could really break out."

Anticipating the stimulus money, Crist supported another big spending project that was opposed by the hard-line Republicans, not as much for political reasons as for the fact that some of the big Florida corporations opposed it—commuter rail in Central Florida. Universal Studios and Sea World were against the project because the rail line wouldn't be stopping at their amusement parks.

Even so, in January 2009 things were running smoothly for both Governor Crist and Chairman Greer. "People were calling and complaining, but the real revolution hadn't yet started," Greer said.

On February 9, Greer's mother broke her hip and was scheduled for surgery two days later. Greer was with his mom at the hospital when he received a call from Eric Eikenberg that would start the snowball rolling towards an avalanche of disaster.

Eikenberg was talking in a very low voice. He said, "The governor is telling us that he's going to Ft. Myers to see Obama. Erin is all excited about being with Obama."

Erin Isaac was Crist's communications director. "She was a young girl," said Greer, "and sometimes a bit giddy. She didn't realize what was at stake, what the repercussions would be."

Eikenberg wanted desperately for Governor Crist to speak with Greer. "I need you to talk to him. We can't go down and meet Obama. It's going to be a mess, and it's going to be a mess for you, Chairman."

Greer completely agreed with Eric. The right wing of the Republican Party, especially the Tea Party crazies, hated Obama so much that in their minds anyone who came within a mile of him automatically became radioactive. Eikenberg knew what would happen if Crist showed up at an Obama rally. He feared a nuclear winter.

The problem, again, was that Crist was being arrogant, blinded by his high poll numbers and underestimating his enemies. Crist, a moderate, often would say, "My mother and father taught me to respect people."

Meanwhile, Carole Crist naively was pushing her husband to embrace the president. Not seeing the raging storm that was brewing inside the Republican Party, she felt a meeting of her husband with the president would be good for Florida and for Crist's career, making him more of a national figure.

Greer thought such a move would amount to suicide.

With LeMieux gone, Greer had become Crist's sounding board, one of the few people he would listen to. Observers knew that when Crist was on the cusp of doing something stupid, Greer was one of the few people who could talk him out of it.

A panicked Greer called Crist.

"Chairman, how are you?" was the familiar refrain from Crist. "I bet you've heard I'm thinking about going down to Ft. Myers."

"Yes sir," Greer said. "I sure have. I don't think it's a good idea, Governor."

"You think it's going to rile up some of the crazies?"

"Yes sir, I sure do. It's going to cause a lot of problems with our Republican Executive Committee."

"Obama's just gotten elected," said Crist. "He's the president of the United States. It's his first visit to Florida."

"Governor, I understand that," said Greer, "but you're supporting the stimulus, which already has the crazies agitated. This could be very damaging. Here's what I think you ought to do. I think you ought to greet Obama's plane and meet him at the foot of Air Force One. *But do not go to the rally.* The rally is a totally different thing. Joining the rally to promote the stimulus package and getting completely behind it—then you'd be all in, and that would be a big problem."

"It's something to think about," said Crist. "Not a bad idea. Let me give it some thought. How's your mom?"

"She's fine," said Greer, who was pacing furiously in the parking lot outside the hospital where his mom was being operated on.

A few minutes later Eikenberg called Greer back. "What happened?" asked Eikenberg.

"I told him I thought he should just go to the plane," said Greer. "Call me back if anything else comes up. My mom's about to go into surgery."

The surgery went well—good news for Greer. The rest of the day—not so much.

When Eikenberg called back, he said, "We're going to the rally. We're in the bubble, and we're going, and it's going to be a bad day for you, Chairman."

All Greer could do was shake his head. "I was sitting in the waiting room with my wife and brother, and I'm watching TV," said Greer, "and there's Charlie on stage, standing at the podium, and he's introducing the president. I'm watching this and thinking, *This is absolutely terrible. This is going to rile the crazies up as never before.*"

Greer watched in horror as, after Crist introduced the president, Obama strode over to Crist and gave him a man-hug as the photographers snapped away.

That afternoon Greer got a call from Jim Stelling, the chairman of the Seminole County Republican Party. Stelling was a close friend from Oviedo and a strong supporter, the sort of friend who wasn't afraid to tell Greer exactly what he thought. "What the fuck is up with your boy?" he asked. "Do you have any idea what this is going to do?"

"Probably," said Greer.

"It wasn't enough, chairman," said Stelling, "that he put a stick in the eye of the Republicans. It wasn't enough he went out of his way to distance himself from Jeb Bush . . ."

"I know, Jim," said Greer. "I know."

Gary Lee, an ultraconservative from Lee County, also called Greer.

"He went off on me," said Greer, "so I knew this was the start of something. But remember, Charlie still had a 73 percent approval rating. Senator Cornyn, the head of the national Republican Senatorial Campaign Committee, was talking to him about running for the Senate. I had just been reelected chairman by a wide margin. I had just co-chaired Michael Steele's transition team. All those things countered what I was now concerned about."

The real fall-out didn't come for about two weeks, but the one photo of the president of the United States and the Florida governor embracing ignited the conservative bloc of the Florida Republican Party like nothing anyone had ever seen.

Until then there had been no direct confrontation of Crist by the Republican right-wingers because he was still so popular. "People weren't yet smelling blood in the water," said Greer. "But I believe they knew it was coming. The Bush people, with some Romney and McCain people—in many cases they were the same people—started strategizing. Marco Rubio sent out mailers to Republicans statewide with the picture of Obama hugging Crist on the return envelope.

Stories began appearing in the newspapers detailing the GOP's opposition to Crist's position on the stimulus. Republicans were quoted anonymously, or occasionally a Tea Party state committee member would state, "What Crist is doing is anti-Republican. Republicans are for less government, less taxes—not for stimulus money, or for government solving our problems."

Crist would reply, but these stories were rubbing the shine off his patina, particularly as he related to his fellow Republicans and the hard-core members of the state committee.

Greer was sitting with Crist in the governor's mansion when Crist asked what he thought the repercussions would be.

"Governor, I don't know," answered Greer. "We still control the executive board. Delmar is there working hard to get us a closer relationship with the members."

"Charlie never asked me, 'Was it the right decision?' said Greer. "He just wanted to know what the fallout would be."

"Governor, you should have just met him at the airport," Greer told Crist.

"Florida needs the stimulus money," Crist replied. "It will provide jobs for Florida. It will help with the budget. And it was the right thing to do."

"It was clear to me," said Greer, "that Charlie wasn't interested in revisiting the decision."

28

THE DARK SIDE LAYS THE GROUNDWORK

IT WAS FEBRUARY 2009, AND CRIST'S POLITICAL ADVISERS WERE CONFLICTED over whether he should run for the U.S. Senate seat Mel Martinez was vacating. Part of the problem was that the legislative session would begin in March, and if he announced now he was going to run for the Senate, automatically he would become a lame duck.

It was the governor's responsibility to provide a budget for the coming year, and Republican legislators were livid when they saw that Crist was filling budget gaps with stimulus money from Washington.

"I was getting calls," said Greer. 'What's he doing? This stimulus money isn't recurring money, it's just one-shot money.' But that was always Charlie's approach. 'Let's solve the problem today. We'll worry about tomorrow, tomorrow.' It was his political philosophy. He's able to make you feel good now. He gives you the shot today. But he doesn't quite tell you that in six months you're going to be dead. For *today* you're going to feel great.

"Let me be clear. I supported his using the stimulus, not that anyone cared what I thought. The Obama administration, though, wasn't being completely honest. There weren't going to be recurring stimulus funds. But I agreed with Charlie that if they were handing out money in Washington, Florida ought to get some. The Republican legislative leaders went after Charlie and his budget director for not telling the whole story. "

In the first week of February 2009, Crist informed the *Palm Beach Post* he would decide in May, right after the end of the legislative session, whether to run for the Senate.

The way the Florida legislature works, there are committee meetings in December, January, and February, and the legislature convenes on the first Tuesday in March. The session runs for 60 days ending in May. During that 60-day period there's an unofficial taboo prohibiting the governor and legislators from soliciting or collecting campaign contributions—everyone is supposed to focus on the legislative session. Hence Crist's May announcement.

"Of course that wasn't true," said Greer. "We weren't going to decide in May. He had decided, only we didn't officially announce it."

When the legislature convened, Crist did other things that infuriated many of the Republican legislators.

The Allstate and State Farm insurance companies—both heavy contributors to the Republican Party—were seeking large rate increases, and Crist was threatening to oppose the legislation. Carole's influence was always lurking in the background, Greer saw; Crist was turning into a Democrat.

"Many actions Crist was starting to take showed me how far from Republican Party philosophy he was edging; he wasn't demonstrating any real allegiance to what the party and the party leadership stood for. And it was real easy for him to do it because in the back of his mind he knew, *I have Greer watching my back.*"

Stories began appearing in the press about Crist's slide towards a more moderate position and tone and that he was considering a run for Mel Martinez's Senate seat.

In mid-March 2009, the conservative rebellion against Crist began with an attack on his use of private jets.

"It started off legit," said Greer. "And what I mean by that, the way the law reads, a person can make an in-kind contribution to the Republican Party of the use of a jet. But the jet must be used for Republican Party business, not for personal use. The first couple of years Charlie would do actual events and raise money for the party near Fisher Island, where he was spending his weekends. Then it got a little ridiculous. One time he flew on a private jet with Carole to a Jimmy Buffet concert in Tampa when there was no real Republican Party business there. Dane Eagle, his travel aide, called me up. Dane's father had given Charlie a million dollars. Dane said, 'Listen, we have a problem. The governor flew to Tampa today on a private plane, and he needs you to do something to legitimize his flight. Can you come over here and deliver him some papers?'"

Greer said he came up with the idea that he had a briefing paper for an upcoming Seminole County Republican meeting that Crist had to sign off on, so he then flew in his own plane to Tampa, met Charlie and Carole at the hangar, and watched Crist go through the motions of reading the document.

"I got right back on my airplane and flew back to Tallahassee," said Greer. "The governor knew I was there simply to cover his ass."

And he didn't even invite Greer to the concert.

"Charlie was flying on private jets back and forth to California to visit Arnold Schwarzenegger, then the governor of California," said Greer. "Everything was generally legitimate because I was usually with him. Sometimes he would be going to fundraisers for the party. But somebody—we never knew who—was getting the press to look into these trips and stories started appearing, '*Crist Defends Corporate Jet Use.*' Crist would always refer the reporter to the Republican Party of Florida.

"One headline read, '*Crist Keeps Details of Jet Use Under Wraps.*' But he was complying with the law as I was the one who was accepting the in-kind contributions."

Greer said, "You can see that the 'Dark Side' was beginning their attacks on him. They were laying the groundwork."

TOWARD THE END OF March, Greer received a phone call from his friend and Republican party rules committee chairman Jim Stelling, the county chairman from Greer's home county of Seminole.

"I want you to know there are some state committee members who are starting to put together a grievance against Charlie Crist," said Stelling. "They're going to ask you to censure him."

Greer was being put in a difficult position. He would have to choose sides between the governor and the Tea Party and ultra-conservatives lining up against him. For Greer, the decision was easy. Crist had chosen him to be chairman, and he vowed to go down with the ship, if need be, to be loyal to the governor.

This was the first test.

Within the rules of the Republican Party of Florida, a provision allowed any Republican to file a grievance against a Republican leader or any other Republican. Once filed, the Republican Party must address the grievance.

If a Republican precinct person from a little neighborhood wrote a $100 check to a Democratic candidate and a disgruntled Republican found out about it, he could submit a grievance to the chairman of the party. If the chairman chose, he could forward the complaint to the grievance committee of the party. That committee met quarterly in Orlando. It could dismiss the case, hold a hearing with witnesses, or recommend expulsion from the party. The resolution then went back to the chairman, who could accept it, modify the penalty, or send it back to the grievance committee to have it looked at again.

"By the end of the legislative term, oh my God," said Greer, "I had a stack of grievances on my desk, with one Republican after another filing against other Republicans. Most of the time it was petty bullshit."

Word was circulating through the party that certain Republicans, angry with Crist, were planning to file grievances against him. Not coincidentally, this was the same time period when the Tea Party was beginning to flex its muscles around the country.

It's not easy to define the Tea Party movement, except to describe what the ultra-conservative supporters of the Tea Party are against. They are opposed to the federal government, spending, taxes, bailouts, stimulus, immigration rights, gays, women, blacks, Obama, and compromise. The latter became important because one of the major objectives of the Tea Party was to oust moderate Republicans from the party.

You might ask what the Tea Party supports. It is for a balanced federal budget and for audits of federal governmental agencies. On the state level in Florida, as we will see, Tea Party members called for audits of the books of the Republican Party of Florida as well as those of the Florida Senate and House side of the party.

The Tea Party started as a grass-roots movement after the election of President Obama. Its supporters included white supremacists and run-of-the-mill racists fearing the country was being taken over by *them*.

Around the country the Tea Party was finding its voice with politicians like Sharon Engel of Nevada, Michele Bachmann of Minnesota, Sarah Palin of Alaska, Darrell Issa of California, Rand Paul of Kentucky, Jim DeMint of South Carolina, and in Florida with Congressman Allen West and state

House Speaker Marco Rubio. They were generally opposed to everything Obama and Crist espoused.

"The Tea Party was starting to cross the country," said Greer, "and they were seeking to censure Republican politicians, especially the moderates. They began censuring Arnold Schwarzenegger in California. The Republican Speaker of the House in Kentucky was censured for passing legislation they saw as un-Republican. Nationally there was a movement to censure or defeat in the primary any Republican who supported the stimulus."

Crist, naturally, became one of the Tea Party's prime targets.

Stelling had warned Greer that some Florida Tea Party grass-roots Republicans were about to file grievances against Crist. "They're going to demand that you stand at the podium as chairman of the Republican Party and tell them, 'I hereby censor Charlie Crist,'" said Stelling.

"That's a joke. I'm not doing it," Greer said. "This man raises tons of money for the party. He shows up on Saturday at five o'clock to raise $100,000. He's done everything the party has asked him to do."

"Chairman," said Stelling, "Charlie is causing a real problem for you. These guys are going to force your hand at the next meeting."

Greer knew exactly who "these guys" were. "There was a small band of them. Allison DeFoor from North Port, Deborah Cox Roush out of Hillsborough County, Gary Lee of Lee County, David Rivera out of Miami and a close ally of Rubio, Peter Feaman of Boynton Beach, chairman of the state committeemen and state committeewomen, Bob Starr, chairman of the chairman's caucus, and Allen Cox, my vice-chairman. All had organized to cause me trouble."

Like Crist, Greer underestimated their resolve and ruthlessness.

The Palm Beach County local Republican Party was to hold its meeting the first week of April 2009. Greer was told that a vote on whether to censure Governor Crist would be taken then.

"I thought that was outrageous, that a county REC would vote to do that to our governor," said Greer. "It was the first step in forcing me to take action in Tallahassee."

Greer called Sid Dinerstein, the Palm Beach county chairman.

"I have to let it go forward," Dinerstein said. "I can't stop it. I'm not saying how I'm going to vote, but as the local chairman, I have to let the people have their say."

Greer was furious. "To me, this was a total lack of leadership, a total lack of controlling his REC," said Greer. "He wanted to have a big night of controversy."

Greer told him, "'Sid, you're going to have to man up and make that committee delay a vote.'"

Greer ordered his political staff to travel down to that committee meeting that night to talk to each person quietly to get them to delay a vote.

Greer's tactics were successful, but some people, including Peter Feaman, a state committeeman, began telling others, "Greer and Tallahassee interfered with the democratic process in the local Palm Beach County REC to censure Crist."

AROUND THIS TIME A different complaint about Crist's performance as governor surfaced as the right-wingers of the Florida legislature began to smell blood. Crist was criticized for a lack of leadership when it came to tough budget decisions.

"Without George LeMieux, there was no strong leader in that office," said Greer. "A joke was floating around, 'What's the biggest difference between Jeb Bush and how he dealt with the legislature and Charlie Crist?' Answer, 'With Charlie Crist there *is* a legislature.' When Jeb was governor, the legislature did exactly what Jeb wanted. With Charlie, legislative leaders were on their own—with no guidance from him. Charlie let them duke it out among themselves."

Crist would also at times double-cross the legislators, vetoing bills he had signaled he was going to sign.

"2009 was really a year of mixed messages," said Greer. "Everything was based on politics, nothing on merit. The legislative leaders would say to Crist's legislative affairs director, 'This bill is moving forward. How does the governor feel about the bill?' And the governor would simply respond, 'I don't have a problem with it.' When that happened, the bill would move forward. Then months later when the bill crossed his desk for signature, Charlie would veto it, making the legislature look stupid.

"The one they really went ballistic on was the bill relating to property insurance—raising rates for property insurers in Florida. How much could the insurance companies raise the rates by? Crist signed off on the legislation that allowed them to raise rates to a high level. The legislation passed and was then sent on to the governor. He vetoed it, even though he had already given the go-ahead. Members of the legislature began to see that Charlie was not a leader but rather a total opportunist. Everything they had whispered about him privately was proving to be right.

"At this time Eric Eikenberg was the chief of staff. Many of these public policy issues were discussed between Eric and Charlie. Eric and I would have drinks at the Ale House in Tallahassee, and he'd tell me what was going on, and he would be pulling his hair out. Eric would tell me, 'He's talking to people who are giving him really bad advice.'

"Crist was beginning to move away from his Republican advisers," said Greer. "He began consulting with people who would tell him what he wanted to hear. I was right smack in the middle. I didn't hesitate to tell him what I thought, but he would respond, 'I talked to Mitch today, and Mitch thinks I need to go ahead and do this.' Mitch was Mitch Bainwol, a wealthy friend of his from Washington, D.C. They had both worked for Connie Mack Sr. many years earlier. Bainwol was the chairman and CEO of the Recording Industry Association of America. He was a Republican, but he was a moderate Republican.

"Or he'd tell me, 'I talked to my dad today.'"

And, of course, he was listening to Carole.

"It was crystal clear now," said Greer, "Charlie was starting to talk to only those who leaned to the left or agreed with him."

Meanwhile the gap between right-wing and centrist Republicans was growing. In May 2009 Greer was holding a press talk at the Republican National Committee meeting in Annapolis, when a reporter asked whether he thought President Obama was really a citizen.

The Birther movement had begun, as Tea Party bigots did everything they could do to deny Obama legitimacy. Pretending he didn't have a birth certificate and therefore was not really an American was part of the Tea Party dogma.

Greer didn't ingratiate himself with the right-wingers when he replied, "This is a ridiculous question, and anyone within the Republican Party who is still talking about it is ridiculous. I saw Obama being sworn in. He's the president of the United States. So that issue should not be discussed, and quite frankly, anyone who is still talking about it is an idiot."

When Greer returned to Tallahassee, Sharon Day, the national committeewoman who had been a thorn in Greer's side from day one, told him that his comments had upset a lot of people.

"I really don't care, Sharon," Greer told her. "I cannot believe we're still talking about whether Barack Obama is a citizen. The matter is closed. He was sworn in. The Marines salute him when he gets off the helicopter. He can order a bombing. He's the commander in chief. The issue is done."

Greer, failing to see into the future, was drawing a line in the sand. He had no clue what was about to hit him.

29

A Fateful Appointment

"The Republican Party was now in open rebellion against Charlie," said Greer, "and I wasn't about to let the state Republican Party or any county Republican Party censure the governor. One night I went over to the mansion and told Charlie that things were getting bad. I told him about Palm Beach and their vote to censure him. I told him about Jim Stelling's warning that certain ultraconservatives were out to embarrass him."

"We still have high approval ratings," Crist said. He told Greer that Senate Republican leader John Cornyn was still saying he would support Crist "over Rubio or anyone else who might run against me for the Senate."

In March 2009, Rubio had not announced his own candidacy for the Senate, but the Tea Party favorite surely was running for something; he already was actively and aggressively campaigning around the state.

Crist, meanwhile, was trying to balance being governor with his behind-the-scenes maneuvering towards a Senate campaign. Greer wanted Crist to announce his candidacy for the Senate and then go on a bus tour of the state, but Crist felt that because of his popularity, all he needed was an announcement in a short press release. Greer disagreed.

At the same time, George LeMieux, now a lobbyist, was still trying to keep Crist in the governor's office and he saw the criticisms by hard-liners who were aware that even with the 2008 presidential campaign behind him, Crist wasn't spending very much time on state business.

The newspapers were running stories commenting that Crist rarely was in his office. LeMieux kept calling Greer, telling him, "You need to tell him to fill up his schedule. His schedule looks terrible."

As much as Crist was bored with the job, his wife loved being the governor's wife. She loved riding the private jets, loved not having to go through security at airports. One problem was that as a Manhattanite, she thought Tallahassee too tame and boring, and she spent most of her time either in New York or at her Fisher Island condo. As a result, Crist rarely was in Tallahassee on weekends. He was either at Fisher Island or at his St. Petersburg condo, where he'd often go to a local bar and watch football or go out on his 28-foot center-console fishing boat. He kept his boat behind his father's house.

Carole also enjoyed the boat, so they'd go out for four or five hours at a time on Saturday and Sunday. Anything to get out of Tallahassee.

"I could tell after the McCain campaign, Charlie had a bad taste in his mouth," said Greer. "He was no longer as interested in being governor. He was just drifting in his job."

IF CRIST HAD ENRAGED the Tea Party and the right-wingers when he hugged Barack Obama, he made an appointment in April 2009 that made his enemies even angrier.

There was a vacancy on the Florida Supreme Court. Among the nominees sent to Crist for consideration was Circuit Judge James Perry, a Democrat and an African American who once had been involved in the civil rights movement. The right-wingers couldn't believe that Crist would dare appoint Perry, but after the Obama hug, they were no longer so sure. To let him know how they felt, they called from all over Florida warning that if he appointed Perry, heads would roll.

"I was getting a lot of calls from county chairmen," said Greer. "They didn't want Perry on the Florida Supreme Court. Gary Lee, the chairman of the Lee County REC, was one of them. He was a former Congressman who was defeated for reelection because he allegedly was caught in a scandal. He had moved to the Naples-Ft. Myers area. The guy was arrogant and obnoxious. He thought because he was a former member of Congress that he knew everything and anything. He berated me about Crist, loudly complaining about all the things Charlie had done as governor. Lee said, 'Tell him that Perry better not get on the Supreme Court.'"

Lee wasn't the only bellyacher about the possibility of Crist appointing a black Democrat to the Florida Supreme Court.

Greer and Crist were together in New York City when Greer received a call from Paul Singer, a multi-millionaire who ran a capital investment firm and was a major contributor to the Republican Party of Florida. Singer, Greer knew, had given big dollars to every race that Crist ever ran.

"He's a very nice man," said Greer, "and if I ever needed $100,000 for the party, I'd call Paul up or his assistant, and the money would be on its way. Paul asked for a meeting while we were in New York."

Lobbyists were throwing a small dinner for Charlie that night at Spark's with the proceeds going to the Republican Party. Spark's was where mobster Paul Castellano had been shot to death.

Crist said, "You and Lisa go to the restaurant first and find out what Paul wants. Carole and I will follow."

"Charlie had good intuition about whether something was going to be a good time or a bad time," said Greer. "If he sensed a good time, he'd be the first one through the door. If he was headed toward any kind of confrontation, he had someone else smooth it over, if not handle the whole situation. On this day I was that person."

Lisa and Jim Greer arrived early and immediately spotted Singer who told them, "Listen, I want to explain why I'm here. If Charlie puts a liberal Democrat on the Supreme Court of Florida, I'm done with him. And I'm going to give a million dollars to Marco Rubio. Perry votes anti-business. He's a liberal Democrat. We don't give a shit about the circuit court or even the appellate court, but my friends and I do not want him on the Supreme Court."

Greer replied, "But Paul, I don't understand why your business is concerned. Why do you care who's on the Florida Supreme Court? I could understand your caring about who's on the United States Supreme Court because you deal with anti-trust issues."

Paul said, "Many of our business-related issues stop first at the state Supreme Court. And we don't want Perry. And I intend to tell Charlie that when he gets here."

After 20 minutes the governor walked in with a big smile on his face. "Hey, Chairman. Hey, Paul."

"He had that Disney World look on his face," said Greer. "Lisa immediately got up, as my dear wife did on many occasions, left the table and went to sit at the bar by herself, so we could talk to Singer alone. It was the first time I had ever seen someone talk to Charlie Crist like he was a dog. Singer didn't pull any punches."

"I don't know what you're doing," Singer said. "I'm hearing things that concern me and concern other people as well. What's happened to you, Charlie? What's going on? Do not put Perry on the Supreme Court. If you put him on the Supreme Court, I'm done with you. And I and my people are going to raise money for Marco Rubio."

Said Greer, "Charlie went into his, 'Oh, Perry's a good guy. You ought to get to know him. He's a great man.'"

Singer left, and when Greer and Crist got up from the table and were going down the stairs, Crist stopped, looked at Greer, and put his hand on his shoulder.

"What the fuck was that?" he said.

"What that was," said Greer, "was a message."

As CHARLIE CRIST'S NEW *consigliere* Jim Greer was meeting with the governor several times a week and almost every weekend with their families.

On a day when the two families were in New York and the kids wanted to go to a wax museum, Crist asked Greer to come with him to talk. The two men sat at a long mahogany bar in a little Italian restaurant in Times Square and ordered martinis.

Greer was horrified when Crist said he was "thinking seriously" of putting Perry on the Supreme Court because it was "the right thing to do." Greer warned Crist that would be a major mistake.

Greer recalled, "I'm a moderate Republican. Or so I've been accused. But as party chairman I had an obligation to advise the governor. Even though I saw no reason personally not to put Perry on the Court, as chairman of the party I knew the outrage that was coming. And I told him so. I said, 'It's like the Ten Commandments that Moses brought down from the mountain. There are two things Republicans will remember for the next ten elections you run in. One of them is raising taxes. And the second one is appointing the wrong judges.'"

Said Greer, "Rudy Giuliani had demonstrated that. Rudy was a conservative Republican, but when he was mayor of New York he had supported a liberal judge, and the conservatives beat him over the head about it. John McCain in his maverick way alienated the Republican Party after he voted for a judge they didn't consider conservative enough."

"Charlie," said a concerned Greer, "if you appoint this liberal Democrat to the Supreme Court, it's going to be one of the final straws. It's going to be ugly."

Crist laughed. The governor's approval ratings were in the 70s. What could the crazies in the party do to him? He put his hand on Greer's knee, and in all sincerity he said, "It's all going to be good, Chairman. It's all going to be good. Don't worry about it. It's going to be fine."

The way Greer saw it, Carole's influence over his decision-making had become total. She was in his ear every night. Greer saw that nothing he could say could change Crist's mind.

He thought to himself, *This is going to be a train wreck.*

IT WAS THE GOVERNOR's task to interview the three candidates for the Florida Supreme Court. During the interview process, Greer got a call from Jason Gonzalez, general counsel to the governor. Gonzalez said, "I'm very worried. I'm being called by numerous people around Florida begging me to tell the governor not to appoint Perry."

All Greer could do was commiserate.

Gonzalez called Greer another day to say he had just sat in on Crist's interviews with the three judicial candidates. "Jim, we have problems. The governor interviewed the first two candidates for just two or three minutes, then shook their hands and sent them on their way. When Judge Perry came in, Crist was enthralled by his stories about his march with Martin Luther King, his civil rights involvement, his activism. They talked about his Marine Corps sharpshooting skills. It was a long interview. I've learned that if Crist spends a lot of time with an interviewee, that person gets the job."

Greer knew the train wreck was coming.

The next day, the governor's office announced that Judge James Perry was being appointed to the Florida Supreme Court.

It was one more major affront to the conservative Republicans. "The same Tea Party group," said Greer, "Peter Feaman, Gary Lee, Bob Starr, Allison DeFoor, Allen Cox, and Debbie Cox Roush went crazy."

Greer couldn't believe that Crist could be so unconcerned about the backlash from his own party.

"The first six months of 2009 it seemed that Charlie was just trying to do anything he could to put a stick in the eye of the Republican leadership in the Republican Party of Florida," said Greer. "He honestly believed that his approval ratings showed that he was governing the way the public, including the Republicans, wanted him to. He started the mantra, 'I'm a Republican, but I'm the people's governor.' If you had said that to a member of the Republican state committee, he'd have said, 'We made him the governor, not the people.'"

The headlines were trumpeting, *Teflon Charlie Remains Popular.*

DURING THIS TIME GREER was still in touch with Rob Jesmer, John Cornyn's man at the Republican Senatorial Committee.

"Jesmer told me that as soon as Charlie announced, they would endorse him—that all the polls showed that Charlie Crist would win. They also saw how effective he was at raising money and that they wouldn't have to put much money into Florida, if any. They felt he was the guy. "Everything looked good for us," said Greer.

Then in April 2009 a charismatic presence appeared on the horizon as a potential challenger to Crist. Marco Rubio, the handsome, youthful face of the Tea Party wing of the Florida Republican Party, announced that he intended to run for Martinez's U.S. Senate seat, whether or not Charlie Crist was a candidate.

Greer wondered who Crist was going to choose to run his Senate campaign. He was hoping it would be himself. The two had gotten close, and Greer felt he had the experience and the passion to lead Crist to victory. Of course, as head of the Republican Party of Florida, Greer wasn't supposed to back any one candidate. He was supposed to be neutral. But Greer believed in Charlie Crist. He couldn't help himself.

One night Greer was sitting in his office at the Republican Party of

Florida headquarters when Crist walked in. The governor had been on the floor above making fundraising calls.

"I want to let you know," said Crist, "that George LeMieux is going to run my Senate campaign."

"Well, I understand that," said Greer, "but I'm sorry to hear it. I was hoping I had a chance to run things."

"I need you here as chairman to cover my back," said Crist, "to keep all the crazies under control. Chairman, I feel sorry for what you go through every day. But George is going to run the campaign."

The next day LeMieux called Greer.

"Listen, I'm sure the Boss told you I was going to run his campaign for the Senate," he said, "but I'm going to need you. You're going to be very involved. We're going to do it as a team."

Said Greer later, "You have to remember, I was the chairman of the party, and the chairman is supposed to be neutral. But I didn't see anything wrong with the chairman of the party helping the incumbent Republican governor. In hindsight, with Rubio out there, it was probably not the smartest thing for me to have done."

That was putting it mildly.

30

Greer Denies the Crazies an Audit

With Crist focused on Mel Martinez's Senate seat, Greer knew preparations had to be made. "We needed a campaign plan," he said. "We needed to strategize about when George would actually take the reins and run things and when Charlie would make his big announcement. Crist disregarded Greer's advice about a tour in favor of a soft opening. And Crist expressed little interest in national policy issues.

"Charlie had a good grasp of Florida policy issues, but he knew little about the national issues he would face. One night I told Charlie he needed to hire a policy person, somebody who could start to develop his positions on issues such as national defense, the economy, education, Israel."

Rubio, meanwhile, began campaigning immediately. He was attending a host of Republican dinners and giving his listeners red-meat rhetoric.

From the very beginning Greer was concerned. He saw that Crist was arrogantly feeling that all he had to do was throw his hat into the ring and he'd win. But Greer knew that the candidate who worked hardest, who went from town to town, shook hands and kissed babies, won elections. Crist wasn't doing any of that. In fact, he wasn't doing anything at all.

"He believed he had plenty of time," said Greer. "He thought that if he focused on being governor and the press ran a slew of photos showing him carrying out his duties as chief executive, then everything would take care of itself."

Greer advised Crist that he needed to develop clear-cut answers as to why he was leaving. "Your critics will say you're abandoning the governor's office," Greer warned.

Crist paid Greer no heed. "In general Charlie just didn't listen to anything substantive. He felt we had plenty of time, but I was certain that we were headed into the race unprepared and disorganized. It was a mess from the very beginning."

ON MAY 13, 2009, Crist announced his candidacy for the Senate. Although Crist was not yet campaigning and Marco Rubio was, Crist was leading Rubio in the polls.

"All the polls were showing Charlie kicking Marco Rubio's ass left and right," said Greer. "But Rubio was quietly going to every Republican Party Lincoln Day dinner, and Charlie had stopped going to them the year before. In 2007, his first year as governor, Charlie went to a ton of them and was the keynote speaker, and I went with him. The second year he went to fewer, and I went to fewer. By 2009 most counties weren't inviting him to be their guest speaker, and a lot of them stopped inviting me. I would say to my scheduler, 'How come I don't have a lot of invitations this year to speak at Lincoln Day dinners?' 'Well, sir,' she'd say, 'Governor Crist isn't too popular in that county, which means you're not too popular either.'"

Crist faced a serious problem in his battle against the conservative Rubio. After Crist's nomination of Judge Perry, the pushback from the ultra-conservative Tea Party wing was immediate. The ever more conservative Florida legislature let Crist know its members were in rebellion by refusing to confirm or even take up many of his appointees to various state agencies and boards.

Said Greer. "In that third year in '09 the legislators started badmouthing Crist openly, calling him an opportunist, accusing him of providing zero leadership to the legislature."

Greer said many legislators also, anticipating that Crist was going to announce for the Senate race, considered him basically a lame duck and quit paying attention to him.

Further, the grass-roots conservatives were voicing their displeasure. When Greer called Tony DiMatteo, the REC chairman from Pinellas County who had been a strong supporter of Crist in 2006 and who had backed Greer, the chairman got the cold shoulder.

"The governor called and asked me to get a get in touch with Tony to get him on our team," said Greer. "This was probably not a wise thing for me to do. Here I was, the party chairman, calling Republicans across the state asking them to join the Crist campaign. I was supposed to be neutral, and it didn't take long for the word to get out that I was supporting Charlie.

"So I called Tony, but he declined to endorse Crist. Tony had once asked Charlie's assistance in getting his son a job in New York, and Charlie had failed to do it. Later, Tony came out publicly for Marco Rubio and was a major supporter. Tony's stated reason for the Rubio endorsement was that 'Charlie's not a Republican.' But the real issue—and Tony told me this—was that Crist hadn't called any of his friends on Wall Street to get his kid a job.

Other legislators had more political reasons for their anger at Crist. The legislature had pushed through two bills it wanted Crist to sign and pass—a bill allowing leadership funds and a bill that made it harder for teachers to get merit pay raises. Crist had told legislators he would support both bills; he vetoed both.

Leadership funds—which allowed legislative leaders to put hundreds of thousands of dollars in bank accounts that let them pay for most living expenses including travel, dinners, entertainment, and even dry cleaning—had an interesting history. They were outlawed in 1989, when Tom Slade became Republican Party of Florida chairman. He saw that the Republican Party of Florida wasn't doing well financially because the legislative leaders kept their money to themselves. Slade told the legislators that he was going to get rid of all the House and Senate staff on the Republican Party payroll if they didn't bring their money back to the party. As a result, leadership funds were discontinued.

As chairman, Greer gave assurances that if they brought those millions of dollars back to the Republican Party of Florida, he would not bother the House and Senate about how they spent it. The leaders wanted leadership funds back because in the spring of 2009 Tea Party ultraconservatives were making noises about auditing how the money was spent by the Republican Party of Florida. Party leaders were getting nervous.

"They wanted to take all their money out of the party," said Greer. He was told that it wasn't because of him but "because of those crazies." Both houses passed the leadership funds bill by huge margins.

The other issue was part of the Florida Republican legislators' war on teachers. If student performance was subpar, the legislators declared, it was because of bad teaching. If FCAT (Florida Comprehensive Assessment Test) scores were low, they were certain it was the teachers' fault. More to the point, teachers belonged to a powerful union hated by Republicans. The bill the legislature was proposing would tighten requirements on merit increases for public school teachers and make it less certain a teacher would get tenure.

"According to the legislature, Crist had signaled that he would not veto those issues," said Greer. "But as was his way, Charlie stuck his finger in the wind and decided he needed the teachers' support. He also determined that leadership funds were not a good thing for him, that they would get him bad publicity. He also recognized that if he vetoed that bill, he would make the legislature look bad."

So in June 2009, Crist vetoed both bills.

Immediately Greer received a phone call from his friend, Representative Chris Dorworth. "Crist is a fucking liar," said Dorworth.

Crist's chief of staff Eric Eikenberg also received a string of nasty calls from legislators.

"By June," said Greer, "the legislature had had it with the governor."

In addition, the grass-roots Tea Party types grew louder. They spoke not only against Crist and Greer, but against the paid political consultants in the House and the Senate. As small government advocates, the Tea Party called for audits of House and Senate spending, as well as that of the Florida Republican Party. Here was another reason that the House and Senate members wanted leadership funds—a way to keep their money clear of any grass-roots audits or the RPOF oversight and audit committee.

"Animosity was mounting between elected officials and the grass-roots," said Greer, "and it had to do with who ran the party. The elected officials— the governor and the members of the House and Senate—raise the money for the party. The grass-roots volunteers generally do not have money to give, but they give their time. So members of the state executive committee believe it is their party. They trumpet, 'We tell the elected officials what to do. They don't tell us.'"

In response to the Tea Party's call for audits, Chairman Greer told the press, "We have an audit once a year. Nothing is ever out of the ordinary."

But the calls for audits were infuriating the heads of the House and the Senate and the staff of the Republican Party of Florida. Rubio, as Speaker of the Florida House, had told Greer, "We eat what we kill," meaning whatever money was raised by the Senate was nobody else's business as to how they spent it. But here were Rubio's Tea Party followers calling for an audit to see how the money actually was being spent.

In response the Republican legislators wanted to know, "Who are these state committee members demanding an accounting of what we've spent on the House and Senate campaigns? Who the hell are they? Who is this guy Eric Miller down in Vero Beach, Florida? Who told the *Vero Beach Press Journal* that members of the House and Senate are 'out of control'?"

"Well, he's a state committee member."

Said Greer, "It got so bad that Dorworth and incoming Speaker Dean Cannon told me the legislature was considering abolishing the state political party structure, which would have been huge. They had had enough of these county committee people acting like they ran the party. Their attitude was, 'We're the legislature. We're the elected officials. We raise all the money.' And, quite frankly, most of the state and county committee people across the state were a bunch of kooks. The legislators felt, *We can't be angry and upset like the Tea Party wants us to be. We have to govern. We have to pass laws.* The flip side was that the grass-roots activists were trying to send a message to me to tell the legislators 'they better stop spending money like we're reading about in the *Miami Herald* or there's going to be a change in the structure of the Republican Party.'"

The tug of war between the elected officials and the grass-roots activists was fierce.

One night Greer sat in his car in the parking lot of a Tallahassee CVS talking on the phone with Bob Starr, the chair of the chairman's caucus of the Florida Republican State Executive Committee. Starr said, "At the next committee meeting, we're going to go after the legislators who have spent so much money. This is *our* party."

Greer replied, "Bob, I want to tell you something you need to clearly understand. The legislators are threatening to bring back leadership funds which will bankrupt the party—if the crazies keep demanding an audit."

Among those crazies was Allen Cox, Greer's vice-chairman, who was also chairman of the budget committee. Cox was in a unique place to cause trouble. Other Tea Party activists like Eric Miller, Gary Lee, and Allison DeFoor kept saying there needed to be an audit.

Greer kept reminding them there already was an annual audit. Meanwhile the legislators would call Greer up and say they had read an article where Cox said there ought to be an audit. "You're not going to let there be an audit, right, Chairman?"

Greer would reassure them there would be no audit. "We're not doing anything improper here. They may not like the way you're spending the money, but it's your money, so you can do whatever the hell you want with it.'"

Chairman Greer was being very protective of the elected officials.

"And quite honestly," said Greer, "most of the people who were calling for the audits, the ones throwing up these red flags, were not Jim Greer supporters. So I was not about to give them any ammunition. I was also being loyal to the House and Senate leadership and to Crist."

At that time everybody loved him for that.

State Representative Will Weatherford asked to meet Greer for dinner at the Governor's Club in Tallahassee. During the meal, Weatherford said, "Dean Cannon and I want to express our sincere appreciation to you for taking all of the arrows for us over in the House regarding spending and American Express charges. You're loyal. You take the hits for us. We think you're a fantastic chairman."

"I believe that's what a good chairman does," said Greer. "When things get tough, a good chairman will always take the hits for you."

Greer had always been consistent when it came to spending. His attitude was, "Anyone who's spending money on behalf of the Republican Party, I'm approving it. In reality, nobody ever asked me for permission to do anything on the House or the Senate side. In fact, I never saw their American Express bills—not ever. I never approved any of their expenditures, but in theory it was all done in the name of the chairman."

As the year went on the Tea Party rebellion would grow and become more of a threat to Crist and Greer.

31

McCollum for Governor

ONCE CRIST ANNOUNCED HE WAS RUNNING FOR THE U.S. SENATE, LEAVING the governorship up for grabs in 2010, the succession scramble began. The main contenders were Jeff Atwater, then the president of the Florida Senate; Vern Buchanan, a congressman from Sarasota; Lieutenant Governor Jeff Kottkamp (for a short while before he decided he wanted to run for attorney general); Charlie Bronson, the agricultural commissioner; and Attorney General Bill McCollum.

Recalled Greer, "In May 2009 we started polling internally for the Republican Party of Florida among likely Republican voters, and Bill McCollum kept winning almost every poll for governor. Bill and I got along. He was always polite. When I saw him, he called me 'Chairman,' and I called him 'General.' He wasn't a Crist fan, so that meant we were cordial but not that warm."

In truth, McCollum and Greer didn't like each other, and McCollum and Crist liked each other even less. "The governor called McCollum 'Howdy Doody,'" said Greer, "because McCollum has big ears and looks like the TV character. He also called him 'Weirdo.' Charlie thought him strange. They didn't see eye-to-eye from the time Crist proposed giving felons back their rights."

Neither Crist nor McCollum wanted to be seen on the campaign trail with each other.

"Crist didn't want to be seen with McCollum because he represented the wacky views of the party," said Greer. "McCollum didn't want to be seen that much with Crist, but McCollum's problem was that Charlie was still the most popular elected official in Florida so McCollum couldn't afford to do or say too much to offend him. McCollum needed the volunteers of the Republican State Committee, so his people had to try and placate the anti-Crist people within the party while at the same time not directly attacking Crist publicly."

In mid-May McCollum and his campaign manager, Matt Williams, came to see Greer. McCollum asked Greer if he would use his station as chairman to get the other potential gubernatorial candidates to drop out.

Greer, who didn't want a primary fight before the general election, said he would. "Kottkamp was easy," said Greer. "Jeff never caused any trouble and was loyal to the governor and me. He was going for attorney general. Vern Buchanan was sending out messages he was going to run, but he was being investigated by the Congressional Ethics Committee. He owned a car dealership, and he was accused of having his employees write checks for campaign contributions and then reimbursing them, which is illegal. Ultimately he announced he wasn't going to run. And Jeff Atwater didn't run. He remained president of the Senate and then was elected chief financial officer of Florida, a post he still holds.

"Charlie Bronson was a different story. He's the agricultural commissioner out of central casting. Charlie owned a lot of land in Osceola County, owned livestock and cattle, has a Southern drawl, and wears cowboy boots. Normally the agricultural commissioner doesn't run for the governor's office. But Charlie had been around. He'd been on the Republican Executive Committee as a precinct person for years and years. He was seriously thinking about running. When I called him, I said, 'I'm trying to avoid bloodshed in the primary where we spend all our money, and then Alex Sink, the Democrat, is sitting there with millions of dollars. Bronson didn't take it too well. He got very mad at me."

Bronson told Greer, "'I paid my dues. I've got a lot of support. I can win this thing, and I think what you're doing is just a bunch of bullshit.' But he said, 'If you're telling me the party is getting behind McCollum, then there's nothing I can do. I'll call you back. But I think it's a hell of a shame, and I don't think it's right.'"

Greer told him what he had told the others: "Bill McCollum is making the announcement he's running for governor next Tuesday at the Embassy Suites in downtown Orlando, and I'd like you to come and stand behind him at the announcement to show we're a unified party."

Greer recalled that all of the other candidates agreed to go except Bronson. "He called me back and said, 'All right, I'm not going to run, but I'm not committing to coming down and standing with him.'"

Greer thought McCollum had only one real problem as a candidate—he was dry and had no personality. And the political people were concerned that his wife, who was very nice, had gray-streaked hair and wore unstylish clothes. "They felt she didn't come across well as a governor's spouse."

TWENTY ELECTED OFFICIALS STOOD behind McCollum when he announced his candidacy. Dean Cannon endorsed him, and so did Mike Haridopolos, the president-designate of the Senate. The press came and so did some of the grass-roots Republican volunteers. Greer introduced McCollum to great applause.

Greer had made McCollum's candidacy easy.

"I cleared the field for Bill McCollum," said Greer. "I did everything I could to help the man. I made it clear when I stood at the podium that day that I was behind him for governor. And that meant unofficially the Republican party was behind him, too.

"McCollum in *realpolitik* would have owed me. McCollum was loved by the right-wing extremists, the conservatives of the party. When I was taking sides in helping to pick the gubernatorial candidate, no one complained I wasn't remaining neutral. They only complained when I was supporting Charlie Crist."

From a public standpoint, Greer did more for McCollum than he ever did for Crist. Of course, behind the scenes Greer did a great deal for Crist, but on this day he went before the press and said, "My candidate for governor is Bill McCollum."

Later McCollum sat on Greer's leather couch and said, "Jim, I will never forget what you've done for me."

Too soon, Greer would find out that never wasn't forever.

ONE OTHER REPUBLICAN CANDIDATE for governor surfaced, Paula Dockery, a state senator who was married to C. C. "Doc" Dockery, a Lakeland, Florida, businessman and GOP fundraiser.

"Dockery said she was going to run for governor, raise money, and park her money with the party," said Greer, "and McCollum saw her as a problem. Matt Williams, McCollum's campaign manager, came down to my office and asked me not to let her park her money with the party."

Greer said she was going to be a Republican candidate, so he couldn't do that.

Williams asked, "How about charging her a really high administrative fee, much more than you charge anyone else who keeps their money here?"

Greer said he couldn't do that, either.

Dockery, who would join the Tea Party group in criticizing Greer and the spending of the party and the House and the Senate, eventually got out of the race.

In July, McCollum visited Greer to talk about his campaign for governor. He said to Greer, "I'm hearing people aren't happy with my campaign. Who have you heard that from?"

Greer said, "I heard it from Brian Ballard, one of your major fundraisers, for one." Greer recalled that he didn't mean anything divisive by his casual answer, but as happens in politics and life, McCollum called Ballard and told him what Greer had said. Not long afterward, Greer's cell phone rang. It was Ballard.

"Let me tell you something," said Ballard. "If you ever fucking get between me and Bill McCollum or Charlie Crist again, I will cut your fucking head off, put it in a plastic bag, and throw your body in a ditch. And I'm not kidding. I can have it done."

"Brian," said Greer, "What are you talking about?"

"You know what I'm talking about," said Ballard through gritted teeth. "You told McCollum I wasn't happy with the way the campaign was going."

"You told me that," said Greer.

"I don't want to talk to you about it," said Ballard, "but you better understand, if you ever fuck with me again, I'm going to screw you but good."

When Greer told Lisa what Ballard said, she told him to call the police. Instead Greer sent a text message to LeMieux and Eric Eikenberg reporting the conversation. He kept other evidence of the phone call.

Greer later called both LeMieux and Eikenberg, and he told them, "Listen, Brian is pretty pissed off at me. He threatened to kill me. I'm telling you, he wasn't laughing. He's mad. He was going to cut my head off, put it in a plastic bag, and throw my body in a ditch."

"You know Brian," said LeMieux. "He's power-hungry, egotistical. He thinks he's the kingmaker in Tallahassee."

Brian Ballard was to be another one who would cause Greer a ton of trouble.

As McCollum traveled the state running for governor, he didn't run into Crist very often because Crist wasn't going to Republican Club dinners. Crist was paying very little attention to the grass-roots Republican Executive Committees, many of which were snubbing him anyway. Using TV and radio ads, Crist was appealing in a broader-based way to attract voters, which is not as effective in a primary as it is in a general election.

Out on the stump, McCollum was hearing the real feelings of the grassroots and the base of the party against Crist, and he was seeing firsthand how many Republicans disliked him. McCollum was getting a strong feeling that the party had turned on Crist. Knowing what he knew, McCollum, the presumptive Republican nominee for governor, then tried to take over the party from lame duck Crist.

One of the people McCollum tried to boss around was Chairman Greer.

"When Charlie won the primary in August 2006," said Greer, "Jeb Bush was still the governor, but he went silent, because he was on the way out. Jeb wasn't telling the party much about what to do. It was now Charlie Crist's party. McCollum tried to do that before it was truly his party."

One night in Tallahassee Greer was eating dinner with Eikenberg at the Ale House when his cell phone rang. It was Matt Williams, McCollum's right-hand man. The Republican Party membership cards that go out to donors bore Governor Crist's picture. "How do you feel about taking the governor's picture off and putting McCollum's picture up there? The General had thought it would help raise some cash," said Williams.

Greer realized that McCollum was trying to push Crist out before it was time.

"Absolutely not," said Greer. "Charlie Crist is still the head of the party."

"What if we put both their pictures on there?" Williams asked.

"Let me check with the governor and see what he thinks," said Greer.

By this time Crist didn't care what the party did. "If you want to put his picture there too," he told Greer, "go ahead."

Even so, Greer refused to give McCollum and Williams the go-ahead.

"I just felt they were trying to get the camel's nose under the tent, and the next thing they would be asking me to move out of my office so McCollum's campaign manager could move in," said Greer. "I knew that McCollum wasn't a fan of Charlie Crist or of me, and I just wasn't going to let them have the keys to the castle before it was time."

In June 2009, six months after Greer's reelection as chairman and one month after he "cleared the field" for McCollum, McCollum went behind Greer's back and called Crist to ask him to get Greer to resign so he could put his own man into the chairman's office.

Crist told him no.

"Everyone's political agenda was coming to the forefront," said Greer. "McCollum's, Crist's, and Rubio's. It divided the Republican Party into so many segments, with all of the fighting and each throwing rocks at each other.

"It was *not* a good time."

32

The LG Gets Stabbed in the Back

The first four months of Charlie Crist's campaign for the U.S. Senate were rosy. He pulled in several million dollars and was applauded as the money-raiser everyone had expected him to be. Rubio was doing badly in the polls and wasn't raising much money.

Crist was the guy.

The Republican National Senatorial Campaign Committee, seeing Crist's strong showing in Florida, formally endorsed Crist. "What a great senator he's going to be," said U.S. Senator John Cornyn of Texas. Crist was also endorsed by influential Republican U.S. Senators Lindsay Graham of South Carolina and John McCain of Arizona.

"We had a tremendous number of endorsements from D.C. coming in," said Greer, "and a few from Florida. Many in Florida were saying, 'Let's hold off and see.' Crist was very popular with the higher echelon of the party, but with the grass-roots people, the Tea Party people, who were becoming major players, Charlie wasn't popular at all. I told Charlie that we needed to get out there and start going to the dinners. But he just wasn't interested in doing that. He wanted to go where he was comfortable, to the Tiger Bay luncheons and the Chamber of Commerce meetings. He didn't want to go into the lion's den of the Republican Party."

In an ominous surprise, one person who refused to endorse Crist was the new RNC chairman, Michael Steele. Greer called and asked for his support, but Steele, himself a moderate, said opposition from the conservative wing of the party made such an endorsement impossible. "I'm getting a lot of pushback within the RNC not to support him," said Steele. "We're getting calls from Florida telling us how pissed off they are that the National Republican Senatorial Committee has stuck its nose into Florida's race. They're telling us, 'You better not put the RNC in it.'"

During this period when Crist was raising millions and leading in the polls by impressive margins, members of the Crist campaign tried to figure out a way to get his struggling opponent, Rubio, out of the race.

In May 2009, while Greer was in a hotel room during an RNC meeting, he received a call from Eikenberg who asked, "What would you think of resigning as chairman and coming over to the campaign? The governor would like you to do that."

"Why?"

"Because Rubio is putting out feelers about his becoming party chairman."

Though still smarting that LeMieux would be running Crist's Senate campaign, Greer was ever the good soldier.

"I'll do it, Eric," he said, "but I'm a little pissed off that once again I'm being thrown to the curb. I love being party chairman, but I'll do it for the good of the campaign. Tell the governor to call me directly."

A few minutes later Crist called.

"Hey, Chairman," Crist said, "Good news. Good news. I'm hearing from Al Cardenas [a former party chairman under Jeb Bush and then president of the Conservative Political Action Committee (CPAC)] that Rubio might be interested in becoming state party chairman because it pays $130,000 a year, and he needs the money."

Greer told Crist he would resign. But a week went by, and Greer never heard another word about his stepping down. "Around this time you'd hear rumors every week or so that Rubio, who had announced on May 5 he would run for the U.S. Senate, was going to drop out," said Greer.

A lot of important Republicans were saying publicly that Rubio ought to fold his tent and run instead for attorney general.

"That would have caused another problem because the lieutenant-governor, Jeff Kottkamp, wanted to be the attorney general," said Greer. "Kottkamp's future was now in limbo because his term was up with Crist's."

But Rubio had no place to go unless Crist could get Kottkamp to drop out of the attorney general race. "We had to put a knife in Kottkamp's back," said Greer. "It was one of the saddest instances to see this man defeated. I felt very bad for him."

Kottkamp never knew what hit him.

Every year Crist held a fishing tournament in Key West to raise money for the Republican Party of Florida. The big donors paid as much as $50,000 each to spend four or five hours with Crist on his boat. By comparison, it cost a mere $15,000 to be on Greer's boat or those of Lieutenant Governor Kottkamp or Crist's chief of staff, Eikenberg.

"The problem was," said Greer, "that Crist wouldn't stay the full five hours. He'd go out for just a couple hours and want to return to shore. One year when he left the boat after just two hours, all the lobbyists were pissed off that they didn't get to spend the whole day with him as they had been promised. But once again, Charlie did exactly what he wanted to do. Another time after his boat came ashore, he called me on my boat's radio and asked me to meet him at the marina bar. That day I thought the donors really got their money's worth because he took everyone—lobbyists, friends, donors—from his boat and my boat to the bar, and we sat and drank all afternoon. That day they really got some quality time in a very social environment with the governor."

Two weeks before the May 2009 fishing tournament, Kottkamp asked Greer to set up a meeting with the governor for after the tournament. Kottkamp wanted Crist's endorsement for attorney general. The loyal Kottkamp thought Crist's endorsement would be automatic.

"Kottkamp never did anything to embarrass Charlie," said Greer. "Kottkamp was perceived as the more conservative of the two by the REC, and it's why he was put on the ticket in the first place. But he was not treated well by Crist's staff. LeMieux, Arlene DiBenigno, even Eikenberg treated Kottkamp poorly. He was a loyal soldier, and I used to tell them how shittily I thought they were treating him. He would always defend Crist at REC meetings.

"Their offices were down the hall from one another, but they hardly ever saw each other. When Charlie decided to run for the Senate, he never had the courtesy to inform his lieutenant governor before his public announcement. Kottkamp told me he had to hear it from other people. The first person Charlie should have called was Kottkamp, because Jeff's political future was based on Charlie's."

Out on his own, Kottkamp announced that he would be a candidate for attorney general. He didn't foresee that his nomination would be determined by Rubio's political future and Crist's self-interest.

During that fishing trip, Greer informed Crist that Kottkamp wanted 15 minutes of his time. Crist tried to avoid the meeting.

"Charlie was the kind of person who would say 'hello' and then walk away as fast as he could," said Greer. "It was his way of avoiding conversations he'd rather not have. He'd probably say 'Good to see you, Jeff. How's it going? How's the wife? Oh, I gotta go.'"

Everyone knew what Kottkamp was going to ask of Crist when he requested that meeting. On the final day of the tournament Greer again told Crist that Kottkamp wanted 15 minutes.

"What's it about?" asked Crist, knowing full well what the answer was.

"He's probably going to ask you to endorse him for attorney general."

"I'm not going to do that," said Crist. "We're trying to get Rubio into that seat."

The morning everyone was to leave Key West, Crist finally agreed to see the frustrated yet hopeful Kottkamp.

"I sat in the back of this nice private room in the back of the hotel restaurant waiting for Crist and Kottkamp, when Jeff came in a few minutes later," said Greer.

"You know I'm going to ask him to endorse me," Kottkamp said.

"Yep," said Greer, "I sure do."

"I'm going to ask for your endorsement too," he said.

"Jeff," said Greer, "you've always been a friend of mine, and I'll support you any way I can. My hands are tied a little, but I'll be there for you. I know my wife will hold a fundraiser for you at the house."

"I appreciate that very much," said Kottkamp. He asked, "What do you think Charlie will do?" just as Crist entered.

"Good morning, LG," said Crist.

"Good morning, Governor."

Greer heard Kottkamp say to Crist, "The reason I wanted to meet with you, you're going to run for the Senate, and we've done a lot of great things together. You know, I've always been loyal to you. I took some hits for you. I'd like you to endorse me for attorney general."

"Jeff, I just can't do that. I've got my own race to deal with," the governor said.

"As an excuse Charlie Crist then brought up the issue of Kottkamp's use of a state plane to travel back and forth to his home district in Fort Myers," said Greer. "Someone had filed a complaint about it."

"Jeff," Crist said, "you have that thing about the state plane."

"Governor, you know that's not going anywhere," said Kottkamp. "You know that was filed by some guy down south who works for the Democrats. I've been with you. I've stood with you. I've been by your side.'

"Jeff, I just can't do it," said Crist, not telling him that keeping the seat open for Rubio was the real reason. "I'm focusing on my own race. I can't get involved in other races. I just can't do it."

Said Greer, "And that man sank into the chair. Literally, he sank into the chair. He had a hurt look on his face like I've never seen—except later on my own face. The governor then said to him, 'I've got to get back to Tally. We'll talk more.' And he left."

Greer was sitting with his coffee cup in his hand when Kottkamp said, "I just can't believe it. I just cannot believe that man would not endorse me for attorney general."

"Well, Jeff," Greer said, trying to justify his boss's actions, "He does have his own campaign. He's focused on that."

Later Crist asked Greer, "How did it go after I left?"

"Governor," said Greer, "he's devastated."

Recalled Greer, "Charlie and Jeff hardly talked again after that. The relationship for the next year and a half was non-existent. Kottkamp started doing his own stuff, wasn't enthusiastic about supporting Crist, but never came out publicly against him.

"Kottkamp stayed loyal to the end."

33

A Campaign in Neutral

Charlie Crist's announcement for the United States Senate turned everything upside down financially for the Republican Party of Florida and Chairman Jim Greer, but also for Crist. Since Crist was running for a federal office, his fundraising now fell under federal rather than state campaign reporting requirements.

Greer, as chairman of the Florida Republican Party, had purchased about $13,000 worth of swag for the fishing tournament—T-shirts, hats, and beer cozies—things originally meant to help raise money for the Republican Party of Florida. In small print, the items were stamped, "Paid for by the Republican Party of Florida."

Once Crist announced he was running for the U.S. Senate, no longer could the Republican Party of Florida pay for those items. Furthermore, under federal law Crist no longer was allowed to collect corporate checks.

"I begged and pleaded with Crist," said Greer, "to wait a day or two after the fishing tournament to make his announcement about running for the Senate."

Crist refused.

"He wanted to begin raising money immediately," said Greer, "and he wanted all the money from the fishing tournament to come to his Senate campaign, which created all sorts of legal issues. We had to call Ben Ginsberg, the famed elections attorney in Washington, for advice. Ben warned that we would have all kinds of problems if we continued to call it the Charlie Crist fishing tournament," said Greer.

Greer asked Ginsberg about the $13,000 worth of hats, T-shirts, and beer cozies. "If you use it," said Ginsberg, "someone can file an ethics complaint."

Crist came up with a solution. They would still hold the tournament, and donors would still give money, but then the Crist campaign would reimburse the Republican Party of Florida for the $13,000 it had spent on the gifts.

"To this day I'm not sure if that's legal," said Greer, "but it was an idea the governor suggested, and we accepted it. Later on in the quarter the Crist campaign wrote the Republican Party a check for $13,000 as reimbursement."

The $13,000 was relatively small potatoes, but another more important financial problem arose once Crist announced his Senate candidacy. Under federal law, U.S. Senate candidates may not accept in-kind contributions from corporations for things like plane rides. Crist discovered quickly that he wasn't able to get around the state nearly as nimbly as when he was running for state office. He now had to fly commercially for campaign trips, and he'd have to pay for them with his own credit card or with the Crist for Senate campaign card.

"That was a big agitation for him," said Greer. "He hated that. Over and over he'd ask me the same question, 'Can I go here? Can I go there? And have you pay for it?' I'd say, 'No.'

"'Even if I'm going for a Republican . . .'

"'No, you can't. You're a federal candidate now.'"

Often Crist would ask Greer, "If I'm going to a Republican Party of Florida fundraiser, can't you find me a way to pay for the trip?"

"No," was the answer each time. "You're a federal candidate now, and you can't take corporate in-kind contributions of planes."

If Crist didn't want to pay for the plane ride, he would have to drive.

Florida Department of Law Enforcement officers went with him because he was still the governor, and because bodyguards accompanied him everywhere, the media started reporting how much Crist's Senate campaigning was costing the taxpayers of Florida.

It was yet another barb from Rubio's Tea Party followers.

"Rubio was one of those anti-spending Tea Party guys," said Greer, "and so it wasn't hard imagining him calling a reporter and saying, 'Hey, you ought to look into how much it costs the state when Crist goes campaigning.' A call like that would spark headlines like *Crist Senate Campaign Costing Taxpayers a Bundle*.

"The other thing Charlie started doing—it had been a common practice during his three years but became even more of a problem when he ran for the Senate—he was trying to schedule his official duties as governor around the times and places he was having campaign fundraisers. On those occasions he could fly to the immediate area on a trip paid for by the Republican Party and be able to say to himself, *It's 5:01. I'm not governor right now. I'm off the clock. I'm a Senate candidate and there's a fundraiser for me 15 minutes down the road.*

"And so he'd use the taxpayers' money to get there.

"Another tactic of Charlie's: the governor has small one-person offices in large cities all throughout Florida. Most governors have probably never seen those offices. But all of a sudden Charlie would show up at the Miami office, for example, and work at a desk for a few hours, and then, *What a coincidence. There's a fundraiser for me tonight in Miami.*

"That was a common practice—the attorney general did it, too—they all do it—but Charlie did it more than the others."

As THE CAMPAIGN ENTERED June 2009, Greer kept pushing Crist to hire a policy adviser. As a U.S. Senate candidate, Crist was going to be asked about national and international issues, and Greer knew that Crist knew little if anything about issues outside the state of Florida.

Crist's position continued to be, "We'll do that toward the end of the year."

George LeMieux was supposed to be running the Crist campaign, but he had yet to fully take over. Tight-fisted to a fault—with his own money—Crist felt that because of his high ratings in the polls, he could push back the ramping up of his campaign.

One night Crist asked Greer, "Would you fill two positions? I need a fundraiser, and I need someone to oversee field operations."

Greer should never have agreed to it, because he knew as the chairman of the party he was supposed to remain neutral. But this was his best friend asking. He said yes. "I was running dual roles: during the day, I'm Bruce Wayne. At night, I'm Batman. During the day I'm chairman of the party. At night, I'm the de facto campaign manager for Crist because LeMieux hadn't arrived yet."

Greer was doing the campaign work for no pay, but he was doing it because Crist was his ticket to the national stage. Greer saw that Crist was obsessed with raising money but wasn't spending much of it. That was how he ran all his campaigns. Also, Florida is a populous state with a huge number of separate media markets. Crist felt that having millions of dollars to spend on television ads was far more important and effective than speaking to the local Republican clubs.

"He believed you could go to every Lincoln Day dinner and sign up all those people to volunteer, but if you don't have millions of dollars for TV and radio ads, you're not going to win. He had operated under that strategy in every race he ever ran. He was a tremendous fundraiser, and he was frugal. He knew exactly how much money he had and how it was being spent. For the present, he wasn't interested in spending any of the Senate campaign money."

CRIST ALSO NEEDED TO find a new campaign fundraiser because he had fired Meredith O'Rourke as the party fundraiser. (Before she and her wealthy and powerful friends were done with Greer, he wished he and Crist had never let her go.)

Said Greer, "Meredith was getting $30,000 a month from the Republican Party of Florida for her work, and Charlie decided she was no longer worth it."

Another reason for Charlie's decision was because of Carole's jealousy. She didn't like good-looking women hanging around her husband.

"Carole Crist was pushing for something she did several times, getting rid of a woman she thought might be attractive to her husband," said Greer. "She would slyly say to Charlie, 'Did you notice the dress Meredith was wearing at the fundraiser last night?'

"Meredith was well-endowed, and she would wear nice but revealing dresses and very high heels. The donors loved it, but Carole didn't. So I immediately recognized two things: we had a problem, and I had an ally in my desire to get rid of Meredith."

Greer wanted to fire O'Rourke because he was the one paying her salary, and she acted as though he wasn't her boss. When he'd tell her, "There's a fundraising meeting tomorrow morning. Can you show up for it?" she rarely did. Time after time she blithely ignored his requests.

Moreover, Greer wanted to develop alternative ways to raise money for the party. He wanted to start an Eagle's Club program for lower donors who would receive cuff links if they gave $3,000. He wanted to have more regional events than the small in-home fundraisers. Meredith refused to implement *anything* Greer wanted.

"She didn't do one damn thing to help me with the Eagles Club or anything else. She felt I was sticking my nose in her business, and she had no interest in the types of programs I wanted to create. She liked the in-house events where we raised lots of money, or the big dinner events at the Vinoy or The Breakers where the Party would raise half a million dollars. I was the first chairman who tried to bring the fundraiser under the organizational structure. I was the first chairman who tried to provide oversight and supervision to the fundraising element."

Greer would later acknowledge that was a bad mistake.

"Meredith's loyalty was more to Brian Ballard than it was to me," said Greer. "At the same time Charlie had gotten very tired of her. She was so much a pain in the ass. She'd cry if you told her something she didn't want to hear. He felt she was a drama queen, and he started saying he didn't want her around anymore, didn't want 'that crazy bitch' flying on the plane with him to fundraisers. So she started driving to events, or she'd fly commercially, and the last couple months she started sending her finance team, the young girls, to these events in her place. She didn't go herself as she'd clearly lost interest."

"Get rid of her," were Crist's orders to Greer, who tried offering her contracts for less pay to no effect.

"Figuring she was protected by lobbyist Brian Ballard, she kept refusing," said Greer. "She couldn't believe it when she was let go."

Greer was more than happy to fire her.

Crist suggested that upon her termination Greer pay her $5,000 a month for the next year.

"What for?" said Greer.

"To keep the crazy bitch's mouth shut," said Crist.

"Those were his exact words," said Greer.

Greer agreed.

Her firing came after a fundraiser in Clearwater at the home of lobbyist Marion Style. When Meredith told Greer she was thinking of sending her staff to the Clearwater fundraiser, Greer told her he needed to talk with her in person. Meredith drove from Tallahassee to be there.

Crist had ordered Greer to have another person with him when he fired her. Greer called Jay Burmer, one of Crist's political consultants and a friend. They met with her in the conference room of Tampa attorney Richard Burton.

Face to face, Greer said to her, "Meredith, the governor wants to go in a different direction, and I want to go in a different direction. But we want to keep you on board as a consultant. We'll pay you $5,000 a month."

"I expected this," she said, "but I'm a little disappointed I had to drive all the way down from Tallahassee for this."

"We want to keep paying you $5,000 a month," Greer repeated.

"I don't know if I want $5,000 a month," she said.

"Okay," said Greer, "but here's a contract for the $5,000. Think about it. Do whatever you want to do."

O'Rourke left.

"Later," said Greer, "she would tell a fabricated story about being in the hospital in Tallahassee when I demanded she come to Clearwater even though she was deathly ill; that I screamed at her and berated her and pounded my fist on the table and told her she had to sign the $5,000 contract.

"None of that occurred. Jay Burmer was there. What she told people was the furthest thing from the truth. Later when the memo went out from the hardliners, 'We're going after Greer,' she recited that story. Her story made it sound like she had four IVs in her while she was in a hospital bed when I called for her to come to Tampa.

"I don't know whether she was ever in a hospital because you could never believe anything she said. One time at a RPOF meeting she told a group of women including my wife that she had had a hysterectomy and couldn't have children. A year later she said she was pregnant. You never could tell with Meredith what was true and what wasn't.

"But she was a fine fundraiser. She was attractive, which was a good part of it, and she knew how to flirt. She also had very powerful friends, particularly Ballard. Anytime I wanted her to do something that she didn't want to do, she'd call not only Brian but other major donors. I'm sure they were saying to themselves, *What is Greer doing to that poor woman?*"

That night while Greer was driving from Tampa to his home near Orlando, he got a call on his cell phone from Ballard, who was angry Meredith had been fired.

"I'm going to have a talk with the governor," said Ballard, who was pushing for Greer to give her a $15,000 a month contract rather than $5,000.

"Well, Brian, go ahead and talk to the governor," said Greer. "I just talked to him myself. Don't forget that I'm just doing what he asked me to do."

"All right," he said, and he hung up.

In retrospect, "Firing Meredith was something I shouldn't have done," said Greer. "I never would have had any trouble if I had just kept her on board, never bothered her, and paid her the 30 grand a month. I didn't realize that she had so many powerful friends, that the relationship she had with some of them went so deep that they would later take on the governor and me—all because I had gotten rid of her."

When Greer tried to replace her, other professional fundraisers, including Ann Herberger, Jeb Bush's fundraiser, and Gretchen Picotte, Rudy Giuliani's fundraiser, turned him down.

"I could tell what was happening," said Greer. "They were calling around and getting the scoop. Meredith had a reputation of being a cut-throat if need be. Nobody wanted to replace her only to have her destroy their reputations as fundraisers."

Greer had to go in-house, hiring Dane Eagle, who had been Crist's travel aide, to be the head fundraiser for Crist's Senate campaign.

"Dane had wanted to take a hand at fundraising," said Greer. "He had met all the big donors over the years. He had watched how Meredith operated, and he thought he could do a good job. He wanted to give it a shot."

Greer agreed to pay Eagle a yearly salary of $70,000, plus one percent of whatever he brought in. In that Meredith O'Rourke had been making $30,000 a month, this didn't seem unreasonable. Crist approved Greer's salary deal with Eagle.

Then the Crist team reported raising $4.3 million in the first Senate campaign finance report.

"Dane was due to get $43,000, a big chunk of money," said Greer. "But Charlie was angry that Dane's commission was so high. He announced, 'I'm going to rescind that.'

"'Governor, that's the deal I made with Dane, and you authorized me to make it. Yes, we raised a ton of money, but he's due that.'

The governor said, "I'm not giving him $43,000."

"But that's what we've committed to Dane."

"I don't care. I'm not giving it to him."

"It was one of the few times Charlie got angry at me," said Greer. "Crist told me he told Dane, 'I'm giving you a salary, but I'm not giving you a commission on the money.'

"I ran into Dane a few days later, and I said, 'Dane, I'm really sorry.' 'Don't worry about it, Chairman,' he said. 'I know it wasn't you.'

Greer was upset because Crist had authorized the deal in the first place.

"Charlie really cut my legs out from under me by canceling my deal with Dane," said Greer. "What upset me the most was that I had kept him informed of my dealings with Dane all along."

In addition to hiring Eagle, Greer also hired Pablo Diaz, who had been working in the governor's office in charge of gubernatorial appointments, and put him in charge of field operations, hiring campaign staff, and handling the grass-roots aspect. Greer needed someone to help get the campaign off the ground.

MEANWHILE, ROB JESMER, THE executive director of the National Republican Senatorial Committee, had been calling Greer to find out if Crist had put together policy papers.

Greer would say, "No, we're working on those," which wasn't true, because Crist had no interest in discussing policy.

"Innumerable times I went over to the governor's mansion," said Greer, "sat down with him in the evening and said, 'We've got to have a position on some congressional legislation, or on issues the president has supported. We ought to have a position on the Israeli issue, the Palestinian issue. We have to be prepared.' 'Chairman,' Crist would say, 'There's plenty of time for that. Plenty of time.'"

All the while Rubio was traveling the state discussing his Tea Party views on all the national and international topics that Crist was avoiding.

Said Greer, "Marco Rubio had spoken on all those issues in his red-meat speeches to the Republican Executive Committees. He advocated cutting taxes. He talked about judicial appointments. Health care. Immigration. He spoke about all the issues currently on the national scene—something every United States Senate candidate needed to do."

Crist's refusal to act like a candidate running for a national office was beginning to worry Greer and other members of Crist's team.

"Eric Eikenberg and I used to joke about Crist's stump speech where he would talk about how his grandfather came to America, shined shoes for a nickel, put his son through college, how his son became a doctor, and 'do you know who that doctor's son is? It's me, Charlie Crist.'

"That was a great story. But Eric and I would shake our heads when a reporter would follow up with a question about something important like the Israeli-Palestinian situation. Charlie would answer, 'That reminds me of my grandfather who came to American and shined shoes for a nickel.'

"It was the beginning of a real concern. By the fall, it was a major problem."

34

Marco Almost Jumps

In June 2009 while Charlie Crist became a mad man at raising money for his campaign, Marco Rubio was traveling to every dinner of every Florida Republican Executive Committee, Republican Women's Club, and Republican Men's Club, no matter how big or small.

Greer kept expressing his concern to Crist and his team. Nobody cared. Everybody kept reading the polls that showed Crist ahead by double digits. And Rubio just kept chugging along, traveling the state, meeting and talking with the grass-roots workers.

There was still speculation that Rubio wanted to get out of the race. He was broke, facing a serious money crisis, and close confidantes were warning him the polling showed he had no chance of beating Crist. When Crist revealed in the campaign finance report that came out in July that he had raised $4.3 million, the huge sum took everyone by surprise.

"The numbers were saying 'Oh my God, this thing is over,'" said Greer. "It's Charlie Crist all the way. He's winning in money; he's winning in polling."

Rubio was about the only one who didn't believe it. He persevered, continuing to meet with every Republican group that would have him, while Crist wrote off the Republican groups and clubs because they were part of the Republican infrastructure, and because he believed the voters—not the grass-roots members of his party—would ultimately win the election for him.

Greer kept telling the stubborn Crist he was wrong.

Recalled Greer, "One night Charlie and I were having dinner at a restaurant on Fisher Island, and I said very clearly that those people you're counting on don't vote in the primary. The ones who vote in the primary are the ones Rubio is courting. The Republican who's my neighbor, the Republican who only votes in the general election—he will vote for you in November, Governor, but we don't get to November unless we win in August."

Crist's almost casual response was, "It's all going to work out, Chairman. It's going to be fine."

"He thought he knew more than any of us," said Greer. "Everything he was doing now he had done in the past, and it had worked out. He had had a brilliant political compass."

But not this time.

"IN 2009 THE ECONOMY was crumbling, and the American public wanted serious leadership," said Greer. "Other times in Florida's history they loved a guy like Charlie—an optimist, a hand-shaker, a friend to everyone.

"In 2009–10, voters were looking for a candidate who would talk seriously to them about leadership and the direction of the state and country. Times had become difficult and dangerous. People were losing their homes. College funds were being used to feed families. Fathers were out of work. Voters were seeking direction and answers from the candidates running for office. Charlie was not a candidate for that time. Marco was. Rubio was offering in-depth commentary and solutions to the economic crisis."

As the summer went on Jim Greer was still Crist's de facto campaign manager. Over martinis and hors d'oeuvres, Greer would pull out his yellow pad and say, "Governor, there are some things I need to go over with you."

Greer would go over party issues, and then he'd say, "I want you to bring you up to speed on a couple of campaign issues."

"No no no no," Crist would say. "We have plenty of time to do that, Chairman. Not now."

"You're giving a speech on Sunday," said Greer. "You need to talk about the economy."

"No no," said Crist. "People don't want to get bogged down in that stuff, Chairman."

Crist refused to talk about anything substantive.

"I'd prepare memos for him on national issues," said Greer. "I'd write, 'Talk about national defense issues and about economic issues, and I'd put talking points in his speech. He'd sit next to me at the table before going up to the podium, and he'd take a felt tip pen and scratch all of it out. And he'd go up and tell the story of his grandfather and his shoeshine kit. I think he was reluctant to talk about issues because he feared follow-up questions. The follow-ups would expose his ignorance on the substantive issues."

Crist and Greer went to the Panhandle for a now-rare invitation to speak at a Lincoln Day dinner. Greer wrote Crist a red-meat speech saying Democrats were taxers and spenders, we must have a strong national defense, Obama is the anti-Christ, the sort of talk the conservatives feast on.

Greer put the speech in a folder. Crist never looked at it. He was supposed to talk for 20 minutes. When he went on stage, he thanked everybody, told them how great they were. He said to a woman in the front row, "Good to see you, Mary," and then he said, "Florida is great. Florida is the Sunshine State, the prettiest state in the union. We're the state of oranges and sunshine and Walt Disney." After about seven minutes of this pap, he sat down.

Greer thought to himself, *What's going on? What's wrong with him?*

"You see, Charlie had his celebrity star status," recalled Greer. "When he finished his remarks, everyone rushed over to him, wanted to touch him, wanted to shake his hand—everyone except the real conservative Republicans. They remained in their seats. They had no interest in touching Charlie Crist's coat.

"George LeMieux would call me up and ask, 'How did last night go? How did he do?' Sometimes I'd tell him, 'He did fine,' because even though he didn't say anything, the people really loved him. Then George would ask, 'Did he give them any red meat?' I'd say, 'Nope.'"

Greer had a good idea what was behind Crist's refusal to discuss the hard issues or go negative. "A lot of that came from Carole," said Greer. "Carole was always at his side. She had this Disneyland way of seeing things—'everybody is so wonderful, you're so wonderful, I'm so wonderful. Why can't we all just get along?'

"Carole didn't understand that politics is a blood sport. I would think to myself, *You don't know it, Carole, but half this room hates your husband.* She never grasped that. She encouraged Charlie to be the optimist, to say nothing negative or offensive. Charlie told me once that Carole didn't want him to be the 'angry candidate.' But Charlie had lost his way."

ON SATURDAY, JULY 5, 2009, Greer took his family on a seven-day cruise to Jamaica, Haiti, and the Cayman Islands. When the ship pulled into the Caymans, his cell phone started to go off. The caller was Armando Gutierrez, a young man connected to the Miami Hispanic area, part of Rubio's group.

"I'm so glad I got hold of you," Gutierrez said. "Marco says he's going to get out of the Senate race."

"He does?" said a surprised Greer.

"Yup, he's going to run for attorney general. But he needs some commitments. He wants to know that you'll throw the party behind his candidacy, that you'll get Kottkamp out of the attorney general's race, and that you and Crist will stand at the podium and endorse him."

"Yup," Greer told him. "No problem with any of that."

Gutierrez then said, "Marco wants to meet with you on Wednesday night at your office in Tallahassee, but he wants to talk to you today."

Greer went out on a balcony outside his stateroom and called Speaker Rubio.

"I really hadn't had much contact with Marco," said Greer. "I knew he knew I was a Crist supporter. But you never know what you're going to face when you pick up the phone."

After they exchanged pleasantries, Rubio repeated essentially what Gutierrez had said about Rubio switching to the attorney general race if Greer and Crist would endorse him and the Party would put its resources behind him.

Greer recalled that he told Rubio the primary fight with Crist was not good for the party and his job as chairman was "to get these musical chairs in order so we could win in November."

So Greer pledged his, Crist's, and the party's support for Rubio in a campaign for attorney general.

"Okay," said Rubio. "I need to talk to a couple of people, but I'm fairly confident this is what I'm going to do. And I'll meet you at six o'clock in your office on Wednesday."

"I'm on a cruise," said Greer, "I'm talking to you from the Caymans, but I'll be back in Tallahassee on Monday morning, and I'll meet you at six on Wednesday."

"Okay," said Rubio, "That's what we're going to do."

"I'll call the governor," Greer told him. "This is the right move. You'll make a great attorney general, and you'll have a straight shot at the governor's office."

"Let's touch base on Tuesday to confirm everything," Rubio said.

And Rubio hung up.

Greer called Crist: "You won't believe the conversation I just had with Rubio. He's getting out."

"Holy shit, Chairman," said Crist. "You have done a fantastic job."

FOR A FEW DAYS Crist seemed to be heading to Washington. Greer as well.

Greer and his family disembarked from the ship on Monday, and on Tuesday Greer called Rubio, who didn't return the call. Greer called again. No call back. After three calls to Rubio, Greer called Gutierrez, who said he'd look into it.

When Gutierrez called back, he reported, "He's having cold feet, Jim. People are telling him to continue his race for the Senate. Jeb has convinced him to stay in."

Rubio never did call Greer back, and when six o'clock came on Wednesday, Rubio was a no-show for their scheduled meeting.

Rubio later published his own book, and Greer notes that "Marco wrote that there were several times he was close to getting out of the Senate race but that his wife talked him into staying. People never knew that he had told me he was getting out.

"His wife has a strong personality, and so does Jeb. I also think there were people in Marco's camp who saw Charlie Crist as the emperor with no clothes. I believe that more than anyone, Rubio recognized that the poll numbers weren't real and that there was an opportunity to turn the party against Crist. What happened next became a huge issue."

35

Rubio Creeps Up

One afternoon in July 2008 political consultant Jim Rimes called on Greer. A new Congressional district was being drawn in central Florida to account for population changes, and Rimes, RPOF executive director at the time and well-connected with the staff of the Republican National Committee, told Greer that the National Republican Congressional Campaign Committee wanted to know if he would consider running for the new seat.

Greer was intrigued and honored. He flew with Rimes and political consultant Kirk Pepper to D.C. to meet with the political staff of the Republican Congressional committee. Rimes and Pepper felt that Greer had name recognition and could win. When he returned to Tallahassee he sought the advice of Harry Sargeant, RPOF finance chairman.

Sargeant thought Greer should run and could win. Newspaper articles began appearing that Greer was considering a run for Congress. First, though, Greer needed the okay from Governor Crist. And Crist, always putting his self-interest first, said no. "You should stay where you are," said Crist. "You need to be here to watch my back."

It wasn't the first time an opportunity was presented to Greer only to have Crist oppose it. But Greer could never forget that Crist had plucked him from local politics and made him the Florida party chairman, and he felt he owed the governor everything. Greer was sorely disappointed, but he respected the governor's wishes.

As 2009 began, the Republican Party nationally and in Florida was splintering. Despite the incredulity and dismay of some Republicans, Barack Obama was in fact the president of the United States, and the backlash to his election was growing stronger. In the 1950s and 1960s the John Birch Society, led by billionaire oilmen, pushed its far-right agenda. Birchers hated the federal government, hated Franklin Roosevelt and the New Deal, hated the Catholic President John K. Kennedy, and hated Negroes. When Lyndon Johnson became president after JFK was assassinated in 1963, the Birchers lost most of their steam. They never completely went away, but it wasn't until the election of Obama in 2008 that their anti-Washington, anti-tax, anti-the poor, anti-minorities, anti-abortion, and anti-gay agenda came roaring back to life, this time as the Obama-hating Tea Party.

It was an irony that Marco Rubio—a "furriner" whose family emigrated from Cuba—would become the darling of the tea baggers, but he did. Rubio would go on the stump and tell people how his parents had escaped Communism to come to the United States, where capitalism and free enterprise were king and where a Cuban immigrant could grow up to be an important politician. Only later was it revealed that his story wasn't quite true, that his parents had come to Miami more than two years before the communists seized control.

Crist and Greer abhorred much of what Rubio stood for. Like the rest of the Tea Party leaders, his test of loyalty to the Republican Party was absolute. If you didn't believe in a complete absence of gun control, that marriage could only be between a man and a woman, that all abortions were wrong, and that all taxes were bad, then you were to be shunned—purged from the party—like a fallen New England Puritan of the 1600s.

Though Crist and Greer hadn't yet recognized it, a revolution was brewing within the Republican Party. As moderate Republicans who believed in opening the party to everyone, in making compromises with Democrats, and in pursuing policies that would benefit all constituents, they would become ripe targets of the Tea Party's hatred.

Crist—at last—began to sense this change in wind direction. When Sonia Sotomayor, an Hispanic woman from New York, was appointed to the Supreme Court by Obama, Crist called Greer and asked, "What do you think I ought to do? Because I really like her, and I don't see any need to oppose her."

"You'll be asked about it," said Greer, "so this may be an opportunity to give the conservatives some red meat."

The next day Crist called back. "I agree with you," he said. "I'm going to come out publicly and oppose her and see if I can collect some chits with the base of the party."

And so Crist announced his opposition to Sotomayor, but it was too little, too late, and got him nowhere with the Florida right-wingers.

The backlash by Tea Party Republicans against moderate Republicans began during the early summer of 2009 when Mike Huckabee, the former governor of Arkansas, ripped the Republican National Senatorial Committee for sticking its nose in Florida's Senate campaign and endorsing Crist over Rubio. Another Tea Party favorite, U.S. Senator Jim DeMint of South Carolina also attacked the RNSC for backing Crist.

This didn't bode well for Charlie Crist, who was counting heavily on support from the Republican National Senatorial Committee to bolster his candidacy. Greer began hearing whispers that the RNSC support wasn't as solid as it had once been.

Recalled Greer, "We learned that Rubio had visited the RNSC. They had told us from the start that they weren't going to give Rubio the time of day. Then I heard he had met with them. And the press, doing what it does so well, asked John Cornyn and Rob Jesmer, practically on a daily basis, why they were endorsing Crist over Rubio. One night the communications department of the RNSC sent out an email reaffirming its support of Crist, but at the end of the mailing said, 'But Marco Rubio has a great future with the Republican Party.'

That night Greer went over to the governor's mansion. Crist was sitting in his personal quarters. Greer showed him the press release.

"They're starting to weaken," Greer said. "They never should have mentioned Rubio's name in a press release about you. You need to get on the phone to John Cornyn right now, and you need to ask him what the hell they're doing. Don't pussyfoot around with these people. Ask them, 'Are they getting ready to fuck us?'"

Crist agreed, downed a couple of drinks, and then got Cornyn on the phone. Greer was busily writing notes for Crist while Crist paced around the dining room table. Greer, who was following him, wrote, "Are you going to drop your endorsement?" He slid it across the table to the governor. Crist asked the question, and Cornyn replied, "No, Charlie, absolutely not.

But you know we have a lot of people who like Marco. We're taking a lot of heat for coming out so early for you. Marco has a lot of support, so we said something nice about him. Are you going to win this thing, Governor? We're still with you."

When Crist hung up, Greer said, "We've got problems. They're getting ready for something up there."

Greer called Jesmer, the RNSC executive director, who swore to God the line about Rubio in the press release was a mistake. "They shouldn't have mentioned Rubio," said Jesmer.

However, in subsequent emails, the NRSC started promoting Rubio, giving him credibility and stature.

"Either they were with us—or they weren't. And that really pissed me off," said Greer."

36

A MATTER OF POLICY

THE UNITED STATES SENATE RACE OPENED UP A WHOLE NEW WORLD THAT Charlie Crist and his de facto campaign manager Jim Greer had to deal with. Dane Eagle had been hired as a Florida fundraiser, but Crist and Greer agreed that the campaign also needed a national fundraiser, someone who could raise money through national contacts and donors who were interested in gaining influence with a U.S. senator.

"Your world opens up considerably when you run for the United States Senate," said Greer, "because there are people in, say, Wyoming who will contribute to a Senate candidate from another state. There are business people, for example, who will contribute because a senator deals with issues that are of interest to them. And then you have organizations like the AIPAC, the National Jewish Federation in Washington, or the Club for Growth, a large politically active organization. As a candidate you have to convince those organizations to endorse you."

Crist and Greer put out feelers. *Did someone know Arnold Schwarzenegger's fundraiser? Who was John McCain's main fundraiser?*

"These fundraisers exchange lists," said Greer. "You call a friend, say, who is Arnold Schwarzenegger's fundraiser and you ask, 'Listen, I need to raise some money from your people. You can tap my people. Let's exchange donor lists.' And you then say, 'Can we send out a solicitation letter to your donors from Arnold?' A U.S. Senate campaign needs to find that type of fundraiser, a top-notch person."

After interviewing several candidates, Greer hired Lisa Spies, who had worked for the Republican National Committee and for Mitt Romney. Unfortunately for Spies, she and Crist never got along, and it wasn't her fault. The problem stemmed from their different approaches to fundraising—he had one approach that he used to run for governor, and he wasn't willing to adapt to a style necessary to raise money from total strangers from out of the state.

"When you're running for governor," said Greer, "people will write you a check just because they want to meet you Saturday night at the country club and get their picture taken with you. When you're running for governor, people won't question you about policy before they'll write the check. When Charlie ran for governor, Meredith would call and ask a donor, 'I'm having a fundraiser at so-and-so's home, and I need a $500 check,' and the person would say 'sure.' Sometimes Charlie wouldn't even show up.

"What Charlie didn't like was when Lisa would say, 'Governor, there are five business owners of a national energy company, and they're talking about giving you a grand apiece, but they want to meet you first.' Charlie'd say, 'What the fuck do they need to meet me for? Are they going to give money or not?'"

On the national level many people had never heard of Charlie Crist.

While Lisa Spies reported to Crist, and ultimately Eric Eikenberg after he became campaign manager, she often also reported to Greer.

"She would me call up and say, 'Chairman, I've got a group of men I worked with on the Giuliani campaign, and they want to have dinner with Charlie. After they meet with him, we'll be able to get money out of them.

"I'd call Charlie up. 'Hey, when we're in New York next time, Lisa has a group of businessmen who want to meet you.'

"Charlie'd say, 'How much are they giving?'

"'They want to meet you first, Governor.'

"'That's all pie in the sky, Jim. They'll meet me, but who knows whether they'll give us any money or not?'

"'Well, Governor, that's kind of the way things work at this level.'"

More often than not, Crist would say no or not respond at all. And Spies would become very frustrated. Or she would call Greer and say, "Can you have the governor call Ambassador Jones? He was an ambassador under Ronald Reagan. He's a multi-millionaire. He has tons of contacts. He can raise us a lot of money, Jim, but Charlie needs to call him and schmooze him a little. I've asked him to call. I've sent the Jones's contact information to Dane."

The contact information would have Jones's telephone number and a brief description of who the person was and how much money Spies felt he would give. But when Crist would see those contact sheets, he wouldn't call.

Greer would say, "Governor, about a week ago Lisa sent you a call list of big donors. They do donate, but they won't do it unless they talk to you and get to know you."

"Are they going to donate money, or aren't they?" Crist would reply. "Do they want to help me, or don't they?"

"They want to help," Greer would say, "but they don't know who the hell you are."

It was a Mexican stand-off, but Crist would be the loser for it.

As a result of Crist's reluctance to reach out to potential donors, his fundraising dropped precipitously after the initial $4.3 million.

"On the national level big donors want to meet and talk with the candidate before writing a check," said Greer. Many had questions and concerns about Crist's candidacy.

"People donated then because he was still the governor," said Greer. "A lot of the money came from lobbyists and corporate executives in Florida. They didn't give a shit about him becoming a U.S. senator, but they didn't want to get screwed by him while he was still governor.

"When Charlie would call and say, for example, 'Hey, executive of Disney World or Universal Studios, or Brian Ballard, I really need some help in my Senate campaign,' they'd say, 'Yes, governor.'"

After the RNSC endorsed Crist, Rob Jesmer, its executive director, told Greer, "The next thing you need to do is reach out to all the Republican senators' fundraisers and ask them to make contributions from their PACs to Crist's campaign."

Greer and Spies first called John McCain's fundraiser, and he said yes. He called Lindsay Graham and he agreed, as did Senator John Kyle of Arizona.

"In the first quarter a sizable number of PACs were writing checks to Crist's campaign because it looked like he was a winner," said Greer. "But a lot of people in Florida who wanted to keep the governor happy had maxed out. They had written their $4,800 checks, the maximum. But Charlie was becoming frustrated with Lisa because as hard as she was working the money wasn't coming in nearly as fast as he was used to. His expectations were much higher than they should have been for a federal race. Charlie would say, 'Why are we paying her? She only raised $25,000.'"

When Greer then told Spies that the governor was getting frustrated, she would reply, "Why don't you tell him to make the calls I've asked him to make?"

Spies arranged for Crist to speak at a Republican conference at Mackinac Island in Michigan. Republican leaders from around the country would be attending. It was *a big deal* to get invited to speak there. "Lisa had planned a small fundraiser in Detroit before we would all fly off to Mackinac Island," said Greer. The Detroit fundraiser brought in between $3,000 and $4,000. Expecting a lot more, Crist was furious. He had been drinking. He, Greer, and Spies had ridden there in an SUV, and after the event was over Crist didn't want Spies riding back with him.

"He's pissed at me, isn't he?" Spies whispered to Greer.

"Yeah, he's mad," said Greer.

"What's he mad about?" said Spies. "I sent him a call list before he came up here so we could raise money. Do you know how many people he called? None. And he's mad at me? I think I'm going to quit."

"Don't quit," said Greer.

"He needs to get it," said Spies. "He needs to understand that he has to work at this thing and call people."

Recalled Greer, "Part of the problem was that Charlie just didn't like dealing with a lot of people. Even though many were die-hard Republicans, he'd hesitate because he just didn't want to call people he didn't like."

Greer thinks there was another reason, too. "He was afraid that they'd ask him questions about national issues."

After the Detroit fundraiser Crist, Greer, and Spies flew to Mackinac Island where the Republican Party had taken over a beautiful old resort. Cars were not allowed on the island. People rode around in horses and buggies.

At the dinner Greer was seated with Ari Fleischer, George W. Bush's former spokesman. "How's Charlie doing down in Florida," Fleischer asked.

"He's doing great," said Greer.

"That's good," said Fleischer. "I like Charlie."

Recalled Greer, "Here we were at about as Republican an event as you can get. I was sitting across from Charlie, having a good time, and I said to him, 'Governor, you really have to give them some red meat tonight.' He got up, and what did he do? He talked about his grandfather, about the Sunshine State, blah, blah, blah. When he sat down, it was to mediocre applause. It wasn't a bad speech, but he had nowhere to take it, because once he got past the fluff, he had nothing to say.

"And I was thinking, *How are we ever going to be president of the United States if this is what we're going to do? If we're not going to show the difference between you and the other candidates and the other party, what the hell are we doing here?*"

Jesmer, LeMieux, and Greer agreed that Crist needed to hire a policy person—and fast. Greer and Eikenberg interviewed a young woman who had been one of Romney's top policy people in 2008. She wanted $5,000 a month, which Greer felt was fair. She would have prepped Crist on questions of economic policy and national defense policy.

"She was highly respected and she came highly recommended," said Greer.

Greer and Eikenberg met with Crist and told him about the young woman. Greer said, "She's very good, very smart."

"I just don't think we're ready for that," said Crist. "I don't know why we have to spend that kind of money right now."

She wasn't hired.

The absurdity of Crist's position not to hire a policy expert was highlighted at a meeting in Washington with the American-Israeli Public Affairs Committee. "They endorse candidates," said Greer, "and they have money. Everyone running for the House of Representatives or the Senate wants their endorsement.

"Charlie was all excited because he was taking Carole, who is Jewish, to this meeting. He asked me to go with them. We were all in an SUV, driving to the meeting, when I tried briefing him on the questions they were sure to ask. At that time Lebanon was shelling Israel. He was kind of listening but he was reading the paper and Carole was giving him some advice.

"When we got there, we were ushered into a big conference room. Three gentlemen from the organization came in. One introduced himself as the political director and the other as the eastern affairs director. This wasn't my meeting. I took my chair and sat in the corner away from the conference table."

Crist introduced Greer as the chairman of the Republican Party of Florida who was helping with his campaign.

"Charlie had gone to Israel in 2007 and had visited the Wailing Wall," said Greer. "While there he had written on a piece of paper, 'Please let there be no hurricanes to hit Florida this year,' which he then folded and tucked into the wall. And there had been no hurricanes that year because of it, he would say. Charlie loved to tell that story."

During the meeting the men brought out a map of Israel and Egypt and the surrounding countries, which they laid out on a table. They started asking Crist questions about Israel, Syria, the Iran situation, and the governor replied, "Do you all know that Carole is Jewish?"

"That's nice, governor. Great."

"Carole, tell them about growing up Jewish."

Said Greer, "She started talking, and we were about ten minutes into the meeting when they said, 'Governor, what do you think the United States should do as it relates to Iran getting nuclear weapons?'

"And Charlie said, 'That's a very good question. Chairman, come on up here. Pull your chair up here.' And he said, 'The chairman and I were just talking about that in the car on the way here. Chairman, tell them what your view is.'

"And I said, 'It's going to be very dangerous if Iran gets nuclear weapons. I'm not sure sanctions are going to work. And the governor just said to me something I think is right, and that is, 'If Iran gets nuclear weapons, the U.S. is going to have to respond militarily.'"

His hosts nodded their heads in agreement.

Said Greer, "I was doing what Charlie wanted me to do, but I was thinking to myself, *I should be running for this office.* They asked him a few more questions, and he said, 'I don't know if you know it, but we went to Israel last year. And I went to the Wailing Wall, and I put a note in the Wailing Wall praying not to let any hurricanes hit Florida. And you know what, gentlemen? No hurricanes hit Florida. That tells you a lot, doesn't it?'

"He was able to deflect every question they asked him. He must have told them Carole was Jewish five times. He must have told them about his trip to Israel two or three times. By the time we were done an hour later, we were all shaking hands as we walked out the door. The whole thing was comical. Charlie just didn't have a clue."

They later wrote the Crist campaign a $1,000 check.

"Charlie's way of campaigning had worked for him in every election. Why wouldn't it work for him this time?"

It wouldn't be long before Crist and Greer would find out why.

37

'The Party is Angry'

Charlie Crist was riding high in June 2009 when he was endorsed at a meeting of the National Republican Senatorial Committee chaired by influential Texas Senator John Cornyn. Later that month, supporters of Marco Rubio answered with a Rubio endorsement by Senator Jim DeMint of South Carolina, an ultra-conservative leader of the Tea Party movement. DeMint made known he had checked with Cornyn and other senators before making his endorsement.

"I don't agree with those endorsing Charlie Crist," DeMint said. "He's not conservative enough." Shortly after DeMint's endorsement, the neo-conservative *Weekly Standard* did a big feature story on Rubio, praising him to the skies.

Recalled Greer, "DeMint was the first time anyone of any prominence had gone against the flow of all the endorsements of Crist. People were still standing with Charlie. He had raised $4.3 million, breaking all kinds of records. That first reporting period, Marco Rubio had raised $340,000. Kendrick Meek, the Democratic candidate for the Senate had already raised $1.2 million.

"Everyone believed the seat was a Republican's to win. The consensus was that Crist would beat Meek handily. And the poll numbers supported that. They also showed Crist far ahead of Rubio."

In the second quarter Crist raised $2.1 million, and Rubio, buoyed by Tea Party followers around the country, raised $1 million.

"Rubio was getting a lot of money from out-of-state DeMint supporters," said Greer. "And the Tea Party activists began sending him a lot of money in low-dollar amounts. Rubio was getting grass-roots support from little old ladies who gave him $50 from their monthly Social Security checks. We were getting major donors who had an interest in keeping Crist happy, while Rubio was getting hundreds and hundreds of small donors to give $10, $15, $20. In many ways, Rubio was mirroring the Obama campaign's grass-roots support in 2008."

In July 2009 the Christian Coalition, the powerful organization founded by television evangelist Pat Robertson, with members numbering in the many millions, endorsed Rubio. Then Arkansas Governor Mike Huckabee announced his endorsement of Rubio.

Rubio, growing confident, called for multiple debates with Crist.

"Charlie wouldn't respond," said Greer, "because he knew he couldn't debate Marco. Charlie and I would meet, and I'd say, 'The Rubio campaign has issued a call today for three debates.' Charlie'd say, 'I'm not fucking going to debate until next year.' Rubio knew he was boxing Charlie in. The press began to report that Crist was running away from Rubio."

WHEN GREER WOULD HEAR Rubio's angry rhetoric against big government, taxes, Barack Obama and Charlie Crist, he would say to Crist, "They're angry, Governor. The Party is angry."

And Crist would reply, "I'm not going to be the angry candidate, Chairman."

As Crist and Greer would find out, just about the only candidates who won in 2010 were the angry ones.

"Marco Rubio had a specific plan," said Greer. "He was opposed to all taxes. He favored a strong national defense. He was in support of a strong Israel. He wanted to cut entitlements. He advocated closing borders and enforcing strict immigration laws. He was saying everything conservatives wanted to hear. And he was railing against Obama and the Democrats. He was able to convey in a very articulate way the frustrations Republicans were feeling about government, the economy, and the Democratic Party."

Crist was unable to convey those frustrations.

Said Greer, "People were desperate to know, 'How are you going to get me a job? What will you do to spark the economy? How are you going to prevent my home from going into foreclosure?' And Charlie didn't know how to answer those questions. So he told the story about his grandfather coming from Greece. Two years earlier that story got him a standing ova-tion. In 2009 it got him nothing."

Greer was acting as Crist's campaign manager and traveling with Crist continuously, so newspaper articles began quoting Rubio's supporters ques-tioning the Republican Party chairman's neutrality:

"Why is Greer in Washington today? Why did he go to New York City with Crist?"

At certain events Greer even stood in for Crist, such as when Crist was supposed to appear at a fundraiser in Chicago but his flight was canceled and Greer spoke in his stead. I felt he was the head of the party, and I should do as he wished.

Meanwhile, Rubio was driving himself to as many political events in Florida as possible. Initially, he didn't raise nearly as much money as Crist, but he was pushing his grass-roots ground game hard, telling Republicans what they wanted to hear: "Barack Obama is bad. Democratic policies are bad. We must defeat them at all costs."

Crist continued to contend he didn't need a ground game.

During the summer of 2009, Greer tried hard to convince the penny-pinching Charlie Crist that he needed to hire staff. Crist finally allowed Greer to hire a full-time press secretary—Andrea Saul, who had a great deal of experience with the national press. A true Republican, she had worked with Mitt Romney and was recommended by the Republican Senatorial Campaign Committee.

However, as with Lisa Spies, Saul and Crist didn't get along. Again, it was almost entirely Crist's fault. Saul would submit press releases for Crist's approval, but he'd rarely get back to her.

"I've called him three times," she'd complain to Greer. "He won't call me back."

Said Greer, "I don't think he liked his own campaign staff. And I don't think he had a clue what was right or wrong to do. Every time he needed to make a decision, he and Carole would have a bottle of red wine, talk it over, and decide what to do. By the time they got around to making a decision, it was too late. It was just a mess, and I was always the one Crist looked to to fix it."

38

LeMieux Demands an Interview

In August 2009, Mel Martinez informed Crist and Greer that not only was he not standing for reelection but he was going to step down before the end of his term. That potentially opened a big door for Crist, because, in the event of a U.S. Senate seat becoming vacant, the Florida constitution calls for the governor to appoint someone to fill the seat until its next scheduled regular election.

Recalled Greer, "The first thing the governor talked about was, 'What if I appoint myself?'" The newspapers immediately began speculating about whether Crist had the *cojones* to do just that.

"One night we had a big discussion about this," said Greer. "The pros were the fact that he would be the incumbent at the time of the election, and that he had the ability to raise a lot of money. Jeff Kottkamp would take over as governor, so there would be a smooth transition. There was some disagreement among our attorneys whether he could actually appoint himself. The consensus was that he could, because it had been done once before, in the 1800s. The problem was that the governor who appointed himself subsequently lost the election."

Greer said he argued that a self-appointment would put a bad taste in voters' mouths. "Charlie agreed with that. He stopped pushing that idea."

The question then became one of whom Crist should appoint.

In a meeting with chief of staff Eric Eikenberg, political consultant Jay Burmer, Crist, and Greer, Greer suggested they put together a small blue ribbon panel to interview candidates.

"I told him to say, 'Bring me two or three names,'" said Greer. "Make like we're letting people decide this. Let's include some elder statesmen heavyweights, too. Maybe have Jeff Kottkamp chair it. The panel would interview the candidates.

"Charlie didn't like the idea from minute one. It would take the spotlight off him. I couldn't get that horse to move out of the gate."

Instead, Crist wanted to put on a show by going around the state to interview candidates himself. The appointed senator would only be in office for 18 months, but Crist wanted to be sure he wouldn't be setting up someone to run for the seat come election time.

Recalled Greer, "The governor's favorite line was, 'We want someone who can get a good table at a Georgetown restaurant as senator but not do anything else.' I told the governor we needed to find an elder Republican statesman, somebody whose time is done, who isn't looking to be a senator for another six years."

Greer suggested Crist interview Dan Webster, the ultra-conservative former Speaker of the House who had "Christian values." He was anti-abortion and anti-gay, too conservative for Crist to actually appoint, but a perfect candidate for the red-meat Republicans. Crist went to Orlando to interview him.

He then went to Jacksonville to interview State Representative Jennifer Carroll, and then to Miami to interview Alberto Martinez, the former United States attorney under George W. Bush.

Greer also called Mario Diaz Balart, a congressman from Miami, but Balart said he wasn't interested.

Crist's staff then set up an interview with Congressman Bill Young of St. Petersburg. The cagey Young, a veteran of 28 years in the House, showed up wearing tennis shoes, a T-shirt, and blue jeans. In a press conference after the meeting Young told reporters he really wasn't interested in the job, that he had just come down to see Charlie.

After the meeting Crist, furious that Young had showed up just to insult him, phoned Greer. "Young made a fool out of me," said Crist.

"Young realized the meeting was a sham," recalled Greer, "and he was calling Charlie's bluff. Charlie was obviously going to appoint someone to do his bidding, someone who would jump back flips for Charlie, and Young knew this interviewing was just a dog and pony show."

"In our inner circle," recalled Greer, "we didn't know who Charlie would appoint, but we doubted it was going to be anyone he was interviewing. The interviewing was a subterfuge. This whole thing was an opportunity to gain points with the conservatives and the press and take support away from Rubio."

While Crist was conducting his interviews, George LeMieux called Greer and Eikenberg, demanding that he be considered for the job. Every day LeMieux would call asking for an interview.

"Remember," said Greer, "George is a strategist. He's the Maestro. I knew every time I got off the phone with him that George was moving political chess pieces because he wanted the job."

Greer told Crist about LeMieux's requests.

"Absolutely not," said Crist. "It would look like I was appointing my campaign manager/chief of staff. It would stink to high heaven. George isn't getting an interview, and he's not getting the appointment. Tell him."

Crist then interviewed John Delaney, the former mayor of Jacksonville and a former state attorney and university administrator. Crist met with him at the governor's mansion in Tallahassee, and the two got along very well.

"He really likes Delaney," Eikenberg told Greer. "I think it's going to be Delaney. The governor says he's asked Delaney to come back for a second interview tomorrow at one o'clock. He's going out of town tonight, and he wants you to come over to the mansion and ride with him to the airport."

Crist was catching a six o'clock flight out of Tallahassee. Crist, Greer, and Eikenberg rode in the governor's SUV to the airport.

"I was sitting in the middle," said Greer, "and the governor leaned over and whispered, 'I really like Delaney. I think we're going to make it Delaney.' I told him, 'That's great.'"

That night Greer ate at a Mexican restaurant in Tallahassee with Erin Isaac, Crist's press secretary, and her husband. Isaac was close to LeMieux, who had hired her. As Crist's press secretary, she knew who Crist was interviewing. During dinner, Erin's cell phone rang. "George is on the phone," she said to Greer. "He wants to talk to you."

Greer left the restaurant and went into the parking lot to talk privately with LeMieux.

"How did today go?" asked LeMieux.

Greer decided to tell him the truth. "He likes John Delaney, George. I don't know for sure if Delaney's going to be it, but he likes him."

"All right," said LeMieux.

Later that night an anonymous website popped up that talked about positions Delaney had taken as mayor of Jacksonville, giving the impression that Delaney had pushed for tax increases.

"The website created a lot of laughter," said Greer, "and gossip. 'You know who did that, don't you?' I was asked several times. Erin confessed to me that George had his people do it. Now all of a sudden there was negative information being posted about John Delaney—for the purpose of boxing in Crist not to appoint him."

Crist swallowed the bait, canceled the interview, and scratched Delaney completely off the list.

LeMieux meanwhile continued to lobby Eikenberg and Isaac for inside information and Greer for an interview.

Greer recalled, "I went over to the mansion and told Charlie that George still wanted an interview. Charlie said, 'I'm done with this. I like George, but if I named him, the press would eat me alive. Plus he's over at the Gunster law firm working with the Seminole Indians on their deal with the federal government to increase gambling in their casinos."

About a half an hour later, Eikenberg joined them. Crist told both Greer and Eikenberg "to go see George and tell him to stop asking for a fucking interview. I want it done now."

Over dinner that night at Andrews Restaurant in Tallahassee, Greer and Eikenberg called LeMieux and asked to see him. He was in Atlanta, but due back at 11:30 p.m. They arranged to meet at a Whataburger on Appalachee Parkway. Then they waited. LeMieux's plane was late. They waited some more.

Finally LeMieux showed up. He ordered a burger and Greer and Eikenberg had shakes. "The place was empty because it was one in the morning. Eric and I sat down across from George. I was the one leading the meeting. I felt very uncomfortable about this, because George had an awful lot to do with my becoming chairman. He had been the governor's campaign manager. He was the governor's first chief of staff. He was a lawyer. He was now the chairman of a prestigious law firm."

For about ten minutes Greer tried not to make it sound like he was speaking for the governor. Finally, he said, "George, he has people he's interested in. He's probably not going to interview any more people. You're just not going to get an appointment."

LeMieux was too smart not to get to the point.

"Did the governor tell you this?" asked LeMieux. "I want to know. I'm asking you, Chairman, did the governor tell you to tell me I'm not getting an interview?"

"George, he thinks it will look bad," said Greer. "It's just not going to happen."

Greer was taken aback by the vehemence of his reply.

"Yes, it is, Jim," LeMieux said. "You don't know what I've done for that man. I've done things for Charlie Crist that would make the hair on the back of your neck stand up. He wouldn't have been elected governor if it hadn't been for me. So I'm getting an interview. And I want you to tell him when you leave here that I want that interview."

39

The Keeper of the Secrets

"LeMieux was firm, not angry," said Greer. "He was clear: *I paid my dues*. I think George knew that if he got the interview, he'd get the appointment. Eric and I shook hands with George, got back in our car, and I said, 'You know what all that's about, don't you?'"

Eikenberg said, "Wow. I sure do He's telling us that he's got some shit on the governor, and he wants that interview."

LeMieux did know where all the bodies were buried. He had always been in charge of making Charlie's problems go away, such as discussed earlier regarding the 2006 campaign and the rumors about two alleged gay lovers and an alleged out-of-wedlock daughter. According to Greer, LeMieux had kept both issues from damaging the campaign.

Greer recalled that in 2007, after Crist was inaugurated, there was additional concern that the alleged daughter would show up at the governor's mansion because she had told reporters she wanted to meet Crist. The girl had applied to Florida State University, Crist's alma mater, in Tallahassee.

"Arlene DiBenigno, Charlie's deputy chief of staff, said the governor's office was in a panic that the girl was going to show up in the lobby and say, 'I want to see my dad.' I got a message from Arlene that George, Brian Ballard, and wealthy friends of Crist were plotting to have a private investigator follow the girl into Bullwinkle's Saloon on Tennessee Street in Tallahassee, surreptitiously grab the glass she was drinking from, and test it for her DNA to see if she really was Crist's daughter. Crist had been denying it to everybody, but George had come to the conclusion that she probably was his daughter because otherwise why would he have signed papers giving over to the reputed mother all his rights to the child."

Greer was alarmed by the whole strategy and asked DiBenigno and LeMieux what they intended to do if the DNA results showed that the girl was in fact Crist's daughter.

"I said, 'That's going to blow up. I think it's best that we just leave it alone, that maybe she is and maybe she isn't.' When I asked later if they ever followed through with this, I was informed that George had gotten cold feet and had backed off, that he was afraid someone would find out and make it public. But I never believed it was called off.

"The one thing everyone was quietly asking was, 'If she wasn't his child, why would he have signed over rights?' Maybe that's what the lawyers told him to do, but there was a general feeling among the staff that he was her father, and that thanks to George he was just able it keep it under control, as was his usual way."

THE EVENING AFTER THE Whataburger meeting with LeMieux, Eikenberg and Greer went to see Crist at the governor's mansion and told him that LeMieux insisted on the interview.

Greer recalled, "The surprising thing was, Charlie didn't blow his stack when he heard that George wasn't backing down. He didn't react at all. That told me that Charlie had nowhere to go on this one. He had tried everything he could, but George wasn't letting go."

The following day Eikenberg told Greer that Crist was granting LeMieux an interview.

The day before LeMieux's interview, Greer got a call from Carole Crist, who was lobbying for George LeMieux or Jeff Kottkamp to be appointed.

"George or Jeff should be the person," said Carole Crist. "They are loyal.'

Said Greer, "Now keep in mind that Charlie had been adamant that George not get the appointment. But now, all of a sudden, Carole was trying to convince me that George should get it. I think Carole realized what George knew."

After a formal interview with Eikenberg present, Crist and LeMieux met privately, then the two of them met with the press in the lobby of the mansion. Crist was filmed with his arm around LeMieux's shoulders.

"George, how do you feel about your interview?" LeMieux was asked.

"I feel great about it," LeMieux said. "I thank the governor for giving me the privilege of an interview."

"What type of Republican do you consider yourself to be, George?"

"I'm a Charlie Crist Republican," LeMieux said famously.

Crist, however, a man who hated making decisions, was still torn about picking LeMieux. On the one hand, he feared how it would look if he appointed his former chief of staff, and on the other he feared what LeMieux might do if he didn't appoint him. Crist continued to say to Greer and Eikenberg, "We need to appoint someone who's loyal, someone who's not going to run against me."

One night, Crist asked Greer, "Chairman, what do you think? What should I do?"

"I think you have two people who are going to be loyal," replied Greer. "You have George LeMieux, and you have Jeff Kottkamp."

"It can't be George," Crist said. "It can't be George. I love your idea about Kottkamp. Tell me why you think Kottkamp."

"First of all," said Greer, "he's been a loyal lieutenant governor. He doesn't have a great, dynamic personality. He's not going to Washington to hold big press conferences; he won't propose legislation. He's just the kind of guy who'll go to those dinners in Georgetown and stay quiet. And when the time comes, he'll step aside for you to take the seat."

"I love it," said Crist. "I love it. Get him on the phone."

Around ten o'clock at night Greer called Jeff Kottkamp. Eikenberg was sitting next to Greer when he called. Crist was sitting nearby.

"Lieutenant Governor," said Greer, "I'm sorry to bother you, but I'm with the governor, and the governor has asked me to reach out to you to see if you would consider serving as the interim United States Senator."

"It would be an honor," said Kottkamp. "I'll do anything the governor thinks I need to do."

"Okay," said Greer, "the governor wants Eric and me to meet with you tomorrow morning at nine o'clock in my office at the party headquarters to discuss this further."

"I'll be there," said Kottkamp.

Greer hung up the phone.

"Fantastic," said Crist. "I want you to make a couple of things clear to him. One, he's not to run for attorney general while he's holding the Senate seat, he has to guarantee he won't run for the Senate seat and, third, he will keep that crazy wife of his under control."

Said Greer later, "Cindy Kottkamp was very strong-willed. She had all kinds of issues about how Jeff was treated. I always liked her, but with Charlie, if you were a woman who voiced your opinion, whether you were staff or not, you weren't allowed to be around much."

GREER, MEANWHILE, WAS RELISHING his role. "I have to be honest, I was enjoying that I had been given the honor of performing this task. Here I was, negotiating and talking on behalf of the governor with people, one of whom was going to be the next United States senator."

The next morning, Kottkamp met with Greer and Eikenberg and was told the three conditions. "I need to talk to Cindy," he said. "She was set on my being attorney general. I'll call you back in a couple of hours."

"Later on," recalled Greer, "it was said that Kottkamp was never offered the job. That is absolute bullshit. The governor told me personally that if Kottkamp said yes to those conditions, he would appoint him the next U.S. senator."

Kottkamp called his wife and told her, "Honey, we're going to Washington."

An hour passed. Greer's phone rang. It was Crist, backpedaling as fast as he could. "Hey, hey, hey," he said, "When you talk to Kottkamp, don't be committal. I want to talk to George again."

"Governor," said Greer, "I've already talked to the man. Eric was there, and Eric is probably in his office preparing a press release. I've already offered Kottkamp the job!"

"Call him back and tell him we're still thinking about it," said Crist, "that it's probably going to be him, but we're also talking to other people. I want to talk to George again."

Oh my God, thought Greer, *they are screwing poor Jeff—again.*

Around 11 a.m., Kottkamp called back to say he had talked it over with his wife and she was on board with his becoming senator.

"I didn't tell him about my conversation with the governor," said Greer.

"I told him, 'I'll be talking to the governor later today. I'll get back to you.'"

Around 4 p.m., Greer's phone rang. It was Eric. "I'm over at the governor's mansion. The governor wants you to come over for a glass of wine. He's made a decision."

"Who is it?"

"Just come over."

A half hour later Greer strolled over to the governor's mansion. The governor was upstairs in his bedroom. Eric was down in the kitchen. Eric said, "It's going to be George."

"George?" Greer said. "I'm losing my freaking mind here. He tells us no way it's George. He tells both of us to go with Kottkamp. We've offered it to Kottkamp. Kottkamp thinks he's going to be the next U.S. Senator. And now he's giving it to George?"

"Yup," said Eikenberg.

The conversation stopped when Crist entered the room.

"Chairman," boomed Crist, "let's get a glass of wine and go outside by the fountain. Eric has called George who's in Fort Lauderdale tonight, but he's on a plane right now to get up here. He'll be here in an hour and 20 minutes. So let's sit around and have some drinks and wait until George gets here."

Said Greer, "We were sitting outside, and I was telling Crist about my growing up on a horse farm. He likes history, and we started to talk a little about Abraham Lincoln. Around seven we went inside. It was a long evening waiting for George to arrive. Finally an FDLE agent opened the door and in came George.

"Eric had told George he was getting the appointment, but George acted like he didn't know. If he didn't know, why would he have flown up to the mansion? So George walked in, and the governor said, 'Senator.' George stopped at the door. 'You know, Senator,' Crist continued, 'you are going to make a great senator. George, my God, I'm so proud of you. You're a great American. You have served me so well.'"

Recalled Greer, "I felt that George and the governor were putting on a show. They knew more than they were saying. George's eyes became a little watery. He sat down and said, 'Governor, I will do a good job for you. I'll serve the state of Florida well.'

"'That's great George,' said Crist. 'Let's have some champagne.' George and I hugged. Everyone hugged.

"An hour later Crist said, 'Well, somebody has to call those people I interviewed and tell them they aren't getting it.' Eric said, 'I'll do that in the morning, sir.' Then Crist said, 'Somebody has to call the LG. Chairman, you're close to the LG. Why don't you call him?'"

And that was that. Greer knew Crist didn't have the *cojones* to call Kottkamp himself.

"I know I contradict myself," recalled Greer, "because there was a point in time when I cared *so* much about this man. But he disappointed me so many times and this was one of them. He didn't even have the character to call his own lieutenant governor and tell him he wasn't getting the appointment. He should have called *all* of the prominent Republican officials he had interviewed personally, but he made Eric call them."

In the end, Greer called Kottkamp and gave him the bad news.

"He didn't get nasty," recalled Greer. "He took it in stride. That's just who Jeff Kottkamp is. I'm sure Cindy was furious enough for both of them. In my mind I could hear her telling him, 'One more time, Jeff, you've gotten screwed by Charlie Crist.'"

THE FOLLOWING DAY CRIST held a press conference at the Old Capitol building to announce his choice for U.S. senator. The news had leaked, so the reporters already knew it was LeMieux. After an impressive press conference in which Crist and LeMieux stood at a podium in front of 50 American flags, Crist put his arm around LeMieux and declared, "What a great United States Senator he's going to be."

Crist, LeMieux, Eikenberg, and Greer then toured the state. They went to Fort Lauderdale, LeMieux's hometown, where he was presented to the local Republicans, and then the delegation flew to Tampa for another rally.

During a private moment on the flight back to Tallahassee, Eikenberg said to Greer, "Have you ever seen anything crazier than what just happened?"

"Nope," said Greer. "Sure haven't.'

"How do you think this happened?" asked Eric.

"I don't know, Eric. I don't know."

But Greer did know.

"This whole situation became a running secret joke between Eric and me," recalled Greer. "After a couple of drinks, we would say what we thought, that LeMieux blackmailed Crist into appointing him.

"While George was in the Senate, one night we all went to dinner at Fogo de Chao restaurant in Washington. Eric was in the front seat of the sedan. George was in the back with me. George looked at me and said, 'You'll never know what I went through.'

"'I'm sure,' I said. Talking about the 2006 gubernatorial campaign, he said, 'It was a very stressful time in my life. Those gay eruptions could have kept us from being governor.'"

Greer recalls that exchange as the only time LeMieux ever acknowledged what he had done for Crist.

"Two times George LeMieux made it a point to tell me something in confidence. I never understood why. Once he told me why he was getting that $10,000 a month contract. He volunteered it one night. And now, in the back of the car, he was talking about 'those gay eruptions.' I guess he felt the need to tell me. Maybe it was just because we were becoming close friends. Maybe he was wondering, *What does Greer think of me?* I'll never know."

40

Now Marco Is Teflon

IN THE FALL OF 2009 WHILE RUBIO WAS CAMPAIGNING ACROSS THE LENGTH and breadth of Florida, Crist was in his bubble, convinced that as long as he raised enough money for TV and radio ads, no amount of person-to-person campaigning by Rubio could beat him.

But as party chairman, Greer saw that Rubio was winning all the county straw polls. He even won the straw poll among the Republican executive committee members of Pinellas County, Crist's home county.

The Crist campaign decided to run radio and TV ads that would position Rubio as less conservative than he claimed, citing his votes on tax increases and cap and trade, to name a couple. The purpose was to permit Crist to crow, "The real conservative in the race is Charlie Crist."

"The whole idea was to make Crist into more of a conservative," said Greer. "The governor had vetoed over $400 million of expenses in the state budget, and we stressed that."

The Crist campaign persuaded Marion Hammer, the Florida representative of the National Rifle Association, to make a public statement that Crist had a better rating and relationship with the NRA than Rubio did.

Greer doubted the strategy could erase from Republicans' memories Crist's public embrace of Barack Obama and the stimulus, but Crist pursued it anyway. Eventually, tired of the drumbeat of criticism that was flooding the blogosphere, he hounded Greer to do something.

"Get Rich Heffley and get him to set up an anonymous website to criticize Rubio," Crist kept telling Greer. Heffley had worked on Crist's campaign in 2006 and he was now a $5,000 a month consultant to the RPOF.

Greer told Heffley what the governor wanted him to do. "He was hesitant at first, but he did it." However, Heffley didn't cover his tracks well enough and the website was traced back to his computer. He was caught red-handed after weeks of blasting Rubio day after day, which infuriated Rubio and his supporters. Here was someone on the Republican Party of Florida payroll—someone who was supposed to be neutral—anonymously attacking Rubio in the Republican primary.

Even though he had pressed Greer to set up the site, Crist denied he had anything to do with it. "He threw Heffley and me under the bus," said Greer.

One of the decisions Crist approved was to hire a firm to do oppositional research on Marco Rubio, which meant digging into every facet of his life, both personal and professional. It would include a public records search done by a third party so no one would know who was behind it.

Stuart Stevens, a media/political consultant who had worked on Romney's presidential campaign, was hired. Stevens, whose job it was to figure out how to attack Rubio, found that Rubio as a legislator had voted for $800,000 in special interest legislation that paid for artificial turf on Miami ballfields where he himself had played flag football. He discovered that Rubio had gotten a six-figure salary at Florida International University as a part-time professor after he had voted for funding for the university as a member of the legislature.

"The research was showing that there were things in Rubio's background that questioned his conservatism," said Greer. "One of the other things he did was give his staff huge raises."

"Crist would get all revved up whenever Stevens came up with one of his gems," said Greer. "He always got animated when people suggested ways to take Rubio down."

But Greer was dubious because Rubio's following was so passionate.

"The problem was that no matter what Rubio might have done, the crazies in the Tea Party and the conservative voters refused to condemn him. When it was revealed that Rubio had charged thousands of dollars for personal expenses, including more thousands to fix up his home, on his RPOF American Express card, nobody cared."

Greer could see that the only way Crist was going to beat Rubio was to find a smoking gun.

That didn't happen. Rubio's transgressions were significant, but they had about the same impact as the proverbial tree falling in the forest.

The great irony was that all through his political career, Crist had been known as Teflon Charlie. Gay lovers? Didn't matter. A daughter out of wedlock? Who cares? No matter what his opponents threw at him, it just rolled off his back. Now, for the first time, a Crist opponent was getting the same treatment. Nothing Crist could throw at Marco Rubio was making a bit of difference.

Florida Republicans were falling in love with Marco Rubio.

IN FACT, THERE MIGHT have been a smoking gun, but Greer's basic decency prevented the Crist campaign from using it and perhaps destroying Rubio's marriage.

"There was an indication that Rubio had an affair," said Greer. "A woman who had worked in his legislative office when he was Speaker of the House abruptly left and got a job at Florida International University as a part-time professor. Emails she had sent him through her college account had become public record. Our opposition research specialist said the emails included things like, 'I have to talk to you right now. I can't take this anymore. Why aren't you returning my calls?'"

To an oppositional researcher the Crist campaign had hired, it appeared there had been a close relationship between the two and that Rubio had broken it off.

"The governor loved it," said Greer. "He wanted us to leak it to the media that Rubio had had an affair.'

Though Greer and Eikenberg resisted, Crist was adamant that Beth Reinhard of the *Miami Herald* be told about it.

Greer told Eikenberg, "I'm not going to tell Beth. You know, I've broken off relationships myself in the last 25 years. I've had girls write letters like that, so I know what they're saying. But there's no concrete evidence of an affair here. And even if there was, do we want to risk this girl losing her job, even if it was a job Rubio apparently got for her?'"

When Crist wouldn't let it go, he pushed Eikenberg to send Reinhard emails so she could start tracking the woman down. Reinhard, the smart reporter that she is, called Greer, but he refused to give Reinhard the ammunition she needed to nail Rubio. Greer also kept his furtiveness from Crist.

"Are we moving on that little situation with that girl in Miami?" Crist asked Greer.

"Yes, sir," said Greer, "but I don't think there's anything really there."

"Where there's smoke, there's fire, Chairman," said Crist.

Greer had extinguished the fire before it could get started.

"WE THREW A LOT at Rubio, but nothing stuck. In the 2010 debates, Charlie would state, 'I'm the true conservative in this race.' He said the same thing in his ads. When I'd watch the ads on TV, I'd laugh out loud.

"In the debate Charlie would say, 'Mr. Rubio, I didn't have a Republican Party American Express card, and I didn't put thousands of dollars on my American Express card for groceries, or at a liquor store, or for having my wife's van repaired.'"

Looking on, Greer was thinking to himself, *No you didn't, Governor. You had me do it.*

"During the debates he also went after the fact that Rubio had authorized the spending of $800,000 on artificial turf, and he questioned the high-paying teaching job Rubio had been given at Florida International University," said Greer. "Charlie talked about the big salaries Rubio gave his staff—all things a true Republican conservative wouldn't do.

"All Rubio would say in his defense was, 'When you're a legislator, you have to vote for legislation that includes things you don't like. But I'm conservative, and you're not. You're the one who helped President Obama. You're the one who couldn't wait to get the stimulus money.'"

Rubio's linking of Crist to Obama and the stimulus was enough to kill any enthusiasm for Crist by most conservatives who knew that Rubio had been officially anointed by Jeb Bush to be the party's "true conservative."

"An important point known to most Florida Republicans," said Greer, "was that Bush had announced when he left office as governor that Rubio was his successor as the leading conservative. He even presented Rubio with a ceremonial sword on the floor of the Florida House of Representatives. The sword was intended to anoint him 'my subject to carry on what I've been doing as a conservative.'"

As a result Greer knew that trying to paint Rubio as a moderate wouldn't get the Crist campaign any traction.

"It failed miserably," said Greer. "One night I told Eric, 'If we went to a Republican Executive Committee meeting and told them that Rubio had voted to raise taxes, that he put liberal judges on the court, that he was the worst thing to ever to happen to Florida, and then they took a poll, Rubio would still beat Charlie Crist.'

"I said, 'They love him, Eric. They hate Charlie. They have lost all respect for Charlie because of Obama and the stimulus. They are obsessed with their hatred for Barack Obama and anybody who's in support of him. They're going after Charlie.

"'Marco Rubio is their symbol of what the Republican Party should be.'"

41

Good Advice Not Taken

With George LeMieux headed for the U.S. Senate, Charlie Crist would no longer have "The Maestro" to advise him. The person who would replace LeMieux as his right-hand man, Crist decided, would be his hand-picked chairman of the Republican Party of Florida, Jim Greer.

"Remember," said Greer, "Charlie still didn't have a campaign manager—he was set to hire Eikenberg but hadn't done it yet. I had been filling that role."

Greer also met in Washington with Mitch Bainwol, chairman and CEO of the Recording Industry Association of America. Bainwol had been Senator Bill Frist's chief of staff and before that had been a budget analyst for Ronald Reagan. He and Crist had been friends for years.

"Mitch was becoming Charlie's adviser," said Greer. "Wherever we were, Charlie was always talking on the phone to Mitch. He'd say, 'I talked to Mitch last night. Mitch thinks we ought to . . .'"

That Crist was listening to someone else didn't bother Greer. He just wished that Bainwol wasn't so far away. "I liked Mitch," said Greer. "I had no problem with Mitch. He had political experience. He had worked for Connie Mack Sr., as Charlie had. But Mitch was in Washington and giving Charlie advice about Florida. He didn't realize the inroads Rubio was making into the hearts and minds of Republican Floridians."

"'You don't have to worry about the grass-roots,' Mitch was advising Charlie initially. 'Just keep raising money.'

"Mitch called me occasionally. When Charlie went to see Mitch in Washington, I'd go with him. I give Mitch some credit for giving Charlie good advice. And he did come to realize we needed more than money.

"Bainwol would tell him, 'Charlie, have you put together a policy paper on the economy? Have you framed your position on the federal reserve?'

Charlie would say, 'No no, I haven't done that yet, Mitch, but those are good ideas. I'll get to it.' So Charlie was hearing this from people other than me, although when he got back to the office, he'd never do it."

Bainwol, like Greer, was concerned about the lack of a manager for Crist's campaign.

"Eric had been designated to leave his position as chief of staff and come over to become the Senate campaign manager," recalled Greer. "But once Charlie made the decision to do that, Charlie would have to start paying him. He had been waiting as long as he could before bringing Eric over to run the campaign."

As SUMMER TURNED INTO fall Bainwol was beginning to see that Crist's campaign was in trouble. "I'm getting reports in Florida," he'd say to Greer, "that things aren't going as well as Charlie is telling me. He's too focused on money."

Greer acknowledged the problems even as he tried to reassure Bainwol they would be overcome. Privately, he knew "it was a rudderless ship that was making major decisions over martinis. That's not how you run a successful Senate campaign."

Greer was not being paid by the campaign but he was Crist's constant traveling companion as they sought funds for the campaign. There was another financial reason for Crist to take Greer with him: as long as Greer was along, Crist could justify having the Republican Party of Florida pick up the tab. "He would often hand me the bill at the end of an event and say, 'The party is going to take care of this, right, Chairman?'"

Greer's devotion to Crist was beginning to bring undue attention from his conservative critics who didn't want the party chairman supporting a particular candidate in a contested Republican primary for a U.S. Senate seat, especially when the other Republican candidate was Marco Rubio.

"There were people in Tallahassee," said Greer, "who did not believe I should be traveling with the governor when he was campaigning. There were mumblings and rumors."

Greer was taken aback when Haley Barbour, the head of the Republican

Governors Association and a veteran campaigner, expressed his concern about all the time Greer was giving to the Crist campaign.

"Haley is hearing that the grass-roots are upset with your support of Charlie," Bainwol said to Greer. "Haley says you need to resign as chairman and come over to the campaign full time or quit the campaign."

This was the "aha" moment for Greer, the moment when he should have taken Barbour's advice. But Greer was sure Barbour had an ulterior motive. He knew that Barbour and Crist didn't like each other.

Greer went to the governor's mansion and told Crist what Haley Barbour had said about him.

"Fuck Haley Barbour," said Crist, "and tell him to keep his nose out of Florida."

"I don't think I'll tell him that," replied Greer. "I'll just ignore the advice."

It was a serious mistake. Greer was too public a figure to do work for Governor Crist without notice. By continuing to work for Crist, Greer was siding with the governor against the entire Tea Party movement. The tsunami was coming and Greer was not moving to higher ground.

Greer, ignoring Bainwol's advice, accompanied Crist on a fundraising trip to California, Colorado, and Nevada. He might have escaped unscathed had he chosen to be less visible, but before that trip, Greer had become even more of a national figure when on July 30, 2009, he was elected the chairman of the Standing Committee on Rules by the Republican National Committee.

Recalled Greer, "I had been to the Republican National Committee meeting in San Diego. I was co-chairman of Michael Steele's transition team, and he had asked me what role I would like to play in the RNC. I told him I wanted to head the Standing Committee on Rules, the group that handles the penalties and the scheduling of the primaries. It was a position of power, somewhat prestigious, and it would be a good, good thing for Florida."

To celebrate Greer's ascension to the post, Delmar Johnson announced that he, Brett Prader, and Kirk Pepper were treating Greer to a round of golf at the famed Torrey Pines Golf Course by the cliffs overlooking the Pacific Ocean in LaJolla, California.

"I was on top of the world," said Greer. "That was the high point. I was traveling with Charlie, and we believed we were going to win the Senate race."

Greer's victory in San Diego was followed by a visit to Las Vegas to meet with billionaire casino owner Sheldon Adelson, who was hosting a fundraiser for Crist.

"Lisa flew in from Florida with our kids," said Greer. "Charlie was there, and Carole and her girls joined us. We were all to stay at Adelson's Venetian Resort Hotel Casino. That evening around six, we went up to Adelson's three-bedroom penthouse suite. The governor went with body-guards. Adelson had his own bodyguards. As you entered, you could see glass doors that opened onto a huge balcony overlooking the Las Vegas strip and west to the mountains. It was a clear, clear evening. The governor and I walked onto the balcony and watched an orange sun set behind the mountains. We were so high up it felt like we were part of the mountains. I told Lisa later it was the most gorgeous sunset I've ever seen."

Crist spoke briefly, thanked everyone for being there, and then everyone left. Charlie, Carole, and Greer had dinner that night at the elegant steak house in the Venetian Hotel. They sat at a corner table. Crist began telling Greer that things at the governor's office weren't going well.

"I'm not happy with Eric as the campaign manager," said Crist, and he began asking whether Greer would join the campaign.

Greer should have said yes. This was yet another chance to save himself from a great deal of heartache. But he loved his job as chairman too much.

WHEN THAT CONVERSATION ENDED, Carole began talking about what Re-publicans in Florida needed to do.

"She told us that the Republicans just needed to start accepting abor-tions," said Greer. "They needed to stop being pro-life, and they should embrace Obama more. She basically eradicated every difference there was between the Republican Party and the Democrats. She went on about how well Michelle Obama dressed, how the Republican Party was totally off the mark on its positions, and how 'Charlie needs to be more like Obama.'"

Greer, flabbergasted, didn't know what to say.

"We were in the heart of a U.S. Senate race," said Greer. "We were being attacked everywhere. We were losing the straw polls. People were starting to rear their heads and endorse Marco Rubio, and here was Carole talking this crazy talk."

Greer saw how much she was influencing Charlie and how much difficulty it was causing him. "She was a *bad* influence," said Greer. "I had seen it before, but on this night she was really off the charts."

AFTER THE TRIP TO Las Vegas, Charlie, Carole, Jim, and Lisa went to California for a week of vacation. Crist and Greer then left their wives for a short trip to Aspen, Colorado, where Brent Sembler, the son of Ambassador Mel Sembler of St. Petersburg, Florida, was hosting a fundraiser for Charlie's campaign. Brent had been in the same fraternity as Crist at Florida State University.

"We flew to Aspen. I couldn't believe how beautiful it was," said Greer. "Brent Sembler's home was a rustic home in downtown Aspen. Over 300 people were there. I didn't speak, but Brent got up and talked about Charlie. People wrote checks, and we left."

They then flew to New York for a fundraiser at the home of Woody Johnson, the millionaire owner of the New York Jets, and then flew back across the country for a fundraiser at the home of California Governor Arnold Schwarzenegger and his wife Maria Schriver. Lisa Spies, Crist's national fundraiser, had worked out a deal with Schwarzenegger's fundraiser to host the event at the "Governator's" home.

"We went out by the pool," recalled Greer. "Arnold had a cabana, with a big-screen TV and big couches, where he smoked his cigars. Arnold took Charlie and me for a tour of the house. Maria is John F. Kennedy's niece, so there were pictures everywhere of all the Kennedy kids. I thought how neat it was. Maria didn't come down until the end of the event. She looked very agitated at having to be there and host the event. She went to the cabana, had her picture taken with Arnold, Charlie, and Carole, and then she returned to the house."

Other than that, said Greer, "everything was great."

Great, that is, until Greer got home to Florida to face stinging criticism because Charlie's fundraising for his Senate campaign meant a corresponding lack of fundraising for the Republican Party of Florida.

"At the peak we were spending $500,000 every month to run the party," said Greer. "I got it down to $200,000 a month, but still, I had to pay staff and I had to pay the mortgage on the building. After Charlie became a Senate candidate in May, he stopped having any interest in raising any money for the Republican Party, and this was a blow because the governor is the major fundraiser for the state party.

"He just didn't care. He was all about his Senate campaign. He raised $4.3 million in the first quarter of his own campaign and hardly anything for the RPOF. As a result, the party was going broke."

The grass-roots state committee members were starting to complain. They'd say to Greer, "Crist is no longer raising money for us. Jim, you used to tell us we should put up with his shit because he's out raising millions of dollars for us. Well, Jim, he's not even doing that anymore."

Greer would schedule fundraising events for Crist to attend, but three or four days before the event, Crist would say, "Something came up." Or, "Chairman, you need to find other methods of raising money for the party because I need to focus on my Senate race."

Greer would say, "Governor, there is no other method. You're it. Nobody is going to give 50 grand to talk to me."

By August 2009 the situation was growing drastic. Greer had been doing everything he could to keep gubernatorial candidate Bill McCollum from usurping Crist's position as the number one Florida Republican, but Crist's refusal to raise money for the party was forcing Greer to rely more and more on McCollum.

"Without any money coming in, I had to go to Bill McCollum's people and beg them to make a contribution of about $75,000 a month from their campaign just to keep the party going," said Greer.

The result was a major shift in power from Crist and Greer to McCollum, the front-running Republican candidate for governor.

"It shifted who was calling the shots," recalled Greer. "Now they were able to say, 'We're paying for the lights, so don't tell me that Charlie Crist is in charge of this party.' When I attended meetings with McCollum, they would start telling me things rather than asking me. I could understand why—they were having to keep the party going."

Greer was also having to borrow money from the House and Senate campaign funds, and that was making the legislators nervous. State House and Senate leaders were telling Greer, "Hey, Chairman, we don't mind your borrowing from us, because we've borrowed from you in the past, but will you guarantee us that the governor will raise enough funds to replenish the money we need for elections next year?"

Greer was powerless to extricate himself from being caught in the middle. He knew Crist wasn't interested in raising more money, but he couldn't tell the House and Senate leaders that.

"Absolutely," said Greer, throwing caution to the wind, "Absolutely."

Said Greer, "We were drawing down the money we had in the House and Senate campaign accounts, and they were getting pissed off. They had raised half a million dollars. Three weeks later they were told by finance that 'the general party has used a hundred grand of your money to make payroll last week.'"

Dean Cannon came to see Greer, as did Senate President Mike Haridopolos. Each said point blank, "Chairman, you're spending our money. Is the governor not raising any money for the party anymore?"

Once again, Greer had to choose between his loyalty to Crist and his good sense. "Yes, he is," Greer equivocated. "We're going to do something next month."

By September 2009 the pressure on Greer from Senate and House leaders brought him to demand a clear-the-air sit-down with Crist over his refusal to raise money for the party. Greer called Eikenberg to set it up.

"Eric," Greer said, "I have to have a serious conversation with him tonight. They are all over me. They know he's not raising money for the party. They know it takes $200,000 a month to operate this party. They know I'm having to live off the Senate and House money. I've been fighting this for a year. They hate me. They hate him. And the Rubio people on the budget committee are now calling the chief financial officer demanding numbers."

Greer later found out there was a snitch in the party finance office feeding Rubio information about the party's financial condition. So Rubio knew the numbers, and he meant to crucify Crist and Greer with them.

At the meeting with Crist, Greer said, "Governor, we were scheduled to do an event in June to raise money for the party, and you canceled it. We scheduled another event, and you canceled that one. I've got to have help."

Eikenberg was sitting in on the meeting, but even though he was Greer's buddy, he didn't go out on the limb for him. Rather he sat there quietly.

Crist stopped Greer in mid-sentence.

"Fuck the party, Jim," Crist said. "I don't give a shit about the party. What do you call those people, Jim? Wackadoos? They're a bunch of wackadoos, Chairman. I've got to win a U.S. Senate race here. So you're going to have to find some other way to solve this problem."

Greer thought, *I'm going to get run out of town on a rail.*

42

A Mess

Jim Greer left the mansion angry. "That didn't happen often, but there were times when Charlie'd get frustrated with me, or I'd get mad because he'd shut me down," said Greer.

"The next day he called me, and he acted like the night before hadn't happened. 'Hey Chairman,' he said, 'I know you're in a tough bind over there. Put some things together for me, and I'll do them.'"

Greer, summoning false hope, organized an event at Wake Forest on a day Florida State was to play football at Wake Forest. Crist had always said he was once a quarterback at Wake Forest—he had gone to school there for a short time.

"According to some media reports, that turned out not to be true," said Greer, "but Charlie used it for years in every campaign."

Delmar Johnson arranged for a private box at the Wake Forest stadium, and lobbyists were to pay $10,000 to sit with the governor at the game. Three days before the event, Charlie backed out. "Something's come up," he said.

Once again Crist was putting Greer in an embarrassing, difficult position.

"I had to lie and not tell the lobbyists he wasn't coming until the last minute," said Greer. "I still wanted to get their money. It's a terrible thing, but there are times when a politician cancels and only the fundraiser knows. Unless the event is a long way off, you have to hold it. Then you make an announcement, 'We've had an emergency. The governor's plane couldn't be here tonight.'"

At the same time Greer was being lambasted for not raising enough money for the party, he continued to be under fire for spending too much time working for Crist's senatorial campaign. The Tea Party scolds and other conservatives were complaining bitterly.

Crist, contemptuous of the Tea Party 'wackadoos,' could not have cared less about the problems the party was facing. But why he wasn't more considerate of the difficult position he put Greer in was a different matter. If Crist thought his relationship with Greer was a problem, you wouldn't have known it. In fact, it seemed that Crist was doing all he could to make it obvious that Greer was mostly campaigning for him.

For one thing, Crist began insisting that Greer introduce him at every fundraiser or rally. Crist generally wasn't happy with the amateur introductions offered by his hosts. "When you're dealing with donors at their homes, some of them aren't very savvy," said Greer. "A lot of them knew Charlie from the old days, when he was attorney general or state senator, and they were very casual in their introductions. We went to an event in Broward County. There were a hundred people in this home. The host got up and said, 'I want to thank everyone for being here tonight, and we have Charlie. Charlie come up here and say a few words.'"

At the end of the event, Crist sarcastically said to the host, "That was a hell of an introduction."

Said Greer, "I knew as soon as we got in the car that I'd hear his favorite line, 'What the fuck was that?' He liked the way I introduced him. He wanted to hear the build-up I always gave him, with words like 'high approval ratings,' 'Cato Institute support,' 'conservative governor of the year,' 'lowering property taxes,' and 'fighting for the people.'

"Whenever I'd introduce him, he'd say, 'Chairman, a great introduction. No one does it better than you.' After the Broward event he said he wanted me to introduce him at all the events from then on. Some hosts got irritated at this, which I can understand. It's your house, and you should decide how things go.

"Also, everything coming out of my mouth was supposed to be neutral, and here I was at a Republican event building up Crist, who was just one candidate in a Republican primary. If we were holding a big rally, I'd do it up big. I had a great knack for motivating a crowd. I'd drag out my remarks a little bit, build to a crescendo, and by the time I introduced Charlie, those people would be on their feet. They'd be whooping and hollering."

BUT BY BOOSTING SENATE candidate Crist, RPOF Chairman Greer was doing himself no favors. And what he did next was even more self-destructive.

Greer had gotten nowhere finding someone to take Meredith O'Rourke's place as RPOF fundraiser. She had been let go, but she was still being paid $5,000 a month, and potential fundraising candidates would ask, 'Is Meredith still on the payroll? What will be her involvement?' When they found out she was, they would decline to take the job because they didn't feel they could do their work with her still around, given her cutthroat reputation.

One day LeMieux suggested, "Jim, why don't you and Delmar Johnson take over fundraising and pay yourself a commission?"

"George was the first person to raise that with me," said Greer. "I had interviewed all these people for the job, and nobody wanted it. I told George I would think about it and then I told Delmar about George's idea."

Greer also discussed his taking over fundraising for the party with Harry Sargeant and Jay Burmer.

"No one saw anything wrong with it," said Greer. "In addition to his being executive director, Delmar could also focus on fundraising. We would pay ourselves a 10 percent commission, which would be considerably less than the $30,000 a month we had been paying Meredith."

With O'Rourke out of the picture, Greer had been able to set up some of the small fundraisers that she had rejected. One was a Charlie Crist golf tournament—small potatoes, she had said. At the golf tournament, Greer confirmed with Crist that he and Johnson had agreed to take over the party fundraising with a 10 percent commission. "Charlie shook my hand, and said, 'You'll do a good job, Chairman. You deserve it.'"

Crist later denied this conversation ever happened. But Sargeant, Brian Ballard, and Burmer swore that Crist was aware of Greer and Johnson taking over fundraising and being paid a commission.

Greer and Johnson formed a corporation, Victory Strategies, to do the fundraising. They did it for tax purposes and also for the future when he and Delmar Johnson would open a political consulting firm.

"I thought Victory Strategies was a great name for a consulting firm," said Greer. Later he would be accused of forming the corporation for the express purpose of concealing its existence, but nothing could be further from the truth.

MEANWHILE, THE LEGION OF Crist and Greer enemies continued to grow. A Tea Party activist continued to feed Rubio information that the Florida Republican Party was living off the House and Senate money and that the governor had stopped raising money for the party. Now they were learning that Greer, the RPOF chairman, and Johnson, his executive director, had a contract to become the party's fundraisers.

A crescendo of criticism rang out. Not all of it was fair. The Tea Party critics, looking for any nit to pick, were loudly complaining that the Charlie Crist Senate campaign was renting space on the third floor of the RPOF building.

"Just like the Bill McCollum campaign was renting space on the second floor," said Greer. "I wasn't giving it to Charlie for free. But some of the state committee people were just pissed off Crist was there. When they'd phone and complain, my staff would tell them, 'They're paying us four grand a month.' They didn't care."

Greer started getting complaint letters from Tea Party types on the county Republican Executive Committees from around the state. "The letters would say, 'It has come to our attention that the Republican Party of Florida is in dire financial condition. You have to cut costs, eliminate staff positions. Your fundraising is down.' Then they'd tell me what the real issue was, that I, as chairman of the party, was assisting Crist in his campaign against Rubio, and that that was a violation of party rules."

Greer would go to the mansion and talk to Crist about the situation.

"How are things going?" Crist would ask.

"Not good," Greer would say. "I got a letter from the Hillsborough County chairman today, and she's demanding an audit of the party finances and that I stop doing anything with you."

"Man," Crist would say, "I feel sorry for you. I don't know how you do it, Chairman. I don't know how you put up with those people."

CRIST, IT SEEMED, WAS living in his own bubble. To him, everything was hunky-dory. To everyone else, including Greer, Crist's campaign appeared to be the *Hindenburg* as it was about to dock in New Jersey.

By early November 2009, Pablo Diaz, Crist's grass-roots director, looked ready to jump off the Skyway Bridge. "He was so depressed," said Greer. "Anytime I went to see Pablo, he'd say, 'Oh, Chairman, it's bad. It's terrible. I don't know.' 'Pablo,' I'd say, 'Take the noose from around your neck and calm down. What is wrong exactly?'

"'I'll tell you what's wrong,' he'd say. 'The Sarasota County chairman just sent me a letter telling me that Charlie Crist isn't welcome at their local REC meetings. What are we going to do? How can I run field operations? This is terrible. They call me up every day . . .'"

Recalled Greer, "Pablo was always a bundle of nerves. He didn't handle stress well. You could see it on his face. About every third day you had to talk Pablo down from the ledge as we neared the end of 2009."

Andrea Saul, Crist's press secretary, wasn't faring much better.

"Andrea was trying to respond to press inquiries on the national level," said Greer, "and Charlie wasn't giving her the attention she needed. Charlie hardly ever came by the campaign office. There was just a disconnect."

It was the same with Eric Eikenberg. "Eric and I went to lunch at a Mexican restaurant in Tallahassee," recalled Greer, "and I will never forget it. Eric, who wasn't much of a drinker, ordered a margarita. That's okay if you're playing golf, or if it's Friday afternoon. But when it's a Tuesday for lunch? I said, 'Eric, what's wrong?'

"'I'm the campaign manager,' he said, 'and I can't even get the governor to return my calls. I left a message for him yesterday—a group wanted to meet with him. He never called me back.' He sat there the rest of the afternoon and drank with me."

Things had gotten so bad by late 2009—Crist was refusing to acknowledge that his Senate campaign was going badly and worse was refusing to do anything about it—that he and Mitch Bainwol had a falling out.

"Mitch called me at home," recalled Greer, "and he said, 'I just want to let you know, I don't know if I'm going to be around. You may not be talking to me any more, because I'm getting ready to tell Charlie how fucked up his campaign is, and how he's going to lose this thing if he doesn't get his head out of his ass.' The next day I was in the car with Charlie as we headed to an event, and I put a teaser out there: 'I think I'll call Mitch and see what he thinks,' I said.

"'No need to call Mitch,' Charlie replied. 'Let's lay off talking to Mitch for a while.' Then I knew they were no longer talking. He had shut Mitch out of his world, even though they had been friends for years. But that's what Charlie did. If you told him something he didn't like, you were put on suspension from the team."

THINGS AT THE CRIST for Senate campaign headquarters became even more bizarre when one day a man named Dan (Greer can't remember his last name) showed up. Dan told Eikenberg he was a college friend of Crist's.

"When things get tough," said Greer, "Charlie has a habit of going back to buddies he's known in years past. They may not have a clue what's going on or be in our same world, but Charlie reaches out for people. It's like going back to an ex-girlfriend."

So this Dan, a real estate guy, a lawyer by trade, showed up, and Greer told Eikenberg that he knew nothing about the guy. Eric, a little paranoid at this point, said, "He says he's from Atlanta and that Charlie asked him to come down and help with the campaign. I bet he's here to replace me."

"Eric," Greer said, "I'm being totally honest with you. The governor has never expressed any frustrations with you."

Recalled Greer, "Actually, he had, but never to the point of firing Eric."

Greer called the governor asked him about Dan, and Crist said, "He's an old college buddy. Good friend, trustworthy. A hard worker. I've asked him to come down and work in the campaign."

"Between you and me, Governor, are you thinking of making a change?" asked Greer.

"No. Not at this time."

Greer knew, of course, that in the world of politics, that meant *Yes, I am, just not now.*

"A campaign has a structure, and it becomes a problem when the candidate's buddy comes down and says he wants to help out," said Greer. "Nobody understands why he's there. He hadn't been hired for a specific job. He was just there 'to help out.' It was yet another example of how disorganized this mess was. Now Eric was unsure whether he was supposed to run things past Dan. What the hell did this guy Dan have to do in the campaign?"

One thing Greer saw: the mysterious Dan was talking to Charlie every night. "Charlie had a habit of calling a lot of people in the evenings, and he liked to have people out there letting him know what was going on," said Greer. "I think Dan was brought in for two reasons: I suspect Charlie had the idea of eventually replacing Eric. And I think Dan's primary purpose was to be a presence at campaign headquarters so he could feed information to Charlie about anyone perceived to be disloyal."

Ironically, it didn't take long for Dan to see how bad things were, and he became an advocate for those who were wanting Crist to right the ship.

"He talked to me about how sorry the state of affairs was," said Greer. "Dan said, 'This is not Eric's fault. It's not your fault. This is Charlie's fault.' One of the things Dan would ask was, 'Is all this coming from Carole? Is all this because of her?'

"Dan had been warning Charlie that there were a lot of problems and that he needed to be calling Eric back more often. 'You guys should be talking five times a day,' he'd tell him. And Charlie reacted as he always does. When he found out Dan was speaking his mind, he'd say he didn't need this shit. Dan never had a role, and the governor was never prepared to give him a paid position. After a while we noticed that Dan wasn't talking to Charlie nearly as much. Dan eventually left and went back to Atlanta.

But Dan was right, said Greer—"Charlie's campaign was really fucked up."

43

STILL IN THE BUBBLE

WHEN THE GRASS-ROOTS ACTIVISTS WHO ATTENDED THE MONTHLY MEET-ings of the county Republican executive committees began talking about holding straw polls on the upcoming Senate race, Greer knew it was trouble. As noted earlier, Crist lost the one held in his home county of Pinellas.

The straw polls were especially ominous for Crist, Greer understood, because the people who voted in them were the same passionate Republicans who voted in primaries.

When Greer learned that Pasco County planned a straw poll in early September 2009, he phoned Chairman Bill Bunting because Bunting had always supported Crist. Sure that Rubio would trounce Crist, Greer asked Bunting to call off the poll. "No," said Bunting, who made it clear he no longer was supporting Crist, "People want the poll. Nothing wrong with having a straw poll."

The outcome of the Pasco County straw poll was Marco Rubio 73, Charlie Crist 9.

As more counties held straw polls, the results were similar. Rubio beat Crist in Pasco, Broward, and Duval (Jacksonville) counties—one domino after another.

"We didn't even have field staff enough to send to the county meetings to work the rooms," said Greer. "People were holding up Rubio's signs in the back of the meeting rooms. We didn't have anybody because the governor refused to organize his campaign, and he didn't want to spend money."

Crist's grass-roots director, Pablo Diaz, was increasingly depressed because he couldn't hire field reps to work with volunteers in the counties.

"Rubio had an army of such volunteers who would work almost as hard as paid staff," said Greer. "The ones we had were merely passing on information about things going in their counties. And they were warning us that Charlie had big problems in their counties."

After Crist lost the straw poll in Pinellas, Greer urged him, "You've got to get out in the field. You've got to let me hire three or four field reps."

On top of losing the straw polls, county chairs and state committee members began openly telling the press why they were no longer supporting Charlie Crist. They said he wasn't Republican enough. He had supported the stimulus. He had his photo taken with Obama. He's an Obama lover.

Through it all, Greer felt that Crist continued to stick his head in the sand.

"These people are just a bunch of wackadoos," Crist would say.

"Many of them *were* weirdos," said Greer, "but we were trying to win a Republican primary, not the general election. Again and again I told Charlie, 'You've got to move more to the right. You've got to offer them red meat. You have to attend these REC meetings. You can't keep losing these county straw polls which are showing lack of support within your own party.'"

AWARE THAT THE CAMPAIGN was in free fall, Greer called together all the major players in the Crist camp—among them Stuart Stevens, Jim Rimes, Rich Heffley, and Eric Eikenberg. They met on September 13, 2009, in Orlando. Greer had asked everyone to bring positive ideas. He told Crist about the meeting.

"Remember there still was no campaign manager," said Greer. "Eric Eikenberg wasn't given permission to move over from the governor's staff until December."

Ten of Crist's people sat around the conference room. "It felt like a meeting to kick off a campaign," said Greer.

Stevens, who had worked for W. and Romney and had been hired by Crist as media/political adviser, said in his slow Southern drawl, "I think we have real problems here. We're not out campaigning like we need to be, and we need to start focusing on and discussing policy issues." Everyone in the group, of course, recognized that Crist had been averse to discussing policy issues.

RPOF Chairman Greer should not have been chairing that meeting along with Eikenberg. Greer should have remained neutral. But blinded by his loyalty to Crist, he couldn't help himself. In a way, Greer was operating in his own bubble. For months he had been attacked for his support, primarily because the members of the ultra-conservative Tea Party despised Crist.

In any case, Greer's convening of the meeting of all the senior advisers to the Crist Senate campaign was a first. In that meeting, the participants composed a campaign action plan, discussed the campaign's message to voters, and outlined Rubio's strengths and weaknesses. But what the advisers mostly wanted to discuss were the shortcomings of their candidate: Crist's lack of engagement in the campaign and his resistance to formulating any national policy positions. Everyone wanted Crist to step up his game while there was still time.

"Just having that meeting gave me hope that we were getting somewhere," said Greer.

GREER SAW THAT STEVENS, who had gotten so much of Crist's attention early in his hire, was now getting less and less of Crist's attention. The governor was perturbed that Stevens was complaining about Crist's lack of involvement in his own campaign. The governor began saying things like "we don't need to talk to Stuart" about whatever might have come up.

"Again, anybody not seeing the picture the way Charlie did was not going to be on the inside," said Greer. "He started ignoring Stuart. I'd tell him things Stuart said to me, and he just wasn't interested in hearing them."

Meanwhile Bill McCollum, the leading Republican candidate to succeed Crist as governor, kept pestering Greer to get Charlie and Carole Crist to donate $500 each to his campaign. Even though McCollum despised Crist, McCollum wanted the governor's public endorsement demonstrated by a contribution.

"I don't want to," said Crist, "I think he's goofy. I don't think he's one of us, Chairman. We'll do it, but I want you to ask him for a contribution to my campaign."

Charlie and Carole each wrote $500 checks to McCollum.

A few days later Greer ran into McCollum in the hallway outside his office. "General, can I speak to you for a minute," said Greer. "The governor is asking whether you can make that contribution to his Senate campaign."

"Oh oh no," replied McCollum, "I just don't think I can do that. There are problems out there with Charlie and the base of the party. If they find out I've given him a contribution, it would cause me problems. You know I'm with Charlie, but I've got to win my race, and so I just can't do it."

When Greer reported the conversation to Crist, the governor said, "Fuck him," Crist said. "I hope he loses."

In the fall of 2009 Greer visited the Crists at Fisher Island. As Greer sat out by the Jacuzzi on Saturday morning reading the paper and eating breakfast, Crist sat down next to him. Greer's phone rang. It was former Congressman Tom Feeney from Seminole County. Feeney had been Jeb Bush's running mate for lieutenant governor the time he lost. Though Feeney was ultraconservative, he and Greer were close friends from the same hometown of Oviedo.

"He said, 'Jim, I just want you to know, the conservatives are really upset. The base of the party has had it with Charlie. And you're too close to him. I'm giving you some friendly advice. They're coming after you, Jim, if you don't distance yourself from Charlie.'"

Crist was sitting across from Greer, so Greer replied, "Tom, I appreciate your calling me, but the governor is doing good things."

When Greer got off the phone, Crist asked who was calling.

"That was Tom Feeney," said Greer.

"What was he telling you? To get away from me?"

"Well, yeah," said Greer. "That's exactly what he was telling me. He said they're getting tired of you, Governor, after some of the decisions you've made, and they're coming after me."

"Chairman," said Crist, firmly ensconced in his bubble, "Don't you worry about it. I'm the governor, and you're the chairman of the party. And we're doing great things for Florida. And we're going to be going to Washington together, so don't let that call bother you one bit."

LATER THAT FALL GREER flew to Washington to meet with John Cornyn, the chairman of the Republican Senatorial Campaign Committee. Crist had asked Greer to find out whether the committee was still behind his candidacy.

"I sat in Senator Cornyn's beautiful office with elegant chandeliers and flags behind his desk," said Greer. "He was wearing boots embossed with the seal of Texas."

"Senator," said Greer, "it's a pleasure to be here. You know I'm the chairman of the Republican Party of Florida and a big supporter of Charlie Crist.'

"That must be causing you a lot of stress," said Cornyn.

"It causes a lot of difficulties holding down both jobs," said Greer, "but Governor Crist will be a great senator. The reason I'm here, Senator, is that you've been very supportive of the governor, but recently your press releases have tended to praise Marco Rubio. That's concerning to the campaign."

"Yes, we're still with Charlie," Cornyn said, "but Charlie is giving us concern as well."

Recalled Greer, "When he said that, I knew we had problems and possibly were going to lose our biggest asset, the endorsement of the Senatorial Campaign Committee. Although Cornyn denied any change in endorsement and said positive things, he told me, 'Rubio is a great guy. He's the future of the Republican Party. We're behind Charlie, but we're not against Rubio.' When they say stuff like that, you know things are falling apart."

Greer returned to Florida and told Crist about the meeting.

Crist again refused to take the negativity seriously. "It's all going to be fine, Chairman," he said. "We've raised a lot of money."

GREER, MEANWHILE, WAS BEING attacked viciously and often by the Rubio people—the Tea Partiers—on the Republican Executive Board. The board had 32 members. Fifteen supported Rubio. As others had before them, they were calling for Greer to distance himself from the Crist campaign or quit as chairman. They also requested that the Crist campaign leave the Republican Party headquarters building in Tallahassee.

"I certainly wasn't going to resign," said Greer. "And I again tried to explain that the Crist campaign was paying rent. But it didn't matter. They didn't care."

The Tea Party's other major concern was the RPOF's finances, which indeed were in dire straits. The party was living off money raised by the House and Senate Republicans, and though Crist constantly promised to raise money for them, he never did.

Crist had promised Greer that he would attend RPOF fundraising events so Greer set up one at a University of Florida football game. Crist didn't show. Greer organized a fundraiser on the presidential yacht in Washington. Crist canceled.

"It happened time and time again," said Greer.

Then Crist's tune changed, putting Greer in an even more dire position. He started telling Greer, "It's really up to Bill McCollum to raise money for the party now. He's the guy. As the presumptive nominee, it's his responsibility to raise the money."

Greer would reply, "McCollum is contributing to the party each month. Governor, you've asked me to make sure McCollum doesn't take over the party, and now you're opening the door for him. If he starts raising money for the party, eventually he'll want a say in how the party runs."

"Yeah, you're right," Crist would say. "We'll do something. Put something together, Chairman."

And Greer would set something up, but Crist would never come through.

One time while Greer and Eikenberg were in a car together, Eric said, "Jim, you were almost pleading with him tonight to raise money for you."

"I know," said Greer, "he doesn't get that he's our number one fundraiser for the party. If he doesn't become engaged soon, then the wolves at the door will take over."

"I was so irritated," said Greer, "Charlie just didn't care anything about the party any more, and in effect was telling me: *I don't care anything about you. I know they're getting ready to lynch you, and best of luck. Now, let's talk about my Senate campaign.*"

44

A Toxic Partnership

As 2009 came to a close, and as Rubio and the Tea Party were gain-ing strength with their anti-government, anti-Obama, anti-Charlie Crist messages, the pressures on Crist intensified.

On the campaign trail with Crist, Greer noticed that the governor was drinking too much; one of the worst effects was that often he would be late for appointments. "There were times we would drink until the early afternoon when we were supposed to be somewhere at six or seven," said Greer. "There were many times when we'd be flying to some fundraising event and Charlie would down two bottles of red wine. Then, after we landed and checked into a hotel, he'd say, 'Let's go get a beer at the bar.' Or he'd say, 'I'm exhausted. I'm going to take a nap.'

"He was also often late because he and Carole had overslept. They never cared much about other people's schedules. He was never down in the lobby when he was supposed to be. Sometimes the staff would argue: 'Who's going to knock on his suite door?' If we were on a trip and Dane Eagle, his travel aide, was along, I'd tell Dane, 'We're supposed to be leaving now. The cars are here. Have you heard from him?' And Dane would say no. And some-times Dane would text back, 'He won't be ready for another 30 minutes.'

"A governor can do what he wants, but there is a schedule. If we were to leave at five, and it was five-thirty, everyone would look to me. Sometimes I'd have the guts to pick up the phone and call him. Most of the time my call went to voice mail."

To ease his stress from the campaign, Crist spent almost every weekend at Carole's multi-million dollar condo on Fisher Island with Jim and Lisa Greer.

"Our wives also were becoming close," said Greer. "We were spending weekends at Carole's condo that she had acquired when she divorced Todd Rome."

Their time together gave Greer the opportunity to really talk to Crist, either while they were boating or drinking together. After downing his martinis, Crist often would excuse himself—"Time to go." And he'd take his afternoon nap.

"The way it worked," said Greer, "was if it was just Carole and her girls, Skylar and Jessica, we'd all have dinner together—Carole, her girls, Lisa, and my kids. Charlie would sometimes come to dinner, but on many occasions he'd join us later after the kids had gone off to watch videos or TV.

"On Saturday morning he'd usually say, 'Jim, let's meet for lunch.' Carole and her girls, Lisa and my kids would go off to play tennis or work out at the gym. I'd get up early and walk around the island because I loved that. But Charlie wouldn't join us until around lunch. Carole, Lisa, and I would be down by the bar or out by the pool, and Charlie would show up. He'd order a Bloody Mary or a martini and have a little nosh. He never really ate lunch. Often Charlie would say, 'Let's have some crackers and cheese.' Lisa and I, meanwhile, would be chowing down with a ham sandwiches and fries.

"Sometimes their kids would come back to the table and ask, 'Hey mom, what are we doing?' Charlie would occasionally inquire, 'How ya doing, Skylar?' But it was very clear the girls were to go away. There was not a lot of warmth there, which, hey, is not uncommon with a lot of stepparents. The problem with Charlie was that he had no clue how to be with kids. He used to say my kids were so well-behaved, and sometimes he'd say it in front of Carole. I'd think, *You're insulting Carole and the kids.*

"By about two o'clock, after Charlie had had a lot to drink, he'd say abruptly, 'I gotta go take a nap. Good-bye.' Literally in the middle of the conversation sometimes. Or he might say, 'Come on, Carole, let's go up and take a nap.' Sometimes she would, or if she was having fun with Lisa and me she wouldn't."

Every once a while Charlie and Carole would quarrel over whether she was going to accompany him when he abruptly left. "One time while Carole was having a drink with us, Charlie came to get her, and they had a big argument at the table," said Greer.

"Come on," Charlie said, "You're coming back to the room."

Recalled Greer, "Here they were, the governor of Florida and the first lady sitting out by a bar going at it in front of all those people."

The worst argument between Charlie and Carole that Greer witnessed happened while the Greers and the Crists were spending the weekend at the Disney World Contemporary Hotel. John Morgan, who ran the giant law firm of Morgan and Morgan, had held a fundraiser for Charlie in his home in Orlando.

In his speech Morgan was effusive in his praise of Crist. He then turned his attention to Greer. "While I'm not in the habit of praising Republican Party chairs," he said, "Jim Greer has done a great job and has worked hard to make this a more inclusive party."

Carole and Lisa didn't go to the fundraiser. They arrived at the Disney hotel before Charlie and Jim.

"Carole had been doing shots of Tequila," Greer said. "When Charlie and I arrived, he kept saying, 'Let's go, Carole. It's time to go.' But Carole didn't want to go.

"I'm not going," she said sharply.

Crist left in a huff to go up to his room.

"What is wrong with him that he doesn't want to be with me?" asked Carole. "Why doesn't he want these? You don't know what it's like. I didn't sign up for this. He's not the man I thought he was."

Greer had to help Carole to her room and put her in bed. Greer thought it odd that Crist was nowhere to be found. Lisa waited outside the room with an FDLE agent while her husband put the buxom Carole Crist to bed.

"It was a very uncomfortable situation," said Greer. "Lisa got angry because Carole kept talking to me and I was taking time away from being with Lisa. The point was, Carole was drinking and she was having second thoughts about the marriage. It wasn't the first time, and it wouldn't be the last time."

FOR THE GREERS, THERE was another irritating aspect of their relationship with the Crists. Often they felt abandoned.

"Before Charlie and Carole would go off to take their nap," said Greer, "they would never let us know what their plans were for the rest of the day. I always thought that was weird. After all, we were all supposed to be in there together. Charlie would just say, 'We'll call you later.' Sometimes he wouldn't get back in touch with us until ten at night. At seven I'd say to Lisa, 'Let's just go and have dinner. I think they're in for the night.'"

When Carole's kids were around, sometimes Carole would call and say, "'Listen, I want to have dinner with you guys, and the girls want to have dinner with Amber and Hunter. Charlie isn't coming with us.' That meant they had had a fight, and he was staying in, or he was too tired, or he was going to watch a football game and drink beer."

Crist's disposition often would dictate whether the Greers had a fun weekend. "Some weekends we had the greatest time in the world," said Greer, "and other weekends Lisa would say to me, 'Why did we come here?'"

Nevertheless, Greer's loyalty to Crist would not allow him to refuse a weekend invitation if he was summoned. There were times when Lisa resented having to take a back seat to Charlie Crist.

Said Greer, "After a bad weekend, Charlie would call and invite us to come again, and Lisa would say to me, 'The kids don't want to go, and I really don't either. I don't enjoy watching Charlie and Carole get drunk and then abandon us for the rest of the weekend.'

"I'd say to Lisa, 'He's the governor, and he wants us to come.'"

THE FISHER ISLAND WEEKENDS did allow Greer to run important campaign issues by Crist.

Crist now was a candidate whose poll ratings were dropping steadily but who had little interest in the nuts and bolts of his Senate campaign. When the Republican National Senatorial Campaign Committee began saying nice things about Rubio, Greer advised Crist to call John Cornyn, whose backing was crucial. Crist had little interest in doing so.

What did interest him was hitting up the residents of Fisher Island for campaign contributions.

"This drove Carole a little crazy," said Greer, "and it was a little embarrassing to Lisa and me. The residents of Fisher Island are wealthy, and Carole knew many of them. Charlie's evaluation of people generally dealt with how much they could give to his campaign—not who they were, but how much they had to give. Carole would say to Charlie, 'Tonight the Ridingers will be at the Tiki bar.' Or 'Courtney Thompson will be down for happy hour. You need to meet him, so you can raise some money.'

"Charlie would say to Carole the exact same thing he always said to Lisa Spies, his national fundraiser: "Okay, I'll meet them, but why don't they just write me a check? Why do I need to go down there and meet them?'

"So Charlie started going around the Tiki bar, ordering a beer, shaking hands, slapping some backs, and immediately asking for contributions. Carole would cringe at this. "'Charlie, I know these people,' she'd say. 'They'll give us $4,800, but they want to get to know you first.'"

"'You have to talk to him,'" Carole would say to Greer.

Recalled Greer, "Those people on Fisher Island looked at the governor as if he were a street cleaner. They came from Big Money. To them it was no big deal that Governor Crist was on the island. They were used to seeing Kennedys five tables away. Famous and wealthy people inhabited Fisher Island. Crist's presence didn't mean as much as Charlie thought it did."

Crist didn't entice the Fisher Island residents to give him as much money as he thought they should. He'd say to Greer, "Chairman, I saw these people out by the bar tonight; get with Carole and put together a little something."

As Greer soon discovered, the Fisher Island regulars had little interest in such an event. "They all had known Carole before Charlie, and there was talk behind the scenes that Carole was a ladder-climbing socialite, a partier. I heard that from a lot of Carole's girlfriends. And second, when Charlie came on the island, he never dressed the part. He never fit in very well."

Greer concluded that he got along with the Fisher Island residents much better than Crist did. Greer would shoot the breeze with them about sports or the topic of the day. On his birthday, two of the resident families, the Thompsons and the Delphos, invited Jim and Lisa to join them on Bill Delphos's huge yacht. Delphos was the founder of Delphos International, a private investment company.

Greer was told, "We don't want Charlie and Carole to come."

Said Greer, "Over drinks at the back of the deck Courtney Thompson, a friend who runs his own company in Coral Gables, said to me, 'Any time I talk to Charlie, he asks about money.'"

Greer recalled that on another occasion Carole went out with the Delphos and Thompsons on the yacht. "They took her for a ride, and they had dinner. The next day Charlie ran into Bill and Betty Delphos. Bill, trying to be flip, said, 'Hey Charlie, I took care of your wife last night when you were gone. We had a great time.'

"Crist bristled and said in a cold and aggressive tone, 'What do you mean by that?' 'I didn't mean anything, Charlie,' Delphos replied. 'I just meant we all went out to dinner and had a great time.' 'I don't like what you're implying about my wife,' said Crist. 'I'm not implying anything,' said Delphos."

Said Greer, "When Charlie is drinking, he can be hostile, and in this instance he was hostile with Delphos. I'm not sure why. Did he think Delphos was telling him he was screwing his wife? I don't think so. I think Charlie was thinking, *Carole was having a good time without me.* At times, alcohol turned him into an asshole."

Greer saw this as an example of how Crist could turn off some potential supporters. "That night I was sitting out by the water with Lisa. Charlie had gone back to his condo. My cell phone rang, and it was Betty Delphos. She told me how much she enjoyed spending time with me and Lisa and asked when I was heading back.

"I said, 'Hey, let me ask you a question. Would Bill be willing to help out on this fundraiser the governor wants to put together on Fisher Island?'

"'I don't think so,' she said, 'but you ought to talk to Bill.' Bill got on the phone. 'Hey, Jim, good seeing you,' Delphos said, 'I really don't want to do anything for Charlie, and there are a lot of people here on the island who are getting sick of him.'

"'Why?' I asked. 'What's happening?'

"'I'm going to be honest with you,' Delphos said. 'I haven't said anything to you yet because people like you. They like Lisa. You're welcome out on my boat any time. They enjoy Carole. She's been down here for a lot of years. But most of the people here don't like Charlie. I'm going to tell you what happened this afternoon.' And he described the scene when he ran into Crist earlier. Delphos said, 'I just think he's an asshole. He bothers people for money.'"

When Carole came down the next day for breakfast, by herself, she brought up the incident to Greer: "'I don't know if you heard, but there was a little altercation between Charlie and Bill Delphos.'" Greer said he had heard. Carole said Crist had been drinking and "'misunderstood what Bill was saying, and it was very uncomfortable. Have you talked to Bill?'"

Greer said he had, and acknowledged that Delphos was "pretty mad." An hour later Crist joined Greer at the Tiki bar, ordered drinks, and started making small talk, including that "'the Delphos are mad at me. Would you do me a favor? Will you call them up and apologize to them for me?'"

"I told Charlie, 'It might be best if you called and apologized yourself.' And he said he didn't know them well, but he knew I got along with them. 'Tell them I'm very, very sorry. Tell them I look forward to seeing them next time. Would you call them?'"

As always, Greer did as Crist asked.

WHILE CRIST AND GREER were living it up on Fisher Island, Crist was ignoring the political unrest in Florida, and Greer ignoring Crist's faults, rationalizing them away. His loyalty to Crist was paramount, no matter how badly Charlie behaved around him or treated him.

One afternoon Greer and Crist wanted to rent a boat so they could have an outing with their families. Greer found a captain who rented boats in Key Biscayne. He handed the captain his personal American Express card and paid for the boat rental of almost $400. Crist never chipped in a dime.

"Back then, did I mind?" said Greer. "No. I was making a lot of money. But Charlie was frugal and cheap.

"We got the boat, and we were going to go out with all the kids, and Carole said, 'Charlie doesn't know whether he's going to come, whether he wants to spend the time on the boat with the girls. So I need you to do me a big favor. I need you to talk to Charlie about how to be a father.'"

"'I don't feel comfortable doing that,'" said Greer.

"'You're the only one he listens to,' she said. 'You're like a brother to him. You're so good with your kids. The girls like you, and they like Amber and Hunter, but . . .'

"And then Carole started saying things like, 'I didn't sign up for this. He's not treating my daughters well. I don't think this is going to work out.'

"Toward the end of 2009 the issue with the girls became even more tense," said Greer. "The chinks in the armor of the marriage began to show. The more drinks she had, the more she talked about having made a wrong decision."

Though he didn't know how to do it without feeling out of line, Greer decided he'd better have a try at talking to Crist about his marriage and his relationship with Carole's daughters.

He tried to make it seem like a guy-to-guy thing. "Governor," Greer said, "I know you never had any kids, but if you want to get closer to her kids, you have to do things with them. You like boating. Skylar and Jessica are from New York, so they probably don't boat much. You ought to show up tomorrow, go out, and take the wheel. I'll sit back with my kids, and you be the guy in charge of the boat."

The next morning Carole, Lisa, Jim and all the kids were down by the boat when Charlie strolled up and got on. Said Greer, "He was on the boat with the girls that day, and he tried as best he could to interact with them, but it didn't really work."

Greer recalled another occasion when Skylar had picked out a Miami restaurant she wanted to visit because it was her birthday—her 10th. "But Charlie absolutely refused to go there. We went instead to Mr. Chow's in Miami Beach, where Charlie wanted to go, and the kids had no real interest in the place, because it was a more grown-up restaurant, and Skylar told my kids all night long what a miserable time she was having. It was always all about Charlie."

Greer said he believed "that Carole was scared that Charlie would leave her. I often wondered why Carole never spoke up for her girls. There were times, when Carole would say, 'The girls would like to stay,' but then Charlie would put his foot down and say, 'I really think we should leave,' and off they'd go. Carole reminded me of a turtle: she'd stick her head out a little bit but then she'd fold.

"Charlie made Carole choose between her daughters and him, and in the end she chose him."

Carole's ex-husband, Todd Rome, later filed for and for a six-month period won full custody; the judge ruled that Carole had abandoned her girls.

"There was a two-year period when she didn't even write to them, didn't call them when they were ill," said Greer. "Todd Rome himself called me and said, 'Do you know how to get in touch with Carole? She's not returning my phone calls. I need to get some papers signed so Skylar can get back in school. She was expelled because of disciplinary problems.' Rome said he and the girls hadn't talked to Carole in over a year."

Said Greer, "That tells you a boatload about that weird relationship. What mother would not want to know where her daughters were, would let birthdays go by without a word, would not even call them? Most likely Charlie had led her to understand, 'It's them or me.'"

45

CAROLE HAS HER WAY

ERIN ISAAC WAS CRIST'S PRESS SECRETARY DURING THE GOVERNOR'S RACE and later during his administration. The press secretary travels with the candidate and controls the press conferences and the day's campaign message. The press secretary is with the candidate all the time, so a bond develops. Sometimes jealousies pop up within the team.

When the campaign began, communications director Vivian Myrtetus, Isaac's boss, stayed back in her office and monitored what was going on. Her job was to look at communications from a macro perspective. How do we disseminate information about a policy? Which reporter should we give a heads-up to?

Then one day with no advance warning Myrtetus quit. "I'm going to work for a communications firm in Tallahassee," she told Greer, "but the real reason I'm leaving is because Erin has completely forgotten she works for me. Erin and the governor have become best buddies."

"That was true," said Greer. "Charlie and Erin had developed a flirtatious, overly friendly relationship—not that I believe they ever had relations. Erin has a great personality. He liked her."

After Myrtetus left, Crist promoted the bubbly Isaac to be his new communications director.

But Carole Crist also noticed how chummy Crist and Isaac were. The bad blood started at a meeting at the Jacksonville airport. Carole arrived after the meeting had begun, and in front of everyone Erin addressed her as Carole, not Mrs. Crist.

"In one way Carole and Charlie were very much alike," said Greer. "Once you go off their good list, it's very hard to get back on. Time and again Carole would ask Lisa and me, 'What do you think of Erin Isaac?' Which already told you there were problems in paradise."

"I'd say to Carole, 'I like Erin. I know she's loud sometimes, but she does a good job.'

"Carole would say, 'I think some of Charlie's approval problems are because the press doesn't like Erin.' I wanted to say, 'Charlie's approval problems have to do with the Republican voters, not with Erin,' but I didn't. Carole was really telling me was that Erin needed to start looking for another job. When your wife or your girlfriend tells you, 'I don't like your secretary,' you have a choice to make. Then Carole started pressuring me to make Charlie do something about Erin."

Greer resisted. And then one day Eric Eikenberg, Crist's chief of staff, called Greer to report that the governor wanted to get rid of Isaac that very afternoon.

Recalled Greer, "Erin had been with Charlie from the beginning. She cared about him. She had a loyalty to him almost as much as I did. Eric called her in and told her she was fired, and Erin broke down, crying hysterically. She said she didn't understand what she had done wrong. She was devastated. She packed up her things and left.

"Erin Isaac was the first casualty of Carole Crist's influence over the governor."

46

A CALL TO RESIGN

The straw polls were coming in hot and heavy in October 2009, and Crist suffered one ignoble defeat after another at the hands of Rubio and his Tea Party acolytes. Crist had not attended many of the county Republican Executive Committee dinners, but he did go to the annual dinner of the Republican Executive Committee in Ocala, a festive, well-attended event held in a big barn—male attendees traditionally wear a tuxedo jacket over blue jeans.

The three speakers were Greer, Laura Ingraham, the right-wing radio star and Fox News talking head, and Crist. When Crist walked in with Carole, there were boos. When he spoke, hecklers in the back shouted out, "Obama lover." As Crist left, he said to Greer, "What the fuck was that?"

"They're upset, governor. But don't worry about it. Despite the hecklers, you got a pretty good round of applause."

Still, Greer knew that getting booed at a major Republican event spelled trouble. He just didn't yet see it coming that the real target of those Tea Party zealots was himself. Crist in essence had become a lame duck governor now that he was running for the Senate, but Greer, as chairman of the party, had, as far as the Tea Partiers were concerned, abandoned the Republican Party to cast his lot with the hated Crist. He and Crist were no longer raising money for the party, and he was spending his time counseling Crist at the governor's mansion. Why, the Tea Party people were asking, was Greer still in office?

In November 2009 the Rubio faction of the party demanded a private meeting with Greer that he knew would be for the purpose of twisting his arm to resign as chairman. Among those demanding his resignation were Rubio's protégé, David Rivera, the state committeeman from Miami who later went on to become a congressman, and Peter Feaman, the state committeeman from Palm Beach. Greer had already sought advice from the party's legal counsel, who advised him that, "You were elected to a two-year term. There's no provision in the constitution for removal. There is nothing they can do."

Greer's staff scheduled the meeting at Howey-in-the-Hills, a small, exclusive golf course between Ocala and Orlando. "We kept it very quiet," said Greer. "We kept the location a secret."

GREER WENT TO THE meeting with his political staff. The room had a long U-shaped table. The Rubio board members sat on the left side of the room; Greer's people on the right.

Greer told Feaman, Gary Lee, and Sharon Day, "We're going to talk about other things as well. I want to discuss the Victory offices that we'll open in 2010, and steps we can take to make the party more inclusive."

The Rubio people made it clear the Tea Party had no interest in the party being inclusive. The Tea Party members also had no interest in those outside the four walls becoming involved in the discussion.

"In the past, board members who couldn't make a meeting could call in by phone, but Rubio's people now objected to that," said Greer. Greer's supporters were cut off while they were on the line. It was a coup.

Greer opened the meeting by having his political staff gave a presentation of their plans for 2010 and how the Republican Party would win the upcoming elections.

About 30 minutes into the presentation, Tony DiMatteo, once a strong supporter of Crist and Greer, stood up and said, "This is not why we are here today. I don't want to hear this stuff about what the party is doing. We're here to talk about your relationship with Charlie Crist."

"Let's finish up first," answered Greer, and he directed his political director, Bret Prater, to finish his remarks. When Prater was done, the Tea Party members asked Greer's staff to leave the room. "Because my staff would be witnesses," said Greer. "This was going to be an inquisition. They were going to lynch me."

"I understand some of you have issues," began Greer. "I fully understand your anger at the party having to borrow money from the House and the

Senate campaign funds. But let me remind you that when I came in as chairman, the House was in debt to the general party for over a million dollars. The governor has committed to me that he will raise the funds to replenish those coffers. Now let's talk about the other things you're upset about."

DiMatteo stood up and said, "This is not about you personally, Chairman. This is about Charlie Crist. You have got to go."

"Well, I want to discuss your grievances," said Greer.

Feaman, an attorney with a one-man practice, stood and read his bill of particulars against Greer. In addition to Greer's having used Senate and House campaign funds for the general party, Feaman cited Greer's support of one Republican candidate over another, and also charged him with allowing the Crist campaign to use party resources—the Republican Party headquarters—without payment—meaning rent.

As Feaman talked on and on, Greer took notes.

Greer asked Feaman for a copy of the list of grievances so he could respond to each one of them. Feaman refused and after reading them put the list back in his coat pocket.

"It was terrible," said Greer.

Sharon Day, another Tea Party activist who had had it in for Greer since the day he was elected chair over Carole Jean Jordan, stood up and said, "And you tried to get me to sign Rule 11 to knock Marco Rubio out of the race."

"Yes, that is true," said Greer. "I did. The governor asked if I could get Rule 11, and I see nothing wrong with trying to get Rule 11 for an incumbent Republican governor." And there was nothing wrong, of course, except that his Rule 11 would have knocked Day's candidate of choice out of the race.

"You threatened me that if I didn't sign it, you were going to do everything you could to hurt me politically," said Day.

"Sharon," said Greer, "that's the biggest lie I've ever heard. We never even had a hostile conversation. You said you weren't going to sign it, and I replied that I thought you should be a team player."

Greer continued. "Let's take one thing at a time. The Crist campaign is paying rent. I offered that same relationship to the Rubio campaign, but they declined it. And the reason they declined it was so they could run around the state and say, 'Chairman Greer and the Republican Party is helping Charlie Crist.' But everything we've done for Charlie Crist was offered to the Rubio campaign, but they declined. This is not about the money because what's going on now has been going on for years. Yes, we have a deficiency in fundraising . . ."

"This is the Republican Party," interrupted Day, "not the Charlie Crist party, and you've made it the Charlie Crist party."

"That's not true," replied Greer, "but he is the incumbent Republican governor. He has raised millions of dollars for this party. You've all forgotten everything he's done for the Republican Party."

Gary Lee, another Tea Party activist, the chairman of the Republican Party of Lee County, stood up and said, "Is it true that major donors' contributions to the party have decreased significantly?"

"Yes, but that's not because of me," said Greer, "and not because of anything the party is doing. It's because the number one person who has dealings with major donors has stopped raising money for the party." Greer didn't name Crist and hoped his answer would suffice. It didn't.

"Is it really true the governor has stopped raising money for the party?"

Greer, loyal to the governor, danced around that question, too. "Not true. He's still doing a lot of events for the party."

Recalled Greer, "I made up excuses, even though they weren't true. Charlie had told me, 'fuck the party,' but I was still trying to keep them on board as much as I could."

The Greer supporters, including Jim Stelling, his buddy from Seminole County, counterattacked the Rubio contingent.

"Greer has been a great chairman," said Stelling. "Maybe he has helped Charlie Crist a little too much, but it's nothing other chairmen haven't done. We won every major race in Florida. We returned every House and Senate member and picked up a couple of Congressional seats."

Lee and Allen Cox got up together to complain about Crist's appointment of James Perry to the Florida Supreme Court. Lee started yelling that Crist was not a Republican.

The rhetoric heated up, as both sides became emotional. At the end the call came: "We are asking you to step down."

"I'm not going to give an answer today," said Greer. "But I don't believe

I've done anything wrong. We raised a lot of money. I tried to reform the party as best I could. I know some of you aren't happy when I tried to create attendance requirements . . ."

The Tea Party scolds just kept on and on.

"We want you out." "We want you to resign."

Greer supporters were giving it to the Rubio people as well. Stafford Jones tried to explain how Greer had brought technology to the party and had upped the ante as far as communications and the relationship with the national party was concerned. "Greer has made the Republican Party more relevant than ever," said Jones.

AFTER THE MEETING ADJOURNED, Greer and Delmar Johnson went outside with the party's attorney, Jason Gonzalez, and sat by a small pond. It was so calm the water didn't ripple.

"They're all a bunch of troublemakers," said Gonzalez. "There is no provision to remove you as chairman. You don't have to resign. Don't even think about it."

Greer wasn't sure exactly how he felt. It's not fun being the target of a group of strident, relentless attackers. *Do I want to resign?* Greer asked himself. Troubled, he called Crist, who was very clear.

"You are not to resign, Chairman," he said. "Don't let these people do this to you. You've been a damn fine chairman. Put it out of your mind. They're only trying to get rid of you to get to me."

Greer called political guru Jay Burmer in Tampa, who told him the same thing.

"Listen, I spoke to Charlie about it," Burmer said, "and he says the only way you're going out is in a body bag. You cannot resign. They're coming over the walls to get to Charlie, and you're the last Marine at the gate. This is what they do in Third World countries."

One of the tactics of the Tea Party crazies was getting former Republican leaders to issue public calls for Greer's resignation. Al Hoffman, a Jeb Bush follower and the former finance chairman of the party, was one of the first. Allen Cox, one of the leaders of the Florida Tea Party and the vice-chairman of the RPOF, spoke out. So did Tom Slade, a former chairman. They also publicized a list of major donors who pledged to no longer give money to the party.

"When I saw that list," said Greer, "I knew that most of them hadn't given to the party in years. They were major donors from the Jeb Bush era.

"State committee members led by Cox and Debbie Cox Roush from Tampa—the anti-Charlie Crist members of the board—wrote letters demanding my resignation. In every letter they mentioned my support for Crist.

"What I still had going for me was the House and Senate Republicans, led by Mike Haridopolos and Dean Cannon. They were supporting me. And I still had a significant percentage of the general state committee on my side."

Not for long.

SOON AFTER THE TRAUMATIC meeting, Greer was in New York for a fundraising event for Crist's Senate campaign and a small fundraiser for the party. He was in charge of booking the rooms.

"It happened regularly that Charlie and Carole didn't like their room," said Greer. "It was never big enough. This time Carole wanted a bigger suite, so I had to go back down to the front desk and arrange it. The manager knew me well because that was a regular occurrence.

"Charlie, Carole, Lisa, and I went out to dinner at a posh Italian restaurant Charlie and Carole had enjoyed before. It was just a great night. Charlie and Carole told us how much they loved us, how we were their closest friends. Charlie mentioned how kind we had been to Carole, especially Lisa who would accompany a nervous Carole whenever she had to make a speech. He thanked me profusely for standing strong against the crazies who were coming after me, because it was really him they were after."

It was a night Greer would remember, but in hindsight, mostly wistfully.

47

A Vote of Confidence

After the grilling of Greer at the Howey-in-the-Hills meeting, his supporters on the Republican Executive Board understood for the first time that the Rubio-led opposition was much more organized and stronger than they had anticipated.

"Jim Stelling, Stafford Jones, and Allen Miller, the assistant treasurer of the party, one of my supporters, and Paul Senft all decided we needed to have a meeting to organize to protect my chairmanship and to counter what was going on," said Greer.

They met in the first week of December 2009 at Stelling's house. Stelling was the chairman of the Seminole County Republican Executive Committee. He wasn't a Crist supporter, but he was a strong supporter and friend of Greer. Miller was a state committeeman in Indian River County, and Jones was the chairman in Marion County. Paul Senft was the national committeeman and on the executive board. Also present were Chris Dorworth, a state representative who was a good friend of Greer, and Jason Gonzalez, the general counsel of the party.

The group determined that what Greer needed was a formal vote of confidence by the executive board. They also suggested that Greer begin to distance himself from Crist.

"Things are getting pretty bad, and you need to come out and make some kind of public statement distancing yourself from Crist," Greer was advised.

"You have got to stop worrying about and protecting Charlie Crist," Dorworth said, "and you have to start worrying about yourself."

Tone deaf to any call to betray the man who made him the chairman, Greer shot back, "We are not going to throw Charlie Crist under the bus. Whatever happens to me, happens to me, but I'm not going to turn on

Charlie. I'm not going to let my party turn on him, and I don't want to hear any more about it."

Dorworth listened while Greer defended the governor. "I just want to tell you what's going on," said Dorworth in an even tone. "I know how you feel about Charlie Crist, but if you don't make some changes, bad things are coming."

Recalled Greer, "Dorworth always had an opinion that the Tea Party was going to throw the exorbitant spending of the Republican Party on me. He felt I was going to be a scapegoat for the spending. He brought it up that night, and he would bring it up several times later."

Greer, his loyalty to Crist now a noose around his neck, had no idea how right Dorworth would turn out to be.

THE REPUBLICAN PARTY OF Florida held an executive board meeting on December 10, 2009, an annual meeting that was held every year in conjunction with the governor's Christmas party at the mansion. The party was for the Republican State Committee members and major donors.

Close to 30 members of the executive board came to the meeting. Most of the Rubio backers weren't there. They were boycotting the meeting and the governor's Christmas party.

"I thought that was weird," said Greer, "because the Christmas party is a big thing. Everybody wants to be there. You get a Christmas ornament from the mansion. You get to walk around the mansion, the governor shows up, there's an open bar, cocktails. But the Rubio people were so mad at Charlie and so intent on removing me that they didn't show up."

One vocal Tea Partier who did show up was Allen Cox. He was in attendance when Paul Senft got up to the podium.

"There has been a lot said about Mr. Greer," said Senft, "a lot of attacks on him. I've seen this before with other chairmen, but I've never seen it this bad. I make a motion that the board support Mr. Greer and indicate its full confidence in Chairman Greer."

The motion passed 26-2.

After the vote Greer was told, "The board is behind you, and it looks like your troubles are over."

"Yes," said Greer, "but let's see how it goes."

After the vote Cox came over to Greer and asked to speak with him privately.

"I have the support of the board," said Greer. "I'm tired of all the trouble. You're my vice chairman, Allen. You should be my number two man, and you're causing me all of this trouble. You're leading this coup against me. I know you want to be chairman really bad, and I know you're the leader of the wing nuts, but even with all of this, does this war have to continue?"

Cox was very calm. He was not at all hostile. "We want you out," he said, "and we want Charlie Crist out. Whatever we have to do, we're going to do it."

Cox would become the leader of a coalition of Rubio supporters, Tea Party followers, and ultraconservatives. Cox was not only the vice chairman of the party, he was also the budget chairman, and he fed financial information to this dissident element of the party. Other important members were Gary Lee and Allison DeFoor, a former judge and sheriff, who had been brought up on ethics charges numerous times. DeFoor was a member of the state committee. So was Peter Feaman.

"It was a Gang of Five," said Greer, "and they just kept feeding the flames every chance they got. They put out an email to all 200 members of the state committee that said: 'Greer has to go. He's supporting Charlie Crist too much. We need an audit of the party to see what he's done to help Charlie Crist.'

The vote of confidence at the December 10 meeting hadn't slowed them a whit. "Allen Cox's biggest issue was that I was too supportive of Crist," said Greer, "and that Crist wasn't raising any money for the party. Allen told me he wasn't going to stop. So I kept the governor apprised of all this. I was with him all the time. I'd tell him, 'They're demanding my resignation.' Charlie'd say, 'You aren't going anywhere. You can't let them take over the party.'"

Neither Greer nor Crist could see the approaching political firestorm.

NOT LONG AFTER THE December 10th meeting with the Tea Party faction, a group of conservative former House legislative leaders published a letter demanding that Greer step down.

"These were people literally going back to the 1980s," said Greer. "The Rubio people were very organized. The drumbeat continued for me to step down."

As before, a large part of Greer's difficulty came from the fact that Crist was refusing to raise money for the Republican Party, putting the party in serious financial difficulty. But Greer, in his own bubble, continued to stress that the party had been in similar situations in the past.

"Where my mistake came," said Greer. "I should have cut expenses. I should have shut the party down."

One problem: it was an extreme measure, and no one wanted him to do it.

Greer had met in his office with Delmar, his executive director, and Richard Schwartz, the CEO of the party, about cutting expenses to the bare bones. Both were rigidly opposed. Anytime Greer took a step to cut expenses, the word would come back to him, "The press is going to crucify you if you do that. The party will appear to be weak if you do that. Bill McCollum will become more powerful if you do that."

Greer recalled, "Every time I talked about cutting expenses, my staff would tell me, 'Oh no, that's terrible.' But we did cut expenses. We didn't fill some positions. I didn't give out raises. I stopped flying my plane. I flew commercial or drove, and on many occasions took money out of my own pocket to pay for party expenses."

But because Crist had stopped raising money for the party, the cost-cutting wasn't enough.

Greer had known the dire straits the Republican Party was in when Crist was running for governor and Carole Jean Jordan was the chairman. The party was in debt a million dollars to the House side of the party. George LeMieux had worked it out that Crist would raise the million and make the party whole again—which he did.

But in December 2009 the Rubio faction rewrote history. Their mantra became, *The party is in dire straits and the spending is out of control.*

Stories began appearing in the media about the specifics of outrageous spending by party leaders. And Greer was deemed responsible.

"These were terrible stories that had some truth to them," said Greer, "but not much accuracy."

One story had to do with Greer flying to Washington for LeMieux's swearing-in ceremony as interim U.S. senator.

Recalled Greer, "George invited all of us to his swearing-in. And it was appropriate for me to go. I was the chairman of the party. He was the Republican senator, Governor Crist's appointee. He invited Jim Rimes, Rich Heffley, and me. We were scheduled to fly commercially out of Tallahassee, and the flight got cancelled, which happens. Rimes suggested we charter a small jet. Delmar called Bear Air, the leasing company that had my plane. They had a small jet, and we chartered it for $12,000. Rimes said he would put in $5,000 from Enright Consulting. Heffley said he'd put up $5,000. I said the party would pay $2,000.

"We went up there and came back, and I later found out that Rimes and Heffley didn't put up their share. So the papers wrote stories about my chartering the jet. But they didn't write that Rimes and Heffley were supposed to pay $10,000 of it. I would have my press secretary, Katie Gordon, call the papers to show them the facts, but it didn't seem to matter. It was entertaining that the chairman of the party was under attack, so they weren't about to correct the record."

The truth was that Greer was more interested in supporting Crist than dealing with the serious problems facing the RPOF chairman.

"Every time I tried to respond with the truth or take corrective action, but nothing seemed to work. After my reelection, it was just not a fun job anymore," said Greer. "It had been a rewarding job in 2007 and 2008. I loved being chairman of the party. And I really believe we did a lot of good things. And I believe I was making the party much more relevant and inclusive.

"But shortly after my election—I won by 77 percent of the vote—when it should have been the best time, when Crist decided to run for the Senate, when the dominoes started to fall, McCollum wanted his own guy in, and Rubio wanted me—and Crist—out."

48

Don't Leave Home Without It

Charlie Crist's 52nd birthday was July 24, 2008. The Crists and the Greers were staying at The Breakers hotel in Palm Beach, where that night there was a fundraising dinner for the RPOF.

"The major donors, the ones who give between $50,000 and $100,000, don't want to stay at the Holiday Inn with the continental breakfast," said Greer. "They want to be at the five-star resorts and hotels."

Greer came up with the idea that he could raise money for the Republican Party of Florida by celebrating Crist's birthday. Meredith O'Rourke got Crist buddy and major GOP donor Scott Rothstein to sponsor the cake for $52,000, and lobbyists chipped in $5,200 per candle. More than 200 persons attended the successful event.

Rothstein was an interesting character, though Greer didn't yet realize how interesting. Rothstein was a wealthy lawyer-real estate-investment-philanthropist with multiple law offices and mansions across south Florida. "Scott always said 'yes' whenever we asked him to do something as far as raising money," recalled Greer. "It turned out he was saying 'yes' with other people's money, because he was sentenced to 50 years in 2010 for what was called the fourth-largest Ponzi scheme in history."

In retrospect, Greer sees Rothstein as an example of the pay-to-play relationships between wealthy donors and candidates that have corrupted the political process. In early 2008, O'Rourke told Greer that Rothstein's donations hadn't been purely out of love for the RFOF; he wanted to be appointed to the Florida Supreme Court Nominating Commission. She asked if Greer would speak to the governor. Crist told Greer, "The timing isn't right. Also Rothstein needs to do more."

Meanwhile, Greer and George LeMieux were getting nervous over rumors that perhaps Rothstein was connected to the mob, that he owned a vodka bottling company, and that he also may have been involved in pornography.

Then in July 2008, Rothstein paid $52,000 to sponsor the Crist birthday cake at the fundraiser. In August 2008, Crist appointed Rothstein to the commission that nominated judges to Florida's 4th District Court of Appeals, not exactly what Rothstein asked, but it covered judges in south Florida where he lived and his law firm was.

Recalled Greer, "No governor appoints someone to a powerful, influential position that isn't on their team or hasn't supported them financially. When I was chairman, I would regularly get calls from the governor's chief of staff who would call Meredith directly or would call me, and ask 'How much has a particular individual contributed?' Because they were considering appointment to positions."

Rothstein's fall, when it came, was swift and hard. "I don't believe Charlie ever really considered him a close friend," Greer recalled "but he ignored all the warning signs about Rothstein because of Rothstein's ability to give big money when it was needed."

AFTER THE GOVERNOR'S JULY 24, 2008, birthday dinner was over, attendees could walk over to one of the other ballrooms in the hotel where the Republicans in the Florida Senate were having a fundraiser presided over by Senate President Jeff Atwater. Greer got up on the stage and said a few words. That night one of Atwater's entourage sought out Greer. "President Atwater says his suite is too small," Greer was told. "He wants to have meetings upstairs, and we need your American Express card to get him a bigger suite."

Greer handed up his RPOF American Express card and he never gave it another thought. Atwater's larger room cost $2,000 for the night, and later Greer would be accused in the newspapers of recklessly spending the $2,000 on himself. It was a setup, and the accusers knew it wasn't true, but no one came to his defense.

In reality, $2,000 for a room for Atwater was small change for bringing the party and the Senate candidates millions. Had it not been for the Tea Party troublemakers, no one would have noticed or cared. No one ever had before. This was business as usual because Greer and Crist had learned an important truth: to raise a lot of money, you had to spend a lot of money.

"You ended up doing a lot of traveling," said Greer, "a lot of wining and dining of major donors at five-star hotels like The Breakers, the Vinoy, the Don Cesar, and the Boca Raton Country Club. We were raising millions and millions of dollars, but we were spending a lot of money. All the private dinners where we asked for $50,000 and $100,000 checks were held at five-star resorts."

Greer would say to his staff, "Three weeks from Saturday we're doing an RPOF fundraiser at The Breakers." His staff would book the rooms.

"People might argue I should have stayed down the street at the Ramada Inn and walked to the fundraiser at The Breakers, but the governor had a room at The Breakers. The finance chairman had a room at The Breakers. Most of the major donors had rooms there, too. And so did I."

In truth, Greer had no idea what the rooms cost; he wasn't booking them. "Delmar Johnson always booked me, or my secretary did, in very nice suites. That was the way everyone else was doing it. The governor had a suite on one floor. I had a suite. The office of the chairman was always considered one of the three or four top offices."

Greer felt justified with the spending for fundraising dinners.

"When the dinner was over, my staff would always come over, lean over, and ask for my American Express card," he said, "and I would give it to them to pay the bill. Delmar Johnson had my credit card number and personal identification information and frequently acted for me in making charges and communicating with American Express and with airlines, hotels, and restaurants.

"When we'd fly to an RNC meeting in Washington or San Diego or wherever, my secretary would say, 'I have Delmar's and your flights booked along with the executive director and the political director. Can I get your American Express card, Chairman?"

These were common, proper expenses, and he'd hand over his card. After a while his secretary didn't even need the card. She knew all the information on the card, so she would make the charges without even asking for it.

"In my opinion it was all party-related," said Greer. "All the Republican Party leaders, including Dean Cannon and Mike Haridopolos, had the very strong opinion that 'We can spend the money as we see fit if it promotes the party.' I bought into that, too. But I believe to this day I was more conscious about spending than others were. If I had a party dinner for donors and my mother was there, I'd often tell my secretary, 'Make sure these charges go on my personal card.'

Greer was naïve. He believed the "everyone else does it" defense would keep him out of harm's way. He could not anticipate how badly the Tea Party opposition wanted his hide.

"I was very dumb," said Greer, "because many times I let them spend money that could be pinpointed back to me, when the money wasn't for my use, so no matter how conscientious I was, if they were doing what they were doing and they were using my card, there was no way I could defend myself later."

THERE WAS ONE OTHER situation against which Greer was defenseless. For him to stay out of trouble with the spending on the RPOF American Express card, his chief of staff, Delmar Johnson, had to remain aboveboard. As it turned out, this wasn't always the case.

As mentioned earlier, not long after Greer became chairman of the RNC rules committee, he, Delmar, and two RPOF staff members, Bret Prater and Kirk Pepper, were in California for an RNC meeting and a staff training session when Delmar said to the group, "I want to take you to play golf at Torrey Pines in celebration."

Torrey Pines was an exclusive, very expensive course where the pros played, and Greer was excited.

"That's great," he said. "The party isn't paying for it, is it, Delmar?"

"Oh no," said Johnson, "Brett, Kirk, and I are all chipping in to take you out there to celebrate."

At the golf shop, Johnson bought a golf glove. "The party isn't paying for that, is it, Delmar?" asked Greer.

"No, I'm paying for it with my own personal money," Johnson said.

"Make sure, because we don't need any more problems," said Greer. He never questioned Johnson further. He trusted the man totally.

He shouldn't have.

On another occasion Johnson threw his boss a birthday party.

"My birthday is in June, state representative Jason Brodeur's birthday is in June, and Delmar's birthday is in June," said Greer. "So Delmar, as he would frequently do, because he was a friend, would call me up and say, 'I put together a birthday party for you, Chairman, at Del Frisco's Steak House,' a fancy restaurant in downtown Orlando. I walked into the room, and there were 50 people there including a couple of donors, a couple of legislators, and a lot of close friends. There were also friends of Delmar's, so I knew it was a party for him as well. Delmar was always very good at getting in on the act. Halfway through the dinner I leaned over and said, 'Now Delmar, make sure this does *not* go on the Republican Party credit card.'

"'Oh no, absolutely not,' Delmar said. 'I'm paying half, and Fred Karlinsky is picking up the other half.'

"'Great,' I said. "I appreciate that.'"

Greer, Johnson, and Brodeur blew out the candles on the cake, and everyone had a great time. A year later Greer was accused of outrageous spending, and one charge was for the Torrey Pines outing and another was for his birthday party. "Delmar had lied to me," said Greer. "Auditors found that dinner that night had gone on the Republican Party American Express card. And so had our golf outing at Torrey Pines.

An auditor questioned Greer, "Do you think the $580 charge at Torrey Pines was an appropriate expenditure for the party?"

"I didn't," said Greer, "but I had been very clear to Delmar that the party was not to pay for the Torrey Pines golf outing. But we did. And we shouldn't have. When the stories came out, the headlines blared, 'Greer held a birthday party at Del Frisco's and charged it to the party.' Well, I didn't. I was very clear that night. I told Delmar, 'Don't charge it to the party.'"

It wouldn't be the last time that Johnson's actions would get Greer in trouble.

LISA GREER GAVE BIRTH to Aiden James Charles Greer on July 4, 2009. By this point, Greer's critics were so obsessed that they accused Lisa of waiting until the 4th and then inducing labor to make the child's birth look patriotic. In fact, Aiden had entered the world without any outside help.

Jim and Lisa gave him the middle name of Charles in honor of Charlie

Crist. As godparents they chose Delmar and Jamie Johnson. At the time, both honors seemed right.

"The governor and Carole were ecstatic and very happy, and we were very happy we did that," said Greer, "because they had become our closest, closest friends."

The Greers invited a host of friends, including the Crists, the Johnsons, Chris Dorworth, Richard Schwartz, and all sorts of legislators and political friends, to Aiden's christening. After the church service, everyone repaired to the Greer home. Clicking away was the official RPOF photographer, Joe Reilly, who had driven to Oviedo all the way from Fort Lauderdale.

In the kitchen Greer said to Johnson, "'What is Joe doing here with all his camera equipment?' 'Oh, he's doing this for you as a gift,' Delmar said. He told Lisa, 'He's going to put a disk together and give it to you.'"

Two weeks later a disk arrived with all the photographs and a book. Jim and Lisa talked often about how wonderful it was that Reilly had come to take the pictures. A year later an audit revealed that Johnson had authorized a $5,000 payment to Reilly on Greer's RPOF American Express card.

Recalled Greer, "I don't think any photographer would charge $5,000 for three hours of time at a baptism. So what I always thought was that Delmar used Joe to photograph his family and used the baptism to cover for it, because that was Delmar's way. I was infuriated when I saw the baptism pictures on the list of charges. So when you read a story that said, 'Greer paid his son's baptism photographs through the Republican Party of Florida,' it's an absolute damn lie. I never told him to do it. I was told the photographer was doing it as a gift.

"People might say, 'Why didn't you march up to Joe Reilly and ask if that was true?' Who does that? Besides, I trusted Delmar. He's my son's godfather. He was my campaign manager. We go back years."

OTHER QUESTIONABLE CHARGES TO the RPOF American Express card were related to Greer's spending on weekends at Fisher Island with Charlie and Carole. Crist would say, "I want you to come to Fisher Island this weekend, because we're going to set up a meeting with J. R. Ridinger, a big millionaire. Bring your family down."

"As I look back," said Greer, "I saw on my personal American Express card that I paid about $22,000 over a year's time to stay at Fisher Island. And I had the party reimburse me about $9,000, because I was there with the governor having meetings on official business. I didn't think it right for me to take money out of my own pocket to pay for a meeting he wanted on a Saturday or a Sunday.

"The argument is, 'When the meeting was over, you still stayed there and socialized and had the Republican Party pay for the hotel,' and the answer is, 'Yes, I did. So did everyone else. That's nothing new.'

"And there were times in hindsight that it was questionable whether I should have paid out of my own pocket. But it goes back to one factor: the Tea Party didn't like Charlie Crist. They didn't like that Crist was running against their hero, Marco Rubio. If I had been a Rubio supporter and had been traveling with Rubio as chairman, none of them would have had a problem with what I was doing. But I was on Crist's team, and therefore I was a target.

"Dean Cannon was using his party American Express card to buy clothes and suits in a men's store. Rubio used his party American Express card to put in new floors in his home in Miami. He used it to buy groceries and to repair his wife's damaged car. I consider that to be a *flagrant* violation of the party's trust. But when he was asked about it, he said, 'I just got confused when I pulled out my credit cards. I thought I was pulling out my personal American Express card.'

"And everyone said, 'That sounds logical.' If Charlie and I had said that, the response would have been, 'What a bunch of bullshit, a pack of lies. Those guys are corrupt. Put them in jail.'

"With a few exceptions, the media went along with Rubio while they pointed all the missiles at me. Richard Nixon said in one of his David Frost interviews, 'I gave them the sword to stab me with.' And that's exactly how I feel about the American Express charges. I gave my enemies what they needed to stab me with. They weren't interested in the facts. Or the truth. They had no interest in asking me anything so I could clear myself. All they wanted was something to use against me."

49

TWISTING IN THE WIND

IN MID-DECEMBER OF 2009 THE FLORIDA TEA PARTY'S GANG OF FIVE, LED by Allen Cox, began circulating a petition to throw Greer out of office at the quarterly RPOF meeting to be held January 9, 2010. The petitioners needed signatures of 25 members of the state committee to get the motion for expulsion onto the agenda. But for there to be a vote, the subject matter had to be legal.

That was the issue: Could Rubio's Gang of Five legally remove Greer as chairman?

The party's legal counsel, Jason Gonzalez, had already told Greer the Tea Partiers didn't have the ability to do that.

"There is no provision to remove you as chairman," said Gonzalez. "You were elected to a two-year term. They can have the meeting, but as soon as they start talking about removing you, you need to gavel them out of order."

A showdown was coming, and Greer knew it.

Greer noticed one other disturbing sign. Whenever Senate President Mike Haridopolos or the House's Dean Cannon spoke to reporters, their support for him seemed to be fading. Without their backing, Greer was cooked. Each controlled ten votes in the executive committee, and if it came to a vote, he would not be able to survive without their support.

The crux of the problem was still the $1 million the Republican Party of Florida owed the House and Senate campaign funds. The only way Greer could regain support, he knew, would be to raise the million dollars. Only Governor Crist had the star power to raise that kind of money fast, but Crist seemed to have no interest in helping his chairman and friend.

Crist had spit in the eyes of Haridopolos and Cannon. He had vetoed bills he had promised the legislative leaders he would sign. Crist had accepted the stimulus money and had embraced President Obama. And once

Golfing buddies, sure, but Greer was going to need a mulligan.

he announced his candidacy for the Senate, he became a lame duck. Ha-ridopolos and Cannon were willing to back Greer, but only if Crist raised the million dollars.

Greer approached Crist and told him that Haridopolos and Cannon wanted to talk to him. "This was one of the few times I was trying to get Charlie to focus on *my* problem," said Greer later.

"They need you to raise the million dollars," said Greer.

"All right, fine," said Crist. "But what about Bill McCollum? McCollum's going to be the next governor. Why isn't he raising money?"

"He is," answered Greer, "but you're still the governor and if we reach out to Bill McCollum, we'll lose control of the party. I'll be reporting to him as chairman."

"Okay, I got it," said Crist. "I got it. I got it."

It was Friday, and Jim and Lisa were heading to Fisher Island to spend the weekend with Charlie and Carole. Joel Springer, the Senate finance campaign chief of staff, and Andy Palmer, chief of staff of the House finance campaign, were talking with Greer on the phone. They were worried that Crist wouldn't go out of his way to help Greer.

"Does the governor know what he needs to say to Haridopolos and Cannon to get them to stick with you?" Greer was asked.

"Yes, I told him," said Greer.

Greer and his wife got in their Navigator for the drive to Fisher Island. Their kids were in the back. It was raining. Crist was to talk to Haridopolos and Cannon at 6 p.m. Around 5:30 Greer called Springer, Palmer, and Jim Rimes in Tallahassee and left a message to confirm how the phone call was to go, and by about 7:30 no one had called him back. Greer called them to get an update. There was no answer. He left a message, and he began to worry when no one called back.

Greer again called his office. They were all there. They put Greer on speaker.

"Hey, guys," said Greer, "how did the call go?"

"Not well, chairman," said Palmer.

"Not well?"

"No, the governor didn't do what he had to do."

"What happened?"

"They asked him," said Palmer. "Haridopolos said, 'We're going to stick with Jim if you will assure us you'll raise the million dollars."

"So what did he say?" asked Greer.

"He said, 'I'm really busy raising money for my Senate campaign, and Bill McCollum is the one who should take the lead in replenishing the coffers of the party.' That really causes you a problem, Chairman. I think you've lost them."

Greer immediately tried to call Haridopolos and Cannon. Neither picked up. His calls went to voice mail.

That night, after Greer and Lisa had arrived at Fisher Island and checked into their room, Charlie Crist was nowhere to be found.

"He and Carole met up with us the next day," said Greer. "He had that smile on his face and said, 'Hey, Chairman. How's it going? Good to see you. Are things calming down for ya?'"

"Not really, governor," said Greer.

"Why? What?"

"That call you had last night," said Greer.

"Yeah, yeah, it went fine," said Crist.

"Not in their opinion it didn't, sir."

"What are you talking about?"

"They didn't hear you say you'd raise the million dollars."

"I told them I'd help out."

"That's not what they were looking for, governor. They needed a guarantee. And Governor, that has really caused me a problem. I think they'll pull their support of me as chairman."

"Well, hasn't legal counsel told you they can't do anything to you?" asked Crist.

"Yeah, but who wants to go through a huge battle at a meeting where they'll try to recall me? I need the Senate president and the speaker to tell the Gang of Five they're sticking with me. If they did that, they might not try a move against me."

"I don't understand," said Crist, who surely did understand.

Greer put Crist on the spot.

"Here's what I need you to do, Governor," he said. "I'm going to dial their numbers right now, and I need you to tell them point blank that you'll raise the million dollars."

Greer dialed Mike Haridopolos. Crist took the phone. He got voice mail, and Crist left a message in which he said, "Hey, Mr. President, this is Charlie Crist calling on Chairman Greer's phone. Must have been some misunderstanding last night. I will raise the money for the party."

Then he called Speaker Cannon and said the same thing.

Crist was sure the matter was settled.

"This is all going to pass," Crist said assuredly.

Greer wasn't so sure. He became deeply worried when neither Haridopolos nor Cannon returned the calls.

"Once they saw it was the governor calling," said Greer, "I assumed they'd call back."

But they didn't.

"With the House and the Senate abandoning me," said Greer, "I was now in real trouble."

50

'It's Time for You to Go'

The Rubio/Tea Party/ultraconservative-led attacks on Greer continued unabated. One morning Greer awoke to a story in the newspapers that claimed the RPOF was paying the mortgage on his twin-engine airplane.

The story was a fabrication, but it even got the attention of Governor Crist.

"Hey, Chairman. The plane of yours. Who pays for it?"

"I do," said Greer. "I have a mortgage. The Republican Party pays for the fuel and the time in the air, but I'm paying the $3,000 a month mortgage. If you'd like for me to get the mortgage book, I'd be glad to show it to you."

Said Greer, "The Rubio crowd threw anything they could at me, including the plane, the American Express charges, the five-star hotels, money my staff was spending, plus Delmar's and Jim Rime's spending on their American Express cards. Anything and everything."

Among the charges that Greer would be accused of making was thousands of dollars spent on portraits of Crist, Greer and Delmar Johnson.

Greer first became aware of the paintings when he noticed a beautiful new portrait of Crist in Johnson's office in the fall of 2009.

"I said, 'Delmar, that's a great portrait. Where did that come from?' Delmar said he had noticed a woman painting portraits, 'and I asked her to do one of the governor. I thought you might like to present it to him at the Republican Party of Florida Christmas party.' 'That's fantastic,' I told him. 'I think he'll love it.'"

Greer then asked Johnson if the party had paid for it, and Johnson said, no, it had been "donated in kind." The portrait sat in Johnson's closet until the December 10 Christmas party, when it was presented to Crist.

At the RPOF Christmas party, Johnson called Greer to the front of the room before the whole staff and said, "Chairman, we want to give this to you. We've all chipped in for it." It was a portrait of Greer, painted by the same artist who had painted Crist's portrait, with American and Florida flags behind Greer in the picture. It was beautiful. Greer loved it.

Shortly thereafter, an item in a political blog said, "Somebody should tell Chairman Greer about Delmar Johnson's house in Tallahassee, and the painting."

Greer called Johnson down to his office. "What is this?" he asked.

"I don't know," said Johnson. "I don't have any idea what it means."

"Are we paying for your house in Tallahassee?" Greer asked.

"No," he said.

"Delmar lied to me," said Greer. "I later found out he was having the Republican Party pay his rent in Tallahassee."

When the article said "painting," Greer thought Delmar had had his house painted, and he asked him about that. "Hell, no, I didn't have my house painted," said Johnson. It didn't occur to Greer to ask if Johnson had commissioned a third portrait of himself. But Johnson had.

As Rubio and his Tea Party followers kept leaking rumors and stories, Greer's political friends were recommending different courses of action.

On December 22, 2009, Jim was shopping at the Millennium Mall in Orlando with state representatives Chris Dorworth and Jason Brodeur, and political strategist Alex Setzer.

It was a Christmas tradition for the friends to shop for their wives together. "It was usually a great time," recalled Greer. "This Christmas, though, it was miserable because the talk was all about the attempts to remove me as chairman."

Dorworth, Stelling, Stafford Jones and other members of the state executive committee recommended that Greer use his power as chairman to remove all the Tea Party naysayers. As previously mentioned, a state statute gave party chairmen the power to remove anyone who "takes action detrimental to the party."

Dorworth was pushing hardest, telling Lisa and anyone who cared to listen that "Jim needs to get rid of these people. He should just get a pen and remove them all."

Greer was reluctant because he feared such a move would lead to additional headlines like "Greer Purges the Party."

His allies also suggested that Crist get on the phone and admonish the troublemakers, but Greer knew that Crist avoided confrontation at all costs. "Had the party been attacking Governor Jeb Bush's chairman this way," said Greer, "Bush would have just told them all to 'shut up,' that 'this is my party chairman.' And that would have been the end of it. Still, Charlie was supporting me. Whenever he was asked about Greer by reporters, he'd say, 'Greer has been a good chairman.'"

During the Millennium Mall shopping trip, as Greer and his political buddies were eating chicken wings and drinking beer at a restaurant, Greer took a phone call from Speaker of the House Dean Cannon.

During their conversation Greer was struck by the fact that Cannon kept referring to the governor as "Charlie," and not as "Governor." The lack of respect struck Greer as ominous, and he was right.

Cannon finally said, "Chairman, it's time for you to go. Charlie has lost the party's support. I no longer support the governor. The party base no longer supports him. And you have drained the House and Senate's general account. There'll be a lot of accusations about spending."

"Mr. Speaker," said Greer. "Let me ask you one question about that. You spent over $200,000 in questionable expenses. Why is it me and not you and others? And Speaker Rubio has spent a lot of money on himself."

"First of all, Chairman," said Cannon, "I've checked with our legal counsel, and I can spend money on anything that I believe furthers the Republican Party. I'm not doing anything Rubio didn't do before me."

"Okay, I'm not arguing with that," said Greer. "But why am I the target?"

"This is all about Charlie Crist," said Cannon. "Charlie has lost the support of the party, and you've got to go. Listen, I like you. I endorsed you for reelection."

That was true. Cannon had held a fundraiser for Greer's reelection.

"Here's what can happen," said Cannon. "If you go quietly, I'll get you a lobbying job in Tallahassee, and you'll make a lot of money. Or what about Michael Steele? You got Michael elected with your endorsement. He owes you. What about getting a job with him?"

"Mr. Speaker, I really don't know," said Greer.

Cannon then said to Greer, "How do you really feel about Charlie Crist? Charlie has fucked you, Chairman. How do you really feel about him?"

Greer had to think about that one.

"Listen," said Greer, "I'm not always happy with Charlie Crist, but I'm loyal to him. I think the party should be loyal to him, too."

"Well," said Cannon, "the party is gone. I've been asked by President Haridopolos to speak to you about all of this. I want you to know that I can't guarantee the ten votes from the House and the ten votes from the Senate."

"That's very disturbing," said Greer, "because I've worked my ass off to be a good chairman."

"I'm sorry," said Cannon, "but that's just the way it is. If you go quietly—here's the other thing we want you to know—we'll give you a severance agreement. We'll pay you as a consultant to the party for the remainder of your term. We'll pay your health insurance. We'll praise your chairmanship. We'll say you were one of the best chairmen the party ever had."

"How about a hold-harmless agreement?" asked Greer. "I'd like to make sure when I go out the door that I'm not accused of everything you've ever done."

"Yes," said Cannon, "we'll give you that too. Let's make this as painless as possible."

"Mr. Speaker," said Greer, "I'm not telling you I'm going to do it, but it gives me something to think about."

51

A Vote of No Confidence

Greer, succumbing to the frustration and the pressure, started having nightmares, anxiety attacks, and shortness of breath. In his dreams they were removing him as chairman. He just couldn't believe it. He felt he had contributed so much to the party. One night he broke down in the living room of his home, and became very emotional.

Whenever he spoke to Crist, the man in the bubble would respond blithely, "Aw, it's all going to pass."

Recalled Greer, "It was terrible. No matter what I did, I couldn't end it. Things were moving too fast. The Tea Party had orchestrated something I just couldn't prevent."

What Greer was yet to understand was that the Tea Party was taking over the Republican Party not just in Florida, but in many parts of the country.

When Allen West was running for Congress from West Palm Beach in 2008, his rhetoric was so over the top anti-government, anti-Obama, anti-poor, anti-choice, anti-gay, and anti-spending that observers wondered whether he was actually crazy. West had been a lieutenant colonel in the Army, and he had been accused of torturing prisoners of war. He had been honorably discharged from the Army, but he had so much baggage that moderate Republicans were loath to endorse him.

Now in January 2010 West was becoming a golden boy of the Republican Party. He was on Fox News every night, exhorting Congress to impeach Obama, to keep the Guantanamo prison camp open, and to bomb the hell out of every Arab country.

In just two years Florida Republicans had gone from "Stay away from Allen West, he's crazy" to fully embracing him. And like the other rigid Tea Party scolds, West called for the Republican Party to expel Republican moderates.

At the top of the list were Charlie Crist and Jim Greer.

Greer, not understanding the Tea Party's new strength, tried to rally support. He called on state committee members loyal to him, and some continued to back him. Paul Senft, the state committeeman from Polk County, wrote a letter to the newspapers testifying to what a fine job Greer had done. Jim Stelling wrote to all the state committee members in support of Greer.

Despite such support, the current was too strong and was sweeping Greer downriver. It would be impossible to survive.

The calls for him to step down increased in number and intensity. Congressman Jeff Miller, a Tea Party backer from the Panhandle, made the demand. So did Tom Feeney, Greer's friend who had warned him about what was coming.

Greer was particularly upset about the latter. Feeney and he had been close. Greer had helped him become a member of the Florida House and supported him when he became its speaker. Feeney then became embroiled in a political controversy when it was revealed that one of his financial backers was Jack Abramoff, the disgraced lobbyist. When Feeney ran for reelection most of his friends turned their back on him, but not Greer, who hosted a fundraiser at his home for Feeney.

"Lisa always reminds me that when nobody would hold a fundraiser for Tom for his reelection, we did," said Greer.

Former party chairs also began calling for his resignation.

"IT'S GETTING BAD," GREER reported to Crist, holed up in the governor's mansion.

"I cannot be any clearer," said Crist. "You are *not* to resign."

Apparently something was beginning to occur to the governor, and it had nothing to do with Greer's position as chairman. He realized that if Greer resigned, they'd be coming after him next.

Crist said to him, "They are going to come over the walls and take over the palace. You have to be the last man at the gate."

Crist had said to Jay Burmer, "Jim has to go out in a body bag."

George LeMieux was another one advising Greer to hold his ground in order to protect Crist. But none of them understood the toll the constant barrage was taking on the mild-mannered Greer. As a successful company CEO, a local politician and community leader, Greer had encountered many challenges over the years—but nothing like this.

"Listen, George," said Greer, "I just can't take this anymore. Every day they're beating me up, planting untrue stories about me in the newspapers."

"If you resign," advised LeMieux, "they're going to accuse the Boss and you—and all of us—of all kinds of things we didn't do."

"We've done nothing wrong," said Greer, who still didn't understand that being right had *nothing* to do with it.

"Whenever someone warned that we'd be accused of things," said Greer, "I'd say, 'Accuse us of what? Of staying at a 4-star hotel instead of a 3-star? That's not a crime.' Since the day I got here, everyone advised me that if we raised $5 million, we could spend it anyway we wanted."

Greer asked LeMieux, "What are they going to accuse us of, George?"

"They'll bring up the $10,000 a month contract you gave me," he said.

"I'm the chairman of the party," said Greer. "The governor told me to give you a contract for $10,000 a month, and George, you did consulting work for me."

Unfortunately, recalled Greer, "George and I both knew that wasn't true."

Burmer, his close friend and adviser, also told him not to resign.

One time Crist told Greer, "I don't use this term often, Chairman, but I'm ordering you not to resign."

Greer was in a serious quandary.

"I felt the governor had the power, but I also saw the entire structure of the Republican Party leaving him," said Greer. "The party had no love for him, and worse, they were coming after *me*.

"They were after the keys to the palace."

The determined Gang of Five, stymied temporarily by Jason Gonzalez's legal opinion that Greer could not be removed as chairman by the Tea Party, announced it had hired an attorney to challenge the ruling.

To orchestrate his defense, Greer was on the phone several times a day to Gonzalez, Delmar Johnson, political director Kirk Pepper, and Jim Rimes.

They were telling him, "There'll be a hell of a meeting, but when it's over, you're still going to be chairman."

Greer wasn't so sure. He questioned whether staying on was worth it. The attacks were relentless, and he had been told he'd get a severance and be praised by everyone as he walked out the door. Mike Haridopolos and Dean Cannon had both promised Greer that he would go out as a statesman. They were going to say he had resigned to unify the party. And they were not going to say a word about the spending of the party's money.

BACK HOME LISA PLEADED with him not to resign. So did most of his friends. But Greer could see he was being railroaded out of town, and he felt powerless to stop it.

On December 27, 2009, Greer agreed to have Gonzalez draw up a proposed severance agreement. Gonzalez put in calls to Allen Cox and the other members of the Gang of Five to ask if they would raise objections to the agreement.

Greer was told, "If the House and Senate want to give you a severance agreement, we won't make a big deal with the state committee. We feel like you've served the party well, and now you're resigning for the sake of the party. We'll end this and give you a severance agreement."

Gonzalez faxed the first draft of an agreement to Haridopolos and Cannon. It stated, "The party will pay him as a senior consultant $11,200 a month." It had a hold-harmless clause that said, "Any and all payments made to Victory Strategies are hereby ratified, lawful, and appropriate."

Greer demanded that Haridopolos, Cannon, and John Thrasher, who was going to replace Greer as chairman, all sign the agreement. Gonzalez would also sign it, as would Delmar Johnson, Richard Schwartz, the party's chief financial officer, as well as Greer.

"I wanted seven signatures that would bind them all to the severance agreement," said Greer.

All the while a scared Governor Crist, needing a firewall, continued to pressure Greer not to step down as chairman. Over dinner one evening at Fisher Island, Crist told him, "The only thing between them and me is you."

Recalled Greer, "A lot of people have the idea that Charlie Crist stuck with Chairman Greer all the way to the end. And some people see that as loyalty. Others question why he did it. I'll tell you why he did it. He did it because it was entirely in his self-interest. I think there was some affection and loyalty to me. We were friends. But he knew what was coming—if I left and they put Thrasher in my place, it would be very bad for him."

The severance agreement was bandied about for several days. The final agreement called for Greer to step down on January 9, but would not take effect until February 20th, upon the election of John Thrasher as chairman.

In theory Greer would be chairman for six more weeks.

Jim and Lisa were visiting Charlie and Carole on Fisher Island on December 29th and were planning to spend New Year's Eve together. When the governor arrived he called Greer on his cell phone and said, "Listen, I want you to call my dad and talk to him. My dad doesn't think you should resign either."

I'll call him," said Greer.

"I have an idea for you that my dad suggested," said Crist. "Why don't you call Mel Sembler and Al Hoffman, the major donors who wrote letters last week asking you to resign. Go see them and tell them I will raise money for the party and that you'll cut expenses to the party. Try to talk to them."

Recalled Greer, "When I came in with Crist, I entered with a new crowd, and I didn't give the old crowd as much attention as I should have. The Al Hoffmans, the Mel Semblers, the people who had raised a lot of money under Jeb Bush were the elder statesmen of fundraisers. As chairman, I dealt with a new group that funded Charlie Crist. I should have gone around and kissed the old guard's rings. But I didn't. And neither did Charlie."

"Governor," said Greer, "I'll do whatever you want me to do, but they've already signed the letter and sent it over to the *St. Pete Times*. It's on the blogs. That ship has sailed. Three months ago you told me to ignore these people, and now you want me to deal with them?"

"My dad said you should talk to them," said Crist," but you do have a good point. Why don't you call my dad, and I'll meet you in a couple of hours by the pool."

It was a sunny day. Greer called Dr. Charles Crist and talked to him as he walked around the Fisher Island marina. "Hey, Jim, sorry to hear what's happening," said Dr. Crist. "Charlie just briefed me."

"It's bad," said Greer. "Doctor, they hate your son. And they hate me. They want to remove me as chairman so they can turn the whole party against him. The Rubio lovers have taken over the Republican Party. And they've got the media buying into it. They are writing stories that aren't true. My board has flipped, and many, if not the majority, are Rubio supporters. It's bad."

"I had no idea," said Dr. Crist. "What if you reached out to some of these people? What if you went to see Al Hoffman? What if you talked to Ambassador Sembler?"

"Doctor, this is December 29. They've been calling for my resignation for the last month and a half. They're having a big meeting in two weeks, and they're going to try to remove me. I don't think seeing those people will amount to a hill of beans."

"If you resign, won't they just come after Charlie left and right?"

"Here's where I am right now, Doctor. During World War II, we fought for islands that at the time had no strategic benefit. Thousands of soldiers died. We're fighting for an island we don't need any more. The party is gone. I'm being beaten to death every day. I want out."

"It's that bad?"

"Yes, doctor. The House and Senate membership have told me they no longer support the governor. The speaker and the president told me they no longer support the governor."

"I had no idea," said Dr. Crist for perhaps the third time. "Well, I guess you're right. There's no reason to hang onto something that's not going to come back to us."

They spoke for over an hour.

"Charlie doesn't want you to resign," Dr. Crist repeated.

"I know that," said Greer. "They want the keys to the building. I say let's give them to them."

"I had no idea the base of the party had left him so badly," said Dr. Crist. "I'll have to talk to Charlie."

ERIC EIKENBERG, NOW CRIST's campaign manager, flew down to Fisher

Island on December 30th to meet with the governor about campaign issues and to discuss Greer's precarious position. He met Greer for lunch first and said, "Boy, the governor has really put you in a bad position. What are you going to do?"

Eikenberg's phone rang. It was State Senator Mike Fasano, a strong supporter of Crist and Greer and a member of the Republican state executive committee. He was also holding back Tea Party crazies who didn't like him because he was perceived as being too moderate.

"What's the word on Greer?" Fasano asked Eikenberg.

"The governor really wants Greer to stay as chairman."

"Okay," said Fasano, "If that's what the governor wants, then I'm still with Greer, and I'll do my best to keep him as chairman."

Toward sundown, Jim and Lisa joined Charlie and Carole.

Greer began talking about his problems despite Crist's aversion to unpleasant topics. "They're going to give me a severance agreement," said Greer. "I'd like to come over to your Senate campaign and be a senior adviser."

At this point Greer was in his own bubble, still convinced despite all that was going on that Crist would win the Senate election against the smart, ruthless, and always scheming Rubio. Crist had told Jim and Lisa that if he won his primary, Greer would be a senior member of his Senate office and afterwards would run his national political action committee and raise money around the entire country.

"I felt I really had a future with him," recalled Greer. "We were going to Washington."

"You know what they'll do, don't you?" asked Crist. "They'll accuse us of things."

LeMieux and even more forcefully Dorworth had predicted the same eventuality. Greer, targeted by the Tea Party wing of the Republican Party, was going to be the scapegoat. "It's going to be bad," Dorworth had said.

Greer told Crist, "The Rubio people have taken over the party."

"I don't want you to resign," said Crist.

"I don't feel I have any other choice," said Greer. "I'm going to do it."

Crist was furious, and the two didn't talk for the next two days.

"He didn't even come around me," said Greer.

52

A Nixonian Moment

When Greer told Crist that he intended to resign, Crist threw a fit, only he did it in a passive-aggressive way. He let Greer know he was angry by avoiding him.

It was New Year's Eve, 2009. The Crists and the Greers were supposed to celebrate together on Fisher Island. Greer got out his tux, and Lisa wore a long gown. They were getting ready to go to a party hosted by Mary Ann Portal, a friend of Carole's, when they were informed that Charlie wasn't going. Around 11, a sheepish Carole popped in.

"Carole had had a few drinks," said Greer. "She said, 'I'm not supposed to be here, but I wanted to come down. I'm sorry we didn't join you guys tonight.'"

Carole went with them to the party. Greer could tell it was against Charlie's wishes. The room was packed with partiers wearing tuxedos and fancy clothes. Crist appeared just before midnight wearing a T-shirt, flip flops, and blue jeans. He didn't walk over to the Greers, but rather went to the concession stand outside and got a sandwich to go. He then left by himself without saying a word.

"Did you see the look he gave me?" said Carole. "He wants me back at the condo. I have to go."

And she left.

Despite Crist's clear displeasure about what he was about to do, on New Year's Day 2010 Greer told Gonzalez that he would step down. He waited two more days before he told Lisa, who cried hysterically and begged him not to. He informed Delmar Johnson, who also begged him not to quit.

Greer was sitting in his office in Tallahassee when Gonzalez arrived with the current draft of the proposed severance agreement. Greer determined that several changes had been made. The sentence that had said "All payments to Victory Strategies were ratified, appropriate, and lawful" was changed to "any and all payments for any fundraising agreements, service agreements, consulting fees are hereby ratified, appropriate, and lawful."

Greer thought to himself, *They took out the name of the company, but they broadened my protections.* He didn't object, though events might have turned out differently if he had.

The original agreement also said that if the Republican Party of Florida were to violate the agreement, Greer would be entitled to a million dollars damages. It was subsequently changed to say only that he'd be entitled to damages.

I can live with that, thought Greer.

Greer didn't sign it immediately; not trusting them, he wanted the other parties to the contract to sign it first. He sent it to his attorney, Damon Chase, who advised him not to sign it.

Then, with his senior staff standing around his desk in a Nixonian moment, Greer affixed his signature to the letter of resignation. He was resigning from a job he had loved and was walking away from what under other circumstances might have led him to an important role in Washington. He didn't want to do it, but the pressure from Rubio and the Tea Party Republicans and other Crist haters was too much to bear.

"That night I was very upset," said Greer. "I couldn't sleep."

THE NEXT DAY, TUESDAY, January 5, 2010, a noon press conference was called to announce his resignation. Delmar Johnson and Eric Eikenberg arrived at Greer's condo before eight to console him. Greer was angry at what was being forced on him, lashing out at the man who was largely responsible for this debacle: Governor Charlie Crist.

"I cannot believe I'm having to resign because Charlie Crist refuses to raise money for the party or even stand up to them," he said.

Johnson and Eikenberg were sympathetic. "Doesn't the governor care about any of this?" asked Johnson.

Greer could only throw up his hands. He couldn't answer. He paced, recalling the highlights of what had been the best job of his entire life. "I thought I was good at it," he said. "I can't believe this is happening. We've done so much good for the party over the last three years, why are they doing this?"

Around 8:30 a.m., Lieutenant Governor Jeff Kottkamp called to say he didn't think Greer should resign.

"I appreciate that," Greer said over the phone, "but I'm ready to get out. The party has financial trouble, and I can't get any help fixing it. Every charge that's ever been made in this building is being blamed on me. To be honest with you, Jeff, the governor has pretty much abandoned the party."

"Yes, I know," said Kottkamp. "If I had any pull as lieutenant governor I would have helped you."

"I appreciate that," said Greer.

A few minutes later Crist called. It was a three-minute conversation. "Are you going to do it?" Crist wanted to know. "Are you sure you want to do it?"

"Yes, sir," said Greer. "I've got the documents prepared."

"Jim, I think it's a mistake."

"Well, sir, they're not going to stop," said Greer. "And they want to come after you, Governor. You don't need this. You need to focus on your Senate campaign. Governor, they are just not with you any longer."

"Well, if that's what you think you have to do . . ."

And bam, Charlie Crist hung up the phone.

Later in the morning, Greer sat in his office, the big desk in front of him, the colorful flags of the U.S. and Florida on poles behind him. The large picture of Abraham Lincoln and Greer's many plaques and awards still hung on the walls. He called in his staff and told them of his decision. Katie Gordon, his press secretary, cried as the others shook their heads.

In addressing his staff, Greer warned about the danger the Tea Party posed to the Republican Party.

"There are people who want to destroy the party," he said. "They will do whatever they have to do to do it. They've been against Governor Crist, as you all know, almost from day one. I didn't come up from the ranks so I was never one of them. There are people who will destroy the party if they don't gain control of it. They've pretty much told me they'll do whatever it takes—they'll say whatever they have to say, whether it's true or not. My family, Lisa and the kids, are upset, very upset. So I decided to resign.

"Today I will be handing in my resignation, but I won't be leaving as chairman for six weeks."

Gonzalez arrived to talk about the severance agreement.

Greer would not sign the document unless the other six signatories did, and so after Gonzalez signed it, he had faxed it to Thrasher, Cannon, and Haridopolos for their signatures. All had returned their signatures by fax.

Johnson and Schwartz signed as original signatures. Seeing that all the other signatures were in place, Greer signed his name as well.

The Republican Party of Florida was now locked into paying Jim Greer $11,200 a month for the rest of what would have been his full term. Not only that, but the agreement cleared him of wrongdoing with respect to how he or anyone spent Republican Party of Florida funds.

Gonzalez said to Greer, "I'm going to hand you a copy, and I'm going to take my copy and put it in a safe at my law office for nobody to ever see. They wanted your head on a platter, but by giving you a severance agreement, that's not giving them your head on a platter."

Greer nodded okay.

"Thrasher doesn't get elected until February 20," said Gonzalez. "The Rubio people, the Tea Party, and the grass-roots are going to be upset if they find out you're being given a severance agreement. Each of us has to keep this agreement absolutely secret. It can't get out."

"Okay," said Greer. "Just make sure my payment shows up."

Gonzalez added, "We've also have to make sure Thrasher gets elected chairman in six weeks in case somebody else decides to run against him."

By "somebody else," he meant a member of the Tea Party.

"He went on to tell me there were rumors that Sharon Day was going to run," said Greer. Thrasher was one of the Good Old Boys, a member of the Jeb Bush club that hated Charlie Crist. "Even though Thrasher was ultra-conservative, he wasn't as crazy as some of the Tea Party people, and they wanted to make sure Thrasher was named chairman and no one else."

In a great irony, on the day that Greer officially resigned as chairman, the treasurer of the party and the head of the party's audit committee arrived at Republican headquarters to look through the financial documents of the party. This wasn't the doing of the Tea Party crazies. Greer himself had asked them to come a month earlier because he wanted them to issue a statement that nothing improper had transpired.

When he was downstairs in the lobby of the headquarters, he was met by party treasurer Joel Pate and assistant treasurer Allen Miller, who had arrived to look at the party's books.

"Joel, Allen, you're going to find out before anyone else that I have submitted my letter of resignation," said Greer.

"Oh, Why did you do that?" he was asked. "We were prepared to write a letter saying that everything has been proper and lawful, that there was nothing inappropriate."

"I'd still like you to go upstairs and do that," said Greer. "I'd like you to look at the Victory Strategies contract. Look at everything."

AT NOON GREER HELD a conference call with more than 300 interested Florida Republicans. He read his letter of resignation in which he said, "There are people who wish to burn the house down, and I do not intend to allow the party to be brought down. I have a higher obligation as chairman. Therefore effective February 20, upon the election of my successor, I shall resign as chairman."

Immediately following news of Greer's resignation, as if on cue, the Rubio supporters began asking if Greer had received a severance agreement. Everyone involved denied it.

"They were so stupid," said Greer. "They should have told the truth. You can't keep anything secret."

Gonzalez encouraged him to leave town to avoid the press and any questions from state committee members about a severance agreement, and Jim and Lisa left Tallahassee immediately for the scenic hills of Blowing Rock, North Carolina, where they stayed for two weeks.

Greer was a lame duck, so until February 20, when Thrasher would be elected, there was really nothing for him to do back in Tallahassee.

Even though Greer had been given a severance agreement, it was clear that Rubio and his followers would scuttle it if they could. Why else would the Tea Party crowd be so interested in whether such an agreement actually existed?

"Is there a severance agreement?" was the question asked by all the media, driven by the intensity of the Rubio followers who badly wanted to punish Greer for not being one of them. The party's top brass continued to state, "There is no severance agreement."

Senate President Mike Haridopolos said, "There were a lot of papers going back and forth, but to my knowledge there was no document with my signature on it."

Recalled Greer, "Which was a flat-out lie. His signature was on it. Publicly and directly he lied to the media. The party was stating there was no severance agreement, and they were making a big mistake by doing so," said Greer. "I was watching all of this from afar, when I got a call from on high.

"Chairman," said Dean Cannon, "we want to make sure you're still on the reservation. You're not to talk to the *Miami Herald* and tell them there's a severance agreement."

"Not a problem," said Greer, "just as long as my first payment shows up on March 1. Any talk about a severance agreement will be coming from your side, not mine."

But Greer, who didn't trust any of them, suspected that the higher-ups in the party were hoping to find a loophole to avoid paying him. His first concrete evidence of this came when Gonzalez called and said, "Listen, you really ought to think about signing a new agreement. The agreement you signed has faxed signatures on it."

Greer refused to sign a new agreement, and phoned his attorney, Damon Chase. "Damon," said Greer, "they're saying the faxed signatures are no good."

"They're trying to pull one over on you," said Chase. "Faxed signatures are legal in Florida. Any lawyer right out of law school knows that. This is all bullshit. They're just trying to get out of the agreement."

When Gonzalez called again, he was even more adamant about having Greer sign a new contract. "I don't think the agreement you signed is legal," Gonzalez reiterated, "because of the faxed signatures."

"Are you trying to tell me they don't want to pay me?" asked Greer.

"No, no, no," said Gonzalez. "They want to pay you. I want to be clear. Everyone wants to pay you. But you gotta sign the new agreement. Everyone says it's the right thing to do."

Greer reported back to Chase, who then wrote a letter to Gonzalez stating that under Florida law a faxed signature is legal. "Just pay the man and stop trying to get out of the agreement," he wrote.

While Greer was vacationing in North Carolina, Sharon Day, Carole Jean Jordan's close friend and one of the darlings of the Tea Party, announced she would run for chairman against Thrasher. Her theme was "We shouldn't be told once again who the chairman is by the House, Senate, and by Bill McCollum. We're the state committee and we should elect who we want. Vote for me as the alternative to John Thrasher."

Day, moreover, said publicly that if elected, she would call for a very thorough forensic audit of the books of the Republican Party of Florida, something neither the House nor the Senate wanted, because they didn't want anyone to scrutinize their wild spending. Both Haridopolos and Cannon worked overtime to make sure Day lost.

Day kept asking Gonzalez and Schwartz, the chief financial officer: "Did Greer get a severance agreement?"

Both lied to her and said he didn't. Had she been elected chair, and had learned such an agreement existed, she would have fired them both.

Cannon called Greer in North Carolina once again to warn him not to tell anyone about the severance agreement. "We're going to get through this together," he told Greer. "You're going to get paid by Thrasher. It's the right thing to do."

To emphasize the point, Cannon told him, "I ran into Thrasher in the hall the other day, and John said, 'We have to make sure Jim gets paid.'"

The skeptical Greer couldn't help but wonder what kind of monkey business they were going to pull to make sure he *didn't* get paid.

53

Sucker for the Party

While he was holed up in North Carolina, Greer read the news stories about the denial of his severance agreement by the top Florida Republicans. Some stories contained criticisms of his leadership by Republicans, something he had been promised wouldn't happen. Other reports revealed the existence of Victory Strategies, the company he and Delmar Johnson had set up for the purpose of fundraising for the Republican Party of Florida as a replacement for Meredith O'Rourke.

"This Victory Strategies contract is outrageous," his Tea party critics blared. "The chairman and executive director never should have had a fundraising contract."

The party leaders were not only denying the existence of the severance agreement in the newspaper, they were also denying the existence of the Victory Strategies contract, saying it had been done in secret, making it sound like he and Johnson had done something sneaky and illegal.

Greer found that unsettling, considering that the company name, Victory Strategies, had been specifically written into the first and second drafts of the severance agreement.

What are they up to? Greer asked himself.

On February 10, 2010, Greer sent a long email to Gonzalez stating, "I did everything you all asked me to do. I have done everything Bill McCollum asked me to by remaining quiet. I continue to read about the attacks on my chairmanship every day. I read things you told me no one was going to say. Maybe we ought to invite the press in, tell them all about Victory Strategies, about every spending expenditure of the party. Let's get it out on the table. I'm sick of these media attacks and all the leaks."

Gonzalez never responded. In hindsight, Greer should have done what he threatened to do.

The John Thrasher versus Sharon Day election for chairman of the Republican Party of Florida was scheduled for February 20, 2010. On February 15, Dean Cannon called Greer to tell him that Beth Reinhard, a reporter for the *Miami Herald*, had a lead about the existence of the severance agreement.

"We're going to deny it," Cannon said, "and you shouldn't talk to her."

"How did they get the story?" asked Greer.

"We fucked up," Cannon said. "Al Hoffman called me and Haridopolos to ask if there was an agreement, and we told him yes, but to keep it quiet. Hoffman was quoted in the *Miami Herald* that an agreement existed; that giving Greer severance was the best thing to do to get him to resign."

Reinhard had one source, but to print the story, she needed another one to confirm it. Cannon and Haridopolos wanted to make sure Greer didn't talk to her. Greer would have saved himself serious trouble had he called the *Herald* there and then and told Reinhard the truth about Victory Strategies.

"Listen," said Greer, "the first payment is due in two weeks. I'm not going to say a word to anyone. Just make sure the money shows up."

"Oh, it'll be there," said Cannon. "We're not going to screw you, Jim."

Recalled Greer, "I thought Dean Cannon was my friend. I thought he was an honest broker."

Greer then talked to Cannon about the newspaper stories of his extravagant spending on his RPOF American Express card.

"I'm very concerned," said Greer, "because you too have questionable charges on the card. You bought clothes on it. You bought fuel for your private plane, all kinds of dinners . . ."

"Don't worry about it," said Cannon. "We take the position that we're a private organization, and we can spend money as we see fit. As speaker designate, I can use the American Express card for anything I believe benefits the Republican Party."

"Okay," said Greer, "I'm just telling you that the Rubio people are going to turn on you-all too."

Greer didn't know it then but the only person they would turn on would be himself.

On February 17, the day Greer and his family were getting ready to leave North Carolina, Greer received an email from Brent Prader, the acting RPOF executive director. Prader wrote, "This email shall serve as notice that the Republican Party is hereby revoking the severance agreement and hold harmless agreement it executed with you on January 4. The reason for nullifying the agreement is one, y   ou unconditionally resigned at the January 9 meeting. And two, you failed to return a signed copy to the party when you signed your resignation letter on January 4."

The first reason was bullshit, Greer knew, and the second was a lie—Gonzalez had said he was putting a copy of the agreement in his safe. Greer's fears were coming true. The bastards were trying to get out of paying him.

Recalled Greer, "What I think was going on was that Gonzalez was talking with the McCollum people, with the House and Senate people, and they were trying every which way to avoid paying me."

Greer called his lawyer who told him, "They can't revoke an agreement that they've executed." Greer then called Cannon: "Dean, I've just received an email from Brent Prader, the craziest email I've ever read."

"What does it say?"

Greer read it to him.

"I don't know anything about it," said Cannon. "Prader didn't have the authority to send that. Those people over at the Republican Party don't know their right hand from their left."

Greer thought to himself, *Sure Dean.* Greer later said that he believed Dean knew all about it.

"I'll call you back in three hours after I get this straightened out," said Cannon. Greer never heard back from Cannon, but he did get a phone call from Chris Dorworth, who said, "Dean Cannon just stopped by my office and said, 'Tell Greer we're going to pay him, but tell him not to call me directly anymore.'"

After listening to Dorworth's phone call, Lisa quietly said to her husband, "They are getting ready to screw you, Jim."

Recalled Greer, "This was the usual running for cover that politicians succumb to. I wanted to believe they were being honest. But the handwriting was on the wall."

With the February 20 Thrasher versus Day election fast approaching, Cannon called Greer himself and had the temerity to ask him to do something incredible. "Listen," Cannon said, "I need to ask a big favor. Would you chair the meeting on Saturday until the new chairman is elected?"

"You want me to chair the meeting?" said Greer incredulously.

"Here's our concern," Cannon explained, "Allen Cox is going to be the presiding officer if you're not there." Cox, the vice chairman of the party, was part of Sharon Day's Tea Party faction and was one of the coup leaders that had forced Greer out.

"If you're not there, "Cannon continued, "we're concerned that in the few minutes Cox has the gavel, he will order an audit that will drag in the House and the Senate. He's crazy. He's not one of us. I know it's going to be hard on you, Jim, but we need to make sure you have the gavel until Thrasher is elected."

"Let me see if I have this straight," Greer replied. "You guys want me to come back from North Carolina and humiliate myself even further by standing up there on the day you're actually throwing me out as chairman?"

"If you will do it," said Cannon, obviously not meaning a word of it, "we will never forget you."

I've got to be out of my mind, Greer told himself, but still caring too much about the fate of the party, he reluctantly agreed.

On the night before the election for the new chairman, Greer returned to his spacious office in Republican Party headquarters in Tallahassee. All his belongings were piled in boxes. The large photograph of Charlie Crist had been taken down and placed behind a chair in the lobby.

Greer and Lisa had arrived pulling a U-Haul trailer. Aside from the pile of boxes, the offices were empty. His staff was nowhere to be found.

"I couldn't find anyone to help me move my boxes," said Greer. "You see, everybody had gotten the memo: *Greer is bad. Stay away from Greer. His chairmanship was terrible. We're getting ready to move against him.* It was a ghost town. Even my own aide wasn't answering my phone calls."

While Lisa boxed up what she could from their condo across the street, Greer lugged the boxes containing his personal possessions into the U-Haul.

As Greer was leaving the headquarters, he and Lisa ran into Andy Palmer, the chief of staff of the House campaign and a supporter of Thrasher's campaign for party chairman. Palmer was surprised to find Greer and Lisa in the building.

"Good evening, Chairman. Good evening, Lisa," he said.

"So you guys have this Thrasher election locked up for tomorrow?" asked Greer.

"Yeah, we think so," he said, "but we have Plan B if he doesn't win."

"Really? What's Plan B?" asked Greer.

"Every one of the House and Senate campaign staff is going to resign," Palmer said. "We're coming in after the election if we lose, and we're taking down all the computers and the servers, because we don't want Sharon Day and her team to have access to anything."

"That's almost like destroying documents in the middle of the night," said Greer.

"Yeah," said Palmer, "if she wins, we're getting out of here—the speaker and the president—and we're taking all our documents and stuff, because we're not about to have her and the Tea Party bunch, the Rubio people, questioning our spending or ordering an audit."

"This sounds like Watergate and the Saturday Night Massacre," Greer said.

THE MEETING TO ELECT the new chair of the Republican Party of Florida took place at the Rosen Shingle Creek Resort in Orlando on February 20, 2010. The purpose of the meeting was to elect John Thrasher as the new chairman. Presiding over the meeting was Jim Greer, the former chairman who had been forced out of office by his Tea Party enemies.

"On Saturday morning I put on my good suit, and Lisa and I went down to the meeting," said Greer. "We were ushered in from the back of the hotel because the Republican leadership didn't want me talking to the press. They didn't want me talking about the severance agreement or about Victory Strategies or any of that."

Jim and Lisa were ushered into the area behind the kitchen where presidential candidates usually pass through to get to the main hall. As they stood waiting for the meeting to begin, who should come walking towards them but Governor Charlie Crist. Crist had no interest in the outcome of the election. Either choice would be bad for him. He was there just to make an appearance.

Two weeks earlier Eikenberg had expressed a fear to Greer that Crist would be booed at the meeting or worse. Eikenberg asked if extra security was needed.

"My God," said Greer, "this is the Republican Party quarterly meeting, Eric. You're asking if a Republican governor needs security at a Republican Party of Florida meeting. Is this how bad things have gotten?"

"I'm hearing things," said Eric.

"It's going to be fine," said Greer reassuringly.

No one booed Crist, as it turned out. But no one came over and shook his hand either. The governor was a lone man in front of a nameplate.

Greer and Crist had last seen each other two weeks before at Fisher Island when they were celebrating Greer's son's birthday. Now, when Crist approached Jim and Lisa, he said but five words.

"Chairman," said Crist coldly. "Chairman for another hour."

And he walked on. Greer was stunned.

Said Lisa, "Can you believe how that asshole just acted after all you did for him?"

Recalled Greer, "Did he really know how he sounded with those words? It just showed he had turned the switch. It was all about his own self-interest now."

To start the meeting Greer walked to the podium. He came right to the point. "The first order of business," he announced, "is to elect a new chairman." He ordered the tellers to pass out the ballots. The party higher-ups sat there wondering whether Day was going to win, because if she did, Armageddon was coming. She had threatened to order an audit. All the elected officials would be under considerable scrutiny . . . unless Palmer and his gang could move the computer records and servers out of the building first.

While the ballots were being counted, Joel Spring, the chief of staff for the Senate campaign, walked over to Lisa Greer and told her how sorry he was.

"Your husband was a good chairman," he said, "and we're really sorry." He then turned to Jim and said, "I want you to know something. We might have to do a fake audit when Thrasher comes in, but it won't mean anything. You won't take any hits. But we're going to do it in order to give these crazies something."

"Fine with me," said Greer, still not understanding the ramifications.

Despite Day's "off with their heads" call, Thrasher was elected. The powers that remained in the Republican Party of Florida were now able to breathe a little. Their relief was palpable. The Tea Party and their ultraconservative followers had tried to stage a coup, but they were beaten back, at least momentarily.

Greer took the podium and announced that Thrasher had defeated Day by 30 votes. It wasn't overwhelming, but it was decisive.

"It goes to show," said Greer, "that many of the state committee members had a brain. They understood that it is leadership that raises all the money for the party."

Thrasher had announced that if elected chairman, he would raise a million dollars for the party and get it back on its feet financially. It was a smart campaign ploy. And he actually kept this promise.

Greer had his photograph taken handing Thrasher the gavel. It was his last act as chairman. He was immediately escorted out the back door to a waiting car. As he departed the Rosen Shingle Creek Resort, he was no longer chairman of the Republican Party of Florida. He and Lisa rode in silence and held hands in the car—just the two of them. No aide. Nothing.

As soon as John Thrasher was elected chairman, the party went into a rare closed-door executive session intended to keep the particulars of the gathering secret. The session was called because the Tea Party members on the board continued to demand information on whether Greer had a severance agreement in an attempt to stop it if the rumors proved true.

Jim Stelling, Greer's close friend and a member of the executive board, reported to Greer that when Day, Gary Lee, and others demanded to know if such an agreement existed, Thrasher told them no. Gonzalez also denied its existence.

John Thrasher's first act as chairman, then, was to lie to the executive board. Then Thrasher added, "But if there is such an agreement, I will not enforce it."

Immediately Greer received calls from other executive board members to tell him that Thrasher had said that he wouldn't pay him.

Greer texted Dean Cannon. "I'm hearing things that concern me greatly," he wrote.

"Don't worry about it," Cannon texted back. "Take your family out of town for the weekend. Everything's going to be fine. We'll talk next week."

"I was *still* under the belief they were going to pay me," recalled Greer. "Everyone was telling me so. For a smart businessman, I sure come out of this sounding pretty naive for believing these people.

"They were treating me like shit, but I believed what they had promised: they would praise my chairmanship, which they did after I left. In fact, Cannon, Haridopolos, Crist, and McCollum all issued press releases praising my chairmanship. But I was dumb enough to believe they were going to pay me."

With a week to go before the severance agreement was to kick in and Greer would receive his first $11,200 payment, he got a call from Stelling. Stelling had been approached by Marc Reichelderfer, the political consultant to both Thrasher and Cannon, and Pat Baynor, the political consultant to Haridopolos.

"They are trying to put the money together," he told Greer, "but they're not sure it's going to be here on the first."

"I have bills, Jim. I want that money on the first," replied Greer.

Stelling continued, "Here's what they're proposing—but the stipulation is you can't cause them any trouble. They're going to give you $200,000, which will be wired into your account. It will come from a third party, a political action committee, maybe a major donor. But you can't talk about any of this. You have to promise not to sue the party, not to get angry, not to talk about the American Express cards."

"Jim, they only owe me $124,000. Why do they want to give me $200,000?" Greer replied.

"They want to keep you happy. It's the right thing to do," said Stelling. "It may not be there on the first, but it will be there in a few days."

"All right," said Greer, sensing that it wasn't all right.

The first of March arrived, and no check.

Greer called Stelling who then promised that an initial payment of $25,000 would be wired into attorney Damon Chase's account by Friday.

Friday came. No money arrived.

By St. Patrick's Day, the party was 17 days late with its money. Chase sent the party a letter demanding payment under the terms of the severance agreement and threatened a lawsuit, an interesting development considering that everyone was denying that the severance agreement even existed.

Stelling came over to Greer's house for dinner. While Greer and Stelling were eating the corned beef Lisa had prepared, Stelling said, "Listen, I hate to say this, but I think there are real problems."

"Yeah," said Greer, "it's been 17 days, and no payment has arrived."

"I really did believe they were going to follow through, Jim," said Stelling, "but it appears they are now going through the records looking for a way to get out of paying you."

"They are?"

"Yeah," said Stelling. "They're doing an audit. They're looking at the Disney World trip and they're looking at the portraits of you and Crist."

"What are you talking about?" asked Greer. "Delmar said the artist donated Charlie's portrait and that the staff chipped in for mine."

"And then there was Delmar's," said Stelling.

"Delmar had a portrait done? He's a staff person."

This was the painting mentioned earlier that the anonymous blogger had referred to.

"Yes, Delmar had a portrait done too. And Delmar lied to you. He had the party pay for all the portraits. I heard they cost five or six thousand dollars."

That still didn't give the party an excuse not to pay Greer under the contract they signed.

Said Stelling, "I've heard through the grapevine that they're not going to pay you."

"Then I'm going to have to sue them," said Greer.

And that's exactly what Greer did, through attorney Chase. He attached the signed severance agreement to the filings of the lawsuit. The headlines in all the Florida papers now blared the existence of that agreement.

The media then turned on Haridopolos and others who had lied about the existence of the severance agreement. For a short time the media was on Greer's side.

In response, Thrasher and McCollum, ultra-conservative Republicans who might as well as been Tea Party members, began to unleash the results of an audit that was manipulated to show only Crist, Greer, and Johnson as targets. The auditors were instructed not to look at anything regarding Rubio, Haridopolos, or Cannon. Nor were they to scrutinize anything that happened during Bush's governorship.

Said Greer, "McCollum and Thrasher teamed up, and they were giving orders to the auditors about what to look for and to keep it narrow."

The audit had but one focus: expenditures during the tenure of Chairman Jim Greer.

54

BENEDICT DELMAR

WHEN THE AUDITORS MET WITH GREER IN MAY 2010, HE WAS HAPPY ABOUT it. His lawyer, Damon Chase, felt otherwise and accompanied him. Greer was told that the audit wouldn't impact him, but as soon as they started asking him questions, he realized that Chase was right. It was a setup.

"Did you go to Disney World with the governor in August of 2009, and is it true that the Republican Party paid for dinners for you and the governor?" they asked him.

Greer readily admitted that was true.

"I paid for those dinners because he's the governor," said Greer. "He's also the head of the party, and we were meeting with Disney World people."

"Is it true that on the trip to Mackinac Island you paid for a hotel room?"

"Yes, it is."

"Let's talk about Victory Strategies. Why didn't you take that contract to the executive board?"

"Because I didn't have to," Greer said. "The executive board has never approved any contract or any fundraising contract. The only person who needed to approve it was Charlie Crist, and he approved it."

"Don't you think you should have taken it to the board?"

"No. No contract ever goes to the board. Besides, the executive board is made up of a bunch of nuts. All they care about is whether you're going to have shrimp and an open bar at the quarterly meetings. The party is run by the elected officials, by the governor and the chairman. And most importantly, we didn't make it well known that Delmar and I were taking over fundraising because Meredith O'Rourke would have screwed us in our efforts. She'd have done everything she could to cut our knees out from under us."

Greer couldn't understand what the fuss was all about. "The most Victory Strategies was ever paid was $200,000," recalled Greer, "and what I got was $125,000, 60 percent." (Ultimately the party would ask for restitution of $61,000.)

The auditors then told Greer something that struck him as wrong. They said, "There are invoices from Victory Strategies submitted to the party that they should pay."

They shoved the invoices over to Greer for his inspection.

"I didn't even know Victory Strategies had invoices," Greer said.

Greer said later that he didn't know because Delmar Johnson was the managing partner and handled the business matters.

"So you've never seen these invoices?"

"No," said Greer. "I don't even know what they're for."

"Mr. Johnson was submitting them over the last year to be paid," Greer was told.

"Listen, guys," said Greer. "I've never seen them. I don't know anything about them. Go and talk to Mr. Johnson."

"He won't meet with us," said the auditors. "So you've never seen these invoices?"

"No, guys. I'll say it again. I didn't even know we had invoices for Victory Strategies."

Said Greer, "I was beginning to understand that Delmar had been doing some things he shouldn't have, that he knew the audit was coming. I believe he suspected he'd get caught. On all of the invoices, he had written one line: "Per the chairman. Please pay this."

Greer was never copied on any of the emailed invoices.

There was concrete physical evidence that Johnson was doing this behind Greer's back. One email Richard Schwartz, the party's CFO, wrote to Johnson said, "I know you don't want me to talk directly with the chairman about these payments."

The question was, *Why was Delmar taking money without letting Greer know about it?*

Greer had a very good idea why: In February 2010, before Greer stepped down as chairman but *after* he was offered his severance agreement, Greer and Lisa were spending the weekend with Charlie and Carole Crist at Fisher

Island. Over drinks Greer said to Crist, "Let me talk to you about something, Governor. Delmar is becoming frustrated. The crazies have taken over the party, and he really needs a job."

Carole piped up, "I don't think we should give him a campaign job. He talks too much."

Charlie added, "He does talk too much, he's involved in too much controversy, and I don't think we should spend the money."

Greer said to them both, "Listen, Delmar has been a loyal soldier. He's put up with a lot of shit. I think we ought to find a job for him."

"Why?" said Carole, "Do you think he'll say things?"

"I just think we ought to find him a job," said Greer.

Thought Greer, *A year ago I was told to give Meredith O'Rourke $5,000 a month just to keep her mouth shut, and here's a guy who has actually worked hard and has been loyal.*

Crist said, "I don't think we ought to hire Delmar what with all the accusations swirling around about party spending."

Greer thought, *This is one of your last remaining guys, Charlie. He was here from the beginning, and you're going to hang him out to dry?*

Greer had no choice but to tell Delmar he was out of luck, that there would be no job for him with the Crist campaign.

"After all I've done," Delmar told Greer. "I just can't believe that Charlie Crist would leave me in the lurch like that."

"Nothing I can do, Delmar," said Greer, "but I'll put in a good recommendation for you anywhere."

"That's not going to help me much," said Delmar. "You have a severance agreement that's going to pay you $11,000 a month. Charlie Crist is going to be the next U.S. senator. I have nothing."

Greer could feel Delmar's pain. But only Crist could have made things right, and he had been too cheap to do it.

"I'll do my best to keep looking for you, Delmar," said Greer.

Soon after, Greer called Chuck Drago, his close friend and Governor Crist's new deputy chief of staff, and asked him to find Delmar a job only to be told that the governor had directed him to do nothing to help Delmar.

Greer felt for his friend. He loved Johnson like a son. He loved his bubbly personality. The two had been inseparable. Delmar had been the student body president at Florida State University, and had become a big man in Tallahassee as Greer's personal assistant and later his executive director. Johnson had big plans in politics. When Crist so callously abandoned him, it was a tremendous blow.

Johnson was forced to fend for himself. He decided the best way to do that was to ingratiate himself with the new crowd of Tea Party politicians taking over the Republican Party.

"As best as I can piece together," said Greer, "Johnson showed up at Republican headquarters and announced something like, 'I have some information that you will find interesting, and I want to get back in your good graces.'"

"Apparently their response was something like, 'If you tell us what we want to hear, you'll be one of us again,' said Greer. "He most likely said to them, 'Here's the deal. The chairman warned me to keep Victory Strategies secret. He told me to write myself checks that weren't legitimate, and to pay him certain sums of money and call them commissions. The chairman ordered me to commission the portraits. The chairman . . .'"

Later it would surface that Johnson had written on every email to the CFO for payment, "Per the chairman." (When CFO Richard Schwartz gave a sworn deposition, he admitted he had never verified with Greer that these payments were approved by Greer.)

"Delmar was the gift that the new gang had been hoping for," said Greer's lawyer, Damon Chase.

It was announced that Greer would not be paid his severance. What came next was even worse. The Tea Party took every lie and exaggeration Johnson told them and ran with them. Greer was never given the opportunity to disprove what Johnson was saying. That was because the Tea Party inquisitors were not looking for the truth. They wanted a hanging.

"My dear wife gets angry when I say anything good about Delmar Johnson and my other accusers," said Greer, "but I'm going to tell you what I think happened. During the last six months Delmar hated his job as executive director as much as I came to hate the chairman job. We had to deal with the shit the Tea Party members were throwing our way every day. Delmar saw that I was focusing my attention on Crist's Senate campaign, and he felt that I was leaving him behind.

"I used to sit with him in his office late at night, and I could see his nerves were shot. He too was taking abuse from the Tea Party people, just on a different level.

"This had been his dream job, and for the last six months he hated it. When you're the executive director, you're the one they scream at. When the state committee members of Alachua County wanted to bitch and moan about something, they called Delmar. When a state committee member of Pinellas County wanted to complain about a Republican Party of Florida field staff person, he called the executive director. And when they wanted to bitch about the chairman, Delmar heard about it first.

"The other reason he did it was that he had been stealing from the party. Delmar felt it was part of his compensation. There's no legitimate way to explain it, but he felt under attack and had convinced himself that he was entitled to a little bonus here, a little bonus there—without me or anyone knowing about it

"What sealed it for him was that he couldn't get a job after I got my severance agreement, that Charlie wouldn't lift a finger for him, and that I had abandoned him. He saw his world crumbling, that I was going to land on my feet, and he would be left with nothing.

"Ultimately, we both got left out."

55

BETRAYAL SINKS IN

AFTER GREER STEPPED DOWN AS CHAIRMAN, HE STILL BELIEVED THAT CRIST would appoint him a senior adviser to his Senate campaign. With this understanding, he moved his boxes of personal belongings from storage into Crist's campaign headquarters down the street from the party headquarters.

He wasn't there very long.

Negative stories about him splashed across the media in late February and early March. Amid the cacophony of negative press, Greer got a call from Eric Eikenberg.

"Hey, Jim, I hate to tell you this," said Eikenberg, "but the governor told me to box up all your stuff at the campaign office and have you come and get it, that you shouldn't come in any more."

Recalled Greer, "Charlie was protecting the campaign and his interests. I could understand that, but Charlie never had the courage to act himself. I was now a victim of what he'd done to others. Erin Isaac had been with Charlie through everything, and he had Eric to get rid of her. When Charlie didn't appoint Jeff Kottkamp to the Senate after promising he'd be the appointee, he had me deliver the news. Now here I was, Crist's best friend, his brother, the person he promised to stick with, and Eric was telling me they were boxing up everything in my campaign office, and I shouldn't come in any more. It was obvious that I was to be the scapegoat."

Greer told Lisa, "It's getting ready bad, and the only person who can stop it is Charlie, and he's sticking his head in the sand."

Greer didn't yet know just *how far* Crist had moved away from him.

News stories appeared in late March 2010 that Republican Party auditors were looking closely for evidence that Crist and Greer had spent party money on themselves.

Rumors swirled that Greer would be indicted. But whenever he asked his lawyer or a lawyer friend, he was always told the issue was a civil dispute over a contract, not a criminal case, and that he was protected by the 'hold harmless' clause in the severance agreement.

Greer's lawyers might have been right but for the vindictive natures of the ultra-conservative John Thrasher, the new chairman of the party, and Attorney General Bill McCollum, who controlled the Florida Department of Law Enforcement.

In 2009, when Greer was chairman, he and McCollum got into a spat over McCollum's use of the FDLE. Brevard County Republican Chairman Jason Steele, a Tea Party troublemaker, discovered that someone was impersonating him on Twitter. The impersonator posted vulgar comments about party officials and was making it seem that Steele, a recovering alcoholic, was drinking again. Steele called the local sheriff's office, who tracked the Twitter account to a computer in the Palm Bay home of Tim Nungesser, a hard-working party field representative loyal to Crist. Steele had criticized Crist in REC meetings, and Nungesser was getting back at him.

When Greer heard about this, he fired Nungesser, over the objections of Delmar Johnson and other party staff. (Later Greer discovered that Johnson, a close friend of Nungesser, gave him a $10,000 severance without consulting Greer.)

"No matter how much I hated Jason Steele and loved Tim Nungesser, there was no way a field rep could be allowed to create a false account about a Republican county chairman," said Greer.

McCollum, whose sympathies lay with Steele, told Greer, "I think to calm the party down in Brevard, I'm going to ask the FDLE to investigate the issue."

Greer, pissed off, argued to McCollum—in a conversation in front of Eikenberg—that it was an internal party matter. "We're not having the FDLE come into the Republican Party headquarters and start looking around. Second of all, General, with all due respect, this is not your decision. The governor runs the party."

McCollum had steamed. As Greer would come to find out, McCollum was the wrong person to have as an enemy, and now with Crist the lamest of lame ducks, and gubernatorial candidate McCollum still the attorney general, Greer was dead in his sights. There was no one to keep McCollum from going after Greer criminally for alleged personal spending on his RPOF American Express card or any other payments made on behalf of others, even though by all accounts this should have been a civil matter.

McCollum ordered the FDLE to launch an investigation and referred the matter to the statewide prosecutor, who was appointed by McCollum.

"It had never been done before," said Greer. "It will probably never be done again. But McCollum was using the state police to find a way to get me and Crist."

Greer said Jay Burmer told him "that if McCollum could have indicted Charlie Crist, he would have." But McCollum found that pinning something on the elusive Crist was easier said than done. Crist never paid for anything; he always had Greer do it for him. As a result there was no Crist paper trail for McCollum to follow.

It began to seem that to McCollum, indicting Greer would be better than nothing. News stories in early April 2010 cited a "possibility" Greer was going to be arrested and indicted.

On the Friday before Easter, Greer received a phone call from his close friend Chris Dorworth. "I hear Charlie Crist isn't saying good things about you," said Dorworth.

Greer, crushed and feeling betrayed, called Crist and left him a voice mail. "Charlie," he said, "I've heard you've been saying unkind things about me. This is really upsetting because I've done everything for you. I'll tell you what, Charlie. I don't want to ever hear from you again."

Around midnight Greer's phone rang. Caller ID indicated that Crist was the caller. At 7 the next morning Greer's phone rang again. It was Crist. Greer clicked *Ignore.* "He called every 30 minutes," said Greer, "and I wasn't picking up."

Jay Burmer called Greer at noon. "Charlie's in a panic," said Burmer. "He thinks you've gone off the reservation. He's worried you won't be loyal to him anymore and that you may say things that will hurt him. Take his phone call. Call him."

"Listen, Jay," said Greer, "I had to resign because of Charlie. There are all these rumors I'm going to be arrested, and I don't see any public statements coming from Governor Charlie Crist supporting me. Now I'm hearing from Dorworth that he's not saying great things about me."

"That's not true," said Burmer. "At least I don't think it's true. It's just the rumor mill. You know Charlie loves you. You need to take his call."

"Jay, all he cares about is whether I've turned on him. Do you really think he cares about me? He just wants to know if I'm still on the 'Charlie Crist team' because there aren't many of us left."

"All right," said Jay, "But would you please take his call? He's been calling me all morning."

As a favor to Burmer, Greer finally called the governor.

"Chairman, how are you?" said Crist. "I've been trying to call you."

"Yeah, I know you have," said Greer without warmth.

"I got your message," said Crist, "and I want you to know I'm not saying anything bad about you. I'm saying you were a great chairman. I'm saying what happened to you is terrible. All these rumors are terrible."

"It's April," said Greer. "I resigned in January. They haven't paid me."

"I was worried about whether they were going to pay you," said Crist. "Remember that time at the mansion I told you to make sure you get it in writing."

"I got it all in writing," said Greer. "but they're still not paying me. Here's the thing: There are all these rumors that they're going to have me arrested and indicted."

"What could they indict you for?" asked Crist.

"I don't know, but they're doing a big audit, and I think they may try to come after you too," said Greer.

"There's nothing I did that they can come after," said Crist. "I've never done anything . . ."

"The party has paid for a lot of your stuff," said Greer.

"Well, yeah, but it was all legitimate. You paid for it. You were the chairman."

"Yes, I know that," said Greer.

Crist changed gears. He wanted Greer to give him some political advice.

"I'm thinking of running for the Senate seat as an independent," said Crist. "What do you think?"

"I think it's a good idea, because you're going to lose in the primary," said Greer. "If you do lose in the primary, you're done. It's not like Joe Lieberman losing in the Connecticut primary and then running in the general. You can't lose the Republican primary and stay on the general ticket. Florida doesn't allow that. You have 30 days to declare you're running as an Independent."

Added Greer for emphasis, "And you *are* going to lose."

"You think so?" said Crist.

"Yeah. The whole party has left you, and they're trying to hang me. Listen," said Greer, trying to be as respectful as he always had been, "They're trying to destroy me because of my loyalty to you. They think if they can destroy me, it will embarrass you in the election."

"Yes, I know that," said Crist.

"And there are all these stories out there about Victory Strategies, that no one knew about it, and that it should have gone through the executive board."

"That's horseshit," said Crist. "You saved the party money. Meredith was making $30,000 a month, and you only got ten percent."

"Yes, I know," said Greer.

Crist changed the subject back to his favorite topic—himself.

"What do you think I should do, Chairman?"

"I'll tell you what I think you should do," said Greer. "I think you should pull out and run as an independent. Because if you do that, at least you'll be alive until November. You're going to lose the primary to Rubio. Then it's going to be Rubio against Kendrick Meek in the November election. If you pull out now and run as an independent, you'll at least live to fight another day. You'll have two or three more months to campaign in the general election against Rubio and Meek."

"We're trying to get Meek out," said Crist.

"I heard that," said Greer, "but I don't think Meek's getting out."

"People are talking to him about getting out," said Crist. "Then it will just be me and Rubio."

"I've heard you have people pressuring Meek, but he's not going to be forced out after he's been running for two years."

Crist returned to the matter at hand.

"Where are you and I?" asked Crist.

"You and I are still good," said Greer. "You know I care about you. But if you start saying things like, 'He wasn't a good chairman,' or if you start trying to cover your own ass, I'm never going to forgive you for it."

"I would never do that," said Crist. "I would *never* do that. You were a damn fine chairman. You were the best chairman the party ever had. This is terrible what they've done to you."

"They're talking about arresting me," said Greer.

"They can't arrest you," said Crist. "There's nothing you've done. You were the chairman. You could enter into any contracts you wanted to. And anything we spent money on, we did so legitimately. They don't remember how much money I raised for them."

"Yeah, I know," said Greer. "They don't. They want to embarrass you by arresting and indicting your former chairman."

"Chairman, you're right," said Crist. "So are we good? Are you going to take my calls when I call you?"

"Yeah," said Greer. "We're good, Governor. I'm glad you called me."

"I want you to know, Jim, I haven't said one bad thing about you."

"Okay," said Greer. "I'm glad to hear that, because I've heard from more than one source that you have."

"That's a lie," said Crist. "I haven't."

Greer hung up the phone, not sure what to think.

56

Delmar Is Wired

Unsettled by the rumors that McCollum and his FDLE minions intended to have him indicted and arrested, Greer decided that he should hire a top-notch criminal attorney. He made an appointment in late February 2010 with Marcos Jimenez of Miami, a former U.S. attorney with a sterling reputation as a hard-nosed defender. Hiring Jimenez, whose specialty was government relations, was costly—$20,000 just to look at the case.

When Greer met with Jimenez for the first time at the offices of Becker and Poliakoff in Miami, he brought with him a stack of documents, including the Victory Strategies contract and an accounting of the RPOF's American Express charges.

After inspecting the documents, Jimenez concluded, "There is no crime here. If they prosecute you—if they try to do anything to you—it would be prosecutorial misconduct." (This would not be the last time Greer would hear this term.)

The attorney told Greer, "Go home, and don't worry."

Greer wasn't convinced. He told Jimenez, "I'm hearing all these rumors. I'm scared. I was told John Thrasher and Bill McCollum held a conference call on March 30 with the state committee in which they said they were auditing Governor Crist and me."

"They're just political rumors," said the lawyer. "You haven't done anything wrong."

During the conversation, Greer mentioned that his longtime friend and protégé, Delmar Johnson, had stopped communicating with him. "At the end of February he got angry with me because I hadn't found him a job," said Greer. "He has stopped returning my calls."

That did alarm Jimenez. "You need to stay away from Delmar," he advised Greer. "If they're looking at anything, and Delmar isn't returning your calls, Delmar may have flipped."

"There's nothing to flip on," said Greer.

"Just don't talk to him," repeated Jimenez.

Greer just couldn't believe that Johnson, the man Greer had brought into high-level politics, a close family friend who had spent many a night at Greer's home, godfather to their son Aiden—the man Greer made his field director, travel aide, special assistant, deputy executive director, and ultimately the RPOF executive director—would do anything to harm him. Greer's basic decency made it impossible for him to wrap his arms around the idea that Johnson would betray him. What he didn't yet realize was that to get at Jim Greer, McCollum had threatened to indict Johnson, and that Johnson had agreed to cooperate in McCollum's investigation against Greer in exchange for total immunity for himself.

Johnson, no longer liable for anything he himself had done, made sure McCollum had plenty of information to bury Greer. Never mind that most of his stories lacked a factual basis, as Johnson told tales of prostitutes and wild parties at Crist fundraising events, stories that made for big headlines in newspapers all over Florida but which had little or no truth to them.

"None of that happened," said Greer. "Some men brought women who weren't their wives to these events, but there were no prostitutes, no wild parties. Delmar was telling these stories to ingratiate himself with McCollum and the FDLE."

Johnson, it turned out, had taken many thousands of RPOF dollars for his personal benefit, but with a promise of total immunity from McCollum, he was free to blame everything—including his own spending—on Greer.

Said Greer, "His testimony basically boiled down to: 'Everything I did, Chairman Greer told me to do it.'"

In exchange for immunity, Johnson agreed to tape phone conversations with Greer to get Greer to implicate himself. Unfortunately for McCollum, there was nothing incriminating for Greer to talk about. If anything, from the transcripts Johnson looked like the one who was playing fast and loose with the spending rules—which in fact was what had occurred.

Delmar Johnson, presumably not wired, holding his godson, Aiden Greer.

ON MARCH 14, 2010—OUT of the blue—Johnson phoned Greer. Despite Jimenez's admonition to be wary, Greer was glad to hear from Delmar.

"Hey, Chairman, I'm sorry I haven't been around," he said. "How've you been? What's been going on?"

During their conversation Greer discussed with Johnson a bill Victory Strategies owed to the Orlando law firm of GrayRobinson. Under their Victory Strategies agreement, Greer and Johnson split their earnings and their expenses 60 percent for Greer, 40 percent for Johnson. Johnson had been in charge of the accounting. He was also responsible for opening a post office box, a bank account, and calculating all commission payments due. Johnson ran the entire Victory Strategies business office.

Concerning payment of the Gray Robinson bill, Greer asked whether the Victory Strategies bank account was still open. Johnson couldn't—or wouldn't—give him a straight answer.

"You don't have a checking account, right?" asked Greer.

"Right, but I can deposit money into it," said Johnson.

"Is it still opened?"

"No," said Johnson. "I closed it. I'm trying to think. The bank account for the campaign, it closed then reopened."

Johnson was talking gibberish.

"It's closed and . . .?" said Greer.

"I will call them and make sure I . . ." said Johnson.

Johnson hadn't closed the account.

Later in the conversation Greer said to Johnson, "Why don't we go ahead and let everybody know that you and I are Victory Strategies?"

"No, no, I don't want to do that," said Johnson. "I don't think we should do that."

"What does it matter now?" asked Greer. "We have to get the taxes done. Have you hired an accountant?"

"Yes, yes, I've hired an accountant," said Johnson.

"Have you ever told anybody that we owned Victory Strategies?" asked Greer.

"No, no, not at all," said Johnson. "No, no."

"Because you know," said Greer, "if Meredith had found out a year and a half ago about it, she'd have killed us."

"Yeah, yeah, you're right," Johnson said. "You're right. Absolutely. She would have Brian [Ballard] call every major donor and tell them not to write any more checks."

According to Greer, fundraisers are notorious for sabotaging their successors in order to preserve their reputations.

"Do you think McCollum and Thrasher will use the Victory Strategies contract and the American Express card payments to embarrass us so they don't have to pay my severance?"

"Yeah, that could be," said Johnson.

Johnson changed the subject, asking Greer if he thought Crist would run as an Independent. He ended the conversation with, "Give my godson a big kiss."

AFTER THE TAPE OF the phone conversation was revealed during legal proceedings and Greer's lawyer Damon Chase heard it, he told Greer, "This tape is great. It shows you didn't know what Delmar Johnson was doing.

How many criminals are concerned about getting their taxes done?"

Johnson showed up another day at Greer's home with a stuffed bunny for Greer's son Aiden, and evidence later showed that Johnson was wearing a wire for the FDLE at the direction of Bill McCollum.

By this time Greer understood that some of what Johnson had told him about spending wasn't true. Now Greer wanted straight answers. During the taped conversation, Johnson repeatedly implicated himself, but of course he had been given immunity from prosecution.

"Did you have a portrait done? I heard you had a portrait done," Greer asked Johnson.

"Yeah," said Johnson, "but I paid for it myself."

"That's not what I'm hearing," said Greer. "Did you also have the party pay for your house in Tallahassee?"

"Well, yeah," said Johnson, "I deserved a relocation package."

"That might be true, Delmar, but you should have asked me first."

Greer then asked, "Delmar, is there anything else at the party that I should know about?"

"Well, no, no. Of course not," he said.

"What about all those commission checks you wrote to me from Victory Strategies, were they all legitimate?"

"Yes, yes. Except for a couple of consulting checks I wrote . . ."

"From Victory Strategies?" Greer asked in surprise.

"Yeah."

And then Johnson abruptly changed the subject.

"MCCOLLUM AND THE FDLE had now entered the case," said Greer, "and they were recording me. They hadn't counted on the fact that I would say nothing detrimental. During that conversation Delmar never said to me, 'Remember when we stole that money from the party?' He didn't because he knew if he had, I would have replied, 'What are you talking about.'"

There was absolutely nothing on the tapes that could implicate Greer in anything illegal. If anything, the tapes implicated Johnson.

"Is there anything that you did that I didn't know about?" Greer had asked Johnson.

"No," said Johnson.

"What was on your AMEX that could be a problem?" asked Greer. "I mean, tell me. Just between you and me. We need to be honest with each other."

"I don't know," said Johnson.

Greer pushed, trying to discover if Johnson had done anything improper. "Tell me. What's out there that hasn't come out yet that might look bad if discovered?"

"The only thing that the AMEX was used for after August was travel," said Johnson. "That's all it was used for. I didn't use mine at all. I didn't even have it in my wallet."

There had been news stories that the audit revealed that the Republican Party of Florida had paid for Charlie Crist's wedding.

"Is there anything on the wedding that I need to know about," asked Greer.

"No," said Johnson. "That was all paid for personally. Nothing."

"Because they keep writing about the wedding," said Greer.

"Yeah," said Johnson. "Well, maybe just the flowers for Carole Crist . . . That's the only thing I can think of."

Johnson would later be accused of stealing $42,000 from the RPOF. But in exchange for his testimony against Greer, he would be granted immunity and given five years to make restitution. (As this book was going to press in the spring of 2014, Johnson had paid no restitution.)

Greer had no idea he was being taped. Afterwards he called his lawyer and told him that Johnson had just paid a visit.

"Oh, my God," was Jimenez's reaction.

Jimenez told him, "The number one rule in these kinds of situations is that when someone disappears and refuses communication, and then suddenly shows up, they've flipped."

"They can flip all they want," Greer said. "I've done nothing wrong."

"You should never have talked to him," the lawyer said.

The clock was ticking.

57

UNDER ARREST

GREER HAD SIGNED A SEVERANCE AGREEMENT WITH THE REPUBLICAN PARTY of Florida. Every important figure in Republican politics in Florida had signed it. Under the agreement he was to be held harmless for anything he or anyone else might have done while he was chairman, and he was to be paid $11,200 a month until the $122,000 that would have been due to him by the end of his term was paid by the party. And now the new party leadership was reneging.

Greer added his Seminole County attorney, Damon Chase, to his legal team. After Chase read all the documents Marcos Jimenez had gathered, Chase came up with the same conclusion: "There's nothing here. This is all about their trying to get out of the severance agreement that they signed with you."

Chase and Greer concluded that the only way Greer would get paid was if he sued the RPOF for breach of the severance agreement. Chase filed a lawsuit on Greer's behalf asking for $5 million in damages and penalties.

Meanwhile, two of Greer's closest friends, Jim Stelling and Chris Dorworth, were telling him that Attorney General Bill McCollum was working hard to figure out a way to arrest both Crist and Greer.

"Despite the rumors," recalled Greer, "I was feeling comfortable because every lawyer I was talking to told me there were no crimes, that this was a civil dispute about a contract."

Greer was also being advised that even if McCollum was intent on accusing him of a crime, he couldn't be prosecuted because of the hold-harmless clause in the severance agreement, a clause that ran on for more than a page.

"It says the Republican Party can't bring up anything you did, and you can't raise anything they did," said Chase. "It's all to create political rumors meant to embarrass you and Crist."

But Greer's lawyers didn't anticipate the ruthlessness of McCollum and the anti-Crist faction now running the RPOF. In May 2010 Greer received a phone call from his lawyers telling him they had received a letter—from the statewide prosecutor's office that reports to McCollum—requesting that Greer appear before a public corruption grand jury investigating the Republican Party of Florida. The prosecutor was looking into American Express charges and also wanted to ask Greer about the Victory Strategies fundraising contract.

"Let's go," Greer responded immediately.

Meanwhile, Marcos Jimenez had brought another veteran attorney onto Greer's legal team, former U.S. attorney Greg Miller from Tallahassee. Both Jimenez and Miller offered the same advice: "You never testify in front of a grand jury. A grand jury is a prosecutor's tool."

Said Jimenez. "Haven't you heard the statement, 'A grand jury can indict a ham sandwich'?"

"Yes, I have," said Greer.

"There's nothing more truthful than that," he was told. "You're not allowed to take a lawyer with you to the grand jury room. The prosecutor makes all the rulings and answers the questions that the grand jury might have. Their aim is to trip you up."

"I want to get in there and talk about all these things," said Greer. "Yes, we kept Victory Strategies quiet, but that was because Meredith O'Rourke and Brian Ballard would have kept us from raising money. The governor knew of and approved of my taking over fundraising and paying myself a commission."

"That may be," said Jimenez, "but I'm telling you: you don't want to go in front of a grand jury and say anything."

Jimenez and Miller instead wrote a long letter to the foreman of the grand jury explaining that this was a political case, that the statewide prosecutor's office should recuse itself because it was under the authority of Attorney General Bill McCollum, a Tea Party candidate for governor who had it in for Greer. The lawyers suggested that the foreman take a look at the RPOF's website where he would see McCollum's picture and the criticism of both Crist and Greer.

"It is highly inappropriate," the lawyers wrote with great logic. "The entity that is initiating this is partisan, and we believe the attorney general and the statewide prosecutor should recuse themselves."

They were whistling in the wind.

GREER'S ATTORNEYS MAY HAVE been telling him he had nothing to worry about, but Greer knew how spiteful and vindictive McCollum, Thrasher, and their Tea Party bullies could be, and he was in a constant state of nervousness.

The Greers had bought a two-bedroom condo on the beach in Cape Canaveral, Florida, in 2007 after he sold his company. On Memorial Day 2010 Greer and Lisa decided to ease the tension by spending the weekend there.

Greer's friend Jim Stelling, meanwhile, was keeping an eye on the machinations of McCollum, Thrasher, and the other leaders of the Republican Party of Florida to see what they were up to with respect to Crist and Greer.

Stelling phoned Greer and said, "I got a call from someone on the state committee and he told me they were going through all your charges and all of Charlie Crist's expenses, and they're upset about the Victory Strategies fundraising contract. They don't care whether it saved the party money or not. They're upset about it, and they're upset Delmar did the portraits. They're angry that you were traveling with Charlie for his Senate campaign events. They're searching for a way to prosecute you to get out of the severance agreement."

Another party friend, Chris Dorworth, called and said, "I told you before you resigned that this would happen. They're looking at any way to come after you. Some mean, evil people have taken over this party."

"By 'mean evil people,'" said Greer later, "Dorworth was talking about John Thrasher and Bill McCollum, Bret Prater, the interim director, Mike Haridopolos, and Dean Cannon. My lawyer told me, 'When they're trying to build a case against you, they don't let anyone say anything good about you.' It was all bad."

Hearing the rumors of his imminent arrest, both Jim and Lisa were so rattled they were having difficulty eating and sleeping. When they returned home to Oviedo, on a Tuesday around ten at night, Greer received a phone call from his lawyer, Marcos Jimenez, who tried to calm him.

"Listen, Jim," he said, "I know there are a lot of rumors out there, and I truly believe you committed no crime based on everything I've looked at and everything you've told me. Go to bed. Rest easy tonight. I don't think anything is going to happen, and even if it does, the prosecutor's office will call me first because you have a lawyer, and you're not a flight risk."

Greer's lawyers were confident that if McCollum and the FDLE were going to move against him, they would call his lawyers first so Greer could turn himself in. It was a courtesy almost always given to high-profile defendants.

McCollum and the statewide prosecutor didn't have the decency to give that courtesy to Greer.

AT NINE THE NEXT morning. Lisa was in the kitchen with two-year-old Aiden. Jim was in his pajamas in bed with five-year-old Austin, sick with a cold, snuggling in his arm. The two older children were off to school.

Lisa came running into the bedroom.

"Jim, Jim, get up," she screamed. "There are police climbing the back fence of the house, and they're pulling up in the driveway, and there's a helicopter over the house."

Jim jumped up out of the bed, put on a pair of pants and a shirt, and made a quick stop to the bathroom while Lisa opened the front door.

Immediately a posse of plainclothes FDLE agents pushed her aside and stormed into the house. They went to the bathroom door, which was closed, and announced, "Mr. Greer, we have a warrant issued by the grand jury for your arrest."

Greer, shaving quickly, cut his lip, and he stood there bleeding while sons Austin and Aiden were crying in fear. Lisa's mother, who was visiting, picked them up in her arms.

"Stand over here, Mr. Greer," he was ordered. "You're under arrest."

Greer, trying to make everything less stressful for everyone, put his hands behind his back. As he was led out the front door of his home in handcuffs, he could hear his young children screaming.

The press was there to take it all in. "They had been tipped off," said Greer. "There were cars blocking my driveway and there were the helicopters. It was all for show."

On the ride to the county jail, Greer sarcastically asked one of the FDLE agents, "All of this for a former chairman of the Republican Party?"

There was no reply.

The remaining officers spent six hours searching his home for evidence. The officers pulled his kids' books off shelves and dumped them on the floor. They went through letters that Jim and Lisa had written to each other when they were dating. "All of the relevant documents I had were in possession of the Republican Party of Florida in Tallahassee," said Greer. "The FDLE had the same copies I had. They didn't need to rummage through my house."

Lisa, infuriated, got into a shouting match with the FDLE agents.

"You're just Bill McCollum's Gestapo," she screamed. "Bill McCollum should go fuck himself."

Greer knew almost all of the Orlando FDLE agents and found it odd that he hadn't recognized the agents who raided his home. He later learned that most of the agents had been brought down from Tallahassee because many of the Orlando agents wanted nothing to do with Greer's arrest.

Jim called Lisa from the county jail. The call was recorded. He told her he wasn't put in a cell. "Everything's going to be fine," he told her. "Be nice to the agents. They're just doing their job. What they're looking for is information on Victory Strategies, and it's in a box in my office."

"Why are you being so nice?" Lisa wanted to know.

"They're just doing what they've been told to do," he said.

"Most of the agents were professional and courteous to Lisa," Greer said later. "A couple were real jerks. One wouldn't let her go to the bathroom without an agent standing in the bathroom with her. My kids were crying. It was a bad scene."

Greer directed his contempt at McCollum, who was going after Greer with the same viciousness with which he had once pursued President Bill Clinton over Monica-gate. McCollum, then a member of the U.S. House of Representatives, had led the Republican demand that Clinton be impeached. It was overkill, as Greer knew this was toward him.

"When I met with my lawyers at the jail, they were astounded," said Greer. "The prosecutors knew I had a lawyer, and they knew I would have turned myself in. Why did they have to raid my house, spend all that tax-payer money, and terrify my little kids?"

As FOR McCOLLUM AND the Republican Party leadership, who were looking for this public arrest of Greer to help catapult McCollum into the governor's office—it turned out to be all for nothing. In the end McCollum didn't even become the Republican nominee.

Greer was not surprised by that. He recalled that in late 2009 he was having a discussion with political consultants Jim Rimes and Rich Heffley about the upcoming governor's race when they told him they had heard about a group of business people looking for an alternative to McCollum. Greer was intrigued, because he felt such a search was unusual given that the entire Republican establishment had gotten behind McCollum.

"There were people going way back to his congressional days who didn't like or trust him," said Greer. "He had once backed anti-business initiatives. He had also done things as attorney general that pissed off some business leaders in Florida. I was told they were looking for someone with money to run against him. Money was essential because the donor base had gotten the message that McCollum was the guy. These backers of an alternative candidate had to find someone with money of his own to make up for the financial backing he wasn't going to get from the Republican Party."

They found him in Naples, Florida—Rick Scott. At one time Scott had owned Columbia/HCA, the largest privately owned for-profit health care company in the country. In 1997, he resigned after the company was accused of cheating Medicaid out of $1.4 billion dollars. Columbia/HCA admitted to 14 felonies and agreed to pay the federal government almost a billion dollars in fines. Scott denied any involvement.

After he resigned, he started Richard L. Scott Investments. He was worth $200 million and vowed to spend a significant chunk of it running for governor.

"In three and a half years as RPOF chairman, I had never heard his name even mentioned as a possible candidate," recalled Greer. "They found him in southwest Florida, and not only did he have the money to run against Mc-Collum, he had the backing of the Tea Party. It was all over for McCollum."

58

STABBED IN THE BACK

AFTER GREER'S ARREST THE FDLE DEMANDED THAT HE BE PUT IN A CELL, but Seminole County Sheriff Donald Eslinger assigned him to a chair in the lobby until he could post bond, which was set at $100,000, more than it should have been considering Greer's ties to the community. To get out he would have to post $10,000 in cash.

"The judge set the bail," said Greer. "He did what the prosecutor asked him."

Greer should have had a bail-reduction hearing, but the hearing was set at one o'clock in the afternoon, and the FDLE claimed it couldn't find the paperwork, which magically appeared not long after the one o'clock deadline. The next bail hearing wasn't scheduled until the next day.

Greer had two choices. He could either pay the $10,000 or wait until the next morning, when he might have had his bond reduced or eliminated.

"But who wants to sit in jail overnight?" said Greer. Lisa Greer and Melanie Chase went to a bail bondsman, obtained the $10,000 in cash, and later that afternoon Greer was freed. Damon Chase met Greer at the back door of the sheriff's department in his SUV. A gaggle of reporters was waiting to film it all. His arrest made the national news—CNN, FOX, the *Washington Post*, and the *New York Times*.

The Orange County circuit court in Orlando was assigned jurisdiction. The presiding judge was Marc L. Lubet of the 9th Circuit.

Chase aggressively recommended that Greer hire attorneys Cheney Mason and Don Lykkebak to try the case as they had experience going in front of Judge Lubet.

Mason and Lykkebak met with Greer at Chase's office in Lake Mary, north of Orlando. After Greer showed them the Victory Strategies contract and the severance agreement, Mason reacted to the injustice of it all. "This is the biggest bunch of bullshit I have ever seen. It's outrageous," he said. "You have a hold-harmless clause in the severance agreement that says that every expenditure of fundraising made through the consulting contract is approved and ratified."

Mason concluded, "This damn case is going to be dropped."

Notwithstanding his optimism, Mason said he needed $100,000 to take the case. What could Greer do? He was in a terrible bind. Paying Mason would take the last bit of money Greer had left. Even so, to pay his legal costs he had to withdraw the money in his two older children's college funds that he had paid off years before.

Mason learned that to obtain the warrant for Greer's arrest, McCollum and the FDLE had gone to Peggy Ann Quince, the chief justice of the Florida Supreme Court. "I've never seen anything like that," said Mason. "Usually you get the search warrant from the county where the accused resides. No one ever goes to the chief justice of the Supreme Court."

"They were spending millions arresting and prosecuting me," said Greer. "And remember this is over a fundraising contract that had been approved, ratified, and determined to be lawful, according to the severance agreement. They organized a raid on my house with agents whose guns were visible to my wife and children. They went to the chief justice of the Florida Supreme Court. All because they wanted to embarrass me and Charlie Crist. They wanted revenge. This was all about revenge."

GREER WAS SITTING AT the bar in the Black Hammock Restaurant in Oviedo about five minutes from his home with some of his Seminole County politico friends—Chris Dorworth, Jason Brodeur, and Alex Setzer, men who got where they did in politics in large part because of Greer. The Black Hammock's bar is on the water, with alligators looking on menacingly from nearby cages.

At this time there were stories in the newspapers about the party's credit card spending, not just by Crist and Greer, but by Dean Cannon, Mike Haridopolos, Ken Pruitt, and Marco Rubio as well.

"These guys are so stupid," said Greer to his friends. "They've caused so many problems. If they had just paid me my $125,000 severance, if they hadn't gone to all the trouble to attack me and embarrass me and arrest me and try to destroy me and Charlie Crist, they certainly wouldn't have had so much negative press. It's pathetic how much harm they've done to themselves. There's a resounding opinion now of, 'Why didn't those idiots just pay Greer his severance agreement'? Because as much damage as they've done to me, they did more to themselves."

All his friends could do was shake their heads.

Mason had continued to advise Greer that the case would be dropped. "All we have to do is prove that Charlie Crist told you to take over fundraising and that he knew about Victory Strategies," he said to Greer.

"I can tell you where I was when I informed Crist of the arrangement," Greer replied. "We were at a golf tournament in February of 2009 when he approved of the arrangement. He also approved my paying myself a commission."

Greer added, "George LeMieux was the first person who suggested we make this arrangement. If you check with Harry Sargeant, the finance chairman of the party, or with Jay Burmer, the political consultant, they'll tell you the same thing."

"When we prove this," said Mason, "the case will be dropped."

Not long afterwards as Greer sat with Dorworth and Setzer at the Black Hammock having a drink, his Blackberry suddenly went off. Greer looked down at a news alert printed on the small screen that said: "Charlie Crist gave a sworn statement today to the FDLE that he knew nothing about the fundraising agreement or Greer's Victory Strategies contract."

Stunned, Greer read it over and over to make sure he was comprehending what he was reading. He knew that Crist could be calculating, but to lie in such a way that would put a friend in jeopardy of going to jail was just unthinkable to Greer.

In shock, Greer passed out and sank to the floor of the restaurant. When Greer came to after several minutes, Setzer and Dorworth drove him home. Lisa saw that Greer's face was red, that he was short of breath, and that his blood pressure was extraordinarily high. She dialed 911. The Oviedo Fire and Rescue Team responded and rushed him to South Seminole Hospital.

At one time, Greer was the deputy mayor of Oviedo. The members of

Fire and Rescue Team knew and liked him. When he arrived at the hospital, the rescue team members signed him into the hospital under the name Bob Reynolds to shield him from the news media.

Crist's back-stabbing denial had so unnerved Greer that his blood pressure was "off the charts." His doctor advised him to take medication to keep his blood pressure down, and to take pills to ease his depression.

"No," Greer told the doctor, "I'm not taking any of that stuff."

They let him out after two days.

"I was crushed," recalled Greer, "absolutely devastated that Charlie would give that affidavit. I couldn't believe it. I still can't. I knew Charlie was still in his Republican primary, but I also knew he was thinking of becoming an Independent. So if he was thinking about doing that, why did he have to bow down to the Tea Party and try to keep them happy? I bet he thought he could still win the Republican primary. He knew he couldn't win it if he came out in defense of Jim Greer—whether it was the right thing to do or not. I have no doubt whatsoever that was why he did that.

"One of my close friends, Jay Burmer, said to me, 'Do you think I would ever sign an affidavit that the FDLE put in front of me that was against you?'

"'Of course not,' I said.

"'What kind of person is he?' Burmer said. 'He's your best friend who you've done so much for. How could he sign an affidavit like that?'

"I told Burmer that Charlie knew they'd attack him. In his mind he had not yet lost the Republican primary. I wonder what Charlie would say today. Since then he's done several other things to betray me, so I don't think he'll ever change. Once Charlie pulls that switch and he's done with you, he's done with you."

Recalled Greer, "From that day forward Lisa became absolutely disgusted with Charlie and with Carole, especially after all we had done for them and after Charlie had told me so many times: 'I'm going to stick by you, Chairman.' All those times he would say to me, 'Evil prevails when good men do nothing.' He would know."

GREER'S LAWYERS KNEW THEY would have to prove that Crist was lying. It wasn't going to be that difficult. Greer's friend Harry Sargeant, a fraternity brother of Crist at FSU, had witnessed Greer talking to Crist about taking over fundraising. And he heard Crist tell Greer to "go ahead."

Sargeant immediately agreed to give a sworn affidavit supporting Greer (see Appendix). "I was on those phone calls with you," Sargeant said to Greer. "I was in conversations with you, George LeMieux, and with Charlie. Charlie is not remembering, and I'll give a sworn affidavit. What they are doing to you is terrible. I like Charlie, but what's happening to you is wrong."

When Greer called Burmer and told him what had happened, Burmer was convinced that the charges would be dropped. Greer responded that he didn't think so, that the prosecutor who worked under Tea Partier Attorney General Pam Bondi wouldn't drop anything.

Burmer, who was involved in the conversations between Crist and Greer, also gave a written affidavit in Greer's support.

The clincher for Greer was Brian Ballard, who had been close to O'Rourke and never close to Greer but who recognized the injustice. He too agreed to state in a deposition that Crist was lying and that he had been told by Crist that Crist had authorized Greer to take over fundraising and earn a commission.

"I was greatly relieved," said Greer, "because Brian Ballard's a big guy. He's very important. He's the number one donor to the Republican Party of Florida, and Charlie Crist's number one guy when it came to raising money. I was excited that he was going to give a deposition and I hoped he'd tell the truth. After Ballard finished being deposed, I got a text message from my lawyer.

"'Great deposition,' it said.

"Don Lykkebak and Damon Chase were damn excited about this," said Greer, "and based on what he heard Ballard say, Damon sent me a text that read, 'This case will be dropped by five o'clock today.'

"I think this nightmare is going to end."

59

A FINAL HELLO

An old political friend's son was getting married at The Breakers hotel in Palm Beach in March 2011. Jim and Lisa were invited, and they were excited about going. They would be back among old friends, some of whom they hadn't seen in over a year since Greer was forced out of his chairmanship and basically out of Florida politics.

Greer wondered whether Charlie and Carole Crist would be there. Greer hadn't talked to Charlie for over a year. Yes, Crist had given a deposition in an attempt to save his own career and had wrecked Greer's. But during the past year Greer had talked to his friends Jay Burmer and Sargeant, and both of them had told him of their conversations with Crist who would ask, "How's Jim? Isn't it terrible what they're doing to him?"

Greer, focusing on their past friendship rather than the betrayal, sent Crist a text message. "Hey, Charlie, would you like to meet up with Lisa and me down at the seafood bar at The Breakers?"

Crist wrote back, "Yes."

Lisa wasn't nearly as forgiving as her husband. "Why are you meeting this son of a bitch?" she said. "Don't you remember the affidavit he signed stating he knew nothing about Victory Strategies? How far up his ass are you going to be? When are you going to stop? When will you see that he doesn't care about you, only himself?"

It wasn't the first argument Jim and Lisa would have over his loyalty to Crist, and it wouldn't be their last.

Greer and Lisa waited at the bar. Charlie came down first, and a few minutes later Carole joined them. In her bubbly manner, Carole said, "How are you, guys?"

Lisa, fuming, refused to play along. "How do you think we are, Carole?" she said.

"Well, Charlie," said Carole, "I guess the Greers aren't going to be the fun Greers today."

Greer kicked Lisa under the table because he could tell she was about to erupt. She barely felt it. Her anger masked a different pain. "Where have you been as our friends?" asked Lisa. "The police burst in on us, raided our house in front of our little boys. What do you mean, 'How are we?'

"Aren't you happy that you don't have to deal with those crazy people in the Republican Party anymore?" asked Carole brightly.

"Carole," said Jim, "I'd much rather not have been indicted and arrested."

"I don't understand," said Carole, not listening. "You're free of them."

"It was as though she and Charlie were oblivious to reality," said Greer later.

Seeing Lisa's rage, Jim suggested that she go up their room to get ready for the wedding. Lisa got up and said, "It was nice seeing you two again. Good-bye."

After Lisa left, Carole asked, "What's wrong with Lisa?"

"It's been a really bad year, Carole," said Greer.

"Oh, you're going to get off," she said. "It'll never go to trial. Oh my God, is that what's bothering Lisa?"

Recalled Greer, "It was like she and Charlie were living in la-la land. They didn't ever want to hear bad news. They are two people who believe that negativity breeds negativity regardless of whether it's reality or not. Whenever anything negative came up, Carole would say to me, 'Chairman, you look stressed. Is something wrong?'

"'Well, yes, Carole, they're running a negative story in the papers tomorrow about the governor.'

"'Oh don't tell him.'"

"'I have to tell him, Carole,' I would say. But if you were not bubbly and giggly and living in their fantasy world, they didn't want to be around you."

RATHER THAN BITE HER tongue or explode, Lisa had gone up to the room. Jim, Charlie, and Carole continued to sit in the bar of The Breakers, drinking wine. Suddenly Crist said, "Boy, we really had some good times, didn't we?"

"Yeah, we sure did," said Greer, meaning it.

"What was your favorite thing we did?" asked Crist.

"That's a hard one," said Greer. "I really liked our trip to the Hearst castle out in California. And I really enjoyed meeting George Schultz. We had a lot of good times, Governor."

"Yes, we did," said Crist. "You and I were a team. Don't worry about anything. You have great lawyers. This will be taken care of."

Greer was looking for an explanation as to why Crist had denied knowledge of Victory Strategies. He approached it from an oblique angle.

"Let me ask you," said Greer, "are you angry because I urged you to run for the Senate instead of running for reelection as governor? Everyone wanted you to run for a second term, but Jay and I were the ones who encouraged you to run for the Senate?"

"No, no, no, not at all," said Crist. "I wanted to run for the Senate. I was tired of being governor."

"Good," said Greer, hiding his emotions.

Inside, he was thinking, *Hey, I was indicted. My house was raided. The party failed to pay my severance agreement. You signed an affidavit that said you didn't know about Victory Strategies and you damn well know you knew about it because you told me to do it. Now you're rewriting history. You're oblivious. Yes, it's a sunny day. Yes, I know there are blue skies on the beach, but Charlie, this is one of those times when you like to ignore things. I lost my financial security and everything I had earned from selling a company that I had built for 23 years. I was forced out as chairman. Am I glad to be away from these people? Well, yeah, but I would have preferred finishing my term."*

Their wine glasses empty, Greer hugged Carole and hugged Charlie, and they parted.

Greer sauntered down to the beach where he ran into Robert Wexler, a congressman from the Palm Beach area. Wexler, a liberal Democrat, was a good friend of Crist's.

"Congressman," said Greer, "How're you doing?"

"Hey, Jim, how are you?" asked Wexler. "Boy, this is just terrible, isn't it?"

"Yeah, it is," said Greer.

"I really can't believe it," said Wexler. "People on my side of the aisle can't believe what your party has done to you."

"Yeah, well, it is what it is, Congressman," said Greer.

Greer went up to his room, and he and Lisa got ready for the wedding. During the ceremony, the Crists and the Greers sat on opposite sides of the aisle. They never saw each other again.

ONE NIGHT ABOUT TWO months after the Sargeant wedding, Lisa was having a very bad time. She was crying hysterically. This was no longer unusual. Many times during the three years he faced criminal charges, when Jim woke up in the morning Lisa's side of the bed would be empty. Jim would find her in the garage bawling.

On this particular night Greer was traveling. When he called home to check in on his family, Lisa was crying uncontrollably.

"She was telling me how this whole thing had destroyed our life," said Greer. "How it's ruined our kids' lives. How we had to cash in our kids' college funds to pay my attorneys. She was lambasting me for putting Charlie and Carole Crist above my own family, and she was saying what a bastard Charlie was. I couldn't get her to stop crying."

Lisa's hysteria and tears goaded Jim—finally—to tell Crist off.

"I texted Charlie," said Greer. "I wrote, 'Charlie, I cannot believe you would deny knowing anything about Victory Strategies. I cannot believe, after everything I did for you, after all the bills I paid for you, after all the hits I took for you, everything I did for you, that you would do this to me. My family has fallen apart. I am just astounded that you would do this to the person you called your brother, that you would lie in an affidavit and not tell the truth about this whole matter. I want you to know that our friendship is over. I don't intend to be loyal to you anymore. When people ask me the truth about you, I'm going to tell them. I'm not going to be like George. I'm going to tell you directly.'"

Greer said he had to make the point that Crist had finally lost Jim Greer's loyalty—"This was Charlie's thing. He always wanted to know if you were still on the reservation."

Unbelievably, when Crist received Greer's text message, rather than take to heart what Greer was saying to him, Crist took the message to the FDLE. "I think this is a threat," he told them. "What do you think?"

They told him it wasn't. "There's nothing here except a person telling you he's not on board anymore."

"Are you sure?" Crist asked.

"Yes, there's nothing here."

"I just thought you ought to have it," said Crist.

Said Greer, "He's like a whiny little girl. He just couldn't have it out man to man. I thought to myself, *You keep asking Jay Burmer and others whether I'm still on the team. Well, Charlie, I'm no longer on the team.*"

GREER SENT CRIST ONE last message.

After Crist announced he was running for the U.S. Senate as an Independent, George LeMieux, the Maestro, the guy Crist put into the U.S. Senate seat, endorsed Marco Rubio.

"George put the biggest knife in Charlie's back that anybody could have. So in a voice mail, I said to him, 'I'm not going to be like George. I'm not going to put a knife in your back and not tell you I'm doing it. So I'm telling you—you and I—we're done. You needn't worry about whether Jim Greer is your friend anymore.'"

Said Greer, "That was the last I communicated with him. He went on to lose the U.S. Senate race to Rubio."

60

The Deck Is Stacked

GREER EXCITEDLY CALLED LISA TO TELL HER, "MY LAWYER SAID THIS NIGHT-mare will be over soon. Brian Ballard just gave a sworn deposition that Charlie was lying, that Charlie knew all about Victory Strategies."

While Greer was talking to Lisa, Damon Chase was meeting with state prosecutors Mike Williams and Diane Croft. "You now know what is true about this case," he said. "Here's a sworn deposition from a guy who doesn't even like Jim."

Chase didn't anticipate—couldn't conceive of—the political nature of the case. This wasn't about law or justice. It was about revenge from the rigid right-wing of the party that exacted vengeance on its enemies.

"We don't see it that way," said Williams. "We're not dropping anything." No matter what evidence Chase presented to Williams and Cross showing Greer's innocence, the statewide prosecutors refused to drop the case. They had their marching orders.

Chase couldn't believe it. "I had never seen a case like this," Chase said. "This was outrageous. I wanted to take this case and jam it up their ass. I intended at trial to destroy the Republican Party. It wouldn't have been Jim Greer on the stand. It would be the Republican Party on trial and the liars who have done this to you."

Jim's other attorney, Cheney Mason, added, "And I'm still not sure a Supreme Court justice has the authority to sign a search warrant." He told Greer, "A lot of these charges are bogus, and we're going to file motions to throw them all out."

Mason did just that, but the judge ruled against every one of them.

Mason continued to claim that this was a civil dispute over a contract. He insisted to Greer that the charges eventually would be dropped. When they weren't, Mason told Greer he needed more money.

"I don't have any more to give you," said Greer.

"I don't know if I'm going to be able to stay on this case any longer," Mason said.

About two weeks later Chase did something he shouldn't have. He felt that for the $100,000 Mason was charging Greer, Mason should have been doing more for his client. In Greer's deposition about Crist, which Chase had taken and which he never intended to make public, Greer had cited an episode when Crist had gotten drunk and fallen out of a golf cart. Greer had described another incident when the governor was drinking, and emotional, and his actions made Greer very uncomfortable.

Chase was frustrated because Greer's case would have ended if Crist had only told the truth about his giving Greer permission to become the party fundraiser. Chase thought it possible that if Crist's lawyers were told about the golf cart and the uncomfortable situation, Crist might admit the truth about Victory Strategies. The quid pro quo would be that the negative stories about Crist would never become public, and Chase would not ask those embarrassing questions in Crist's deposition.

"The reason my attorneys were proposing Crist revise his affidavit was because people close to Crist were telling me that he wanted to do so," said Greer, "that he was looking for a way to help me."

Chase called John Morgan, Crist's attorney, and said, "Listen, Jim doesn't want to say anything to embarrass Charlie, but on the stand I'm going to ask Charlie some questions he's not going to like. And here are the questions I'm going to ask him."

After Chase read him the questions, he asked Morgan, "Would Charlie like to revise his affidavit?"

"Maybe," said Morgan. "Send over a revised affidavit that you'd like him to sign."

By taking this action, Damon was falling into Morgan's trap.

The next day Crist went to the Florida Department of Law Enforcement and said, "Jim Greer and his attorney are trying to extort me into changing my testimony by bringing up embarrassing stuff against me."

When Greer learned of this, he thought to himself, *What is wrong with Charlie that he runs to the FDLE like a little baby.*

"Damon," Greer asked, "did you threaten him?"

"No," Chase said. "I didn't do anything like that. Morgan asked me what kind of embarrassing questions we were intending to ask. I was trying to do the guy a favor by avoiding a deposition."

"They turned the tables on you," said Greer.

The FDLE subsequently ruled that Chase had not extorted Crist, but Crist made sure the press knew what Chase had done by calling in reporters and putting it in the newspapers.

Mason, for one, was furious at Chase.

"Goddamn it," Mason shouted to Greer. "I can't believe Chase divulged those things to Morgan. And now we're getting all this bad press. I'm getting out of the case. I can't stand Damon Chase. I can't believe he did this."

"Cheney," said Greer, who was at the end of his rope, "at least Damon is doing something. Nobody has heard from you in three weeks."

"The case is fucked up," said Mason. "I thought it would be dropped over a year ago. I'm going to need another $30,000."

Greer said he was broke and didn't have it.

"I'm pissed off," said Mason. "I'm not mad at you, Jim, just pissed off at Damon. Don and I are going to have to withdraw from the case."

"In the middle of my case?"

"Yes," Mason said. "You have Damon, so stick with Damon."

And he walked out.

WHEN MASON QUIT, CHASE and his attorney wife, Melanie, immediately took it on, determined to keep their client from going to jail.

"Damon delved into this case like you wouldn't believe," said Greer. "His whole house was covered in files. He learned every piece of evidence. And he was absolutely confident we would win the case at trial. He discovered how Delmar had given bonuses that I hadn't known a thing about. He saw that Delmar was doling out bonuses to Richard Schwartz, the party's CFO, the person whom Delmar was submitting the Victory Strategies invoices to for payment. Because Delmar was giving Schwartz performance bonuses—one for $20,000 and two each for $10,000—Schwartz wasn't about to reveal this to Greer. [Damon Chase got Schwartz to admit to these bonuses during a deposition.] He learned that Delmar had lied over and over again."

Chase, meanwhile, wrote to Mike Williams, the prosecutor:

From: Damon Chase

Sent: Wednesday, December 19, 2012 2:40 PM

To: Michael.Williams@myfloridalegal.com

Cc: diane.croff@myfloridalegal.com; nick.cox@myfloridalegal.com

Subject: Greer

They are reviewing the RPOF servers today, and I am told the IT guys have discovered that most of the records for Delmar Johnson, Richard Swartz and Jim Greer from August through December of 2009 have been intentionally deleted.

You guys are prosecuting the wrong guy. How can it possibly be justice if we have said from the beginning that those records will exonerate him? I immediately requested them in the civil case, but they have ducked us for two and a half years. Upon taking over the criminal case, it was the first thing I requested. They still fought it. Then when I finally got a court order, they continued to fight. Then they said they wanted $104k, knowing that Greer was broke and had given his last $94k to Cheney Mason. Then when the $104k was impossible to defend, they finally caved on the day of the hearing. Now when we go there, the records have been intentionally deleted. Their own guy says they were intentionally deleted. Just for those three guys and just for those few months.

How can you possibly continue to prosecute Jim Greer? Every witness against him has been proven to be lying. Your "victim" intentionally destroyed evidence. Let the poor guy get on with his life. This is just messed up.

<image005.jpg>

DAMON A. CHASE, ESQ.

CHASE | FREEMAN

1525 International Parkway

Suite 4021

Lake Mary, FL 32746

Chase also visited Williams in person to say, "You have destroyed Jim Greer. He was a wealthy man, and now he has no money left. His reputation has been destroyed. The Republican Party has called him every name under the sun. You've vilified the man. He has nothing left. Drop the charges and let him go," he pleaded.

Chase said the prosecutors just sat staring at him with stone faces.

TRIAL SEEMED IMMINENT, BUT for over a year kept getting postponed, fraying Jim and Lisa's nerves. In September 2011, Steven Dobson, the attorney for the Republican Party, contacted Chase and asked for a settlement agreement. (Dobson contends that Chase called him.) Dobson wanted a secret, confidential meeting to settle the $5 million civil suit that Greer had filed against the party for reneging on the severance agreement.

"If we can settle the civil suit," Chase was told, "they will tell the prosecutors to drop the criminal case or at the very least refuse to cooperate."

"But before they would do that," recalled Greer, "they wanted Lisa and me to sign a confidentiality agreement. It was another "secret deal," like the secret deal with my severance agreement. It was amusing, their accusing me of having a secret contract when *everything* they did was a secret contract."

"Isn't this really odd?" Greer said to Chase. "On Monday they call me a thief, and on Tuesday they want to have a secret meeting with me to settle the case."

A five-page confidentiality agreement that the Republican Party sent to Chase included subjects that would be discussed in settlement negotiations including those that would prevent Greer from writing a book or getting a movie deal. The agreement discussed his never divulging information about any fundraising events that had not been authorized by the House or the Senate campaigns going back to years before Greer became chairman.

The party lawyers also demanded that Lisa Greer sign.

"She wasn't even a party to the severance agreement, so why does she have to sign?" asked Greer.

"She knows too much," was the reply.

"We'll give him $100,000," said Dobson, who fudged by saying the executive board and the chairman had to approve it. As a result, Dobson was always able to tell the press there was never a formal agreement to settle the case.

Chase should have taken the money and been done with it. He didn't. He didn't think a hundred grand was enough for all the heartache and pain the Republican Party of Florida had put his client through. And there'd be very little money for him.

"No," said Chase. "We want $3 million for what you've done to him."

No agreement was reached.

"No formal offer ever came from the Republican Party," said Greer, "other than their saying that if something could be worked out, they'd tell the prosecutor it'd all been a big mistake."

The wheels of justice continued to turn.

CHASE TOOK A DEPOSITION from Delmar Johnson, catching him in several lies, including getting him to admit that he had created and submitted invoices for Victory Strategies that Greer had never seen.

"Damon was grilling him, destroying his credibility, demonstrating that Delmar was blaming me for things he had done," said Greer.

Johnson had said he made phony invoices at Greer's behest and had spent more than $60,000 of Republican Party of Florida money on himself. In other words, Greer was being blamed for his associate's illegal expenditures that Greer hadn't even known about. And the worst part was that the prosecutors had given Johnson immunity to testify against Greer. Johnson would never be charged for anything he had done. Only Greer.

"When it comes down to it," said Greer, "Delmar had actually taken a lot more money than I'd been accused of taking. Even so, they told him he had five years to pay back any restitution to the party. To this day he hasn't paid back a dime. It was what he got for cooperating with them."

At the deposition Chase asked Johnson, "Was there anything else you discussed with prosecutors in private today?"

"Yes," Johnson said, "We talked about the prostitutes in the Bahamas."

"So the prosecutors are interested in prostitutes on a Bahamas trip going back two years?"

"Yes."

"So what did you tell them?"

"I told them there were women in golf carts riding around that to me looked like prostitutes," said Johnson.

"Anything else?"

"Yes," said Johnson. "I told them Mr. Greer had knowledge about some of the people on the trip having affairs with women."

What was interesting was that the prosecutor was talking to Johnson about events that had no connection whatsoever to Greer's case. The prosecutor was focusing on gaining information that he could use to hurt the reputations of the defense witnesses in the case. He didn't care whether the information was true.

"Chase was smart enough to stop asking any more questions along those lines," said Greer, "because he didn't want to hurt any of my friends."

In the depositions the prosecution didn't ask any questions to determine whether what Johnson was saying was at all based on facts. Once the deposition became public record, the newspapers ran stories about Delmar Johnson's scenario of "prostitutes in the Bahamas." Johnson's account, while false, made screaming headlines.

"Delmar was making assumptions," said Greer. "He was making it up, had no idea who any of these women were. He was feeding them what he thought they wanted. The prosecutors must have been sitting there thinking, 'Yes, tell us *anything* that will embarrass Jim Greer and Charlie Crist.'"

For two and a half years Greer and his lawyers had been demanding copies of emails in Greer's RPOF account, in CFO Richard Schwartz's account, and in Johnson's account—to prove that Greer was telling the truth about the finances of the party and that Johnson was lying. Greer, moreover, knew at least one email showed that Crist knew about Victory Strategies and thus that the governor had lied in his affidavit. In another email, Greer questioned Johnson about his truthfulness regarding the party's finances, and Johnson threatened to quit.

Though asked repeatedly for the emails, the RPOF's lawyers never responded. "They refused to turn over the emails," said Greer.

A frustrated Chase went before Judge Lubet and said, "Your Honor, there are emails in the Republican Party of Florida's server that will show that Mr. Greer is telling the truth, that will go even farther than the sworn affidavits we have. They are refusing to turn them over. They are dragging their feet. We need Your Honor to order the Republican Party to give Mr. Greer access to these emails."

The judge agreed. "If the emails will benefit his case and show he's innocent," said Lubet, "he has a right to those emails."

One aspect of the case that unsettled Greer and Chase was that the prosecutor and the attorneys for the Republican Party of Florida were joined at the hip. They walked into the courtroom side by side, and they talked together constantly. Whenever Greer's attorney met with the prosecutor, the RPOF attorney was always in attendance. It was as though McCollum and Thrasher were keeping an eye on the proceedings to make sure Greer got what they felt was coming to him.

"Well, Your Honor," said Steven Dobson, the attorney for the Republican Party of Florida, "if you're going to make us give him those emails, we have the right to charge him reasonable copying fees."

"Yes, that's true," said the judge. "Present a bill to Mr. Greer for the reasonable copying fees, and once you do that, Mr. Greer has the right to come to Tallahassee with his IT people and look at the emails."

"We don't have to do that until he pays the reasonable copying fees, right, Your Honor?"

"Yes, that's right," replied the judge.

A week later Greer was presented with a bill for copying fees—$104,000.

"My attorneys were stunned," said Greer. "They howled over how outrageous it was."

Explained the attorney for the Republican Party, "Well, you know, we have to have an IT person sit there, and we want our attorney fees while we're there when you guys go through all the emails."

They were stalling for time so they could erase the files important to Greer's case.

The two sides were scheduled to go back before the judge in November 2012. Right before the hearing was to begin, Greer's attorneys were informed that the cost of the email copying would be less than a thousand dollars.

"You can come to Tallahassee," his attorneys were told.

Greer was broke, so Chase paid with his own money for his trip to Tallahassee.

When Chase and his IT expert opened Greer's file of emails, it was completely empty. All the emails had been scrubbed. They opened Delmar Johnson's file of emails. His from August 2009 through March 2010 had been deleted. They opened the file of Richard Schwartz, the chief financial officer. Same thing. His beginning in August 2009 were gone.

If anyone but Pam Bondi had been in charge, those who erased the emails would have been charged with tampering with evidence. But because Bondi, like her predecessor, Bill McCollum, was a member of the Tea Party, nothing was done.

Chase tried to put a happy face on this devastating development. He immediately called Greer—with good news and bad news.

"The bad news is that all the emails which would prove that what you are saying is true have been deleted, or according to the Republican Party of Florida, 'just weren't archived.'"

"What's the good news?" asked Greer.

"The good news is we can't wait for a jury to hear this,'" said Chase.

"Yes, but I would much rather have those emails," said Greer.

Chase got into a heated argument over these deletions with the lawyers for the Republican Party, but to no avail.

Said Greer, "The state and the Republican Party of Florida were hand in hand. They had unlimited money. I was broke. The state spent millions of dollars pursuing this. The Republican Party of Florida spent $800,000 defending my civil suit. It wasn't going to matter what depositions I had. As Damon Chase said to me, 'You have taken on some very powerful people.'"

The erasures of the emails left Greer a beaten man.

Said Greer, "After almost three years of fighting, for the first time I realized there was no way I was going to receive a fair trial."

61

'They Got Me'

It was now clear to Greer that this was a persecution, not a prosecution. This was a fight the prosecutors, hand in glove with the Republican Party of Florida, were determined to win. They were out for blood; justice had nothing to do with it. Greer had supported Crist against the wishes of Marco Rubio, John Thrasher, Mike Haridopolos, Dean Cannon, Sharon Day, Bill McCollum, Pam Bondi, and every Tea Party member who wanted the hated Crist thrown out of office. Their pound of flesh was coming out of Jim Greer's hide.

In November 2012, prosecutors Mike Williams and Diane Croft were encouraging Chase to convince Greer to take a plea. If he did, he would go to jail and his pursuers would have their victory. The prosecutors told Greer's attorneys, "Even if you win on some of the counts, if he is convicted on just one of them, we're going to ask for eight to ten years."

Williams said he intended to do something even more disquieting. "If we go to trial," he warned, "I'm going to publicly destroy and discredit the people who support your story. I'm going to question them about their personal lives. I'm going to do a lot of things that will embarrass these people."

Greer saw that Williams wasn't making idle threats.

Some of my friends may have turned on me to save themselves, thought Greer, *but I couldn't live with myself if I had to do that to my friends to stay out of jail.*

Greer was loyal because his father, Austin Greer, a former master sergeant in the Marines, always told him, "Loyalty determines your character." His compassion came from his mother, Virginia Greer, who taught him to always be considerate of other people's feelings.

Now he saw that his friends would be discredited by an out-of-control prosecutor. Greer felt boxed in.

His attorneys, with intimate knowledge of the facts of the case, argued forcefully that Greer should go to trial.

"I'm going to kick their ass," Chase told Greer. "I'm going to show that Delmar Johnson is lying. I'm going to show that you never knew what Delmar was doing, that you never knew he was falsifying invoices. I'm going to show he was taking bonuses without your permission. And I'm going to show that Charlie Crist is a lying piece of shit. Don't take the plea."

Greer wanted a second opinion.

Chase contacted Hank Coxe, a prominent former Florida Bar Association president and highly respected criminal lawyer from Jacksonville. Coxe was asked to study the case, talk with the prosecutors, and give his opinion whether Greer should plead or go to trial. Coxe made some phone calls to find out what Greer's chances were if he went to trial.

He concluded they weren't very good.

At a meeting at Chase's lakeside home outside of Ocala, Coxe told Greer, "I'm a criminal attorney. I've been doing this for years and years. I think you have a very strong case, Jim. I agree with Damon on a lot of points. But this is a very odd case. The prosecution is not negotiating like they normally would. The prosecutor has told me that the higher-ups, meaning Pam Bondi, have said that you have to pay. They are not going to allow this case to be negotiated like a normal case, where you might get it dropped down to a misdemeanor or you might get probation."

Coxe told Greer that in his conversations with the prosecutor's office he had negotiated a plea bargain that he thought Greer could live with.

"Here is the prosecutor's deal," said Coxe. "You plead guilty to every-thing—"

Chase erupted. "He's not pleading guilty to a fucking thing," said Chase, who had spent three years reviewing every aspect of this case. "This is outrageous."

"Just let me talk, Damon," said Coxe. "The prosecutor says if he pleads guilty to everything, he will, number one, ask for 42 months, not eight years, and that they will not object if the judge wants to go below 42 months. And they'll ask for restitution of only $65,000, not $125,000." (Where the $65,000 number came from, nobody knows.)

"The higher-ups, Pam Bondi, and prosecutors Nick Cox and Mike Williams told Chase, 'Greer has to serve time. We will let him have a short sentence, but he has to serve.'

"Here's the deal," Coxe concluded. "I can work a deal where you'll get sentenced to 42 months, but the judge will suspend 28 of it. The state says it won't object to that. You'll only have to serve six-months probation, and they'll be no restrictions when you get out. And it will all be over with, Jim.

"The flip side is, the prosecutor says if you take this to trial and air all the dirty laundry, everything is off the table, and they're going for years and years and years if you get convicted on the slightest thing.

"I've been doing this for 30 years, Jim," said Coxe. "And you never, ever know what a jury is going to do."

GREER FACED A CHOICE: go to trial with a chance to clear his name, or take the plea, serve the 15 months, and preserve the reputations of his friends. The most convincing argument for taking the plea was that he'd be home to watch his three young children grow up.

All this time Chase kept saying, "I'm going to kick their ass," and Greer loved Chase for saying so. But the restitution the Republican Party demanded was going to be paid for him. And one thing that Coxe had said had resonated within him: "They won't forgive you for talking about voter suppression. The prosecutor is playing dirty. If you lose on just one count, he's going to ask for eight to ten years."

These prosecutors, Greer well knew, would do just that.

ON FEBRUARY 10, 2013, the trial of Jim Greer was scheduled to begin. The media was in court in Orlando in full force. There was a buzz in the air. It's not often that high-profile political figures go to trial. It's rare even when they're indicted. As far as the public was concerned—for this is what they had learned from the media—Jim Greer had secretly started a company called Victory Strategies and had used it to siphon money from the Republican Party of Florida for his personal gain.

The media campaign engineered by the RPOF and the prosecutor working for it had convinced the public that Greer was guilty of all charges.

The morning of the start of the trial, the jury was slated to be selected.

The prosecutor said to Greer's attorneys, "Here is what we'll do, but we don't want it in writing. We don't want our fingerprints on it anywhere. This cannot be perceived as a plea deal. The higher-ups (Pam Bondi, Nick Cox, Rick Scott) don't want it to appear that we agreed to anything."

Said Greer, "It was another secret deal right to the end."

Greer couldn't believe that Governor Scott was even involved. Said Greer, "After one late-night phone call with Hank Coxe, I was taken aback when Coxe was told that Scott's office may even need to sign off."

They adjourned to the judge's chambers. Prosecutor Mike Williams told Judge Marc Lubet, "If Greer pleads guilty to everything this morning, ending the trial before it begins, this is what we'd like to see happen. We're going to jump up and down, putting on a dog and pony show to argue that he needs to serve 42 months. But, Your Honor, we won't object if you sentence him to 18 months, and he'll be out in 15."

"This is a very unusual case," said Lubet, "but I can understand why Mr. Greer is pleading guilty. I will publicly issue the sentence on March 27, even though the courtroom won't know we have already made a deal."

Chase was terribly concerned that nothing had been put in writing, but Lubet mollified him by saying, "You've never been in my courtroom before, Mr. Chase, but when I say I'm going to do something, I keep my word."

There was one other very important catch: Under the law, a civil matter is not supposed to be connected to a criminal matter, but the Republican Party of Florida had one very loose end it had to tie up. Greer still had his outstanding $5 million civil lawsuit against the Republican Party of Florida for breach of his severance agreement.

The Republican Party in civil court had lost all of its motions to dismiss Greer's lawsuit including motions to take Thrasher and Haridopolos out as defendants. Try as they did, the RPOF had not been able to find a way to void its severance agreement with Greer. But with Bill McCollum and John Thrasher pulling the strings, they now had the way.

RPOF lawyer Steve Dobson told Greer's attorneys there would be no plea deal in his criminal case unless Greer dropped his civil suit against the party—a proposal that first had to be approved by the RPOF executive board.

For the first two years of this case, the prosecutor told Greer's attorneys that the civil case had no effect on the criminal prosecution. But in the final negotiations, resolving the civil case became the key to the criminal plea deal.

"There's no deal unless Greer drops his civil suit," Dobson told the prosecutor.

Chase felt that Greer's civil suit would have been a "slam dunk." Settlement money would have gotten Greer back on his feet after prison, and it would have provided fees for Chase, who had worked on Greer's case almost for nothing. Some of the severance agreement money would have gone to pay him.

No longer.

On March 27, 2013, Chase, gritting his teeth at what he was about to do, surreptitiously passed Dobson a notice of dismissal that Greer no longer was pursuing his civil suit against the RPOF.

Prosecutor Mike Williams then got up and began the charade. No one in the audience knew that the scenario about to unfold before them had been worked out in secret weeks earlier.

"Mr. Greer deserves 42 months," Williams stated.

Chase got up and talked about what a good man Greer was.

Judge Lubet was pleased that the case had been settled, but was uneasy that Johnson had not been prosecuted. He even branded Johnson a co-conspirator and raised the fact that "Delmar Johnson had not paid one cent in restitution and that he had been given immunity." He also raised the issue of a recent case where a bookkeeper had stolen over $250,000 from her employer and the prosecutor had not asked for any prison time.

The judge, as arranged the month before, told the packed courtroom, "Mr. Greer has never been in trouble. This case is very unusual, and I don't believe 42 months is warranted. I'm going to suspend 28 months and sentence him to 18 months. In that he only has to serve 85 percent of his sentence, his jail time will amount to 15 months. There'll be no restrictions on him. He'll only have probation for six months. And then this case is over with."

A month before his sentencing, Greer begged Chase and Coxe to talk to Williams about reducing the time he had to serve by two months so he could attend the high school graduation of his two older children.

Williams said he was required to check with Bondi before he could give an answer. He came back and said, "I ran it up the flagpole, and the higher-ups said no."

The Tea Party Republicans had gained their pound of flesh.

Said Greer, "The statewide prosecutor's office, Republican first under Bill McCollum and then under Pam Bondi, spent millions of dollars raiding my house, interviewing God knows how many people trying to get something negative on me, and working this trial like they were prosecuting a member of the Gambino family.

"'For the first time in Florida history,' said Jay Burmer, 'they had a political prisoner.' And the Republican Party of Florida, instead of paying me the $125,000 severance it had agreed to pay, spent $800,000 in lawyer's fees defending my civil case. All for $65,000, which was paid to the Republican Party in restitution.

"Even if you're not a Jim Greer fan, you're just the guy on the street, wouldn't you say to yourself, *Let me get this straight. They've spent millions of dollars of taxpayer money, and they've spent $800,000 of the Republican Party's money—suppose you're a member of that party—just to make the point that we're going to get Jim Greer because he was loyal to Charlie Crist? Did they think getting me was going to lead them to getting something on Charlie Crist?*"

Having pled guilty, Greer was shaken by the unfairness of it all.

"What upsets me more than anything are those people who, over the last three years, said to me, 'Jim, it's awful what they're doing to you. Jim, this shouldn't have happened. This is terrible what they did to you.'

"Some of those people were in a position to stop it. But they never did."

Greer was told more than once, "The people who started this witch hunt would say, 'This got out of hand.' They never intended it to go this far."

One evening Greer told Lisa and Damon and Melanie Chase, "There are a lot of criminals in this case, but I'm not one of them. While I was chairman, the party was taken over by an angry mob, like men and women with torches, running down the street looking for Frankenstein. This mob's Frankensteins were moderates. They hated them and hated having to say to them, 'Your opinion is very important to us.' What they were actually saying was, 'Get out of our party.'

"The Florida Republicans were able to take everything they did wrong, every frustration the grass-roots had against their elected officials, and point it at me. When grass-roots activists would ask Dean Cannon, 'Didn't you spend $50,000 on clothes and a five-star hotel?' Dean could reply, 'Yes, but look over here at Jim Greer.'

"They managed to turn a play with 30 actors into a one-man show. Somehow it all turned on me. The party was even successful in getting law enforcement and the prosecutor involved in what really was a civil matter.

"They got me. It's just terrible. Lisa was sobbing, and I was hugging her, and she said, 'Jim, you promised me when this started that we'd make them pay for what they did to you. Now they're all walking away, and you're going to prison.'

"'You know,' I answered, 'maybe God and the voters will make them pay.'

"When the prosecutors and the Republican Party leadership, and even Charlie Crist, realized I was really going to prison, that my little boys wouldn't be able to have me on Saturdays for father/son day any more, and my six-month old baby was going to miss her dad for 15 months, I wonder whether those people would think about me.

"The sad thing is, they probably don't care. They got me. They really got me. This was the Salem witch trials of 2013.

"I know I made mistakes. This morning I said to my best friend Gene Collins, 'I'm trying to figure out whether I really did anything wrong. I feel like the guy at the Nuremberg trials who said, 'I didn't do anything to stop it.' Is that guilt? Am I the guy who let spending get out of hand and didn't stop it? Am I the guy who shouldn't have supported Charlie Crist?

"I'm trying to sort through all of that.

"Was I a good chairman or a bad chairman? When I was there, I was told I was the best chairman they ever had. And now today they say I'm the worst chairman the party ever had.

"I have a lot to figure out."

62

Musings from a Wewahitchka Jail

During the writing of this final chapter, Jim Greer was a political prisoner at the Gulf Correctional Institution in Wewahitchka, Florida, in the Panhandle, hundreds of miles from his wife and his children. He could talk to Lisa on the phone for 15 minutes a day. He was scheduled to be released on July 5, 2014.

As Jim and I were coming to the end of this project, I asked why he had spent so many hours talking to me about his "nightmare," as he calls it.

Above all, Jim said, he wanted the truth to be told.

In one of his last interviews for this book, Greer said:

If I did the right things for all the right reasons, you have to say that the system is more corrupt than anyone could ever imagine. The Republican Party nationally and in Florida is an organization of criminals that believes everything is okay because "We're in power, and we're making the laws."

We can suppress votes if we want. We can eliminate early voting, and why do we do that? Because it's been shown that Republicans vote on Election Day. So what do Governor Rick Scott and Republican legislators do? They file legislation to reduce or eliminate early voting. And they say they're doing it because of voter fraud. That's an absolute lie. There's very little voter fraud in Florida. When I was chairman, no one ever came to me and talked about voter fraud. It's clearly their manipulating the political process to win elections.

I can tell you right now, the Republican political strategists and political consultants will do whatever they have to do to win on Election Day. If they have to keep minorities from going to the polls, they'll do it. If they have to change the laws for their benefit, they'll do it and then come up with some excuse for why they're doing it, something that sounds good but has no connection to what they're really doing. If they have to use the power of the state police, they'll even do that.

Critics think the Republican Party works to suppress the black vote in order to win elections, but it's only part of the story. Elections have turned into a major business. It's big business for polling companies and mailing companies and consultants. It's incredible how much these mailing companies are making from campaigns.

Huge bonuses are paid if your candidate wins. Recall the $10,000 a month we paid George LeMieux for helping Charlie win the governor's race. What voters need to know is that a lot of money is riding on the outcome of the election, and that's the main reason political consultants are motivated to manipulate the system—for instance, to change the laws to keep minorities from voting.

There are all kinds of strategies used to win an election besides just getting your message out. Among those strategies employed by Republican lawmakers all across the country is voter suppression.

To me, there's a difference within the Republican Party with respect to racism and voter suppression and winning an election using voter suppression.

When I became chairman, I really focused on minority outreach. I created the African American, the Hispanic, and the Jewish advisory councils. One of the things that drove the Tea Party and the crazies crazy was I went to the NAACP annual banquet with Governor Crist. I was welcomed warmly and had a great time.

I really believe we cannot continue to be the party of Old White Men, which is what the Republican Party is coming down to. Deep down many people in the party believe the exact opposite of what they say publicly. The Republican Party talks about wanting to be an inclusive party, but they don't do anything to be an inclusive party. Because the ultraconservatives demand that you stay true and pure and follow everything the party stands for. There's no flexibility, no independent thought allowed.

Appealing to blacks isn't part of Republican Party orthodoxy. Are there racists in the Republican Party? Yes. There are people who do not like blacks and make negative comments about them. We would have one or two blacks at our quarterly meetings only because we needed them for show. If most of the radical Republicans had their way, there's wouldn't be any in the entire Republican Party.

The haters come from two areas, the old-time Republicans in leadership who've been there for years, and those who come from the rural counties. Nationwide if you look at the voters in the rural states, they haven't moved up to the 21st century. Our county voters are the same way. Some of these people still can't accept that the South lost the Civil War. They want things to go back to the way they were. They still don't accept civil rights for blacks.

The other segment of the party trying to keep minorities from voting comes from the professional side, the political consultants and political strategists, the ones who used to report to me. In most cases they are not racists, just professionals doing a job. And their job is to win on Election Day.

We were always looking for voter information, and there's a whole mechanism used by political parties and strategists to identify voters. It sometimes boils down to what magazines you order. In this day and age everything can be traced, and there are professionals who try to identify how you think, what you think, and who you're going to vote for by the products you use. If someone orders Field and Stream or a hunting magazine, the Republican Party knows it. People who fish and hunt are generally conservative and vote Republican, so they will be identified and then encouraged to vote.

It's called the "Get out the Vote" program, and it's very intense.

We discovered that early voting is bad for us. So what Rick Scott and the Republican legislature did in 2010 as soon as Charlie Crist and I were gone was to pass sweeping election laws to reduce early voting days and early voting hours statewide.

The press did a good job reporting that there was no voter fraud, that what Rick Scott and the legislative leadership was telling the people of Florida wasn't accurate. So you see, there's a difference between people who are racist within the Republican Party and Republican political strategists who are simply trying to eliminate Democrats from voting so we can win and they can make a lot of money.

I've never to this day bought into the fact that every black in the entire state will vote Democratic. I believe the Republican Party has a good message of less government, less taxes, and more freedom. I don't agree with everything the party does—in fact I don't agree with a lot that it does—but my philosophy has always been you can't get that voter to vote Republican if you don't talk to him.

I was always told, "At the end of the day they're not going to vote Republican so why even try? In fact, reaching out to the black community could end up hurting us because they could go to the polls and vote Democratic. But I just don't buy that.

Unfortunately for democracy, the Republicans in power today—and not just the ones in Florida—aren't going to take any chances.

They'll do whatever it takes to win.

The Republican Party wants to keep power at all costs. The Republican legislature in Florida and the governor's office under Rick Scott will do whatever it takes to stay in power. They'll gerrymander. They'll discredit anyone who's in their way. They are drunk with power. They no longer think like citizens.

Election Day is not an exercise in democracy any more. It's Bonus Day. The Republican political consultants will strategize to win an election with no regard for the integrity of the election process.

One thing they often said about me: "He's not one of us. He didn't rise up through the ranks. He wasn't a Republican precinct person."

When all is said and done: I don't want to be one of them.

I WANT MY KIDS one day to be able to know that I really tried to be a good party chairman. I also want them to know why in the end I pled guilty even though what I was guilty of was trusting people who weren't worthy of that trust. I want my family, friends, and others who believed in me and supported me through this unbelievable ordeal to know why I did what I did.

Some may ask, "How can you reveal these secrets? How can you divulge such personal details about people who had been my close friends?"

My answer is that I was left no choice. This is the only way I can salvage my reputation in my own eyes and in the eyes of my family and loved ones. It is said that the truth will set you free. In my case, the truth will set me free.

To those people who could have stopped the witch hunt but didn't, to those who could have told the truth but didn't, to those I considered my dear friends but who did nothing to help me, sitting by and letting the Florida GOP press machine destroy my reputation with lies and deceptions, and to those people who privately said, "It just got out of hand," or "We're sorry this happened to you," I forgive all of you—I have to in order to move on with my life.

When asked why I bared my soul to Peter Golenbock, it's because I want Florida Republicans to know that I was honored to be your party chairman and that we accomplished many good things.

Among my greatest regrets are all the hurt and embarrassment this has caused my wife Lisa and my children Hunter, Amber, Austin, Aiden, and Hope. This nightmare has caused me to lose respect and enthusiasm for public service and government. From the time I was first elected to public office, I have had a deep desire to serve my community, state, and country, and I've always taught my children to respect our government and those who serve in it. It's hard to promote and defend those ideals after I have personally witnessed how corrupt and vindictive those in power can be. But no matter what has happened, I will always believe that what was done to me was done by individuals, not by the Republican Party or our system of government.

Yes, I made mistakes, but the mistakes had less to do with what I was doing than who I was doing it with. The good news is that my family and I have survived, and we're looking forward to putting all of this behind us.

Finally, I know all too well the truth about what happened to Jim Greer, the chairman of the Republican Party of Florida, and after reading this book, you will, too.

Appendix

4.   RPOF stipulates and agrees that all RPOF expenditures made during Greer's term as RPOF Chairman were proper, lawful, appropriate, and served the interests of RPOF, and RPOF specifically acknowledges that all expense reimbursements of any kind, American Express account expenditures, consultant fees, fundraising fees, agreements, service fees, travel and dining expenses were proper and authorized and otherwise ratified by RPOF.

5.   RPOF agrees to release a written statement to the press publicly praising and acknowledging Greer's service and accomplishments as Chairman of RPOF. RPOF agrees to release this statement with the approval of Greer on the date Greer, in his sole discretion, chooses to publicly announce his resignation. Such statement may include quotes from any other individuals approved by Greer in his sole discretion.

6.   The Parties, for themselves and their respective parent corporations, affiliates, subsidiaries, successors, agents, representatives, employees, officers, directors, trustees, insurers, subrogees and assigns, hereby release, acquit and forever discharge each other, and each other's agents, employees, officers, directors, trustees, successors, representatives, insurers, subrogees, and assigns, and all other persons, firms, and corporations from any and all suits, actions, causes of action, arbitrations, claims, demands, rights, interests, obligations, liabilities, debts, damages, fees, attorneys' fees, interest, expenses, contracts, costs, covenants, agreements, guarantees, controversies, or promises of every kind, nature and character, now existing or hereafter arising, in law or in equity, known or unknown, foreseen or unforeseen, accrued or unaccrued, arising out of or relating to Greer's service as RPOF Chairman, including any claim related to the appropriateness of any RPOF expenditure, payment, contract, agreement or other action made or otherwise authorized during Greer's term of service as RPOF Chairman.

Page 2 of January 2010 agreement between Greer and RPOF whereby he would resign as chairman, be held harmless on actions during his tenure as chairman, and be paid the balance of salary owed if he had served his full second term as chairman. For complete document, see www.newsouthbooks.com/chairman/supplement.

Jan.04.2010 07:14 PM   PAGE. 1/ 1

Delmar W. Johnson III
Executive Director
Republican Party of Florida

Jason Gonzalez
General Counsel
Republican Party of Florida

Dean Cannon
Speaker Designate
Florida House of Representatives

Richard Swartzz
Chief Financial Officer
Republican Party of Florida

Mike Haridopolos
President Designate
Florida Senate

John Thrasher
Florida Senate

To be re-executed following the election of successor RPOF Chairman:

John Thrasher

From: 01/04/2010 17:50   #006 P.002/002

Delmar W. Johnson III
Executive Director
Republican Party of Florida

Jason Gonzalez
General Counsel
Republican Party of Florida

Dean Cannon
Speaker Designate
Florida House of Representatives

Mike Haridopolos
President Designate
Florida Senate

Richard Swartzz
Chief Financial Officer
Republican Party of Florida

John Thrasher
Florida Senate

To be re-executed following the election of successor RPOF Chairman:

John Thrasher

10/26/2002 03:11 PAX   ⓐ001
From: 01/04/2010 17:47   #007 P.005/005

Delmar W. Johnson III
Executive Director
Republican Party of Florida

Jason Gonzalez
General Counsel
Republican Party of Florida

Dean Cannon
Speaker Designate
Florida House of Representatives

Richard Swartzz
Chief Financial Officer
Republican Party of Florida

Mike Haridopolos
President Designate
Florida Senate

John Thrasher
Florida Senate

To be re-executed following the election of successor RPOF Chairman:

John Thrasher

*Faxed signature pages of January 2010 agreement between Greer and
RPOF; key party leaders attested to the terms. For complete document, see
www.newsouthbooks.com/chairman/supplement.*

AFFIDAVIT OF JAY BURMER

BEFORE ME, an officer duly authorized by the laws of the State of Florida to administer oaths, this day appeared Jay Burmer, who having been first duly sworn to tell the truth under oath, does hereby depose and say:

1. I am Jay Burmer and am over the age of 18 and otherwise sui juris.

2. In late 2008 and early 2009, I was a paid political consultant for the Republican Party of Florida (RPOF) and then Governor Charlie Crist.

3. In late 2008 and early 2009, I had several discussions with Charlie Crist and then RPOF Chairman Jim Greer about replacing Meredith O'Rourke as fundraiser for the RPOF.

4. In late 2008 and early 2009, I had several discussions with Jim Greer and Charlie Crist about Jim Greer having difficulty finding someone to replace Meredith O'Rourke as fundraiser for the RPOF due to concerns from potential fundraising candidates that Meredith O'Rourke would interfere with their professional fundraising relationships.

5. In late 2008 and early 2009, I had several discussions with Jim Greer and Charlie Crist about Jim Greer replacing Meredith O'Rourke as fundraiser for the RPOF and that Jim Greer's need to keep his fundraising efforts confidential in order to avoid Meredith O'Rourke's interference.

6. In early 2009, Charlie Crist requested I attend a meeting in which Jim Greer was going to terminate Meredith O'Rourke's fundraising contract with the RPOF.

7. When Charlie Crist requested that I attend the aforementioned meeting, he advised me that Jim Greer would be assuming the fundraising responsibilities for the RPOF.

8. While I never specifically discussed what Jim Greer's additional compensation would be for accepting the additional duties of fundraising for the RPOF, it always assumed he would in fact be paid additional compensation over and above that which he was being paid as Chairman.

9. In early 2009 and at the direction of Charlie Crist, I did in fact attend a meeting with Jim Greer and Meredith O'Rourke wherein Meredith O'Rourke was advised by Jim Greer that her contract with RPOF was being terminated.

10. From early 2009 through Jim Greer's resignation in January 2010, I was aware that Jim Greer was doing the fundraising for RPOF and no other professional fundraisers had been hired to replace Meredith O'Rourke.

11. At all times when Jim Greer was doing fundraising for RPOF, I assumed he was in fact being paid additional compensation over and above that which he was receiving as Chairman.

12. While I was aware of, and agreed with, Jim Greer receiving additional compensation for fundraising activities, I had never heard the name of his fundraising company now known as Victory Strategies, which I did not consider relevant.

FURTHER AFFIANT SAYETH NAUGHT.

Jay Burmer

The foregoing instrument was acknowledged before me this 9th day of May, 2012 by Jay Burmer, who is personally known to me and did take an oath.

Notary Public

GLENISE SHILLINGFORD
NOTARY PUBLIC
STATE OF FLORIDA
Comm# EE064426
Expires 2/14/2015

Complete affidavit of Jay Burmer affirming that Crist knew of and had approved of Greer's fundraising for RPOF and his compensation.

15.   During the above-described late 2008 discussions, it was suggested that GREER and RPOF Executive Director Delmar Johnson should take over fundraising responsibility and there would be compensation for same in addition to the existing compensation from the RPOF.

16.   As Finance Chairman and a major donor to the RPOF, I did not consider it inappropriate for GREER and/or Mr. Johnson to receive additional compensation for assuming additional fundraising responsibilities, and in fact believed it would be more efficient and beneficial to the RPOF.

17.   I was surprised when GREER was charged with a crime relating to setting up a company to do fundraising for RPOF, as GREER and Mr. Johnson were acting with the knowledge and approval Governor Crist.

FURTHER AFFIANT SAYETH NOT.

HARRY SARGEANT, III

SWORN TO SUBSCRIBED before me this _12_ day of April, 2012, by HARRY SARGEANT, III, who is _X_ personally known to me or ___ produced _____ as identification, and who after being duly sworn under penalty of perjury, did take an oath and executed the foregoing instrument and acknowledged before me that he executed same.

Notary Public
My Commission expires: 10/18/2015

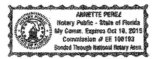

Last page of affidavit of Harry Sergeant affidavit affirming that Crist knew of and had approved of Greer's fundraising for RPOF and his compensation. Full document is online at www.newsouthbooks.com/chairman/supplement.